In this important contribution to the study of industrial relations, Roy Church and Quentin Outram present new research into the strike activity of British coalminers since the late nineteenth century. The authors consider not only the major national strikes and lock-outs which have made the industry a byword for industrial militancy, but also the multitude of small-scale strikes which have formed the routine of British colliery industrial relations. *Strikes and solidarity* is multi-disciplinary in approach and views the industrial relations history of the industry from the perspectives offered by sociologists, industrial relations specialists and economists, as well as social and economic historians. Assessed in the comparative context of the American, French and German experience, the authors' findings are also given an international dimension. Church and Outram have successfully blended quantitative and qualitative investigations to form a new explanation for the long-standing issues presented by the industrial relations of the industry.

Strikes and solidarity

Strikes and solidarity

Coalfield conflict in Britain
1889–1966

ROY CHURCH AND
QUENTIN OUTRAM

CAMBRIDGE
UNIVERSITY PRESS

PUBLISHED BY THE PRESS SYNDICATE OF THE UNIVERSITY OF CAMBRIDGE
The Pitt Building, Trumpington Street, Cambridge CB2 1RP, United Kingdom

CAMBRIDGE UNIVERSITY PRESS
The Edinburgh Building, Cambridge CB2 2RU, United Kingdom
40 West 20th Street, New York, NY 10011-4211, USA
10 Stamford Road, Oakleigh, Melbourne 3166, Australia

First published 1998

Printed in the United Kingdom at the University Press, Cambridge

Typeset in Plantin 9.5/12 pt [VN]

A catalogue record for this book is available from the British Library

Library of Congress cataloguing in publication data

Church, Roy A.
Strikes and solidarity: coalfield conflict in Britain 1889–1966/Roy Church and
Quentin Outram
    p.   cm.
Includes bibliographical references and index.
ISBN 0 521 55460 8 (hb)
1. Strikes and lockout – Coal mining – Great Britain – History.
2. Trade-unions – Coal miners – Great Britain – History.
3. Solidarity.   I. Outram, Quentin.   II. Title.
HD5365.M615C48   1998
331.892'822334'0941—dc21   97–12821   CIP

ISBN 0 521 55460 8 hardback

To Wendy
and to
H. L. B. J.

Contents

Figures and tables

Preface

This investigation into the strike activity of British coalminers attempts to explain the causes of strikes, the regional and inter-colliery differences in strike propensity, and the relation between strikes and social solidarity in the history of colliery communities. It has been inspired by the seminal research carried out by Knowles, Cronin, Shorter and Tilly, and Stearns, which combined quantitative methodologies with more traditional qualitative approaches in a search for generalizations rather than descriptive narrative accounts of strikes. Their ambitious research agendas have included attempts to chart and analyse the strike histories of a wide range of industries in several countries, to elucidate a dynamic of strikes generally, and to place strikes within the socio-political context of a 'modernization' process. The perspectives offered have been sectoral and comparative, inter-industrial and national, and to some extent international, in scope.

While we have adopted a similarly rigorous approach to our research which is both historical and firmly rooted in concepts and methodologies drawn from the social sciences, our study focuses on a single industry and on the experience of the employers, managers and workers in the localities and the collieries within one polity, albeit one comprising a trinity of national cultures. That it does so does not mean that our research is less ambitious or that it lacks the capacity to offer generalizations of comparable interest to those offered by scholars who have chosen wider fields to investigate. Even an attempt to analyse strike behaviour in a single industry, however, reveals the difficulty of drawing generalizations. In Britain, strikes in the coal industry have probably received more attention than any others; yet some of the best historical research of a traditional kind (judged by its methodology, the use of primary sources, the level of detailed analysis, and in particular the presence of a sensitivity to the complexity of the history of miners and of mining strikes) risks the charge, in Crew's rather unforgiving words, of reducing this experience to little more than an 'eclectic explanatory pluralism' (Crew 1986: 308). This is a salutary warning to historians of mining strikes who venture beyond structural, quasi-deterministic explanations; perhaps an awareness of such risks helps to explain why, though they have been subjected to serious criticism, structural and quasi-deterministic explanations of coalfield conflict continue to survive in the literature and why no satisfactory alternatives have been presented. The difficulties of arriving at an alternative analysis are underlined by the reservations expressed or endorsed by Cronin, Perrot, Tilly and Volkman, who have emphasized the limitations of their own statistical analyses in answering questions which extend beyond chronology, location, frequency, duration and participation (Geary 1986: 377–9). With these reservations we concur but the widespread interest among historians of miners and mining, manifest in the recent voluminous and valuable publications orchestrated on an international scale by Tenfelde and his collaborators (Tenfelde 1986; Feldman and Tenfelde 1990; Tenfelde 1992) strengthened our resolve to take the risk in progressing towards a social history of mining in the nineteenth and twentieth centuries (Tenfelde 1992). This we have done by focusing on the history of strikes over a lengthy period, combining traditional historical research methods and quantitative analysis with concepts and medium range theory borrowed from the social sciences.

Our quantitative analyses proceeded from our conviction that the full potential for the statistical analysis of strikes has yet to be explored, our experience that when the primary data are analysed in detail they yield unexpected results, and that the outcome throws light on some of those issues which hitherto historians have assumed or implied were not susceptible to generalization because they were beyond quantitative analysis. In this study we have attempted to combine the statistical approach with narratives which are illustrative rather than descriptive, interpretative rather than synoptic.

Our objectives are more limited in scope compared with those whose work has been alluded to above. We have not attempted to write a history of strikes on an international basis. That is a project which requires large-scale research even to substantiate the dimensions and degree of international differences in strike patterns and propensities, let alone understand them. We have not tried to write, or rewrite, the history of industrial relations in the British coal industry, though it is evident that no interpretation of the industry's strike history would be credible were it to ignore the organizations and events, the people and the communities involved in the industrial relations processes. Among those organizations, the Miners' Federation of Great Britain (and later, the National Union of Mineworkers), and among those events, the great national strikes and lock-outs of the 1912–26 period stand pre-eminent, having captured the imaginations of public and miners alike, whether in admiration or condemnation. While these find a significant place in this study, our focus is on the ordinary local and domestic strikes in the industry which, while undramatic and often brief, were far more frequent. Before the near-national lock-out of 1893 and after the defeat of 1926 these were the strikes which sustained the reputation of the British miner and the British coalowner for industrial militancy and intransigence in dealing with each other.

The analytical depth which our approach makes possible enables us to ask questions which have not been asked before. Were all collieries strike-prone or only some? Why did miners strike frequently at some collieries and in some localities but not in others? Why did histories of colliery militancy often come to a relatively rapid end? How widely did miners participate in strikes? What was the relationship between local, regional and national strikes? How real was miners' strike solidarity and, to the extent that it existed, how much was it a consequence of the peculiarities of the coalmining industry and how much was it created in some sense outside the structural and experiential characteristics of coalmining? Did the pattern of coalmining strikes change after nationalization and, if so, why? And how do the conclusions reached on the basis of our detailed analysis of coalmining strikes in Britain compare with what is known about the history of strikes in other major coal producing countries in continental Europe and the USA? Such questions are central to any history of industrial relations; furthermore the questions we pose might be asked of other industries and of other groups of workers, both in Britain and in other countries. Indeed, some work on such questions has already started (Julia Morris et al. 1994).

We believe that our research has wider resonances both for the study of labour history and of industrial relations, areas of interest which have recently been subjected to critical scrutiny. In an important review of the compartmentalization of labour history and the study of industrial relations, to the intellectual impoverishment of both, the editors of a new journal signalled a mission to revitalize the 'historical analysis of the practice *and* theory of industrial relations' (Lyddon and Smith 1996: 10). Their principal criticism was that labour history and industrial relations have become increasingly narrowly defined, the one ignoring theory, the other history, an analysis which builds on the increasing dissatisfaction expressed by British and American scholars, particularly since the 1980s (Hobsbawm 1964; Zieger 1983; Phelps Brown 1986; Brody 1989; Montgomery 1991). Our review of the literature on strikes specifically in relation to coalmining confirms this verdict, which is why we also explained how we proposed to tackle this problem in the research which then lay ahead of us (Church et al. 1989a, 1991a).

In the same inaugural issue of *Historical Studies in Industrial Relations*, Ackers rejected the notion that the history of labour and industrial relations in the coal industry was an 'exhausted seam'. He argued vigorously that the centrality of the industry for two centuries necessitated much more research if a truer, deeper understanding of the history of miners and mining is to be achieved (1996: 169). Our study, the result of intensive primary research over several years, anticipated the concerns expressed by these three authors. The scope is broad even though the focus is specific, while the methodology employed combines theory-based industrial relations and history in an approach entirely consistent with that which the journal editors insisted was a necessary condition for the future development of both. Like them, we seek to revitalize the historical analysis of the practice and theory of industrial relations. Moreover, in focusing on 'miners [who] remain central to modern British social, political and industrial relations history' (Ackers 1996: 170) we have chosen an important test case for an innovative methodology applied in a historical and comparative analysis. What follows, therefore, is our contribution to a new labour studies agenda.

We are grateful to the many archivists and librarians who have assisted in the location of material and to those trade union officials who kindly allowed access to records in their care and put us in touch with former coalminers. Our indebtedness to Dr. David Smith, who was research associate between 1986 and 1989 is difficult to exaggerate. In addition to his expertise in finding and utilizing sources in the normal process of orthodox research, his flair for eliciting relevant information from personal interviews with former coalminers and trade union officials was of special value. We are also pleased to acknowledge the constructive advice, information and useful suggestions provided by Carolyn Baylies, Sue Bowden, Alan Campbell, Heather Johnson, Gary Littlejohn, Joël Michel, Paul Turner, and by journal editors and anonymous referees who helped in the preparation of articles based on our research at an earlier stage, and to Richard Fisher of Cambridge University Press and anonymous referees whose advice on the initial proposal substantially modified the scope of the book.

The articles upon which parts of chapters 1 and 2 are based were published in *The Bulletin of the Society for the Study of Labour History* and the *Journal of Interdisciplinary History*; that forming the basis for chapter 5 in the *British Journal of Industrial Relations*. Chapter 8 draws on an article which appeared in the *Sociological Review,* and chapter 10 on another which appeared in the *Scottish Journal of Political Economy*. Full publication details will be found in the List of References. Some of our ideas were first put forward at the International Mining History Congress in Bochum, Germany, in 1989 (Tenfelde 1992) and in Golden, Colorado in 1994; we are grateful to the organizers of those congresses and to those participants who were kind enough to offer their views on our work.

List of abbreviations

AA	Amalgamated Anthracite
AAM	Amalgamated Association of Miners
CPGB	Communist Party of Great Britain
DAC	Doncaster Amalgamated Collieries
DMA	Durham Miners' Association
DPLA	district power loading agreement
ESRC	Economic and Social Research Council
FA	Fuel Administration
ILO	International Labour Office
ILP	Independent Labour Party
JNNC	Joint National Negotiating Committee
MAGB	Mining Association of Great Britain
MFGB	Miners' [*after 1933* Mineworkers'] Federation of Great Britain
MMM	Miners' Minority Movement
MNA	Miners' National Association
MNU	Miners' National Union
MSWCOA	Monmouthshire and South Wales Coal Owners' Association
NACODS	National Association of Colliery Overmen, Deputies and Shotfirers
NCB	National Coal Board
NMA	Nottinghamshire Miners' Association
NMIU	Nottinghamshire and District Miners' Industrial Union
NMMCA	Northumberland Miners' Mutual Confident Association
NPLA	National Power Loading Agreement
NRT	National Reference Tribunal
NUM	National Union of Mineworkers
NUSMW	National Union of Scottish Mineworkers
OFD	Owners of the Federated Districts
PR	participation rate
PRO	Public Record Office
RILU	Red International of Labour Unions
SCOA	Scottish Coal Owners' Association
SDF	Social-Democratic Federation
SMF	Scottish Miners' Federation

SWMF	South Wales Miners' Federation
SWMIU	South Wales Miners' Industrial Union
SYCOA	South Yorkshire Coal Owners' Association
SYMA	South Yorkshire Miners' Association
TUC	Trades Union Congress
UA	United Anthracite
UMS	United Mineworkers of Scotland
UMWA	United Mine Workers of America
URC	Unofficial Reform Committee
WAC	Welsh Amalgamated Collieries
WYCOA	West Yorkshire Coal Owners' Association
YMA	Yorkshire Miners' Association
YMWA	Yorkshire Mine Workers' Association

1   Interpreting coalfield conflict: focus and formulations

Mining strikes and 'militant miners': contemporary perceptions and empirical expositions

Miners are not averse to striking on slight pretext. They like to 'play' at intervals, and then return to scrabble harder in the pits, whence they can direct their thoughts with some contempt to the people who have to pass all their hours on the surface. The public takes no notice of these small disputes. They are not even reported in the papers, except by some short paragraph stating that 2,000 men have stopped work because a non-unionist has been discovered, or a foreman is disliked or the appointment of a checkweighman is questioned. The man in the street wonders why such a storm in a teacup should upset so many people, and possibly deems the stoppage to be the work of an 'agitator' or an unnecessary exhibition of strength. (Askwith 1920/1974: 201)

Of all classes of labour, he [the coalminer] is the most grasping and the most combative, the sturdiest fighter in the industrial field, always asking for more. (Bulman 1920: 2)

The miner not only works in the pit, he lives in the pit village, and all his immediate interests are concentrated at one point. . . . The miners' intense solidarity and loyalty to their unions is undoubtedly the result of conditions under which they work and live. . . . Their isolation ministers to their self-sufficiency and loyalty one to another. (Cole 1923: 7)

The British coalminer's reputation for militancy, exemplified in the observations quoted above by Askwith, a leading and experienced industrial conciliator, Bulman, a colliery director, and Cole, a scholar and a champion of labour, endured into the 1990s, when the dramatic decline in the coal industry was accompanied by a spectacular fall in the number of working miners. The bitterness of industrial relations in the industry's history, the miners' periodic clashes not only with employers but with governments, and the industry's extraordinary record of strikes for many years before and after the Second World War has confirmed the portrayal of coalminers as among the most militant of all workers.

   For more than a hundred years the relatively high strike propensity of coalminers has attracted comment from contemporary observers, social scientists, historians, and from miners themselves. Described as 'the traditional battle-

Table 1.1. *Average annual number of strikes per 100,000 employees in employment (broad industry groups, UK 1893–1966)*

Period	Mining and quarrying	Metals and engineering	Textiles	Clothing[a]	Building/ Construction	Transport and communications
1893–1900	18	12	9	4	16	3
1901–10	14	5	6	3	3	1
1911–20	13	12	8	6	12	5
1921–30	13	4	3	3	7	3
1931–38	27	5	6	3	5	2
1938–48	99	12	5	4	5	5
1949–58	171	7	2		7	5
1959–66	161	18	3		15	9

Notes:
Strikes and lock-outs as recorded by the Department of Employment and its predecessors. Data refer to strikes beginning in the years shown. The Census of Population data used for 1893–1920 did not clearly distinguish employees in employment from those unemployed (C. H. Lee 1979). Deficiencies and lack of comparabilities in the employment and strike data render small differences insignificant.

[a] Employment data refer to clothing and footwear for 1893-1920, clothing 1921–48, textiles and clothing 1949–58, and textiles and clothing and footwear 1959–66.

Sources: Strikes: Cronin (1979), appendix table B1. Employment: C. H. Lee (1979) for 1893–1920; Feinstein (1972) for 1920–48; Department of Employment and Productivity, *British Labour Statistics*, table 132 for 1949–66.

ground' by modern investigators (Durcan *et al.* 1983: 213), British coalfields were shown to be particularly susceptible to strikes as early as 1880, when Bevan described the number of strikes as 'out of all proportion to strikes in other trades' (1880: 39). The disproportionate number of strikes recorded in the industry is presented in table 1.1. By the 1950s no less than 70 per cent of all strikes in the UK were in mining and quarrying, a peak from which there was a subsequent decline both in relative and in absolute terms.

Yet serious deficiencies in our knowledge of the historical patterns of strike activity have obscured the nature of 'miners' militancy', and an understanding of its causes has so far eluded both commentators and scholars alike. Attempts to explain the industry's strike proneness have a long history. Some of these explanations will receive detailed scrutiny later in this book. At this point, however, we wish to emphasize how 'problematic' the industry's strike record has appeared to those in positions of power, and in particular to the organs of the state. A history of concern with the industry's industrial relations can be traced through a series of government enquiries from the late nineteenth century forward. These enquiries demonstrate not only the level of concern but also the repeated failure of the state to find an adequate explanation of the problem which confronted it.

Although not explicitly concerned with the coal industry, the *Majority Report* of the Royal Commission on Labour of 1891–4 contained the essential elements of two perspectives which have both remained influential. The first was the contention that strikes occurred because of the absence or inadequacies of institutions for the discussion and negotiation of points of potential conflict (Royal Commission on Labour, *Majority Report*: 98); this is a view echoed in the analysis of industrial relations experts and scholars seventy years later. The second was that the separation of workers from their employers 'in their lives and pursuits' was a major factor in explaining overt industrial conflict, a view which reappeared in sociological models of mining communities in the 1950s.

Such models were more fully anticipated in the remarkable *Report on No. 7 Division (Wales and Monmouthshire)* of the 1917 Commission of Enquiry into Industrial Unrest. This dealt both with the institutions of collective bargaining and with the geological, geographical, economic, demographic, social and ideological contexts of unrest among the miners of South Wales. In summarizing the 'reasons for the greater discontent manifested by the miners as compared with other classes of workers', it drew attention to four specific factors: first, an 'erroneous view of the value of colliery produce' (that is, coal prices and profits) and therefore the industry's ability to pay; second, the tendency towards monopoly in the industry, which it was suggested had 'aroused considerable alarm in the minds of the miners'; third, the very high density of colliery employment in some areas which induced 'an exaggerated view of their [the miners'] indispensability to the employers and to the nation' and also a high degree of commitment to their union; and fourth, the location of the industry away from large towns, which precluded 'intercourse with the inhabitants of such towns and participation in their public life and activities'. The fact that the industry was then considered to have been 'well organized' on both sides and that a conciliation board had long been in operation seemed, in contradiction to the earlier prescriptions of the 1891–4 Royal Commission, to offer no protection against strikes (Commission of Enquiry into Industrial Unrest, *Report on No. 7 Division (Wales and Monmouthshire)*: 21).

Despite the short duration of the enquiry and the relative brevity of the *Report*, this has remained the most substantial official analysis of the 'especially pronounced' class antagonism found in the mining industry. The reports produced by the Sankey Commission in 1919 lacked analytical depth, while the 1926 report of the Samuel Commission, although certainly more substantial, was largely concerned with the economic state of the industry and treated industrial unrest as incidental to this concern. Unrest was examined primarily in terms of the grievances held by workers and employers and, implicitly and naively, the remedy recommended to end the strike proneness in the industry was that of removing 'well-founded' grievances (Royal Commission on the Coal Industry (1925), *Report*: 113). As in previous official reports this emphasis stemmed from an excessive dependence on the evidence of witnesses whose roles in the industry as employers or trade union officials led them to concentrate on the success or failure of the institutions in which they participated, portraying grievances as the causes of strikes. Nowhere in these discussions is it acknowledged that a grievance was not a sufficient condition to precipitate strike action.

Well-founded or not, miners' grievances were not of course removed subsequent to the Samuel Commission's *Report*. Instead, in the General Strike and subsequent Coal Lock-out of 1926, British coalowners and the British state acted on what is probably the oldest theory of strike activity: that strikes will not occur in the absence of strong trade unions. The impoverishment and weakening of the coalminers' trade unions by the events of 1926 took mining industrial relations off the political agenda for many years. But, curiously, although they were defeated in the coalfields the political battle moved gradually in the miners' favour. By the end of the Second World War the propositions that the industrial relations of the industry were very poor, that this situation was the result of 'especially pronounced' class antagonisms in the industry, and that an appropriate and acceptable way to remove these was to nationalize the mines, were widely accepted (Supple 1987).

The failure of nationalization to achieve a 'transforming improvement' (Acton Society Trust 1953: 9) in the relations between workers and management had become obvious by the early 1950s. Although no national or official strike had taken place, local and unofficial strikes took place in extraordinarily large numbers, making mining by far and away the most strike-prone industry group on this measure (table 1.1). After undergoing a radical cure and finding it ineffective, the industry's managers gave every impression of having run out of ideas. By the mid-1950s there was a noticeable diagnostic and policy vacuum in the National Coal Board (NCB) (Baldwin 1955: 63, 83–4). In 1965 when the NCB was asked by another Royal Commission 'Is it possible to specify any principal reasons [for "the rather large number of unofficial stoppages" in the industry]?' it was reduced to saying:

[I]t is not peculiar to this country that there are industrial disturbances in the coalmines. They happen all over the world. It is one of the features of the industry. Maybe it is in the nature of the industry. . . . I am afraid I could not give an answer to it. (Royal Commission on Trade Unions and Employers' Associations, *Minutes of Evidence*, 4, Q720)

The research and investigations, statistical and otherwise, conducted by, or on behalf of, the state have produced analyses of 'miners' militancy' or miners' strikes which have failed to go beyond what one might call an impressionistic empiricism in which questions or perceptions derived from social theory are notably absent. Such approaches to strike activity have not been confined to official investigations, however. Knowles (1952) provided a valuable, exhaustive but atheoretic analysis of the published official statistics confining his investigations to the period between 1911 and 1947. The breadth of his coverage and the aggregative characteristic of the officially published data he used also limited the scope of his research. The self-styled 'update' of Knowles's study carried out by Durcan *et al.* (1983) displayed many of the limitations of the earlier work. Cronin's study of *Industrial Conflict in Modern Britain* (1979) was both aggregative and national in approach, building on the work of Shorter and Tilly on French strikes (1974) and emphasizing the importance of 'the political and organizational resources available to both sides in industrial conflict' (Cronin 1979: 37). He described his analysis of strike behaviour as dynamic, in search of a theory or concepts which might explain industrial conflict. His contribution in identifying a series of 'strike waves' in Britain since 1888 mapped the chronological dimension of strike activity for a period of almost one hundred years; yet partly because the scope of his enquiry was national and included all industries, his conclusion 'that strikes come in waves, in broad explosions of creative militancy' (1979: 194) was essentially descriptive rather than explanatory.

It is evident that while the subject of coalmining and coalminers has generated a vast literature, few explanations for the pronounced temporal and spatial variations in strike activity are well established. In part, our understanding of the history of mining strikes has been obscured because of the tendency of historians to reconstruct the history of industrial relations either from a trade union perspective or in episodic terms which emphasize not variations and patterns but events – the formation of the Miners' Federation of Great Britain in 1889, the lock-out in 1893, the campaign for the eight-hour day, the first national miners' strike of 1912, and the great lock-outs of 1921 and 1926 (see J. E. Williams 1962a; Hobsbawm 1964; Briggs 1966). Although these events were important set-piece battles, the tendency to view the course of industrial relations history solely from this perspective runs the risk of failing to capture the significance of the numerous 'small disputes', often affecting no more than a single colliery, which accounted for most strikes in the industry, and to which Askwith drew attention in the passage with which we opened this chapter.

Theoretical orientations to mining strikes

The empirical approaches we have just discussed contrast with those adopted by Marxist writers, some of whom have cast miners in the vanguard of the class struggle. Despite their diversity, and although the theory is not always explicit, all Marxist writers place theory at the centre of their analyses of industrial conflict. We regard their writings as important not so much because of their specific content but more because their attempt to grasp the whole range of social reality as it unfolds through history serves to demonstrate the often limited and partial nature of the work carried out by non-Marxist historians and social scientists. Because of the diversity of approaches which can be found in the Marxist literature, it is helpful for the purpose of our own exposition to offer a synthesis of Marxist views based largely, though not entirely, on the work of Hyman (1972, 1975).

For Marxists, work relations under capitalism provide a permanent and

inevitable source of conflict, while the strike and lock-out are the most prominent methods by which employer and worker prosecute their mutually antagonistic interests. However, although industrial conflict is 'the central reality of
industrial relations', overt conflict is rare and not commonplace (Hyman 1975:
190). As disputes are constantly occurring, more or less permanent machinery
for the resolution of disputes by direct negotiation, conciliation or arbitration,
often staffed by full-time specialist personnel, is established. In this way the
expression of conflict becomes institutionalized. Moreover, the continual contact between the employer and employee sides of those institutions encourages
the growth of shared understandings and orientations which, in the short term at
least, facilitate the peaceful resolution of disputes. The hegemonic domination
of capitalism, however, ensures that employee representatives tend to assimilate
the world view of the employer rather than vice versa. In drawing closer to the
employer's view of the world, employee representatives, especially full-time
trade union officers, draw away from the outlook of the rank and file membership (Cronin 1989; Price 1989; Zeitlin 1989). This is one aspect of the 'inherent
duality of trade unionism' and one reason why 'industrial peace' is a precarious
state.

Established with difficulty and always provisional, industrial peace is subject
to continual disruptions deriving from the inherent instability of capitalism,
which continually undermines and subverts the technological, economic, social
and political bases of the existing pattern of accommodation between employer
and employee. Industrial relations are thus continually brought to points of crisis
in which conflict becomes overt. The manner in which such crises are resolved
and the terms of their resolution depend greatly on the leadership offered to
workers by their industrial and political representatives. Where, despite the
pressures inherent in their position, leaderships have retained a class consciousness or where they have acquired such a consciousness from political organizations, they are enabled to provide a militant leadership in sustained, overt
conflict. Where leaderships have adopted the views and attitudes of their opponents, however, their predominant concern will be to bring overt conflict to an
end as rapidly as possible, if necessary on terms detrimental to the working class.

This schema has found its most frequent application in the analysis of the very
large national lock-outs and strikes of the British industry in the period after the
First World War which culminated in the General Strike of 1926 and in the large
national strikes of the early 1970s and mid-1980s. In these applications the
emphasis is on crisis as the source of the dispute and on the tension between the
rank and file and trade union and political leaders as a basis for understanding
the course and the conduct of the strike. Thus Foster locates the General Strike
in a general crisis of British imperialism precipitated by the First World War and
exacerbated in the coal industry by the policies of a state dominated by financial
interests (Foster 1976). In two wide-ranging studies Fine et al. (1985a, 1985b)
also locate the General Strike in the contemporary political and economic crisis
but provide little discussion of rank and file relationships with the trade union

leadership until they come to examine the industrial relations of the early nationalization period in the late 1940s and 1950s. Allen's work on the confrontations of the 1970s stresses the importance of changes in the miners' level of political consciousness, in turn attributed partly to the policies of governments, the policies of the NCB and the National Union of Mineworkers (NUM), and to changing economic conditions. For Allen, however, 'The factor with the greatest significance at that time [the early 1970s] was undoubtedly the coterie of Communists and left wing Labour Party members who were active in the union at this time' (Allen 1981: 319).

Marxist-oriented studies of local industrial relations and conflict are rare. The study by Dennis, Henriques and Slaughter of 'Ashton' colliery and its community in Yorkshire in the 1950s emphasized at different points the inherent conflict in capitalist industrial relations and the 'alienation between the interests of union officials and union membership' (Dennis *et al.* 1956: 32, 115). Rigg tested Allen's views on the importance of a class conscious leadership as a determinant of industrial militancy by means of an interview study of the union leadership of two collieries with widely contrasting levels of strike activity. The results tended to support Allen's view (Rigg 1987).

At a more abstract level the history of industrial relations in the British coal industry is, like any other aspect of history seen from this perspective, the outcome of the interplay of structures, organizations, consciousness and action (Giddens 1979; Hyman 1984: 180–8). 'Structures' are enduring constraints on human action. They may be 'natural' or 'social'. Relevant examples of natural structures include the geographical and geological disposition of coal measures and other natural resources. 'Social structures' are economic, social, political and legal institutions which have been created intentionally or unintentionally by human action but, once created, appear as constraints on human action which cannot be removed or relaxed immediately. The demographic and spatial characteristics of mining communities, the market for coal, the available technologies of coal extraction, and the institutions through which state power is shaped, transmitted and expressed, are examples of social structures. 'Organizations' form a subset of the set of social structures: they are defined in terms of the social relations between members of a group. Typically membership is clearly defined so that it is possible to refer unambiguously to people as 'members' or 'non-members', 'insiders' or 'outsiders', 'familiars' or 'strangers'. Typically, also, it is possible to describe the social relations of the members of the organization in terms of relations between superiors and inferiors, leaders and followers, officers and members. As colliery companies, employers' associations, trade unions and work teams are all examples of organizations it is clear that neither formal written rules nor special legal status is necessary for an organization to exist.

'Actions' are of two kinds. There are actions which confirm the reality and rigidity of the constraints offered by existing natural or social structures: the strike for higher wages which fails and confirms the reality of the constraints placed on wage settlements by a free market for coal, or the strike, such as the 1984–5 British miners' strike, which confirms the reality of state power. But there are also actions which change structures: the strike that wins union recognition and thus changes the structure of social relations at the workplace or the political campaign which succeeds in replacing private by state ownership of the industry. 'Consciousness' is the subjective interpretation and valuation of structures, organizations and actions. Consciousness may be more or less coherent and more or less articulate. The ideology of the 'independent collier' with its stress on individualism and job control (Campbell and Reid 1978) is one example; the ideas, attitudes and valuations summed up in the word 'paternalism' as documented in the British mining context, for example, by Waller (1983) is another as is, of course, a Marxist-Leninist class consciousness as studied in our context by Macintyre (1980b).

None of these four elements (structures, organizations, consciousness and action) can be studied sensibly in isolation from the other three. Structures influence actions but this influence is mediated by organization and consciousness. Actions change structures, organizations and consciousness. These processes take place in time and as such cannot be understood without a historical dimension. Today's actions are constrained by structures and organizations put in place by yesterday's actions and have meaning for their participants in terms of a consciousness derived from past experiences, a point underlined by Kenneth Morgan's contemporary commentary on the strike of 1984–5, 'A time for miners to forget history' (1985). These points are all fairly straightforward and uncontentious, yet it is remarkable how much of the previous research relevant to this study has failed to go beyond an analysis of structures or a description of the development of an organization or a celebration of the advanced class consciousness of the mining proletariat. How far the interactions between the various aspects of social reality can be identified and elucidated in the history of British coalmining between 1889 and 1966 is the central problem addressed in this study. The next section explains the methodology we have employed in our attempts to do so and maps out the investigations which follow.

Methods, sources and schema

Theorists claim meaning for their work, though typically it is lacking in historical content. Too often the writings of labour historians and of other empiricists possess content but employ little theory (if at all) and offer interpretation within limits defined by either the organizations or by the specific events which concern the authors. Too few studies of the social history of miners have focused on historical processes. Here we have attempted to combine theory and concepts from the social sciences with empirical historical data. As will become clear in the chapters that follow, one of our principal criticisms of previous work in this field is that, with few exceptions, each contribution has offered only a partial account of its subject. Our work attempts to rectify the one-sidedness of current understandings. Our choices of theories and concepts are based on our judgements of their relevance to the questions we seek to answer and the fruitfulness of their application.

This has resulted in the assembly of quantitative data which is new, qualitative evidence from primary sources, and also the use of secondary sources, including traditional historical narratives. By using an existing literature on the social and economic history of coalmining to supplement our own researches, and with the assistance of concepts and theory from the social sciences, we have sought to inject more meaning into traditional accounts of institutions and events in the industry and to generalize. While the study is national in scope it is not our intention to provide either a narrative history of all colliery strikes between 1889 and 1966 or even of the major conflicts which punctuated the history of the industry. None the less, the descriptions of strike activity contained in traditional histories are susceptible to later analytical interpretations which their authors would not have contemplated. Partly from these sources, and by constructing some of our own case histories, we have juxtaposed the aggregative with the case study and we have analysed both quantitative data on large numbers of strikes and large samples of collieries with qualitative data pertaining to single strikes, collieries, companies and localities. We have found this diversity of approach to be an effective way of compensating for the deficiencies of each approach on its own.

One of the most important differences between our research and that of other researchers is that our focus is on local rather than national, regional, district or county strikes. These other manifestations of conflict find a place in our study, but only in contexts where they can illuminate the strike activity and also the nature of miners' solidarity. The justification for this focus is that the frequency and prevalence of strikes limited to a single locality or colliery are so numerous compared with other kinds of strikes that the local strike may be regarded as 'ordinary'. The questions we explore concern spatial, chronological and inter-colliery differences; the levels and differential patterns of strike activity between collieries and between localities; strike persistence over time; factors which explain both high and low strike proneness; and strike participation and the issue of 'miners' militancy'. In each case the statistical basis is national, but a comprehensive coverage using primary and printed sources was quite beyond imaginable resources and reasonable time required for such a study. Hence the strategy of combining intermediate levels of analysis of a limited population of localities and collieries with a smaller number of case studies. While our study cannot claim to be comprehensive in all respects, we would argue that the methodology we have used to make a systematic selection of our sources justifies the claims we make for the validity of our conclusions.

The period covered in this study begins in 1889. That marked the formation of the Miners' Federation of Great Britain (MFGB) and the beginning of the collection of annual strike data by the Labour Department of the Board of Trade. The bulk of our research has focused on the period up to the Second

World War, but because of the availability of richer data sources we have investigated the period between the wars in greater detail than any other. We were concerned to see how far the conclusions we reached on the basis of these investigations held true for the Second World War and after, when the industry saw major changes not the least of which was its transfer from private hands into state ownership in 1947. We have therefore extended our basic analyses to the post-war period in an attempt to ascertain the historical specificity of our conclusions; we have not attempted to give as full an account of strike activity in this period as is offered for the pre-war period. Just as we were concerned to see how our study looked from the perspective offered by another time so, too, were we concerned to gain the perspective offered by other places. We have therefore considered international variations in miners' strike activity in an attempt to see how the patterns we discern in the British industry were replicated elsewhere.

We have brought this study to a close in 1966. Restrictions on access to the official records which form a major source of data mean that we would have been unable to take this study much beyond 1963 in any case: records from after that year were not open to us at the time of writing because of the statutory closure of official records under the thirty years' rule. However, in historical terms a termination of this study in 1963 makes no sense: it was not a remarkable year and we can be fairly sure that the succeeding three years were not significantly different. The year 1966 can claim to mark the end of an era. That year saw the introduction of the National Power Loading Agreement which, by replacing piece-rate wages by a form of measured day work, had, it has often been argued, a major impact on colliery- and national-level industrial relations, culminating in the 1972 national strike, the first in the industry for almost fifty years.

Up to this point we have taken it for granted that we know what we mean when we refer to a 'strike'. However, as soon as we consider the definition of 'strike', difficulties emerge. We would expect there to be a solution to these difficulties, at least on a pragmatic level, since they must be resolved if strike statistics are to be compiled on a consistent basis. These official statistics are one of the principal foundations on which our research has been constructed. However, it is difficult to discover how the official statisticians decided what was and what was not a strike. No detailed official guide to the sources and methods used in the compilation of these statistics has ever been published. What official material is available is not adequate and almost all of it relates to the pre-1914 period. The accounts published since 1914 have been absurdly brief (see, for example, Department of Employment and Productivity, *British Labour Statistics*: 19). One of the few things to be clear is that the official statistics exclude forms of pressure which do not involve a complete cessation of work: 'go-slows', 'working without enthusiasm', 'working to rule', overtime bans, 'ca'canny' and other forms of output restriction. It is also clear that since 1983 no attempt has been made in the official statistics to distinguish strikes from lock-outs: hence the official term 'stoppage of work due to an industrial dispute', often abbreviated to 'stoppage' or 'industrial dispute'.

At this point we should clarify our own terminology. Unlike the official statisticians we use the terms 'strike' and 'stoppage' inclusively and interchangeably to mean a 'stoppage of work because of an industrial dispute'. In our usage, a 'dispute' or a 'grievance' is not the same thing as a 'strike', however: a dispute may be resolved or a grievance redressed without a stoppage of work, perhaps through the use of grievance procedures or conciliation machinery. We often use the term 'militancy' here simply and only as a shorthand for 'readiness to strike' or 'strike proneness', without, necessarily, any implication of 'class consciousness' or any other highly developed political awareness; our usage is also not intended to imply that strike action is the only manifestation of conflict at work (P. K. Edwards and Scullion 1982; Winchester 1983).

The definition of 'strike' most frequently quoted is that offered by the International Labour Office (ILO) in 1926: 'an economic occurrence, characterised by a temporary stoppage of work . . . wilfully effected . . . with a view to enforcing a demand'. Sometimes this is extended to include stoppages designed only to 'express a grievance' (International Labour Office, *Methods of Compiling Statistics of Industrial Disputes*: 14; cf. Knowles 1952: 301, Hyman 1972: 17 and P. K. Edwards 1981: 287). However, it should not be assumed that the British statistics have been compiled using this, or indeed any, definition. While the official Board of Trade *Report on the Strikes and Lock-outs of 1888* offered a definition of a strike which broadly anticipated the ILO definition, a decision was made subsequently that the statistical definition of 'strike' should conform to the legal definition given in the Trade Disputes Act of 1906 (Ministry of Labour, *Statistics . . . Definition of Strikes and Lockouts*, Minutes by H. H. Cook, 3 March 1921 and 5 August 1926, PRO LAB 17/325), and it is clear that from at least 1921 the statisticians worked with one eye on the courtroom. The problems this practice led to are easily imagined. A legal decision in July 1926 to the effect that the General Strike of May that year was not a strike within the legal meaning of the term appeared to imply that the statisticians should expunge the strike from the records; this, they decided, was 'not practicable' (*ibid.*, 5 August 1926). The passage of the Trade Disputes and Trade Unions Act 1927 which included a new and extraordinarily wide definition of 'strike' caused consternation among the statisticians. Quite how they decided to respond to this is not clear from the surviving records. All one can say is that those records suggest that the strike statistics were compiled by civil servants guided by pragmatism rather than principle.

Problems of definition conceal a deeper source of imprecision in the data which throws doubt on the very meaning to be attached to recorded 'strikes'. It is not merely that it may be difficult to apply a definition of a 'strike' in particular cases but that the people concerned may choose to define a protest as a 'strike' or vice versa and may themselves understand their actions as a 'strike', or as a 'protest', or as a 'demonstration', or in terms of some other socially defined category, and that these presentations and understandings affect the way participants behave. Such a possibility has consequences for how that behaviour can be understood (cf. Batstone *et al.* 1978: 19–20). An example may make this clearer.

Paterson and Willett give an account of a strike at 'Blackford colliery' in 1949. It was a warm spring day and a number of men were sitting in the sun at the pithead waiting to go down on the afternoon shift. The conversation turned to an old grievance that had never been settled but 'the conversation was neither heated nor aggressive. One man remarked that it was "very fine weather for the backshift" and the men immediately and unanimously decided they would not go underground that afternoon' (1951: 63). When the observing sociologist asked what was going on, he was told that the men were on strike and immediately a range of old and new grievances were discussed as if to justify this description. Within half an hour a demand had been formulated which from then on was presented as the reason for and justification of the strike.

One interpretation of these events is that the afternoon shift saw the fine weather and decided to find some way of avoiding work that afternoon: a grievance was found to justify a strike which allowed the men to 'legitimately' take the afternoon off. A case of mass absenteeism was presented, defined and understood by its participants as a 'strike'. The role of social meanings and interpretations is underlined by the contrast provided by another account. Frank Vernon, who started work in a Yorkshire colliery in 1937, recalls

a glorious sunny summer day. All the haulage lads always used to hang back until the last minute and would go down the pit on the last cage. Harry [Fountain] was standing with his mates, grumbling and muttering about having to go down the pit, leaving all this sunshine. All of a sudden he bawled 'Am gonna chuck mi hat up in the air and if it comes down we're going home!' It was a foregone conclusion. We went home. (Vernon 1984: 19)

Vernon does not present this incident as a 'strike' but its resemblance to the incident at Blackford colliery is clear. Thus very similar sequences of events may attract different interpretations. The fact that we understand a 'strike' as something different from an 'absence from work' can obscure the close similarities that may sometimes exist between the two and hence obscure the reasons for the events we observe. When considering our strike statistics we need to remember that what we have before us are details of events which have been socially, not merely statistically, defined as 'strikes'.

These questions arise most seriously in cases of 'spontaneous walkouts' precipitated by what appear to be trivial events. To insist on treating such instances as 'economic occurrence[s], characterised by a temporary stoppage of work . . . , wilfully effected . . . with a view to enforcing a demand' may be to miss the point entirely: far from being rationally chosen means to other ends, such walkouts may directly achieve their end: to gain a temporary respite from work. There is a long history of linguistic usages which seem to imply such motivations: employers and contemporary observers referred to miners 'playing the pits', and to 'play days'; the observations by Askwith with which we opened this chapter are a case in point. That approximately one-third of strikes ended on the employers' terms without negotiation in the late 1920s and 1930s also suggests that walkouts to achieve a respite from work may not have been at all uncommon. However, other evidence suggests that, at least in the more recent period, such walkouts have been less frequent than this. Jencks's industry-wide study for 1953–6 presented data which showed that between 6 and 9 per cent of stoppages and restrictions occurred without any discussion of the strikers' grievances (which the data presume must have existed) with NCB officials (1966: table 6).

While it is important to make explicit the difficulties which the ambiguities of definition and the blurred distinctions between different manifestations of conflictual behaviour present to researchers, they have not deterred us from attempting a systematic, though in the light of the discussion above, cautious inquiry into the 'strike' activity of British coalminers.

As we have already indicated, one of the main primary sources for this study is the official statistical record of strikes and lock-outs held in a series of manuscript ledgers at the Public Record Office. The ledgers cover the period from 1901 and provide more complete information from 1903. These provide case by case details of all officially recorded strikes and lock-outs. For the period prior to 1903 we have relied on the annual Board of Trade *Reports on Strikes and Lock-outs* for the years 1893–1900, and for 1901–2 on the less complete listings contained in the Board of Trade *Labour Gazette*. The importance of the large volume of data contained in these sources lies partly in its unique degree of disaggregation. This characteristic allows a much more detailed examination of the forms and variations of strike activity, not merely for a locality, district or region, but for the industry nation-wide. The importance also lies in the possibility presented by these records of constructing strike 'histories' for the individual collieries and for the places, towns and villages noted in the records.

These data are, of course, by no means ideal. We noted above that there is no clear or consistent definition of 'strike' discernible in these data. The most significant other difficulties are discussed in the general appendix and a detailed account of these and other points is available in Outram (1997). Even readers who are averse to appendices should, however, note the existence of one problem which we have had to bear in mind at every twist and turn of our investigations. This is that the coverage of the data is incomplete to an unknown extent. Some strikes were excluded from the official records on the grounds that they were too small to be of any significance and, undoubtedly, other strikes were simply missed by the official statisticians; these, too, are highly likely to have been small-scale strikes. All our quantitative evidence pertains only to officially recorded strikes; of those that did not enter the official record we can say little. At each stage of our quantitative investigations we have therefore had to consider how far the picture presented by the officially recorded strikes could differ from the picture that would be presented by the totality of coalmining strikes were we able to examine them. While we comment on this problem at the appropriate points in the chapters that follow, here we offer reassurance that while the coverage problem effectively precludes a useful answer to some questions (most obviously, 'What was the true number of strikes in colliery X in year t?') it does not preclude useful answers to *all* questions. We hope that by the end of this book the reader will have been able to accept this reassurance.

A second major source which is critical to our method of reconstructing colliery strike histories is the *List of Mines*, published annually by the Home Office (later the Mines Department). While at first sight not much more than a list of names and addresses, the *Lists* are an enormously valuable source. One reason for this is that by linking the variously named collieries in the strike records with one uniquely named colliery in the relevant *List*, they enable us to treat collieries consistently. Another is that the information contained in this source allows a linkage to be made between collieries and owning companies and between collieries and the administrative areas in which they were situated. Complemented by trade directories, especially *The Colliery Year Book and Coal Trades Directory*, and by census data, it has been possible to answer such questions as which collieries were struck, when, for how long and by whom? Were they rural or urban? By whom were they owned? By whom were they managed? How large was the company? How many worked at the mine? What types of coal were being produced? When was mechanization introduced?

Integrating such factors influencing strike activity as organization among workers and employers into our analysis presented problems because the sources, other than at a national, and for some parts of the country regional, level are few, discontinuous, of variable quality and of limited application. Records of trade unions and of coalowners' associations have contributed to our discussion, while at lodge and colliery level, printed and oral evidence has provided a basis for the interpretation of the origins and outcomes of strikes in the mine and at the coal-face.

The sources described above have been used in statistical procedures in the search for those quantifiable factors that were associated with high levels of strike activity. Those procedures require large samples of data if useful results are to be obtained. This makes it difficult to incorporate non-quantifiable factors into the analysis and so the explanation offered by such procedures is necessarily incomplete. For this reason we attempted to supplement the statistical work by a more detailed examination of a small number of matched pairs of collieries. We identified pairs of collieries possessing similar geographical and quantifiable characteristics but which revealed contrasting histories of strike activity. We then conducted a more detailed examination of the quantitative evidence for each colliery and attempted to uncover qualitative evidence through archival work supplemented by a small number of interviews with miners who had worked at the colliery concerned. In many ways this is traditional historical work; but it is more purposive and rigorous than traditional comparative studies in that we used formal criteria to construct a useful collection of comparator collieries and then sought evidence on them. We have not simply discussed the collieries for which evidence was to hand or was convenient to gather or in which we were interested for personal reasons. Inevitably, we found we could discover little about a number of the collieries we had selected; none the less the evidence assembled has provided valuable information illuminating the origins of strikes at the point of production. The primary sources, both printed and oral, we have used in this exercise, together with the secondary and official evidence we have utilized in our statistical investigations, are central to the themes developed in the following chapters.

We have written this book to reflect the history of our investigation. During our work we encountered a series of puzzles in trying to understand why some collieries were struck and some were not, why some localities seemed very strike-prone and others quiescent, why some regions experienced far more strikes than others. Some puzzles we have been able to elucidate. Often, the new light has revealed new puzzles and we have been led to investigate questions we had not considered interesting or important when we started this research. The most prominent examples of such 'unasked questions' are to do with the 'solidarity' for which British miners have such an outstanding reputation. Despite this reputation, coalmining strikes have hardly been studied from this point of view: they have almost always been treated as conflicts between workers and managements, rarely as occasions of co-operation between workers. Of course they are both and we hope this work will encourage others to investigate this dual character of strike activity.

Before we embark on an account of our investigations we provide in chapters 2, 3 and 4 a survey of the industry's history between the mid-nineteenth century and 1940, describing its structural and organizational features, the evolution of collective bargaining and the changing relations between workers, employers and the state, and the developments in coalowners' and miners' attitudes and politics. This survey is shaped by our interest in how, and the extent to which, the literature connects those facets with industrial conflict which is our primary concern. Chapter 5 measures strike activity at local and colliery levels, and reveals a pattern of frequent but small-scale and localized strikes. Despite the reputation of British miners for militancy and solidary behaviour we find that local strikes were frequently poorly supported. This leads us into an investigation of 'solidarity' as it was manifested in strike activity. The notion of solidarity, its manifestation and interrelations at national, regional and local level are the focus in chapters 6 and 7. We then return to the question of what lies behind the enormous variations of strike activity from colliery to colliery and from place to place and examine the idea that it is the massing of miners in isolated communities which leads to high strike activity. This thesis is examined statistically in chapter 8. We find that this idea has some merit but that the massing of workers at work, as well as outside it in the locality, is also a factor of importance.

This takes us on to an examination of the effects of colliery size on strike activity in chapter 9. Here again we find that a large part of the answer to our questions revolves around the effects of colliery size on worker solidarity and sectionalism; consequently much of this chapter is given over to the investigation of these topics at colliery level. We find that variations in massness in the locality and massness at work appear to explain some of the variations in strike activity; but these structural factors are clearly inadequate by themselves to explain all of the marked variations that existed. Accordingly, in chapter 10, we turn to alternative hypotheses explaining industrial conflict which include other structural factors and organizational characteristics. We have translated ideas contained in the literature dealing with the history of the industry into statistically testable models. Using both historical narrative and statistical investigation we find that the level and forms of organization and the policies pursued by the leaders of associations and trade unions have had discernible effects on the level of strike activity. By this point much of our explanation is in place; but one major puzzle remains. A feature of the industry well known to those acquainted with its industrial relations is that collieries apparently alike in structural and organizational respects may none the less differ markedly in their strike activity. Pairs of neighbouring collieries, to an outsider all but identical, may be hotbeds of activity in the one case and scenes of the utmost tranquillity in the other. Chapter 11 compares the strike histories of a number of pairs of collieries, matched as far as possible for their structural characteristics, paying particular attention to aspects of action and consciousness. By the end of this chapter we are ready to set out our solutions to the puzzles presented by the industry's strike record. However, questions arise as to how generally these conclusions hold true for the later period. Chapter 12 examines the Second World War and the post-nationalization period to see how far our results, derived as they are largely from research on the pre-war period, need modification before they may be applied to more recent years. In chapter 13 we again extend our horizons to ascertain what light the history of coalmining strikes in France, Germany and the United States can shed on our conclusions. Chapter 14 concludes the book.

2 Tradition and modernity: the mining industry 1889–1940

The social and economic history of the nineteenth and twentieth centuries has often been written around one major theme: the emergence and development of a recognizably 'modern' economy and society. Since one of the characteristics of modernity is incessant innovation, the 'pre-modern' period comes to be seen as, or indeed defined as, 'traditional'. The movement from tradition to modernity can be discerned in almost every sphere of social and economic life, and in each sphere different points may seem to be key moments in the transition from one form of life to another. In the relationships between masters and servants or between employers and workers many of the key changes have been perceived at least since the time of Marx. They are the production of commodities by machinery rather than by tools alone, the detailed division of labour, the growth of large-scale organization and bureaucracy, the growth of large-scale settlements or urbanization, and finally the development of an integrated world economy. Many commentators have argued that during this transition relationships between employers and workers became at the same time more distant but marked by an increasing measure of control and discipline by the former over the latter (Burgess 1975; Stearns 1975).

Until perhaps the mid-nineteenth century the British coalmining industry could claim to be in the van of movements towards modernity. Long before the nineteenth century, coalmining had required the investment of large accumulations of capital in order to sink shafts and construct pumping machinery. In Britain the erosion of tradition and custom by the penetration of market forces was well advanced in the industry long before steam power began to transform production processes. Coal mines brought together exceptionally large groups of workers and by the early nineteenth century Babbage expressed his opinion that the system of management and supervision found in the typical contemporary coal mine was a remarkably advanced example of the division of mental labour (Babbage: 1832/1989: 201–2; Dobb 1963: 139–40; Laslett 1983: 11; Fisher 1981).

Possibly by the end of the nineteenth century, certainly by the 1920s, the mining industry had lost this earlier reputation. During the nineteenth and early twentieth centuries innovations of technology and organization in manufacturing industries and transport outpaced those in mining. Machinery for pumping, ventilation and the transport of coal both underground and over ground had been invented and widely utilized during the nineteenth century, whereas the technology of coal-getting at the face hardly changed and seemed stuck in the stage which Marx called 'manufacture' for a remarkably long time, arguably until the widespread adoption of machine mining during the inter-war period. Apparently archaic forms of work organization (the use of subcontracting and the 'butty' system) persisted until perhaps the end of the 1930s. Management methods were direct, personal and at least in some instances marked by traditional paternalism (Gospel 1992). Even in the 1940s only a few firms evinced formal bureaucratic structures which would have borne comparison with those normal in the large modern firms of the times (Clegg and Chester 1953: 50). While most miners worked in large enterprises during the twentieth century, the fifty or so workers who were employed by the many small-scale collieries that continued to exist under private ownership seemed definitive of small-scale rather than large-scale industry. Moreover, such collieries were often located in isolated villages, far from the teeming crowds of the great cities, and their work-forces were marked not by the comings and goings of incessant mobility but by a 'hereditary closed shop' (Hair 1955: 268; Beynon and Austrin 1994: 130–43).

The traditional elements of this picture should not be allowed to obscure the modern, however: in some respects the industry remained in the forefront of movements towards modernity. The industry participated in global economic relations and supported large-scale, 'mass' organizations, both defining aspects of modernity. Some coalfields were more tightly integrated into the world market than was the British economy as a whole: for example nearly one-half of all coal mined in South Wales was exported by the turn of the century, at a time when a little less than a quarter of the output of the UK economy was exported; fluctuations in the world prices for coal were mirrored in domestic prices well before the economic disasters of the 1920s and 1930s (Feinstein 1972: table 3; Mitchell 1984: 279–80, table 2.2). By 1914 the Miners' Federation of Great Britain (MFGB) with its affiliated membership of 673,000 was one of the largest trade unions in the world (Cole 1923: 65). Its membership faced not only a mass of small-scale coalmasters but also some of the largest companies operating in any industry in the country. In some coalfields enormous combines and cartels emerged in the 1920s, and when the industry was nationalized in 1947 the National Coal Board (NCB) became the largest employer in the Western world (Supple 1987: 674; Winterton 1989: 190).

This chapter and the next surveys those aspects of the industry's economic and social structures which most affected relationships between employers and workers. The first section of this chapter considers the implications of technology for mine size and describes the ownership structures of the industry. The second section considers the production technology, the structures of colliery management and, because these structures have often been thought to have clear and substantial effects on the strategies managers adopted to try and

Table 2.1. *The distribution of colliery sizes measured by employment (Great Britain 1913–1955, in percentages)*

Size[a]	1913	1924	1938[b]	1947	1952
1–99	39	40	46	42	38
100–499	33	27	21	24	22
500–999	17	17	18	19	21
1,000–1,999	9	11	11	13	16
2,000–2,999	2	4	2	2	3
3,000+	–	1	1	–	–
Total	100	100	100	100	100

The source of the data for 1913–38 does not state what definition of 'coal mine' has been used, and differing definitions will have an impact which will be most marked in the 1–99 employees range. The data for 1947 are based on counts of all 'mines producing coal'; the data for 1952 are based on the 'colliery units recognized by the NCB for administrative and accounting purposes' together with coal mines not operated by the NCB. It is not clear, therefore, to what extent the data for 1913–38 are comparable with the data for 1947 and 1952. Percentages less than 0.5 are indicated by '–'. Components may not add to 100 per cent because of rounding.
[a] Size is measured by the number of employees. For 1947 these are 'wage-earners employed at 13th December' and for 1952 'wage earners on colliery books'.
[b] There appears to be a minor error in the source data for 1938. The data in the source have been uniformly deflated to force the components to sum to 100.0.
Sources: For 1913–38, Supple 1987, table 9.2; for 1947, Ministry of Fuel and Power, *Statistical Digest for the Years 1946 and 1947*, table 7; for 1952, Ministry of Fuel and Power, *Statistical Digest 1953*, table 29.

control miners' working activities, these are also considered in this section. In this chapter we shall see a clear transition to modernity taking place within the industry. At a later point, in chapter 8, when we consider the implications of the structures of mining localities for mining industrial relations, we shall consider an aspect of the industry which has, however, set it apart from the modern world: the villages and small towns in which miners lived, a 'race apart' from the urbanized factory and office workers of the twentieth century.

Structures of colliery scale and ownership

In the latter half of the nineteenth century the limits to colliery size were set by technology. As the access technologies of pumping, haulage, winding and ventilation developed, colliery size increased. The size of the average mine, measured by output, doubled between 1860 and 1895 to 65,000 tonnes and by another 50 per cent by 1913. While in 1895, employment exceed 1,000 in only 3 per cent of mines, by 1913 this proportion had risen to 11 per cent. A large and growing proportion of miners were employed by the big collieries. Even in 1913 47 per cent of all miners were employed by collieries of over 1,000 workers, the figure rising to 55 per cent by 1938 (Supple 1987: table 9.2). This was a high proportion compared with manufacturing industry and increasingly mineworkers experienced a place of work which was large by manufacturing standards (Prais 1976: table 3.3). Even so, between 1913 and 1952 very small collieries employing fewer than a hundred workers represented roughly 40 per cent of all collieries, whereas in the 100–499 category colliery numbers fell from 33 per cent to 22 per cent of the total (table 2.1).

This workplace was likely to be one of several owned by the company. Some coal companies were extremely large undertakings and the number of such undertakings grew during the prosperous years before the First World War and afterwards as well. In 1894 there were only five undertakings employing more than 5,000 colliery workers and none employed more than 10,000. By 1913 there were five employing over 10,000 and this number increased to nine in 1924; there were the same number in 1938. Although forming only a very small proportion of the number of undertakings, these giant corporations employed nearly 6 per cent of all coalminers in 1913 and 18 per cent in 1938. Both in 1913 and 1938 about half of all British coalminers worked for companies employing over 3,000 colliery workers, and at both dates these companies typically owned six or seven collieries (Church 1986: 400; Supple 1987: 303).

The gradual growth in company size, however, was not accompanied by a radical change in the character of corporate structure and organization. The nineteenth-century pattern of family enterprises, partnerships and private companies continued to characterize the industry throughout the period of private enterprise until 1947. Large-scale public joint stock companies with dispersed shareholding and subject to 'impersonal' buying and selling of quoted shares were exceptional before 1914, limited mainly to a handful of coal producing iron and steel companies and coal exporting enterprises, principally in South Wales and Scotland, though increasingly in the East Midlands and Yorkshire thereafter. Even after 1914 the trend in some other industries towards a bureaucratized corporate structure, in which professional managers took major decisions relating to business rather than to merely production matters, was to be found in no more than a handful of the largest coal producing companies. One implication, therefore, of the highly competitive structure of the industry, its self-imposed reliance on finance from within the industry, and the dominance of owner-management or something similar, was the perpetuation of long-established administrative structures, policies and practices.

These structures of ownership will have affected not only relations between coalowners and miners but also relations among coalowners. Except in the 1912–26 period these relationships were based predominantly on region and district rather than the nation as a whole. The history of regional association among coalowners had been continuous in the major coal producing regions since the 1880s; but the competitive structure of the industry, even at the regional level, ensured that successful association occurred only when colliery owners were presented with effective organization among colliery workers. Where a few owners dominated the output of a district it may have been less difficult for them to act collusively and formulate a joint policy, whether in matters of collective bargaining or coal pricing. The ten largest producers in each region in 1894 employed between 29 and 39 per cent of all miners according to area. By 1913 the biggest ten producers in the East Midlands and Scotland had broken out of this range, reaching 43 and 45 per cent respectively. By 1935 the domination of the districts by the largest companies had certainly increased, although differences in the way the available data have been presented prevent a precise comparison. In North Derbyshire and Nottinghamshire, which formed the bulk of the East Midlands district, the nine biggest undertakings produced 59 per cent of the output in 1935; in Scotland the top nine produced 60 per cent. In both Lancashire and South Wales the top seven produced 68 per cent of output in the same year. However, at national level the picture was much less dramatic, with the biggest 21 per cent of firms producing 31 per cent of the national output: in this arena 'even the giants of the industry hardly dominated it' (Supple 1987: 362). The figures we have quoted may understate the ability of some prominent coalowners to dominate their district and the industry as a whole since they take no account of inter-firm alliances represented either by interlocking directorships, interlocking share holdings and the ownership of formally independent companies by others within the industry (Church 1986: 401; Supple 1987: 373–4). None the less, the complexity of the matrix which resulted was not conducive to widespread and effective co-operation and collusion. The range and complexity of interests which rendered inter-firm co-operation problematic, even when investment or participant links existed, also undermined coalowners' attempts to achieve sustained policy co-ordination at either a national or regional level.

Structures and strategies of labour management

Whereas the implications of structures of ownership for labour relations have received comparatively little attention from social theorists, the 'labour process' has been the subject of a major debate during the last twenty years, inspired and initiated by Braverman's *Labor and Monopoly Capital*. It is now difficult to recall the prevailing assumptions and interpretations which dominated scholarly discourse on labour studies before the publication of this book in 1974. It is consequently worth stating that, remarkable as it now appears, before this time the study of labour management, work, skill and machinery was not regarded as central to the study of industrial relations. Braverman's focus was on the daily experience of work rather than on overt class conflict or strike activity and was centred on a search for 'the causes, the dynamic underlying the incessant transformation of work in the modern era'. He sought this in 'the evolution of management as well as technology' (1974: 4). His treatment of the movement for 'scientific management' emphasized management's drive to wrest the control of work from workers in the interests of raising productivity, reducing costs and raising profits. Braverman insisted that the prime source of workers' ability to control their work lay in their skill rather than in their organization and that the corresponding strategy which that implied for management seeking to take control of work was to destroy workers' monopoly over skill. His treatment of the evolution of technology emphasized that machinery which replaced workers' skills by mechanical or electrical devices could increase management's ability to control work and raise profits. The transformation of work in the twentieth century was thus dominated by the expansion of management and the contraction of control over work by workers.

Braverman was soon criticized by his remarkable failure to explore, rather than merely gesture towards, the role of 'worker resistance' to this 'deskilling' and loss of control over the labour process. However, contributors to 'the labour process debate' showed little interest in removing this lacuna in Braverman's treatment. Instead, labour process theorizing tended to be replaced by empirical observation, largely of management, not of labour. The movement towards empirics was most marked in one of the main areas of debate: the extent to which managerial actions in relation to labour can be conceptualized in terms of dominant and coherent strategies consciously designed to control workers and the labour process. Empirical study of this question in a range of settings and time periods did much to undermine earlier attempts to construct typologies of management strategy, revealing instead a much more complex picture in which management was less omniscient and co-ordinated than had been assumed (Friedman 1977; Richard C. Edwards 1979). For example, the study of the NCB by Hopper et al. (1986) drew attention to the competing strategies to be found at various levels of the managerial hierarchy within the organization (P. K. Edwards and Scullion 1982; Gospel and Littler 1983; Thurley and Wood 1983; Knights et al. 1985; Storey 1985; P. K. Edwards 1986; Friedman 1987).

This is not to suggest that management is typically ineffectual or incapable of initiative, and it remains the case that work relations are heavily influenced by workers' responses to management's initiatives. Although Braverman and subsequent contributors to the debate did not explain why strike activity might occur in some circumstances but not in others they have reminded us that conflict at work may arise not only over wages and hours but also over the introduction of new technology, the pace of work, staffing, supervision and discipline, and safety. More generally, they have succeeded in arguing the relevance of technology, work and labour management to industrial relations. That these now seem like statements of the obvious is a tribute to the change in perceptions which Braverman brought about.

The effects of the labour process debate on studies of industrial relations in coalmining have been to rekindle interest in Goodrich's early studies of job control in the industry and to direct much greater attention than before towards the technology of coal extraction and the management of the labour expended upon it. In Britain *The Frontier of Control* (1920/1975) has become Goodrich's best known study, partly because of its British focus and partly because of the great entertainment offered by its collection of job control anecdotes. But it is markedly inferior to Goodrich's later study, *The Miner's Freedom*, which succeeds in maintaining a steady gaze on the supersession of tradition by modernity in the work processes of the bituminous coal mines of the United States. As we consider the issues raised by Goodrich may assist our analysis of developments in the British industry, the relevant observations he makes are summarized briefly here. He described the transition to modern industry in the United States thus:

> It may be paradoxical to speak of a current coming of industrialism to coal, since without coal there would have been no industrialism. Yet it is true that, so far as the manner of work underground is concerned, 'mining is still in a way a "cottage" industry.' The indiscipline of the mines is far out of line with the new discipline of the modern factories; the miner's freedom from supervision is at the opposite extreme from the carefully ordered and regimented work of the modern machine-feeder. . . . Machine methods of production and factory methods of supervision have already begun to invade the mines, and the industry is apparently in the first stages of a great industrial revolution. (Goodrich 1926: 13–14)

Goodrich made it clear that the 'industrial revolution' in the industry was proceeding along a number of different fronts and that machinery was not involved in every case: as we would say nowadays, different managements pursued different strategies. In one case a degree of regimentation was achieved by transferring bodily the rules and regulations used in a company's manufacturing plants to its mines (1926: 120–2). In another case the system of supervision was changed and the number of supervisors much increased without any change in the technology of production but with a shift, which Braverman's work has made familiar, towards a system in which 'the mine foremen and assistants "are supposed to do the thinking for the men" ' (1926: 126). In other companies the division of labour was increased creating small numbers of skilled workers and larger numbers of deskilled workers (130–1). However, 'the more important movement toward the breaking up of the miners' craft is coming by way of . . . new machines that take over much more of the loader's [filler's] work' (131). These included face conveyors which were often introduced with a new division of labour, which created a large class of unskilled and tightly supervised coal loaders who shovelled coal on to the conveyor and a smaller class of skilled workers involved in undercutting, conveyor shifting, timbering, drilling and 'shooting' [shot-firing] (133–4). The mechanical loaders being introduced at the time of Goodrich's research, would, Goodrich thought, move the industry towards mass production methods turning the coal mine, to quote one union committeeman, into 'nothing but a God damn factory' (155).

Unlike Braverman, Goodrich was concerned to assess the effects of these changes not only on the experience of work but also on the organization of industrial relations. The deskilling of work enabled companies to hire 'greenhorn' labour who, it was thought, would make a 'ready surrender to discipline' (161) and were less likely to form good unionists. But Goodrich thought the threat to jobs created by the new machinery would be the most potent force on industrial relations (172), and this could only temper the expression of discontent caused by the introduction of factory methods 'into the very strongholds of the miner's freedom' (177).

Goodrich's work on mechanization in the United States gives a very useful illustration of some of the many possible influences of technological change on industrial relations. Although technological change may precipitate some conflict directly, its most important effects may be very indirect. Goodrich emphasized the vulnerability of unskilled labour and unemployment but, as we shall see below, others have been more impressed by the impact of technological change on the division of labour and worker–supervisor relations. Goodrich's study also exemplifies the dynamic nature of the relations between structures and actions. The competitive market structures of the US industry forced colliery managements to reduce costs and, at the time when Goodrich was writing in the mid-1920s, the predominant strategy they formulated to accomplish this was based on the introduction of new technology. Once installed, the new technology became an uncontested 'fact' of the industry, affecting, if we follow Goodrich, the strength of the mineworkers' organizations, thereby helping to mould the actions of workers in their relations with their employers.

In the remainder of this section we review the history of colliery mechanization and management in Britain in the light of the issues raised by Goodrich, and later by Braverman. In order to explore whether a labour process of the kind, and with the dynamic, outlined by Goodrich and Braverman can be detected in the coalmining industry in Britain it is necessary to review the history of British colliery management and mechanization.

The management structures to be found in British collieries in the late nineteenth and twentieth centuries were varied but were of essentially two kinds, both of them developments from eighteenth- and early nineteenth-century models. The first kind of structure was based on direct management, the second was based on the subcontract of some or all managerial functions. Direct management was the predominant model of mining management adopted in collieries across almost all the regions during the eighteenth and early nineteenth centuries. Subcontract systems in their most highly developed form were much less common, but elements of this system were present over a wider area and continued until nationalization.

Direct management was the established practice in the largest and most advanced region of the North East, a system which was developed and refined during the eighteenth and early nineteenth century and became a model for colliery operations elsewhere. A royalty owner, who might be a landowner, an ecclesiastical body, or a board of directors of a business organization, normally engaged an experienced mining engineer as a 'viewer', or 'check viewer', who took responsibility for the terms of the lease, accounted for coal worked from the property, ensured that production was maximized, and monitored rental income, all of which would be the subject of lengthy reports to the royalty owners. Particularly before the last third of the nineteenth century the viewer was part-time, often acting in a similar consulting capacity for several other royalty owners. From the mid-century onwards, however, large colliery owners, who by that time consisted mainly of coal companies, increasingly appointed a full-time head viewer, agent or manager. The responsibility of the check viewer and, where no such appointment existed, the head viewer, included advising the owners on all policy matters as well as drawing up plans for sinking the shafts, production, determining the mining methods to be adopted, costing and pricing, and advising on the marketing of coal, employment policy, labour relations and housing (Bulman and Redmayne 1951: 66–74).

The decline of the viewer reflected both the increasing professionalization in coalmining which led to greater specialization between the managing director or general manager, responsible for the business, and the colliery manager, responsible for mining operations. The acknowledged specialist experience, skills and theoretical knowledge of colliery managers implied an embryonic professional status, though the formalization of this did not begin until 1872, when the Mines Act required all collieries employing at least thirty workers to engage a trained, certificated colliery manager. Although the motive behind this legislation was to promote safety, one effect was to provide a powerful impetus towards a centralization of authority in mine managements and a greater degree of supervision and potential control at pit level. The first professional organization, the National Association of Colliery Managers, was formed in 1887 in direct response to renewed legislative intervention (Carr-Saunders and Wilson 1933: 152; Church 1986: 409–22).

Where management was by direct methods, responsibility for the management of coal production underground, including overall labour policy, rested with the colliery manager, though coalowners might also become involved (Church 1986: 409–22). The responsibilities of the colliery manager were often highly diverse and showed little evidence of any attempt to specialize managerial functions or divide managerial labour. In the 1920s the manager of Seaton Delaval Colliery in Northumberland, Richard (later Sir Richard) Redmayne, pointed out that the technical role of the colliery manager, ensuring that satisfactory methods of coalmining were practised, was one of only several functions which he was required to perform personally. These included responsibility for three schools, for inspecting and keeping in good repair nearly 1,000 miners' cottages, 1,100 acres of farming to supervise, and attendance at two parish council meetings of which he was chairman and vice-chairman. He was also involved in the organization of the social and educational life of miners in the villages. In his view the statutorily required daily underground inspections he made did not amount to the supervision of work or labour (Redmayne 1942: 23–5). The colliery manager's 'most harassing and unpleasant' responsibility in the view of Redmayne and H. F. Bulman, another former colliery manager, was that of managing men and avoiding or settling disputes with them. The changes which led them to emphasize the increasing difficulty which labour management presented, from at least the beginning of the twentieth century, was that at that time 'the manager was practically an autocrat; he could at once dismiss any men who made difficulties'. The differences they perceived in the ideas and feelings embraced by miners since that time led them to believe that 'without real sympathy a manager will never get on with his men' and would set an unsatisfactory role model for colliery officials subordinate to him. Former presidents of the National Association of Colliery Managers also urged members to be courteous and to avoid the degrading effects of intemperate behaviour and expression which 'did not assist the manager in controlling those under him' (Bulman and Redmayne 1951: 63–4).

Except in the smaller collieries the face to face supervision of work was the responsibility of 'overmen' or under-managers and it was these and other, lower, officials, rather than the colliery managers, who had continuing face to face contact with underground workers. Overmen, described by Bulman and Redmayne as 'the backbone of colliery management', were usually miners who had worked themselves up to supervisory level, perhaps by becoming assistant or 'back overmen', covering the afternoon or 'back' shifts for the overman. The overman's duties included visiting all parts of the mine daily to ensure overall safety and satisfactory working. Within the pit, each 'district' was in the charge of a deputy overman (usually known simply as a 'deputy' but in some regions of the country known as 'firemen' or 'examiners'), the 'competent person' whom legislation required to ensure the inspection of roads and working places before the hewers began their shift, ensuring that conditions were sound, fencing off dangerous places and sometimes carrying out timber work in broken places. It was the deputy who had to deal with face workers and other underground workers contending with the unpredictable difficulties of mining coal. The 1911 Coal Mines Act required for the first time that the deputy, too, be certificated (Bulman and Redmayne 1925: 74, 1951: 72–4). That it is possible to describe the managerial hierarchy from this period with so few references to regional variation is because much of it was laid down by statute: the internal management of no other industry, with the possible exception of the merchant navy, was more closely regulated by the state (Carr-Saunders and Wilson 1933: 146–54).

In theory, the overman's responsibility was to encourage effective production while the deputy's responsibility was solely for safe working. In practice, this division could never be kept watertight. Many of the deputy's tasks and interventions had impacts on production and miners' piece-rate earnings. Frowen, General Secretary of the General Federation of colliery officials' associations, claimed in his evidence to the 1919 Royal Commission on the Coal Industry that deputies were subject to pressures from both miners and managers to neglect safety in the interests of earnings and production (Tailby 1990: 322) and, as we shall see below, the introduction of machine mining techniques led to allegations that the role of the deputy was being changed fundamentally from that of a safety officer to that of a production supervisor.

This role change, to the extent that it occurred, made the deputy closer to management than to workers and it seems reasonable to suppose that one effect would have been to inhibit strike activity among deputies. Ackers's (1994) study of the National Association of Colliery Overmen, Deputies and Shotfirers (NACODS) and its predecessors documents in detail the distancing of NACODS from the activities of the MFGB and later of the National Union of Mineworkers, and confirms the supposition that strike activity among deputies was restrained by the ambiguity of their position.

Direct management was the dominant practice throughout our period but in the West and East Midlands, and in at least some collieries elsewhere, variations on the second of our models of mine management, the subcontract system, were widespread, especially in smaller collieries. The subcontractor was usually known as a 'butty' and the subcontract system as the 'butty system'. Although butties were usually regarded as 'gombeen men, or half proletarian exploiters' (Samuel 1977: 18), Goffee points out that the etymology of the word suggests that a butty was originally a kind of companion or friend, not a taskmaster, and that usage in South Wales conformed to the original definition as late as the 1920s. This indicates the variety of the arrangements that have come under the label 'butty system' and warns us that miners may have attached widely different meanings to the term (Goffee 1981: 478–9).

It is now usual to distinguish the 'big butty' or 'charter master' system found in the West Midlands from the 'small butty' system which was more usual elsewhere. The big butty system was dominant in Staffordshire until at least 1870 but was also used in other areas, particularly areas worked by ironmasters, such as Derbyshire, Scotland and South Wales (Samuel 1977: 20; Church 1986: 417–20). Under the big butty system, a subcontractor 'assumed broad responsibilities for the production, but not for the distribution, of the coal; for the provision of the working, but not of the fixed, capital of the colliery; and for the maintenance, though not necessarily the initial recruitment, of the labour force' (Arthur J. Taylor 1960: 226–7). Importantly, the butty also had control over wages and discipline of the colliers who worked for him. This big butty system declined both in Staffordshire and other parts of the West Midlands, and, where it had existed, in parts of the East Midlands during the fourth quarter of the nineteenth century (Alan R. Griffin 1971: 32; Samuel 1977: 18, 20, 88 n. 99).

In the small butty system, the butty, sometimes a working hewer and sometimes not, negotiated a contract price per ton of coal with the colliery manager from which he paid up to a half dozen workers, or sometimes more, who assisted him at the face. The small butty's management functions were usually limited to labour supervision and discipline, although in some cases there was also some control over recruitment (Bulman and Redmayne 1906; Jevons 1915/1969: 334, 455–6; Rowe 1923: 63; Arthur J. Taylor 1960; Alan R. Griffin 1971: 32; Neville 1974: 286–7; Krieger 1984: 91–4). The subcontractor's income depended on the difference between the contract price negotiated with the colliery manager and the amount he chose to pay the workers. The system was open to abuses by contractors who, beyond the control of the colliery office

after receiving the contract pay, might, as one miner recalled, 'pay out anywhere
. . . bike shed, under t'arches, land sale . . . out of a tin' (Finch, quoted by
Downing and Gore 1983: 27–8). Another miner who worked under the butty
system at Creswell Colliery in Derbyshire during the 1920s remarked that 'It
were a system that wanted t'union to fight it off, but the union didn't because
majority belonging bloody union were butties themselves' (Lowther, quoted by
Downing and Gore 1983: 28; see also Douglass 1977: 226 and Sunley 1988:
27–8). Nevertheless the district unions in Derbyshire and Nottinghamshire
fought against the system and won its abolition in 1918 and 1919 respectively.
But the victory was short lived and the system was reintroduced shortly after
(Rowe 1923: 64, note 1; Alan R. Griffin 1962: 98, 100; J. E. Williams 1962b:
641, 664–8; Alan R. Griffin 1971: 192; Krieger 1984: 92; Sunley 1988: 28–30;
Tailby 1990: 181–93). In Kent a complex system which appears closer to the
small butty system than the big butty system operated in Snowdown Colliery in
the 1920s and 1930s and some form of subcontracting operated at each of the
other Kent collieries (Goffee 1977: 43; 1981: 479). Arrangements referred to as
'the butty system' but not always precisely described also operated in Yorkshire
and at least some collieries in Scotland until the Second World War (Board of
Trade, *Report on Collective Agreements . . .* [1910]: 37; *Trade Disputes: . . . Strikes
and Lock-outs in 1914*, strike to abolish the butty system at a colliery at Udding-
ston, Lanarkshire, PRO LAB 34/14; Ministry of Labour, *Trade Disputes: . . .
Strikes and Lock-outs of 1929*, strike at Thorne Colliery, South Yorkshire, PRO
LAB 34/47; *Trade Disputes: . . . Strikes and Lock-outs of 1939*, strike at Bedlay
Colliery in Lanarkshire, PRO LAB 34/54; Dennis *et al.* 1956: 58; Douglass
1977: 226–7; Bellamy and Saville 1976, under 'Alfred Smith'; Baylies 1993:
296–8). Despite the claim by one researcher that the butty system was still
present in North Staffordshire in the mid-1950s (C. S. Smith 1960: 97, cited by
Goffee 1981: 493), it seems safe to claim that the system, though not its
influence, withered during the Second World War (see, for example, Peggy
Kahn 1982: 51).

A big butty might have employed many tens of miners, a small butty half a
dozen, but many 'ordinary' hewers in South Wales, Lancashire and Lanarkshire
employed their own assistants, sometimes paid by the colliery office out of the
hewer's earnings and sometimes paid directly by the hewer (Bulman and Redmayne 1906: 258; Jevons 1915/1969: 335; Rowe 1923: 61, 66, 67). In some
Yorkshire collieries haulage workers seem to have been paid by the hewers rather
than directly by the colliery (Ministry of Labour, *Trade Disputes: . . . Strikes and
Lock-outs of 1930–33*, strikes at Birkenshaw Colliery, South Yorkshire, 1932, and
Shuttle Eye Colliery, West Yorkshire, 1933, PRO LAB 34/48). In many cases
hewer and assistant were father and son or otherwise related. With these arrangements for paying wages seems to have gone a degree of supervision and
control of the assistant or haulage workers; they were sometimes referred to as
the 'butty system' even in cases where sons assisted their fathers (Lewis Jones
1937/1978: 119). However, while miners' unions often objected strongly to the

big and small butty systems as we have described them above, they do not appear to have objected to the employment of assistants by hewers.

Subcontract systems of management have usually been presented as 'pre-modern' if not archaic, and their survival in British coalmining well into the twentieth century presented as a problem requiring special explanation (Tailby 1990: 190–5). The late twentieth-century movement towards various forms of flexible work organization (Piore and Sabel 1984) makes us question this perspective. Although subcontract died out, the reasons for this are still unclear. The bias of legislation towards direct management methods and changes in technology may have presented some problems for coalowners who wished to continue with a management strategy based on subcontract, but it is clear that there was neither a statutory nor a technological imperative behind its demise. This will become apparent from an examination of developments in coal-face technology, to which we now turn.

Changes in technology made minimal impact on coal-getting before the 1890s, but for several decades before this mine managers had been seeking improved productivity at the face and higher quality, cleaner coal by switching from the traditional pillar and stall method to longwall mining and its variants. By 1900 it has been estimated that about three-quarters of British coal production came from longwall faces (Church 1986: 336–7). The technical details of these two principal modes of working coal are less important here than the differences which affected the relationships between workers and managers.

Pit working under the pillar and stall system enabled miners to control the pace of work and therefore the amount of coal cut. As hewers were paid at piece-rates, each was in a position to decide on the trade-off between work and wages, and a high rate of absenteeism was a consequence. However, management was still free to sack absentee workers, of course, and where the overman or the butty retained control over who worked where in the colliery a lesser but still substantial power remained in the hands of management: because of geological variations in seam qualities, different stalls offered different earnings prospects and management could punish or reward colliers by moving them to or from the less remunerative places. But in the North East for most of the nineteenth century and in parts of Cumberland until the end of the 1930s, the right of management to allocate labour in this way was limited by one of the most highly formalized and best-documented examples of miners' control over their work: the system of allocating working places by lot known as 'cavilling' (Bulman and Redmayne 1906: 77; Rowe 1923: 165–6; Douglass 1977: 229–39; Krieger 1984: 87–90; Wood 1988: 233, 250; Beynon and Austrin 1994: 149–53). Although usually presented as a system preserved in the teeth of managerial opposition, it was recommended as the 'fairest and best' way of allocating working places by the Yorkshire owners in 1911 and it was the Yorkshire Miners' Association that then categorically rejected the proposal to adopt the system (Baylies 1993: 373–4).

Under the pillar and stall system each stall was worked by one or two colliers on each shift. If there were two shifts this would produce a group of two or four men known in Durham as 'marras' (mates) who, in that county at least, would usually be paid jointly, sharing their earnings; in some other fields the stalls would have been worked by small butty-men (Trist *et al.* 1963: 33; Burgess 1975:159; Douglass 1977: 221).

> Each of these [groups] was a self contained working unit. Its members performed all the operations necessary in winning the coal and loading it into the tubs. Faceworkers under this system were essentially craftsmen; men who had been taught their skill by their fathers, not trained by their employers; men who provided their own tools – even their own powder; men with a strong sense of independence. (Goldthorpe 1959: 214)

This method of working with its small scale and unusual degree of job control was the basis for the concept of the 'independent collier' which, despite changing objective circumstances, survived as a powerful myth in some coalfields, notably Scotland and Lancashire, until the late nineteenth century or even later. One effect was to perpetuate the belief that output restriction, a traditional method of placing pressure on coalowners to concede advances and, more often, to resist wage reductions, was an effective method of resolving a dispute in the colliers' favour (Fisher and Smethurst 1978; Campbell 1979; Daunton 1981: 583; Campbell 1984: 38).

In theory, longwall working afforded both a greater scope and a greater need for supervisory control: a face of up to 50 metres (rarely longer before 1900) provided more opportunity for the deputy to observe operations and required the deputy to ensure that the whole face moved forward at the same pace so that the advantages of longwall mining could be realized and the safety of the miners ensured. One consequence was that the pitman and his 'marra' or the butty and his assistants working in a stall were replaced by a team of between four and six workers working a section of the longwall face. There was no technological reason why this team need not continue to perform its work in almost the same way as it had been performed before in the separate stalls; but firms wishing to maximize the productivity of the new method introduced simultaneous changes in working methods. These might be limited to the introduction of a stricter work discipline to ensure a greater uniformity of work pace and attendance or they might involve more radical changes. Some collieries converted to a double shift system at the face with the first shift undercutting the coal and the second loading the coal into tubs, an arrangement which implied a new and greater division of labour (J. H. Morris and Williams 1958: 258–61; Campbell 1984: 38).

Some owners also took the opportunity presented by a conversion to longwall to abolish the butty system (Goffee 1977: 49). That they did so was possibly because an even advance of the face was difficult to achieve where a number of independent operators were exploiting the seam. For miners accustomed to working under the butty system the introduction of longwall could thus have a transforming effect on their working environment. According to one coalowner who had introduced longwall working, 'The charter [butty] system has been suspended and men are not left to themselves. . . . Now there is more supervision on the part of owners and managers' (Commission on Coal Supply, *General Minutes . . . , Committee C*, QQ 1854–6). However, abolition of the butty system was anything but a technological necessity. Indeed, the President of the Lanarkshire owners' association early expressed the opinion that successful coal cutting was 'often an impossibility' unless the coal filling was performed by a contractor, in other words a butty, and this system appears to have been widely used in Scotland in the early decades of the twentieth century (Campbell 1984: 40).

Although we have already noted that the introduction of longwall methods sometimes led to a stricter work discipline, the abolition or the imposition of the butty system, new shift systems and new divisions of labour, Daunton has argued that the critical change in working methods as far as industrial relations were concerned was not the supersession of pillar and stall by longwall but the introduction of mechanical coal cutting and the use of face conveyors (1981: 584). Tailby has amplified this argument by referring to the contrast which mining engineers began to make during the 1920s between mechanical coal cutting and machine mining 'proper' (Tailby 1990: 211).

Mechanical coal cutting might involve no more than the substitution of machines for hands in the hewing of coal. The term 'machine mining' was employed to describe a systematic approach to coal-getting as a whole, in which the primary process of undercutting was part of a thought-out strategy of mining policy and 'not dissociated from the ancillary services upon which the effective application of machinery at the coal face depends' (Mavor 1924: 1510). It represented an extension of 'managerial control over the preparation and planning of work and over the use of the new technology, with this control employed to direct and increase the productive effect of labour' (Tailby 1990: 211). Based on the contemporary observations of engineers and other commentators, Tailby's account highlighted the system's standardization of method and specialization of labour. 'Management now planned "every detail of the scheme of operation in advance" so that "organisation is built up at the beginning once and for all" and, in theory at least, had thereafter "only to be maintained on established lines" by subordinate officials. The collier's "complete job" was broken down into a series of narrowly defined tasks. These tasks were arranged by management in a rigid sequence over three separate shifts' (Tailby 1990: 121, quoting the *Colliery Guardian*, 31 August 1923: 525). While many variations existed, a description recorded by a mine engineer in 1947 is instructive. The sequence started with the night, or cutting shift, during which a crew of four men, each fulfilling designated tasks, undercut the coal and cleared the cut of 'kirvings' or the loose coal and dust produced by the cutting machine. The morning shift, consisting of borers and shotfirers but mainly of fillers, brought down the coal and filled it on to face conveyors. The afternoon shift consisted of rippers who extended the tunnels leading to the coal-face and timbermen who set supports (Manley 1947: 12–16). This sequence of tasks and division of labour allowed management to allocate the job of filling, the biggest task, to a group of unskilled workers; but in many implementations fillers were also required to set roof supports as soon as possible after clearing the coal from the face (cf. Dennis *et al.* 1956: 40; Trist *et al.* 1963: 42; Campbell 1984: 38). This was very skilled work and in such circumstances one of the main managerial advantages of the division of labour, the separation of unskilled work so that it may be performed by unskilled and cheaper labour, would have been lost.

The transition to machine mining brought about a substantial increase in the size of the work group and an increase in the level of stress. Colliers now worked as members of teams of twenty or thirty or even one hundred men instead of in pairs or groups of four working largely in isolation from each other (Mavor 1924: 1510; Zweig 1948: 22). Contemporary reports of colliery engineers, managers and miners admit or insist that a system which, in the words of Bulman, required performance comparable to 'that of a well-drilled gun squad, each practising in his own special duties and working in full conjunction with each other' at a regular and rapid pace in adherence to a strict timetable, imposed new kinds of stresses on the miners involved (Gallacher 1906: 44; Bulman 1920: 159–60; Greenwell 1933; Joseph Jones 1936: 21; Royal Commission on Safety in Coal Mines, *Report*: 183). Analogies with machine parts abounded: Greenwell referred to the miner becoming 'a cog in a machine' (1933: 303), while the same metaphor was used in a report by Welsh miners (quoted by Boyns 1992: 375). Furthermore, while stress at work increased, the degree of supervision to ensure performance and safety also became more intensive and continuous (Mavor 1924; Royal Commission on Safety in Coal Mines, *Report*: 48). It was these characteristics of close managerial supervision and control that have usually been seen, not only by historians but by contemporary owners and managers, as incompatible with the butty system and in Nottinghamshire, one of the heartlands of the butty system, this was the reason contemporaries gave for its abolition (Alan R. Griffin 1971: 192–3).

Even before the introduction of machine mining, deputies, traditionally and by law under the Coal Mines Act of 1911 responsible for safety, faced increasing pressures to pay more attention to productivity than to safety regulations (Gallacher 1906: 43; Tailby 1990: 339). During the inter-war years the deputy became, in effect, a 'coalface foreman' (Pick 1946: 77), implementing managerial decisions and discipline regarding the pace and progress of production, rather than attending to safety and sound mining practice in accordance with traditional standards and procedures (Trist and Bamforth 1951; Supple 1987: 440–1).

With the advent of machine mining the technology and labour of the British industry finally entered the era Marx had labelled 'Modern Industry' many decades before. Large-scale machinery, powered by steam or electricity, was combined with human labour in a rationally designed process based on the detailed division of labour. This modernization took place over an extended period. It had hardly started in 1913 when only 8 per cent of coal was cut by machine and when face conveyors were still so rare that the Mines Department collected no data on them. The most rapid changes took place after 1927. By 1938 coal cutting by machine had become the dominant method, used to extract 59 per cent of the total coal produced, and 54 per cent of output was removed from the face by conveyors. In some districts the decade after 1927 saw very rapid changes: the proportion of coal cut mechanically increased from 16 to 68 per cent in Lancashire, and from 22 to 78 per cent in North Derbyshire and Nottinghamshire. This mechanization and other developments required almost a doubling of the horsepower of the electrical machinery used underground from 1.1 hp per worker underground in 1927 to 2.0 in 1938. Meanwhile the use of animal traction underwent a slow decline. Between 1927 and 1938 the number of horses and ponies working in British coal mines fell from 54,503 to 32,524 (Mines Department, *Annual Report of the Secretary for Mines 1927*: tables 14 and 45 and *1938*: tables 17 and 45; Supple 1987: 337–85. Supple's numerical data do not tally with those in the *Annual Report for the Secretary for Mines* which are recorded here).

The new system of machine mining has been regarded by some investigators as the basis for a wide-ranging and modernizing transformation of labour relations. In 1951 researchers at the Tavistock Institute published findings which concluded that the social relationships engendered by the machine mining system were equivalent to those to be found in mass production engineering, with the institutionalization of occupational roles associated with it, and the outlook which it encouraged (Trist and Bamforth 1951: 5). This view was echoed and reinforced by Goldthorpe (1959), who argued that under the machine mining system there was a 'pre-disposition' to conflict which had been absent in hand-got mining. In hand-got systems management attempted to secure a fast pace of work by piece-rate payment systems or by the use of butties: 'Discipline in the sense in which it is usually understood in industry, that is as some form of control exerted upon the worker from above, was . . . virtually absent' (1959: 216). Consequently the deputy had only infrequent contact with the colliers and, according to Goldthorpe, conflict was not 'inherent' in the relationship between collier and deputy (217). In machine mining, on the other hand, the rigid arrangement of tasks by shifts required the deputy to exercise close supervision of face workers and to enforce a discipline in attendance, in accepting orders, and in securing a pace of work which would bring about the completion of that shift's task ready for the next to start work. In short, the deputy had to impose a discipline in the factory sense (218–20). Machine mining, according to Goldthorpe, therefore gave 'rise to a variety of situations in which it could be said that supervisor–worker conflict [was] inherent' (222).

The early sociology of Goodrich, Trist, Bamforth and Goldthorpe which the labour process debate revived has informed a number of studies which have nevertheless been firmly historical in their approaches. Of these, one of the most prominent is by Daunton, who compared working practices and social relations in the coalfields of the North East and South Wales before 1914 where differences in the tenor of industrial relations, conflictual in South Wales, collaborationist in the North East, have long presented historians with a puzzling contrast. He described the use of pillar and stall techniques in the North East in contrast to the longwall methods used in South Wales, the organization of ancillary tasks which involved a more detailed division of labour in the North East than in South Wales, the tradition of cavilling in the North East which was absent from South Wales, the differing shift systems and the differing career patterns of underground workers in the two fields. Daunton juxtaposed these descriptions with the contrasting patterns of unionization and militancy and with the differing attitudes exhibited by the respective coalfield trade unions towards legislative interventions in working arrangements before the First World War. While he explicitly denied any intention to treat his description of workplace structures as an explanation of the long-standing difference between the industrial relations of the two fields, his work invited the inference that these contrasting behaviours and attitudes owed much to the differing structural and organizational features of the workplace that he had described.

Goffee's exploration of the nature and implications of the butty system for union organization and for work group relationships at Snowdown Colliery in the Kent coalfield between the wars was both more careful, utilizing oral as well as documentary sources, and more probing. Although the Kent Mine Workers' Association made abolition of the butty system official policy, the branch officials at Snowdown were themselves butties (1977: 43, 47; 1981: 484). These officials were, of course, elected and this points to some ambiguity in the opposition to the system by rank and file miners. For example, Goffee speculated that those who considered themselves well rewarded by butties may have regarded the system as undesirable in general but their own particular experience of it satisfactory. Thus, united rank and file opposition to the system was non-existent:

> The range of subcontracting arrangements and the differing impact of the system, even amongst those employed on the same contract, made a common response unlikely since there was no foundation of common experience. Certainly the men were divided, but not into two clearly-defined groups [butties and their workers]; rather the system splintered the workforce into numerous small, mutually competitive sects. In this sense subcontracting permeated work-place relations and seriously limited the development of solidaristic ties and the potential for colliery-wide collective action. (1981: 488)

Union membership was relatively low at Snowdown, with fewer than half the miners in the union. The implications for strike activity were perhaps the reverse of what one might have expected. The consequence was not quiescence but industrial relations which were 'unsettled and punctuated by small scale disputes . . . which were frequently the result of grievances and disagreements between miners' (Goffee 1981: 488).

Goffee's account of Snowdown's sectionalism, based as it was on interviews as well as documentary sources, is one of the few studies, whether by historians or sociologists, to consider seriously the meanings attached to structures and organizations, for example the butty system, by miners themselves. That this is a crucial omission is suggested by Gouldner's classic account *Wildcat Strike* (1954). Gouldner described the background and origins of a ten-day strike at an American gypsum mining and processing plant at a town, which Gouldner called 'Oscar Center', in 1950. The strike took place without any planning, without a strike vote and without any formal notice: in short, it was a 'wildcat' strike. It was also the first 'real' strike to have ever taken place at the plant; though there had been a brief 'walkout' two years before these were not workers who had developed a routine of striking (1954: 37, 40). The events leading up to the strike were complex. The processing plant had been working on a job that had been transferred from another of the company's plants, a move intensely resented by 'Oscar Center' workers. Changes were being made to some of the machinery to speed up operations and there had been a dispute about the role of supervisors involved in implementing the engineering changes needed to accomplish this. Finally, there was an angry altercation between the production engineer in charge of the changes and the chief steward, the upshot being the steward's announcement that work would stop in two hours, as soon as the plant could be shut down in an orderly manner (1954: 41–3).

On the face of it these events indicate what the strike was 'about' and thereby explain what caused it. But Gouldner suggested that the strike was only intelligible in terms of the different and conflicting meanings which workers and management had attached to a wide-ranging series of changes that had happened at the plant during the previous two years. Gouldner implied that before 1948 the plant's industrial relations were peaceable because both sides shared the same assumptions about the other's rights and privileges and their daily activities conformed to the expectations based on those assumptions (1954: 17). Gouldner identified a number of elements in workers' expectations of management. Workers expected management to provide a safe working environment and to 'take care of' workers who suffered injury at the plant, for example by providing them with light work. They expected management to be lenient, that is to be flexible in its interpretation of plant rules and regulations and to give workers who infringed the rules a 'second chance'. They expected to be able to use plant machinery and materials for their own domestic purposes. Workers expected to be free of close supervision except when it was necessitated by the production process: supervision exerted for its own sake or to assert managerial superiority was resented and met with hostility. Workers expected to have a role in the allocation of labour in that their union agreement with the company allowed them to bid for other jobs in the plant when vacancies arose; as Gouldner pointed out, this enabled workers to escape from unpleasant supervisors and thus weakened the impact of workplace discipline. Gouldner referred to this pattern of expectations as 'the indulgency pattern' and argued that it motivated workers and generated a commitment and loyalty to the company (1954: 20–2).

Although the company's expectations were not identical to those shared by workers' (the company, for example, assumed that workers had an obligation to obey management, whereas workers recognized only a rather different obligation: to work), there was sufficient in common to allow production to carry on at the 'Oscar Center' plant fairly harmoniously most of the time. However, the 'indulgency pattern' was not without its problems. It was recognized by workers to have only a dubious legitimacy; this brought an instability into industrial relations, made it difficult to use formal methods of grievance resolution if the pattern was violated and led to the displacement of grievances to 'legitimate' areas like wages (1954: 24–5). These problems became all too apparent in the two years prior to the 1950 stoppage. A new plant manager had been appointed with instructions to increase production. Under this pressure the new manager introduced a number of changes which violated the 'indulgency pattern'. Strict interpretation came to be applied to plant rules: a miner was dismissed for taking home some dynamite for his own use; a new Personnel and Safety Officer was appointed who took a legalistic view of company obligations; the provision of light jobs for disabled workers was terminated. Hostility to the new manager mounted rapidly and anxiety increased with the announcement that new machinery was to be introduced. By the spring of 1948 a sharp cleavage had developed between workers and management, reactivating the latent hostility that had been dormant since the depression of the 1930s. From this point on a strike was 'just waiting to happen' and was only narrowly averted during the 1948 wage negotiations. While a settlement of the wages issue was finally reached, another replacement of the plant manager and changes of personnel among the middle managers further destabilized the previous pattern of accommodation (1954: 27–39).

That the strike happened when it did, Gouldner argued, could only be understood in the context provided by the 'indulgency pattern' and its violation; in other words it could only be understood in terms of the subjective interpretations workers put on managerial actions. The work diverted from the strike-bound 'Big City' plant helped to precipitate the strike, not because the 'Oscar Center' workers felt a class-conscious solidarity with the 'Big City' workers but because their strike legitimized their own: 'We're not the only ones who feel this way'. The introduction of the new machines aroused workers' hostility not only for the obvious reason that some workers would have to work harder but also because, at least during its introduction, the workers were subjected to close supervision which was carried out in a 'status-emphasizing, deference-demanding manner' (1954: 50–1, 70–1). The production engineer's cursing of the shop steward was not the trivial event it appeared to be from the outside but an event which, to the workers who observed it, was symptomatic of the deterioration of the informal and friendly relations that had previously existed under the 'indulgency pattern': it epitomized everything that was wrong with the new management (1954: 45–8).

Gouldner's explanation of the strike thus stressed workers' attitudes and beliefs, or their 'consciousness', that is the subjective meanings of the social actions in which they participated. Indeed, Gouldner stressed 'consciousness' to the virtual exclusion of all else. Although he gave a brief indication of 'the community context', some basic structural features of the plant and referred to the pressures on management to cut costs imposed by deteriorating product market conditions (1954: 12–17, 27), Gouldner made no attempt to integrate these factors into his analysis: subjective meanings were paramount. This rejection of the structuralism then dominant in sociology and Gouldner's prefiguration of the 'action frame of reference' which became popular in the 1960s (Silverman 1970) seem less extraordinary when one remembers that Gouldner was primarily interested in industrial bureaucracy and as such was well schooled in Weberian sociology, the root of the 'action frame of reference'. Thirty years later a rather similar trajectory seems to have been followed by Krieger, whose study of pit-level industrial relations at ten collieries operated by the NCB was primarily motivated by an interest in bureaucracy but also took it for granted that subjective meanings have to be investigated if social reality is to be understood.

Krieger's *Undermining Capitalism* (1984) examined in detail the history of industrial relations in five Durham and five Nottinghamshire collieries during the period between nationalization and 1980. The focal point of his work was the conflict between, on the one hand, the regionally differentiated colliery structures, working practices, attitudes and traditions, and on the other, the bureaucratic, rationalizing, uniform methods of the NCB exemplified by the introduction of a new wages structure for miners working on power loading coal-faces, the 1966 National Power Loading Agreement (NPLA). Among the factors that differentiated the regions were the cavilling tradition in the North East and the legacy of the butty system in Nottinghamshire, which in these and some other cases could be traced back to the nineteenth century. Krieger concluded from extensive interview and documentary studies of the ten collieries that 'the character of the relations among workers – whether there was competition or cooperation in selection of the most favourable [coal]face positions and work tasks, whether the members of a work team tended to perform the overall task cooperatively or compete for individual high productivity – reflected the pre-NPLA traditions in their distinctive regional patterns' (Krieger 1984: 271).

Krieger's study takes us back to our starting point. While the industry's technology and management structures had largely entered the era of 'Modern Industry' by 1940, his monograph showed that traditional systems of understanding and meaning survived well into the 1960s. While it is possible to link those systems with working structures which once existed, for example the institution of cavilling and the butty system, the conjunction of modern structures and traditional elements of consciousness and action provides a potent warning against attempting to understand one in terms of the other without the knowledge provided by a historical perspective.

3   Employers and workers: organizations and strategies

The geological and economic structures of the industry presented miners and coalowners with enduring problems. From an early date fluctuating coal prices meant that the income generated by the industry was rarely stable from year to year. Coalowners attempted to force at least a part of this income variability and income risk on to coalminers; poorly placed to shoulder such risks, they responded with attempts to stabilize their earnings which often led them into dispute with their employers. Within this inter-annual instability, underground workers often faced great variations in earnings from pay to pay. As we outlined in the previous chapter, managerial problems of labour supervision and control over mining work led to a reliance on piece-work wages systems. Natural variations in geology and other factors caused frequent week to week variations in colliers' ability to earn and incessant local grievances. The history of collective bargaining in the industry is largely the history of conflicts over contesting solutions to these problems. From our standpoint it is important to review the institutional structures and strategies which form the major factors in that history because of their possible ramifications and their effects on the history of strikes in the industry.

In these conflicts both miners and mine owners formed organizations to promote their causes and pursue their conflicts. They each attempted to find institutions which would lead to resolutions of these conflicts in a way which balanced the pursuit of interest with a desire for peace. The creation of these organizations was difficult to accomplish. Each side attempted to change the organizations of the other in its own interests: owners destroyed unions or fomented sectionalism; miners tried to compel the owners to operate national organizations in order to dampen or eliminate the competitive structure of the industry which they believed to be at the root of many of their misfortunes.

Frameworks and processes before 1914

Coalmining labour relations in the mid-nineteenth century were dominated by attempts by the county- and district-level mining unions to resist deteriorations in wages or conditions in bad times or, in boom times, to press for improvements. The tactics were those of the strike and output restriction through the 'stint' or the 'darg', later familiar as the 'go-slow'. Procedural agreements or practices which might have obviated recourse to these tactics were unknown: an employer intending to change wages or conditions would typically post a notice at the pit head announcing the new terms. Workers would resist changes by submitting a letter or putting a notice in the press. Usually a deadline would be attached and strike, lock-out or restriction would follow. Where discussions took place they usually started after, rather than before, the action (Allen 1964: 238).

Up to this time mining trade unions were ephemeral associations, whether organized at county or national level, and none established itself as the accepted and legitimate bargaining agent of its members (Arnot 1949: 34–41; Church 1986: 674–5). There were two reasons behind this failure: the determination of employers in the period before the 1870s to oppose trade unions and collective bargaining, and the constant fluctuations in the selling price of coal. When prices were rising, output was usually rising and labour becoming more scarce; where trade unions were organized they could grow with extreme rapidity in such conditions, their membership drives fuelled by the successes they could show in wringing increased wages out of the coalowners. However, when prices fell and demand for labour dropped workers were unsuccessful in preventing rapid cuts in wages. Defensive strikes were rarely successful and often long; strike pay would lead to a haemorrhage of the union's assets; the victimization of the union's activists and its extinction ensued (for examples see Welbourne 1923: 37–43, 115–24; Arnot 1955: 41–5).

From the late 1850s until the coal boom of the early 1870s coal prices moved gradually upwards uninterrupted by major slumps and providing a favourable background to union organization (Church 1986: 54–6). This period saw the founding of a large number of local and county unions in the industry including county unions in Fife, in South and West Yorkshire, in Cumberland, Northumberland and Durham, that survived as 'permanent' organizations, with a continuous history until nationalization and beyond (Marsh and Ryan 1984; Church 1986: 680–7). The majority of these unions saw their membership slip away to very low levels in the depression of the industry after 1874; only the Durham and Northumberland unions retained a mass membership by the end of the decade (table 3.1). As trade improved again at the end of the 1880s, new unions were established and membership revived, following a pattern that was already long familiar.

By the mid-nineteenth century contemporaries had begun to acknowledge the ineffectiveness of pit-based output restriction in raising coal prices or miners' wages, and the 1860s and 1870s saw attempts to modernize output restriction (Campbell 1978: 97–9, 1979: 265–6; Church 1986: 695). If the main problem with pit-based output restriction was the emergence of inter-colliery and inter-district competition in the market for coal then the obvious solution was to extend the scope of output restriction from the pit to the district or the region. First the Miners' National Association (MNA) in 1863, followed by the Amalgamated Association of Miners (AAM) in 1869, the Scottish miners in 1879,

Table 3.1. *Trade union membership density in coalmining (Great Britain 1890–1938, in percentages)*

Period	Scot-land	South Wales	North East	York-shire[a]	Lancashire and Cheshire	East Midlands	West Midlands	Great Britain[b]
1890	4	3	54	64	37	46	20	42[c]
1895	25	15	59	58	32	51	n.a.	39
1900	69	87	69	80	42	62	73	68
1905	54	67	68	50	37	57	51	56
1910	67	65	76	61	59	74	81	68
1913	80	66	91	79	84	87		81
1920	75	69	74	85	72[d]	77	67	78
1925	67	70	82	74	78	56	67	74
1930	42	44	(80)[e]	60	73	35	28	(58)[e]
1935	34	59	(98)[e]	73	76	40	30	(66)[e]
1938	57	75	89	71	84	64	46	76

Notes:
Membership data for 1920–38 are the figures on the basis of which constituents affiliated to the Miners' Federation of Great Britain; in some cases these data appear to be conventional and remain unchanged for significant periods.

[a] Alternative data for 1920–38 (Andrew J. Taylor 1984a: table 1), based on information supplied by the National Union of Mineworkers (Yorkshire Area), show higher membership numbers and consequently higher membership densities for Yorkshire (except in 1930). The biggest disparity is for 1938: Taylor reports a membership of 139,309, yielding a density of 98 per cent, whereas the Yorkshire Mine Workers' Association continued to affiliate to the MFGB on the basis of a membership of 100,000, yielding the density shown in the table.

[b] Including districts not shown in previous columns.

[c] 1892.

[d] Including North Wales.

[e] Data for membership of the Durham Miners' Association is given as exactly 120,000 for 1925, 1930 and 1935. While 120,000 for 1925 may have been a plausible approximation, an unreduced membership over the next ten years is not plausible. Membership density in Northumberland sank from 69 per cent in 1920 and 77 per cent in 1925 to 58 per cent in 1930 and 61 per cent in 1935. Average membership density for GB excluding Durham was 53 per cent in 1930 and 59 per cent in 1935.

Sources: Church (1986), table 8.2 for 1890–1913; 1920–38 membership from Miners' Federation of Great Britain, Minutes of Proceedings, 1920–38, NUM Library; data were taken from statements of accounts, reports of the Executive Committee or reports of the Credentials Committee to the annual conferences, as available; employment for 1920, Mines Department, *Statistical Summary of Output ... of the Coal Mining Industry in respect of the Three Months ended on 30th September, 1920*, which describes the data as 'workpeople employed'; employment 1925–38, Mines Department, *Annual Reports of the Secretary for Mines*, 1925–38, e.g. *1925*, table 15, which describe the data as 'wage earners'.

and the Miners' National Union (MNU), (a merger of the AAM and the MNA) in the early 1880s, advocated a policy of an eight-hour day coupled with regulation of output (Youngson Brown 1953: 46; Fisher and Smethurst 1978: 119, 122). Though the last serious attempts to use output restriction as a collective bargaining tactic belong to the early 1890s (J. E. Williams 1962b: 319; Burgess 1975: 205), there is a continuity between the traditional policy of restriction and the new policy on hours adopted by the Miners' Federation of Great Britain (MFGB) which campaigned for a legislative eight-hour day from its formation until it achieved its goal in 1908 (Church 1986: 695).

The strike was the most obvious alternative to output restriction; but it was one that few familiar with its realities can have relished, for strikes, lock-outs and the evictions made in consequence could lead to a rapid escalation of conflict sometimes involving riot, personal injury and the destruction of property (Church 1986: 653). The first breakthrough occurred in the 1860s in South Yorkshire. Following consecutive defeats of the coalowners by the South Yorkshire Miners' Association (SYMA) in 1864 and 1865, the SYMA succeeded in enlisting the participation by some of the employers in an arrangement by which either side in a dispute could refer it to a meeting of representatives of the employers and the union (Machin 1958: 342–50). The first formal machinery was the joint committee set up in Durham in 1872 to settle individual colliery disputes, regardless of the issues, and to adjudicate on county-wide issues (Beynon and Austrin 1994: 66). This model was adopted on union initiative in Northumberland and in West Yorkshire during the boom of 1870–2.

These institutionalizations of direct negotiation were overlaid by arbitral procedures (Welbourne 1923: 162, 168; J. E. Williams 1962b: 139; Challinor 1972: 104–5). Although arbitration fell well short of union leaders' ambitions, it served their interests since participation in arbitration would promote the organizational status and legitimacy of the union. That arbitration was accepted by employers so soon after periods when they had rejected any form of collective bargaining was remarkable 'for it was an acknowledgement that independent persons could sit in judgement on what hitherto had been regarded as the private preserve of employers' (Allen 1971: 69). The men chosen to umpire boards of arbitration, however, tended to be 'experts', and were inevitably sympathetic to the conventional 'rational argument' presented by the owners: that miners' wages should follow coal prices. The problem for the miners' leaders was not simply that the arbitration process might well yield outcomes that were unwelcome to their members. The standing of the union as an effective and reliable organization for conducting industrial relations was at best precarious, and preserving its status in this role required the ability to ensure that arbitration awards would be adhered to by their constituents. This in turn meant that rank and file members had to be persuaded of the reasonableness of the arbitrator's case and that there had to be some means of controlling members who, nevertheless, felt inclined to push their dissatisfaction to the point of organizing local strikes, or even to the point of forming a breakaway union. The former require-

ment was met by an elaborate theatre of investigation and due process (Bougen
et al. 1990: 156–8). The latter requirement was met, to the extent that it was, by
central union control over strike funds and inter-branch communications.

Almost without exception, arbitrators had used changes in the price of coal as
the justification for awarding reductions or, more rarely, increases in wages. This
practice was soon formalized in 'sliding scale' agreements. By 1885 sliding scales
were in operation in Northumberland, Durham, Cumberland, Somerset and
South Wales (Munro 1885: 3; Clegg *et al.* 1964: 19). These provided for set
percentage advances or reductions in wage rates for each rise or fall in ascer-
tained coal prices. A sliding scale provided a supposedly automatic way of
changing wage rates which promised to give owners, particularly those of the
major exporting areas of the North East, South Wales and Scotland where prices
were especially volatile, their *sine qua non* of rapid wage reductions on a falling
market, without the evil and delay of a lock-out.

That the unfettered coal market should determine prices and that wages
should follow prices was a view which was also widespread on the union side.
Only MacDonald of the MNA really contested this; leaders in the North East,
Yorkshire and, after 1875, South Wales accepted it. The dominant view ration-
alized brute reality. In the circumstances of the time the only alternative to the
sliding scale was to court the union's destruction by striking on a falling market.
While miners' leaders accepted the terms of the truce which the sliding scale
represented, the harsh and rapid reductions which the scales imposed engendered an undercurrent of opposition and ideological antagonism to the union
leaders who accepted them (Youngson Brown 1953: 48; Clegg *et al.* 1964: 23;
Church 1986: 696). When the coal trade and trade union organization revived
towards the end of the 1880s opposition to the sliding scales mounted. Among
numerous objections undoubtedly one of the most strongly felt was the failure of
most scales to provide any effective minimum below which rates could not fall
(Jevons 1915/1969: 495–8; Porter 1970: 467–9, 1971: 18–20; Church 1986:
699–701). The most important element in the growth of this opposition was the
formation of the MFGB in 1889. Based in the inland fields, where coal prices
were more stable than in the export districts, the MFGB was committed to
securing a 'living wage' for miners. The emphasis of the Federation's leaders on
the maintenance of a 'minimum standard of life' inevitably implied hostility to
sliding scales. This and its other major policy objective, a statutory eight-hour
day, gave the MFGB a 'distinct socialistic bias of a practical kind' which was
characteristic of the rapidly emerging 'New Unions' of the late 1880s (Jevons
1915/1969: 467; Clegg *et al.* 1964: 107).

The MFGB's opposition to sliding scales was first put to the test in 1893.
Facing falling coal prices, employers demanded wage cuts which the MFGB
opposed. The result was by far the biggest strike or lock-out that had ever been
experienced in Britain: 300,000 miners were locked-out for sixteen weeks.
Because of its scale it also became the first industrial dispute in which the
government intervened directly in an attempt to find a resolution, sponsoring a

conference chaired by Lord Rosebery. There the owners argued that the prices at which they had accepted contracts would not allow them to make profits unless wages were reduced. They urged arbitration. The MFGB replied that:

If the employers like to accept contracts at ridiculously low prices that is their look out. They did not consult them before they committed themselves. . . . The miners are not going to work for less than a living wage, and owners should recognise that before recklessly reducing prices. Open arbitration could only be based on these prices, . . . and therefore they are compelled to object to arbitration. (Clem Edwards 1893: 655)

As was pointed out by a contemporary observer, the 'real question at issue [was] whether labour [was] or [was] not to have the right of exercising a voice in fixing prices' (Clem Edwards 1893: 655). The settlement prompted by the government temporarily averted wage cuts; from 1894 wages were to be determined by a board of conciliation. The MFGB had survived and its policy of a living wage remained in place. After this point sliding scales became increasingly anachronistic and conciliation boards became the predominant mode of wage fixing in the industry (Arnot 1949: 219–53; Clegg et al. 1964: 106–11; Church 1986: 736–41).

Boards of conciliation were negotiating committees of coalowners and miners sitting under the auspices of an independent chair or 'umpire' who was normally empowered to issue a binding award whenever the two sides failed to come to agreement: they thus retained an important element of arbitration (Board of Trade, *Report on Rules of . . . Boards and Joint Committees*, 1908; Rowe 1923: 40). Under the conciliation board system the miners made an attempt to insert an effective floor to wage rates and, while still accepting that wages would vary with coal prices, asserted the necessity of a minimum (Phelps Brown 1959: 135). How far the supersession of sliding scales by conciliation boards represented a change of substance and how far merely of form has been a matter of controversy. While it is clear that the course of coal prices remained the predominant influence on wages, Treble's quantitative analysis has demonstrated that where conciliation boards were introduced with minimum and maximum limits to wage rate variation these limits were effective and did indeed reduce the level of wage rate risk to which miners were exposed. Where conciliation boards operated without such limits, as in Northumberland and Durham, the new conciliation boards were no better than the old, unlimited, sliding scales (Treble 1987: 99–100). But, while the conciliation boards therefore usually represented a step forward for the miners, the minima they fixed increasingly came to be seen as inadequate commitments to the concept of a minimum living wage (Church 1986: 740–1).

The formation of the MFGB accelerated the progress of organization and recruitment (Marsh and Ryan 1984). But although district and local unions emerged in the Scottish and Welsh coalfields, it was not until the following decade that permanent, regional trade union organization was established. In both regions the coalowners' associations continued to refuse to recognize the unions after 1889. In these areas coalowners adopted tactics similar to those of English coalowners during previous decades: acting in concert at county or district level to prevent unionization by fixing wage rates, exchanging information on workers, blacklisting, and the provision of legal aid to enforce evictions from company housing (Church 1986: 652–9).

By 1890, trade union members as a proportion of working miners in each of the major regions amounted to 64 per cent in Yorkshire, 54 per cent in the North East, 46 per cent in the East Midlands and 37 per cent in Lancashire and Cheshire (table 3.1). In the remaining regions, the figure for Scotland was 4 per cent, South Wales 3 per cent and 20 per cent in the West Midlands. It was not until the turn of the twentieth century that collective bargaining could be described as firmly established in all the major fields of the country (Burgess 1975: 214). But by 1910 one-half of all coalminers were covered by collective agreements, compared with about one-fifth of British workers as a whole (Clegg et al. 1964: 471–6). Between 1890 and 1913, trade union density in British coalmining as a whole roughly doubled, reaching 81 per cent. While the figure for the North East was 91 per cent in 1913, even more spectacular by comparison with the 1890 figures were those for Scotland, where the Scottish Miners' Federation of county unions, affiliated to the MFGB in 1894, achieved a membership density of 80 per cent. In South Wales, where the South Wales Miners' Federation (SWMF) had affiliated in 1899, the figure was 66 per cent. Aggregate trade union membership grew from 271,400 in 1892 to 885,800 in 1913. Paradoxically to some, but by no means all, contemporaries, miners at once demonstrated both the widest participation in collective bargaining through formal machinery and displayed the highest strike frequency of all workers.

The orderliness of the industry's collective bargaining arrangements was indeed somewhat illusory. The conciliation boards fixed regional or county-wide advances or reductions on the 'standard' or 'basis' piece-work price lists. ('Basis' or 'standard' piece-rates were those price lists which were accepted in each colliery as being subject to the percentage advances or reductions set by the conciliation boards or by other means (Jevons 1915/1960: 346–8; Rowe 1923).) The conciliation board arrangements thus aided the adjustment of wages to the changing circumstances of the industry at regional or county level as indicated largely by coal selling prices, and the changing balance of power between miners and owners. The conciliation boards did not, however, provide any machinery for the resolution of the 'domestic' disputes arising at individual collieries that gave rise to the 'normal' strike activity which is the primary concern of this study. Before 1914, formal pit-level machinery for dealing with domestic issues was almost unknown. Typically, workers with grievances would, either singly or in deputation, take them to under-managers or managers and the management might, or might not, consent to discuss the matter. Even county-level machinery for the resolution of domestic disputes was rare before the First World War, in 1907 existing only in Cumberland, Northumberland, Durham, West Yorkshire and the Forest of Dean. The Durham joint committee was the most active example of such machinery. Established in 1872, this body dealt with several hundred cases each year in the period 1897–1909, which is the only period for which data have been published. All but a handful of these disputes were settled without a strike. The joint committee consisted of equal numbers of representatives from each side sitting with an independent chairman and provided for recourse to an umpire where agreement could not be reached (Jevons 1915/1969: 501, 515). The Northumberland joint committee, established in 1873, usually settled over fifty cases a year in the same period, again with very few indeed proceeding to strike action. By contrast, the West Yorkshire joint committee, set up in 1890, dealt with only a handful of cases, while the South Yorkshire joint committee, established in the same year, apparently conducted no business for many years after 1897. Elsewhere, conciliation boards or a standing sub-committee of the board, as in Cumberland, sometimes acted in domestic cases or were empowered to use their 'good offices'; and occasionally disputes were referred to and dealt with by conciliation boards despite the absence of any provision in their constitutions for doing so. The most prominent example of this arrangement was in South Wales where the conciliation board dealt with eighty-six cases in 1909–10; in sharp contrast to Durham, only sixteen were settled (Board of Trade, *Report on Rules of . . . Boards and Joint Committees,* 1908: 238–9, 254–5; Board of Trade, *Report on Rules of . . . Boards and Joint Committees,* 1910: 32–3, 38–9; E. W. Evans 1961: 200).

In 1912 'domestic' problems and the concern with a 'living wage' brought the MFGB into confrontation with the owners. As we describe in greater detail in chapter 7, the MFGB sought to establish that when daily piece-work earnings failed to provide a living wage, a flat rate daily minimum should be paid in lieu. The objective was to reduce the instability of pieceworkers' earnings arising from abnormal geological and other conditions peculiar to each colliery, indeed, to each working place. With a minimum set in the conciliation board agreement and an 'individual' minimum set to guard against abnormal conditions, pieceworkers would have attained some protection from both sources of the risk to which their earnings were exposed: the market and the geology of the mine. When the owners, for the first time negotiating as a national body, albeit on a temporary and *ad hoc* basis, rejected the demand a strike ensued which lasted seven weeks and involved 850,000 workers (Clegg *et al.* 1964: 44–52). As in 1893, the government became involved and as part of the settlement an Act of Parliament was passed which imposed the principle of an individual minimum on the coalowners and established a machinery to determine minimum rates.

By 1912 the industry had seen substantial changes. Since the 1880s trade union membership had grown very substantially: both employer and trade union organization had become more stable and more widespread. The gradual accession of power to the miners allowed them to put some limit on the fluctuations of wages and earnings. But although the MFGB had demonstrated its strength by successfully weathering a lock-out on a falling market in 1893 and by obtaining the principle, if perhaps not the substance, of a minimum wage in 1912, it was still a long way from ensuring that prices followed wages rather than vice versa. Those local disputes which were settled found resolution outside any formal machinery in most districts and continued to erupt into strikes at frequent intervals.

The coalowners were critical in determining whether formal machinery was used and whether stoppages were the result when that machinery was not invoked. Just as the origins of permanent trade unionism in the industry can be traced back to the period between 1850 and 1870, so too can the origins of the coalowners' organizations that survived until nationalization. Previously loose and informal structures, predicated on networks of personal acquaintanceship and knowledge, were superseded by standing organizations with formal rules supported by continuing subscriptions. These organizations arose not merely simultaneously with the miners' unions but often because of them: the establishment of the South Yorkshire Miners' Association in 1858 resulted in the formation of a South Yorkshire owners' association in the same year; it was a similar story in the North East, in South Wales and in Fife. However, the attempts at a national union represented by the AAM, the MNA and the MNU found no real counterpart among the owners: although the MAGB was formed in 1854 it was concerned largely with representing the mineowners' interests in Parliament (a function parallel with that of the MNA and MNU) but was formally debarred from concerning itself with wages or prices (a limitation not paralleled by the miners' unions) (W. A. Lee 1924: 351–2; Cawley 1984: 128–9; Church 1986: 652–65).

From about 1860 owners' associations became increasingly involved in industrial relations. In 1860 the West Yorkshire coalowners reconstituted themselves to provide strike insurance for their members; the Northumberland Steam Collieries Defence Association, formed in 1864, sought to restrain wages; one of the main purposes of the Durham Coal Owners' Association, established in 1871, was to conduct relations between employers and workpeople; the South Yorkshire and North Derbyshire Coal Owners' Association, set up in 1874, offered strike insurance (Cawley 1984: 83–5; Church 1986: 656–7). These early associations were unstable: they were riven by differences of interest and were unable to control members who pursued their own interests at the expense of the interest of the association as a whole. The structure of obligations and incentives established by many of the owners' associations was bound to cause internal tensions. The strike insurance schemes of which we have details charged premia irrespective of whether the member's collieries were peaceful or not. Consequently, peaceful pits were deterred from joining by the costs of subsidizing the warlike policies of other members; belligerent members were under even less constraint when their association indemnified them against the losses arising from their policies. Owners' associations tried to overcome this problem by agreeing rules under which the association was allowed some involvement in the conduct of disputes (Church 1986: 657). Such rules did not always achieve their aim. Baylies describes a long series of disputes over piece-rates at the Hemsworth colliery in the early years of the twentieth century. For a long time the West Yorkshire Coalowners' Association (WYCOA) was closely involved. But its influence was less than decisive and eventually the owner agreed to one of the miners' demands: 'Members of the WYCOA were aghast' (Baylies 1993: 339).

Coalowners contemplating membership of an owners' association therefore had to consider not only the cost of their subscription and the possibility that much of what they subscribed would be paid out as indemnities to others but also that, in an attempt to limit such indemnity payments, the association would 'interfere' in the relations between themselves and their workers. Unlike the miners' unions, which could aid their recruitment by offering friendly society benefits, there was little to attract an owner into an association, especially an owner with a successful record of industrial peace. In the circumstances it is remarkable that the coalowner association membership was as high as it appears to have been. Few of the larger owners seem to have taken the view expressed by Lord Davies of Llandinam, the Chairman of the Ocean Coal Company, that by 'being a non-associated Colliery we reap all the advantages without any of the responsibilities' (Francis and Smith 1980: 229). In the early 1890s, the Durham association claimed its members produced in excess of 80 per cent of the output of the field; using the same measure, it would appear that membership stood at about two-thirds in Fife and Clackmannan, South Yorkshire, in the South Staffordshire and East Worcestershire District, and in South Wales; in West Yorkshire it was about half (Church 1986: 670–1).

Strike insurance was not the only tactic used by the owners' associations to fight strikes. They recruited strike-breakers, assisted with evictions and aided the victimization of strikers by the use of the discharge note. These aggressive tactics were perhaps more typical of the 1850s and 1860s than of later decades: indeed, in 1896 an agreement was reached in South Wales to abolish the use of the discharge note. However, this did not abolish victimization: it was widespread after the 1926 Lock-out and more than ten years later the leader of the 1936–7 strike at Harworth colliery in North Nottinghamshire was banned from employment by every colliery in the East Midlands, finally securing employment only after the war. Strike-breakers were recruited during the Denaby Main lock-out in 1885, and during the Cambrian Combine strike in South Wales in 1910–11; and hard-line employers in the region continued to use them into the 1930s (David Evans 1911: 64–5; Arnot 1955: 215; J. H. Morris and Williams 1957; J. E. Williams 1962b: 735–6; MacFarlane 1976a: 82; Francis and Smith 1980: 76, 240, note 48, 318–21, 505–7; Andrew J. Taylor 1984a: 49; Clegg 1985: 29; Beynon and Austrin 1994: 329–31). However, the use of eviction appears to have virtually died out by the First World War. Miners at Denaby were evicted from their houses in 1885 and again in 1903, Hemsworth miners were evicted in 1905 and employees and tenants of the Butterley company were given notice to quit in the 1912 national strike. But this action was subsequently repudiated by the company's board and this seems to mark a turning point. In the 1921 and 1926 lock-outs owners appear to have allowed rent arrears to accumulate rather than evict collier tenants (an action which would in any case only have hampered the return to work) and in the unrelenting dispute at Harworth colliery in 1936–7, where the company 'practically owned the village' and applied for eviction orders, the judge imposed a two-month delay, remarking that 'Blood cannot be got from a stone' (Lawson 1941: 150; J. E. Williams 1962b: 420, 765; James MacFarlane 1976a: 81; Supple 1987: 251; Chaplin 1992; Baylies 1993: 321, 345–6; Fishman 1995: 183, quoting the judge's words from a report in the *Daily Worker*, 21 January 1937).

Such were the owners' tactics with regard to strikes but, as we have seen, coalowners' associations also pursued collective bargaining strategies based on arbitration, the sliding scale and conciliation. Just as the mining unions came to be divided between those which advocated or accepted the sliding scale and those which rejected it, so did the owners. After 1882, when the last sliding scale in the inland areas was terminated, until 1894, when the conciliation board for the Federated Area came into operation, there was no formal collective bargaining relationship between the unions and the owners in the inland areas (Munro 1885: 3). This weakened the coalowners' associations that existed in the inland areas and in the late 1880s and early 1890s a number had to be re-established (Cawley 1984: 90–1; Church 1986: 666–71). At the time of the formation of the MFGB there was no corresponding organization of owners to oppose it. The MAGB, the obvious vehicle for opposition to the MFGB, was debarred from considering wages questions and it was not until 1890 that the Owners of the Federated Districts (OFD) was formed. The OFD was formally separate from the MAGB but shared its officers with the MAGB; to a great extent the separation between the two was a legal fiction. It was not until 1920 that the MAGB revised its rules and was empowered to negotiate wages issues with the Miners' Federation (W. A. Lee 1924: 357; Cawley 1984: 152–3).

Trade unions, coalowners' associations and industrial relations 1914–40

The history of mining industrial relations in the ten or twelve years preceding the General Strike has been recounted many times and it would be otiose to give another narrative here: the general historiography can be traced through Arnot (1926), Cole (1927), Crook (1931), Hutt (1937), Arnot (1953), Symons (1957), Mason (1970), Farman (1972), Renshaw (1975), Margaret Morris (1976), G. A. Phillips (1976), Skelley (1976), Clegg (1985) and Supple (1987). But it may still be helpful to emphasize the exceptionalism of the 1914–26 period. During the First World War the state intervened in the affairs of the industry to an unprecedented degree culminating in the *de facto* but temporary nationalization of the industry. The impact of this was to cement the national solidarity miners had slowly built up during the approach to the first national strike of 1912.

Legislative intervention in the industry had always treated it as a national whole, with regional and local differences being accommodated, if at all, by delegated legislation and administrative measures. The First World War saw no change in this practice. Intense government pressure on the industry to increase output led to the nation-wide establishment of pit-level Joint Absenteeism Committees (Cole 1923: 17, 69–70; Bougen et al. 1988: 620–2). A piece-meal but national regulation of coal prices and the industry's finances developed, rendering the pre-war regulation of wages by district coal prices nonsensical. Increasingly fraught wage negotiations in South Wales threatened to lead to a stoppage throughout the coalfield, which was the source of the strategically essential Admiralty-grade steam coals. It was this crisis that persuaded the government to requisition the whole of the South Wales coal industry in November 1916 and the rest of the UK industry early the next year. From this point the government's Coal Controller became the most significant collective bargaining partner for the MFGB. In the absence of any other obvious grounding for negotiations, changes in the cost of living became the central focus of wage bargaining, and for the remainder of the war national flat rate advances were sought and gained from the state. This change, from negotiating on the basis of regionally differentiated coal price changes to national changes in the cost of living, gave concrete expression to the *de facto* nationalization of the industry and helped to concert the interests of miners throughout the polity. The financing of these wage increases by a 'profits pool' through which the more prosperous fields subsidized the less prosperous, demonstrated the possibilities for wage equalization that a permanent nationalization would enable.

These advances were immediately threatened by the Armistice. The MFGB's post-war programme, which aimed to make permanent many of the changes brought about by the war and use them as a springboard for further advances, failed in the face of state and coalowner insistence that the industry be returned to private control and the owners' insistence that wages must once again be determined, district by district, according to the district industry's 'ability to pay', not according to the miners' need for a 'living wage' (Bougen et al. 1990: 160–3). Nevertheless, the undoubted ability of the MFGB to mount a damaging national strike or resist a national lock-out, the post-war context of widespread labour unrest, the fluid political situation and uncertain economic prospects of the industry led the state and the owners to pursue a time-consuming strategy of resistance and delay until 1926 when the latter felt sure the time was ripe for a final show down (Cole 1923: 73; Tawney 1943; Cowling 1971; Kirby 1977; Outram 1982; Clegg 1985; Supple 1987: 122–3, 153–7). After a seven-month lock-out the MFGB finally accepted defeat and instructed the districts to seek district settlements: the era of national collective bargaining, inaugurated in 1912, was at an end.

The First World War had forced the MAGB into a national role not only, as customarily, in relation to legislation but also in relation to its workers. The state treated the MAGB, rather than its constituent district associations, as the representative body for the industry, an arrangement which, despite its alleged constitutional inability to discuss wages and working conditions, the MAGB accepted. But the MAGB was profoundly uneasy with its new role. The president, Evan Williams, took the view that national wage settlements politicized the economics and industrial relations of the industry and rendered a subsequent step towards nationalization all the more likely. Williams was surely right in his assessment. This perspective formed the bedrock of MAGB strategy until at least 1930 (Supple 1987: 158, note 2, 248; Sunley 1988: 15). That the strategy survived for so long, well after it had succeeded in 'putting nationalization to sleep' in 1919 (Evan Williams, quoted in Supple 1984: 231) is explained by organizational imperatives. The fragile pre-war unity of the Association was founded on non-intervention on wages and hours, and when the MAGB was, nevertheless, forced to intervene it encountered serious difficulties (Outram 1982: 10–11; Supple 1987: 163, 416–17). Hence the MAGB's 'famous vanishing trick' (*Manchester Guardian*, quoted in Supple 1987: 415): the insistence that, despite all appearances, it was unable to negotiate nationally on wages or hours.

However, in one respect the 1926 Coal Lock-out did mark the close of an era, not merely the end of an interlude. From the late 1920s it is possible to detect a change in the economics of the industry, at first obscure, but by the mid-1930s in plain view. The seemingly inevitable concatenation of falling product demand, tumbling prices and wage cuts vanished. Although the 1932 depression was by far the deepest experienced since the 1880s, coal prices rose continuously relative to trend and during the late 1920s and early 1930s average real earnings per shift actually rose (Mines Department, *Annual Reports of the Secretary of Mines*, 1923–38; J. Harry Jones et al. 1939: 147ff). Detailed investigations, hampered by evidence which is necessarily indirect, have concluded that, independently of but supported by the 1930 Coal Mines Act, a degree of tacit and voluntary collusion to maintain prices and restrict output became established throughout the industry (Kirby 1977: 116–20; Supple 1987: 208–13). Certainly, by the 1930s the instability of coal prices which lay at the root of many of the conflicts of the industry had gone and there seemed to have been a 'change in attitudes' among the coalowners (Neuman 1934: 383–5, 420, 425, 427ff; Kirby 1977: 116–20, 140–50; Greasley 1995: 56, 61). Viewed in historical perspective, it is remarkable that at a time when miners' fortunes had reached a nadir the owners should have accepted the wisdom of restricting output, a policy which miners had urged vainly upon their employers since the time of the Chartists (Fynes 1873/1972: 50), and that as a result and for the first time in the modern history of the industry a major fall in demand did not bring with it a significant cut in real wages.

The 'de-nationalization' of the industry in 1921 led eventually, in 1926, to a reopening of the inter-regional fissures that had been a marked feature of the industry in the period before the passage of the Eight Hours Act in 1908. The weakness of the MFGB affiliates after 1926 was deepened by the emergence of rival unions. These had their origins in the exploitation of the economic differences between the districts during the 1926 Lock-out in a strategy concerted by the MAGB and the Government (Arnot 1953: 482; Supple 1987: 244; Sunley 1988:14). It had been easy enough to do this. The revenue productivity of the districts varied greatly so that in some areas the owners could offer (relatively) advantageous terms of settlement; in Nottinghamshire the owners failed to post notices of wage reductions and were apparently willing to provide work on the old terms (Alan R. Griffin 1962: 152, 165). The drift back to work in the final stages of the 1926 Lock-out had been strongest where the cuts were least, in the Eastern District (including Nottinghamshire and North Derbyshire), in South Derbyshire, in the Midlands and in the Forest of Dean. The only district to stand out from this pattern was Yorkshire, where despite relatively low prospective wage cuts the strike was virtually unbreached (Sunley 1988: 6–7).

The first organized breakaway came in Nottinghamshire. George Spencer of the MFGB-affiliated Nottinghamshire Miners' Association (NMA) met local owners to negotiate a district settlement on 1 November and soon afterwards the Nottinghamshire and District Miners' Industrial Union was formally established – the term 'industrial union' in implied contrast with the so-called 'political' unions affiliated to the MFGB (Arnot 1953: 444–5, 497; Alan R. Griffin and Griffin 1977: 135). The NMA found that the owners would not negotiate with it and its membership fell rapidly, from 34,767 at the end of 1925 to 10,055 at the end of 1926 (Registrar of Friendly Societies, *Annual Reports* for 1925 and 1926, part IV, Trade Unions). The Nottinghamshire Miners' Industrial Union was by far the biggest of the 'industrial' unions among those established after 1926. The only other of any significance was the South Wales Miners' Industrial Union (SWMIU), which established itself at a small number of collieries in the late 1920s. Although strong at these collieries, the SWMIU appears never to have recruited more than 8,000 members. Elsewhere, small and short-lived 'industrial' unions surfaced, all of them dissolved or submerged in obscurity by the end of 1930. Only the unions in Nottinghamshire and South Wales survived this date (David Smith 1972–3; Alan R. Griffin and Griffin 1977: 142–4, table 1; Alan R. Griffin 1977; David Smith 1978; Alan R. Griffin 1978; Francis and Smith 1980; Waller 1987; Colin P. Griffin 1990; Beynon and Austrin 1994: 335–7). Both came to an end of their independent existence in the late 1930s. The Nottinghamshire union was forced into a merger with the MFGB affiliated NMA and a campaign against the SWMIU launched by the SWMF in 1934 was finally brought to a successful conclusion in February 1938 when the SWMIU agreed to merge with the SWMF, an agreement facilitated by a discreet bribe paid to the SWMIU General Secretary from SWMF funds (Arnot 1961: 201–43; David Smith 1972–3: 366–77; Alan R. Griffin and Griffin 1977: 140–51; Francis and Smith 1980: 379–88; Fishman 1991: 310).

Developments in district-level collective bargaining have been little studied during the inter-war years. In some of the smaller districts, collective bargaining on district-wide questions appears to have been in abeyance after 1926, but in most there was a continuity of organization and institutions. The fate of the joint committees established in the 1870s and 1890s to consider local disputes at district level was varied. The Durham committee was suspended in 1923 and was not restarted before the mid-1930s, but the Northumberland committee continued in operation throughout the 1920s and beyond. Joint committees were also in operation in Cumberland and South Derbyshire during the 1930s but the most surprising development was in South Wales. By 1915 local disputes were being regularly dealt with by the conciliation board or its sub-committees. However, there appears to have been no provision for a recourse to arbitration at this time which may have encouraged the long delays castigated in Jevons's discussion (1915/1969: 513–15). The competence of the conciliation board to deal with 'disputes at the various collieries' was reaffirmed in 1921 and 1931. By the latter date the conciliation board agreement provided for a 'complete scheme' for dealing with domestic disputes. It specified that disputes should pass upwards from pit committees through a number of intermediate committees to the joint standing disputes committee of the board, but that in the event of a final failure to agree there should be not arbitration but 'liberty to tender notices to terminate contracts'. Whether the committee was any more successful in the 1930s than in the pre-war period is not clear (Ministry of Labour, *Report on Collective Agreements* . . . [1934]: 67–70; Arnot 1975: 213–14).

Even less is known about collective bargaining at pit level during these years. It is clear that by the late 1920s the miners' unions had suffered a massive loss of funds and members (table 3.1), but lodge membership appears to have declined very unevenly (Andrew J. Taylor 1984a), in some places to less than a third of employees. In these lodges collective bargaining may have been all but absent, allowing little or no protection for members; certainly few strikes were recorded in such collieries. Elsewhere, lodges retained members and were able to continue to bargain and occasionally to strike.

The industrial relations history of the period from 1926 almost to the Second World War is, at the national level, a history of efforts to overcome the divisions that re-emerged in the wake of the 1926 defeat. By the outbreak of war substantial organizational recoveries had been achieved. 'Non-political' unionism had been eradicated and few coalowners continued to deny union recognition at pit level, even in South Wales and Scotland, removing an important source of grievance. Once again, as in the early 1920s, the MFGB could claim to organize and represent the vast majority of miners.

'United we stand': the traditional battlegrounds of Celtic Britain

Union recognition was denied longest in the coalfields of Scotland and South Wales, and it was the Scottish and Welsh miners who were reputed to be the most militant and the most strike-prone of all. As we shall see in chapter 5 the number of strikes per million workers in these regions far exceeded the levels recorded in Britain as a whole; in some periods more than two-thirds of British coalmining strikes occurred in Scotland and South Wales. It is hardly surprising, therefore, that some of the traditional literature, and that which focuses on the role of culture in historical change, should have offered interpretations of the spectacular strike records of the two regions as evidence of regional – even Celtic – peculiarities, stressing the exceptionalist nature of the historical experience of Scotland and South Wales. Such an approach clearly has implications for our narrower concerns with mining strikes. As a prelude to considering such interpretations we survey briefly both the similarities and the contrasting characteristics of the two regions compared with the English coalfields, before asking the question whether coalmining strikes in Britain were largely a manifestation of cultural exceptionalism.

Numerous similarities in the history of the Scottish and Welsh industries may be identified. The geology of the coalmining districts of South Wales and Scotland produced immense and often unpredicted variations in the physical conditions of working and in the mix of coal and dirt when the coal was cut. Both were important sources of disputes. Producers in both regions exported coal, a trade that was particularly vulnerable to marked fluctuations in demand and, related to this, both regions were strongholds of the sliding scale. In both regions miners were relatively late to establish permanent and county-wide trade unions and these failed to organize the majority of miners in their districts before the late 1890s (table 3.1). In both regions a federal union structure persisted even after the formation of the regional unions: the Scottish Miners' Federation in 1894 and the South Wales Miners' Federation in 1898.

Within both regions sharply contrasting geographies and geologies encouraged fragmented structures of industrial relations despite the semblance of increasing union centralization from the 1890s. After the First World War organizational and financial weaknesses contributed to the formation of militant breakaway organizations: the Miners' Reform Committee in Lanarkshire, the Reform Union in Fife and, later, the United Mineworkers of Scotland (Arnot 1955: 151–70; Macfarlane 1966: 265–6; Long 1978: 330–2; Campbell 1992: 92–103; Fishman 1995: 35). In South Wales, the 'Spencerist' Industrial Union, though opposite in ideology to the militant Scottish organizations, was also symptomatic of divisions in this coalfield. Faced with weak unions until the turn of the century and by divisions after that, coalowners' associations in both regions developed an aggressive posture. While sliding scales became the subject of agreements between coalowner associations and trade unions, unions were often not recognized at colliery level for the purpose of negotiation over pay and conditions (Anthony-Jones 1959: 109–20; Long 1978: 338). The approach of owners' organizations in both regions was noticeably more militant than in most English coalfields. For example, after the Taff Vale decision, the South Welsh association required members to use the law on breach of contract against employees or otherwise forgo financial support; miners who took industrial action without notice had to be prosecuted. Union membership was proscribed in neither region, though where strikes occurred over recognition or where miners took steps to achieve a closed shop, the owners took a hard line. In South Wales, allegations of victimization were permitted to appear on joint committee agendas but invariably the coalowners' policy was to support the colliery management (Scottish Coal Owners' Association, *Minutes*, University of Glasgow Archives, UGD 159/1/1–9; Anthony-Jones 1959: 109–20; Long 1978: 338; J. Williams 1985: table 1, 46).

The greatest concentration of highly strike-prone pits, not only in the regions but in Britain, was, however, in the anthracite mining district of rural West Glamorgan, Brecon and Carmarthen (see below, table 5.10), away from the major coalmining activity and, until the mid-1930s, excluded from the hard-line policies pursued by the MSWCOA. The refusal by local coalowners, whether disposed towards more harmonious relations with their essentially stable, rural work-force or mindful of the strength of the local union, to apply the recommendations of the owners' Special Purposes Committee, which required reprisal, extended layoffs, and the prosecution of all unofficial strikers, drew condemnation from other coalowners (Anthony-Jones 1959: 53, 113–14; Francis 1980: 170–4). A further difference between the history of labour relations in the anthracite district and the rest of South Wales was that, by comparison with the latter, very few disputes found their way to the joint committee for resolution.

Anthony-Jones attributed the militancy of the anthracite miners to excessively difficult working conditions in which seams were even more broken and faulted than those elsewhere in the region. Widespread and comparably difficult geological conditions were to be found only in Scotland. He suggested that until 1914, at least, the rural location of the several small enterprises mining anthracite had enabled miners to continue to farm smallholdings, thus supplementing their income and perpetuating a degree of independence missing elsewhere in the principality. He argued that vestiges of independence, residence in relatively isolated communities, and a shared experience of the threat of silicosis, peculiar to hard rock and anthracite mining, contributed to a strong sense of solidarity (Anthony-Jones 1959, 113–14). One other factor which probably had greater relevance was the buoyancy of markets for anthracite, which enabled miners to pressure the companies into making concessions on allowances (Hare 1940: 14–19, 61–2, 69; Anthony-Jones 1959: 49). From 1923 the disadvantage the anthracite miners experienced because of their inclusion in the same wages agreement as workers in the Welsh bituminous coal mines may also have been a major disruptive factor. This change proved disadvantageous because percentage additions to basis wage rates were determined by the level of profits for the whole of South Wales. The averaging carried out in order to reach a common quarterly ascertainment of profits meant that the heavy losses incurred by bituminous coal producers adversely affected the wages of anthracite miners (Hare 1940: 66–70).

Regional comparisons between environmental, structural and organizational factors affecting labour relations in the two most militant regions highlight important contrasts as well as similarities. The spatial configuration of coalmining communities in South Wales facilitated (albeit within a limited compass) the process of building solidarity in disputes. The earlier, more rapid advance of technology in Scottish pits where the greater prevalence of thin seams rendered mechanization economic (Greasley 1982: 246–54) presented greater scope for disputes resulting from changes in work organization and working practices related to mechanization. The more extensive faulting in South Wales coal seams, on the other hand, created a particular difficulty of 'abnormal places'. In both regions, therefore, a context of uncertainty and potentially destabilizing occurrences was not conducive to stable labour relations.

Regional peculiarities have taken a central place in historians' attempts to identify the differences which have produced the contrasting historical experience of South Wales and Scotland when compared with England. Differences in social structure, patterns of economic control, political orientation and activity, on which the literature on the Celtic societies of the British Isles has focused, may all be regarded as potentially relevant to an explanation of their distinctive industrial relations record as reflected in exceptionally high strike propensities. Stead has described the outcome of industrialization during the early nineteenth century as having transformed South Wales into 'a community in which a pattern of economic control and of social and political values create[d] a labour force with a very distinct psychology' (Stead 1973: 42). The crucial elements in this process, he argued, were rural migration on a large scale, Irish in the mid-nineteenth century and north and mid-Welsh and border counties later, in search of relatively highly paid work in the collieries and ironworks around which numerous industrial villages developed. This resulted in the development of a 'unique civilization of semi-urban peasantry', which Stead also described as an 'industrial peasantry' possessing a strong sense of community and a disposition to take collective action (Stead 1973: 47–8).

Two factors were accorded special importance in his analysis. One was the absence in those industrial villages of a middle class and therefore of 'civilizing' institutions such as churches and chapels, schools, hospitals and almshouses, which was remarked upon by a Royal Commissioner in 1847 (Commissioner Appointed . . . to Inquire . . . into the State of the Population in the Mining Districts, *Report*, 1847). Seventy years later, the Commission of Enquiry into Industrial Unrest in the South Wales coalfield also underlined the 'absence of municipal centres and centralised institutions; the development of civic spirit and the sense of social solidarity – what we may in short call the community' (Commission of Enquiry into Industrial Unrest, *Report on No. 7 Division (Wales and Monmouthshire)*, quoted by Stead 1973: 46–7). The second factor which was central in Stead's analysis was the attitude of employers, whose refusal to deal with unions evoked an equally antagonistic posture on the part of organized labour. This had been a sporadic response until 1893 when Ben Tillet addressed Welsh miners in an uncompromising speech in which he called them a rabble, accusing them of accepting appeals from their leaders which consisted of no more than patriotism and cant; organization and participation, he argued, was imperative if Welsh miners were to escape from their subjection by mine owners and union leaders like 'Mabon' (Stead 1973: 52).

Language continued to be one of the divisive influences among the South Welsh mining communities. 'Mabon' employed the Welsh language, in song and in rhetoric, as a means of appealing to emotion and cultural identity in order to get his own way with union members, while the MFGB encouraged the formation of a rival English-speaking union based in Monmouthshire (E. W. Evans 1961: 57). The failed strike by colliers in South Wales on a rising market in 1898 was the turning point, after which the cultural divide based largely on language began to disappear (Kenneth O. Morgan 1981: 77–9; Mitchell 1984: 187). Thereafter, an 'intensive feeling of solidarity during periods of open conflict' among Welsh workers in heavy industry was the consequence not only of the influence of English trade unions, notably the MFGB, but of the 'spiritual value [which workers in South Wales] placed on camaraderie' (Stead 1973: 53). Thus, Stead asserted the peculiarity of the miners of South Wales, a perspective which David Smith reinforced in his examination of the emergence and character of the Welsh working class in *A People and a Proletariat* (1980: 7–46), and which Francis and Rees adopted as their starting point in their study of the role of Welsh miners during the national coal strike of 1984–5 (Francis and Rees 1989).

Campbell's detailed studies of industrial relations in the Scottish coal industry and Lewis's study of the Rhondda (1959) strengthen this interpretation of a Celtic working-class culture as the result of exceptional historical developments originating well before the period which is the subject of our analysis. As in South Wales, where Glamorgan, Monmouthshire, and Carmarthen formed a core coalmining region within the principality, the central Clyde Valley formed a region in which a middle class barely existed and in which institutions and organizations associated with civil society were largely absent. Within such an economic and social environment pressures arose which triggered political as well as trade union activity (Campbell 1995: 52–3). Campbell identified religious and ethnic differences, essentially the presence and activity of Irish Catholics who came into conflict with the Protestant native Scots, as one of the significant contributions to tension within the Clyde Valley population and which was conducive to conflict, whether in the public house or in the workplace. He found evidence which pointed to an association between Catholicism and support for the Communist Minority Movement in Lanarkshire and Fife, where the two largest county unions were located (54–5).

When such emphases on the evolution of peculiar national cultures in Scotland and South Wales are juxtaposed they clearly convey their relevance to any attempt to account for the exceptional history of strike activity throughout several generations. Our findings based on the history of the coal industry are consistent with the conclusions which Hechter reached in his innovative investigation of *Internal Colonialism: the Celtic Fringe in British National Development*, a study which was sociological in approach but within a firmly historical framework. He interpreted heavy migration and lower per capita incomes together with linguistic and religious differences among the populations of the two nations as providing ample justification for describing them as culturally subordinate relative to English counties (1975: 327) and fertile ground for the development of an 'ethnic solidarity' (345). While certainly adding support to our recognition of the cultural distinctiveness of the Celtic coalfields, this analysis does not also strengthen the credibility of an argument which explains the exceptionally high strike propensity of coalminers in Scotland and South Wales.

Hechter perceived Celtic culture and shared disadvantage as a basis for anti-English political mobilization (343). The fact, however, that both in Scotland, and even, as Hechter concedes (278), in South Wales, at least from the 1880s, the coalowners were predominantly indigenous Scots and Welsh, suggests that ethnicity is a dubious factor among possible explanations for the distinctiveness of their strike histories when compared with the strike history of England. Whereas migration was common to both, notably from Ireland to central Scotland and from England to South Wales, the conflict which the mixture of Catholic with Protestant produced in the Scottish coalfield was not replicated in the principality. Social heterogeneity may have increased the probability of conflict at work as well as in the streets of industrial Scotland, but at the same time the basis for solidaristic behaviour was thereby reduced. This appears to be in contrast with circumstances prevailing in South Wales where the language, rather than religious denomination, was the greater influence for division (Hechter 1975: 186–200). Evidence on the effects of an 'ethnic solidarity', to which Hechter attaches importance in the context of Celtic nationalism, on solidarity at the workplace has not been found.

While in some respects persuasive, therefore, an interpretation which links Celtic cultures with strikes and solidarity must remain provisional. Such an interpretation would gain more credibility had strike activity in other industries in Scotland and Wales been consistently greater than in the English regions, but Knowles's research on this question, based on strike activity between 1911 and 1945, strongly suggested that the role of Celtic culture was at best partial and limited. After adjusting for the effects of industrial structure, Knowles found that workers in South Wales were, indeed, almost five times as strike-prone as workers in the UK as a whole; but workers in central and North Wales were considerably less strike-prone than average. Scottish workers were shown to be little more strike-prone than the UK average, once the effects of industrial structure had been taken into account, while workers in Lancashire and Cheshire and in the West Riding of Yorkshire emerged as at least twice as strike-prone as their Scottish counterparts (Knowles 1952: 185–209). This final finding resonates with the industrial relations history of the coal industry where during the 1930s the large and rapidly growing South Yorkshire coalfield emerged as one of the most strike-prone, and where high levels of strike activity were sustained after nationalization. No one has suggested that the concept of cultural subordination applies to South Yorkshire.

Of fundamental importance is our finding, documented in chapter 5, that when we focus on ordinary strike activity at local and colliery level regional differences are less important than the similarities in strike patterns and characteristics in all regions. Even within the highly strike-prone regions some collieries were much more strike-prone than others, and a high strike propensity, even in the relatively highly strike-prone regions, was normally a temporary condition. This indicates the importance for scholars whose primary interest is that of ordinary strikes, whether in the Celtic coalfields or others, that the prime focus of research be on localities rather than regions.

This was the starting point for Zweiniger-Bargielowska's detailed study of four South Wales collieries during the period between the late 1930s and the late 1950s, one of the few attempts at a systematic comparative analysis of colliery strike histories (1990, 1992–3). The study concluded that strikes in mining could be seen as a specific response to specific circumstances, though the author pointed to the diverse incidence of unemployment and industrial unionism during the inter-war years as important factors affecting strike propensity. A combination of local pit conditions, the balance of power between lodge and management, the degree of lodge leaders' control over the rank and file membership and managerial strategies were seen to have been the factors which explained why miners were militant or not (1992–3: 383). The valuable evidence presented in the course of her study provides further empirical underpinning for our investigation into the national picture. However, the significance of her conclusions for our study is limited by the research methodology adopted which lacks a control element in the collieries compared. Based on only four collieries her exploration of considerably more than four sets of explanatory factors could not be expected to enable her to pin down the precise significance of each factor for explaining the tenor and history either of the labour relations of those collieries or, by extrapolation, of South Wales collieries generally.

Zweiniger-Bargielowska's emphasis on diversity and interaction might be interpreted as a deterrent to others to attempt generalization. Indeed, scholars similarly impressed by the complexity of specific strike histories have offered even more pessimistic verdicts. After detailed research on strikes in South Wales and Yorkshire, both Howells (1979: 244, 388) and McCormick (1969: 181) concluded that inconsistencies evident in collieries' propensity to strike ensured that any generalization would lack validity; that local strikes were multi-causal and therefore defied overall generalization. In chapter 5 we shall see clear patterns within the complexity and by chapter 10 we shall have suggested firmly that such extreme pessimism is unwarranted. However, before this we return to the national context and national influences, asking whether the industry's high strike activity can be explained, in part at least, by the attitudes and ideologies of miners' employers and miners' leaders.

4   Employers and workers: ideologies, attitudes and political orientations

The industrial relations experienced by coalminers and coalowners reflected not only the structures and organizations of the industry but also the attitudes and ideologies which miners and owners brought with them to workplace, meeting room and conference chamber. These attitudes and ideologies were influenced by each miner's own experience in the industry but also and decisively by events and developments in the wider society: the decline of Liberalism and the rise of Labour; the First World War and the Russian Revolution; the Great Depression and the renewed threats of war in the later 1930s. This chapter considers the attitudes and ideologies of coalowners and miners, proceeding to a discussion of the extent to which these illuminate the industry's strike history before 1940: how important in explaining strike activity was the growth of leftist organizations and the role of activists?

As is so often remarked in the modern historiography of the industry there is a huge disparity between what is known of miners and what is known of mine owners. An abundance of material, particularly biographical, is readily available on miners' leaders which permits a detailed examination of their ideas, political affiliations, and activities. On the coalowners we have a great scarcity of material, even biographical material. It may be argued, however, that while it is clear that militancy in the conduct of labour relations was not a monopoly of the miners, such historical evidence as we have (see chapter 3) suggests that coalowners and managers tended to act in response to what they considered to be a challenge to the status quo, specifically to their authority in managing the mines. To the extent that the coalowners tended to be reactive, the unavoidable brevity with which we examine their 'philosophies' and political orientations and the length at which we examine those of the miners' leaders may be justified.

Pressure groups and politics

The coalowners who formed the membership of the district coalowners' associations in the later nineteenth and early twentieth century were mostly descended from colliery owning families or families in which mining engineering or colliery management consultancy was the fathers' (and in several cases grandfathers') profession. Metallurgical enterprise was another significant source of recruitment to the industry's business elite. Many qualified as mining engineers after a period of apprenticeship; few received university education, and the inbred nature of recruitment from within families ensured that even in some of the largest companies key decisions lay in the hands of owner-managers lacking formal training. Few played an active role in politics, though a public role in the local community was not unusual. Increasingly the line between professional and proprietorial interests and influences was blurred, as colliery owning families substituted professional training for learning by doing. D. A. Thomas, for example, chairman and managing director of the largest colliery combine in the country, the Cambrian Collieries in South Wales, was the son of a wealthy coalowner, read mathematics at Cambridge, and then spent time in the sales office of his father's company (Elizabeth Phillips 1925: 210–14; Church 1986: 449–68). The architect of the Cambrian Combine, the result of a series of amalgamations and mergers, he served briefly as an MP, but quit to return to business which he described as 'a modern equivalent of war. Business attracts the man who loves conquest, who loves to pit himself against vast odds, who could not live without strain of effort' (Elizabeth Phillips 1925: 213–14). He earned notoriety for his relentless opposition to organized labour and the scale of the lock-out at the Cambrian Collieries in 1910. In 1916 a leader in *The Times* accused the South Wales coalowners of pursuing a 'grasping policy', and criticized their mismanagement, obstinacy and greed, acknowledging that in no other coalfield did there exist such strife and distrust of the owners (Supple 1987: 75).

While the perception that coalowners, or at least their leaders, have been bulwarks in the defence of *laissez-faire* capitalism seems unchallenged, the view that the miners have always been at the heart of the labour movement is historically inaccurate (Gregory 1968; Howell 1983: 16; Kenneth O. Morgan 1987: 289). The political attitudes of miners' have taken a trajectory which, starting well to the right of the Labour Party at the party's birth, had reached, in some parts of the country, a position well to its left by the start of the First World War. In pursuing what at first sight seems to be a surprising conjuncture in some periods of industrial militancy and political moderation (Howell 1983: 18), we chart briefly the history of miners' politics, examine the electoral history of the mining areas, and the waxing and waning of movements such as the Miners' Minority Movement. By surveying the personalities, beliefs and attitudes in relation to the willingness of British coalminers to strike, it is possible to throw some light on the extent to which attitudes and ideologies interacted with organizations, strategies and events.

In 1885, after the extension of the franchise brought about by the Third Reform Act, six miners' MPs were returned to the House of Commons. These men were the elite of mining trade unionism in their day and they were all Liberals. In the constituencies where the mining unions had not been able to nominate a candidate, Liberals were usually returned. Although the trade unionist Liberal MPs formed a distinct group, known as the 'Lib-Labs', their loyalty to Liberalism was strong. That this was so is not surprising. Liberalism was the leading 'progressive' party of its day: Liberal governments had established legal foundations for trade union activity in the 1871 Trade Union Act, extended the franchise to large parts of the male working class in 1884 and stood for the advance of popular education. The party was associated with Nonconformity and Nonconformist churches were the major religious force in the coalfields. In Wales, the Liberal Party was the party of nationalism and Welsh cultural awareness; in Scotland, where many mining constituencies had a sizeable Irish Catholic population, it was the party of Irish Home Rule (Clegg et al. 1964: 45; Gregory 1968: 93; Saville 1971: 26; Kenneth O. Morgan 1972–3: 311; Stead 1972–3: 331–5; Rubinstein 1978: 105). Support for Liberalism, in some areas entrenched in miners' unions, was one factor behind the slow spread of support for the Labour Party. In an individual ballot on affiliation to the Labour Party in 1906, affiliation was narrowly rejected. However, within two years rank and file attitudes had changed markedly and in a new ballot on the same issue affiliation was heavily endorsed. The Miners' Federation of Great Britain (MFGB) eventually affiliated in 1909 and from that time any candidate sponsored by the Miners' Federation was required to sign the constitution of the Labour Party (Gregory 1968: 29–35).

By the beginning of the First World War the movement towards the Labour Party was clearly in progress but by no means complete. The real transformation occurred in the five years after the end of the war. In the 1923 election which led to the first Labour government, forty-three of the forty-seven candidates sponsored by the MFGB were returned (Arnot 1953: 550–1). The 1924 election, although it led to the defeat of the Labour Party, all but annihilated the Liberal Party, which was reduced to forty seats. Instead of the Liberals, a Labour Party espousing socialist ideas now dominated working-class electoral politics (Cowling 1971: 414; Kenneth O. Morgan 1972–3: 306–9).

But while, for the most part, the electoral identity of the miners and the Labour Party became a fixture from this date, such a crude formulation ignores much of importance. Even by 1910, a year after the MFGB had finally affiliated to the Labour Party and when Lib-Labism was not yet dead, the first stirrings of Marxism could be discerned in South Wales. Where mining trade unionism last established a permanent hold, in South Wales, the labourist tradition was relatively weak and it was here that the new radical Socialist, and later revolutionary trade unionist, or Syndicalist, ideologies took their deepest root (Francis and Smith 1980: chapter 1). These developments became more widely known with the publication of the Syndicalist *Miners' Next Step* in 1912 (Unofficial Reform Committee 1912/1974; Gregory 1968: 133; Francis and Smith 1980: 10). However, the level of support for Syndicalism in the South Wales coalfield is difficult to assess. Four Syndicalists, Noah Ablett, John Hopla, Noah Rees and Tom Smith, were elected to the South Wales Miners' Federation (SWMF) executive committee in 1911; the *Miners' Next Step* sold 5,000 copies, not all of them in South Wales, shortly after publication; and *The Rhondda Socialist*, which Ablett helped launch, claimed a circulation of over 6,000; but there is little other quantitative evidence. In Scotland a 'Miners' Indignation and Reform Committee' was formed in 1912 in which Syndicalist ideas were discernible (L. J. Macfarlane 1966: 45; Holton 1976: 112; Campbell 1989a, 1992: 90). But by 1914 the South Wales Unofficial Reform Committee was 'a declining and localized splinter group'. As Morgan has written:

The turmoil of the years 1908–14 ended with the official union leadership firmly in control of events. . . . Even ILP [Independent Labour Party] activists like Hartshorn and James Winstone, were known to be vehement opponents of syndicalism and industrial indiscipline. . . . Despite the class conflict, despite the massive influx of new immigrants from England, despite the new generation of miners represented by younger men like Ablett, Frank Hodges and A. J. Cook, 'Lib-Labism' remained a dominant and unifying creed in industrial south Wales down to the outbreak of war in 1914. (Kenneth O. Morgan 1972–3: 301–2)

Outside South Wales and Scotland the traces of Syndicalism now surviving are few. Williams wrote that 'there can be little doubt' of Syndicalist influence in Derbyshire during the time of the 1912 national strike, but presented no substantial evidence for this proposition (J. E. Williams 1962b: 395). In Nottinghamshire, despite its reputation for political 'moderation', 'the union's Council took on a syndicalist tinge' in the years just after the First World War urged on by the teachings of Jack Lavin, a miner at Welbeck colliery and a former member of the Socialist Labor Party of America (Alan R. Griffin 1962: 38). In the North East, it is possible to point to Will Lawther, whom Holton has described as 'a leading syndicalist militant' (1976: 113) but whose views appear to have been rather more fluid than this description suggests, and George Harvey, a student at Ruskin in 1908 and a checkweigher at Wardley colliery in Co. Durham just before the First World War (Beynon and Austrin 1994: 242). Harvey accepted the Syndicalist doctrine of 'dual unionism' and consequently had no position in the Durham Miners' Association but Holton claims 'he made a considerable impact in some other parts of the coalfield as a revolutionary propagandist' (1976: 113). By the early post-war period Harvey's views appear to have shifted somewhat and he was reputed to be 'Ney Communist, ye knaa, a Bolshevik, that's what he was' and went by the *nom de guerre* of the 'Wardley Lenin' (Arnot 1975: 156; Coates 1974: 31–2; Holton 1976: 169–70; Douglass 1977: 283; Kenneth O. Morgan 1987: 74–5).

Harvey's trajectory was that of many on the left during and just after the First World War. When South Welsh radicalism resurfaced in political form towards the end of the war it moved towards Communism and the Minority Movement. In Scotland, a previously inchoate industrial militancy among some sections of the work-force moved in the same direction. The Reform Committees of Lanarkshire, Fife and elsewhere in Scotland, set up after August 1917 and at the height of their success in 1919, were influenced by Syndicalists and Marxists and demanded not only union reform but the 'mines for the miners' in place of the more orthodox demand for nationalization (Campbell 1992: 90–1). While Syndicalism had been a parochial enthusiasm, even in the South Wales context,

Communism had a much wider and longer lasting influence (Kenneth O. Morgan 1987: 75).

Tracing the impact of Communism on the miners' attitudes is not such a simple task as the charting of the rise of the Labour Party. The electoral achievements of Communism were always marginal in the UK. At their inter-war highwater mark in terms of total votes, reached in 1923, the Communists gained 77,641 votes for the nine candidates fielded. All but two of these were adopted as candidates of the Labour Party, so that even this short tally exagger-ates the support for Communism. Only two Communists stood in what could be described as mining constituencies, Ashton-under-Lyne, where Ellen Wilkin-son, a member of the Communist Party but adopted by the Labour Party, polled just under a quarter of the vote and Motherwell, where J. T. Newbold, standing as a Communist, polled over a quarter (L. J. Macfarlane 1966: 103, 295–6; Newton 1969: 166–74; Macintyre 1980b: 32–3). Much more important than this was the influence of the Communist Party and associated organizations in the miners' trade unions (Macintyre 1980b: 33–6).

Even before the formation of the Communist Party of Great Britain (CPGB) in 1920–1, the constitution of the SWMF had been amended to include the abolition of capitalism as one of its objects and the Durham Miners' Association, formerly a citadel of Liberal trade unionism, followed suit in 1921 (Garside 1971: 69; Francis and Smith 1980: 30). The CPGB attempted to direct rank and file organizations within the miners' unions and encouraged the affiliation of trade unions to the Red International of Labour Unions (RILU) (L. J. Macfar-lane 1966: 129–32; Martin 1969: 5). A motion to affiliate the MFGB to the RILU was thrown out with very little support from the 1922 MFGB annual conference and despite a campaign for the independent affiliation of the SWMF which continued into 1924, the SWMF never affiliated either (L. J. Macfarlane 1966: 130–1; Arnot 1975: 245–6). In January 1924 the founding conference of the Communist Miners' Minority Movement (MMM) took place and adopted a programme including affiliation to the RILU, the transformation of the MFGB into a United Mineworkers' Union, a weekly wage and a six hour day. These were 'transitional demands' and the ultimate purpose of this programme was to hasten revolution. Its hope was that by leading ordinary miners in their conflicts at work and by demonstrating its virtues in everyday disputes it would wean miners away from Social Democracy. In the 1925 elections for the post of General Secretary of the Lanarkshire Miners' Union, the Minority Movement candidate secured over 40 per cent of the vote but was still defeated (Campbell 1992: 92). In the country as a whole the MMM's most prominent supporter was A. J. Cook and its greatest success was Cook's election as secretary of the MFGB in 1924 (Martin 1969: 24, 33–4, 37).

The historian of the Minority Movement credits it with a number of tactical 'successes' in the mid-1920s, including the promotion of a series of 'no surren-der' tactical decisions during the 1926 Lock-out (Martin 1969: 88–9; see also L. J. Macfarlane 1966: 169–75). Unable to deny the disaster of defeat after the

Lock-out, the MMM blamed this on the collapse of MFGB unity and proposed to mend this by the creation of One Miners' Union. From this point on, the 'One Union' issue became a litmus test of leftism in the miners' unions just like the issues of the legislative eight-hour day and the minimum wage before it. In 1927 eight MMM candidates were elected to the nineteen-person executive of the Lanarkshire Miners' Union and Communists were elected to the posts of general secretary and president in both the Lanarkshire and Scottish unions (Campbell 1992: 93). But the MMM went into decline after 1928. The switch from the 'united front' policy of its earlier years to the 'new line' of 'class against class' in 1928, with its denunciation of the Labour Party and the trade unions affiliated to it as 'social fascists' and its advocacy of separate unions, brought about a distancing of the MMM from its most prominent supporters, A. J. Cook and Arthur Horner in South Wales. Both found themselves forced to decide between following the 'new line' and acting to preserve trade union unity; both put unity first (L. J. Macfarlane 1966: 262, 264; Martin 1969: 119–20).

In this period the CP and the MMM seem to have been unable to lead miners out on strike. Instead, they attempted to lead, control, extend and prolong strikes that had already broken out predominantly by what a later generation would call 'agit-prop' techniques. For example, in response to strikes at Boldon, Whitburn and Harton Collieries in County Durham early in 1928, the CP and MMM produced a special bulletin, *Fight or Die*, and held 'dozens of meetings'. A conference of Durham lodges was organized in an unsuccessful attempt to extend the strikes more widely, and demonstrations were held (L. J. Macfarlane 1966: 260–1). The following year a lock-out of almost 4,000 miners over wage cuts began at Dawdon colliery, again in County Durham. The local lodge's decision to resist the wage cuts was taken without CP or MMM influence: 'the Communist Party had not a single member or contact at Dawdon' but 'within a week contacts had been made, meetings held and a party bulletin issued by the Tyneside district committee [of the CP]' (L. J. Macfarlane 1966: 262). The CP and MMM were unable to gain sympathetic action from other collieries or to displace the existing lodge leadership. The Minority Movement itself concluded that the campaign had been 'without mass content' and demonstrated 'the futility of the approach from the outside' (Martin 1969: 129–30).

The Minority Movement was liquidated in November 1932 after further twists in Communist Party strategy (Martin 1969: 174–5). Henceforth the Communist Party's involvement in industry involved collaboration with, not condemnation of, the existing trade unions. This was 'the approach from the inside' in which CP activists attempted to provide leadership for conflicts at their own place of work; the first step in this strategy was often to gain election to official positions within miners' lodges and at higher levels of the union hierarchy. Membership of the CP, although always very low, rose in the middle and late 1930s and, at least in South Wales, Communist Party organs claimed an increasing role in leading strikes (Newton 1969: 159–61; Francis and Smith

1980: 268; Fishman 1995). In South Wales in 1935 the Party could boast of 17 local councillors, 352 members in the SWMF mainly in leadership positions, and a fortnightly newspaper with a circulation rising to 8,000 (Francis and Smith 1980: 269).

Miners' leaders and miners' militancy

It is possible to gain a more vivid idea of how these political changes affected people's lives by studying the biographies of some of the most prominent office holders in the Miners' Federation: Ben Pickard, president of the MFGB from 1889 to 1904, Thomas Ashton, its secretary from 1889 to 1919, Robert Smillie, president 1912–21, Frank Hodges, secretary 1919–24, Herbert Smith, president 1922–29, A. J. Cook, secretary 1924–31, Ebby Edwards, president in 1931 and secretary from 1932 to 1944 when he became secretary of the National Union of Mineworkers (NUM), and Sir William Lawther, president of the MFGB, and later the NUM, from 1939 to 1954. In this way we also gain some insight into the leadership elected by and offered to the rank and file miner. These eight men were born between 1840 and 1890. All except Smillie and Cook started work in the mines at a very early age, Smillie and Cook in their mid-teens. In their youth they gained office in their local branch or lodge; in their prime, between the ages of 30 and 50, they typically gained high office in their local county unions, although Frank Hodges and A. J. Cook leapfrogged this stage. They reached the presidency or secretaryship of the MFGB at varying ages: Hodges and Cook when notably young, Smillie, Smith and Lawther when notably older.

Pickard was the 'type' of the Liberal mining trade unionist of the founding generation of the MFGB. He had no formal education beyond elementary school and started work in the pit at the age of 12. He was a Wesleyan and a supporter of the Lord's Rest Day Association. His views conformed to Liberal political and economic ideas except where they conflicted with the tenets he had acquired from his experience as a trade unionist; for example he was adamant in his belief in the necessity of a legislative eight-hour day. His speeches deprecated political ideology in general, adversely contrasting 'idealists' with 'practical men' such as himself. He asked of proposals to nationalize the mines not whether they would add to justice and social equality but whether they would make miners 'a penny better off than they are today' (Baylies 1993: 238–40). His constituents and supporters were reported by a contemporary observer to be similarly practical: 'These careless, thoughtless, hard-working, hard-living fellows have only one political belief and that is a belief in Ben Pickard' in other words a belief in unity and loyalty (Montague Blatchford in *The Clarion*, 30 October 1897, quoted by Rubinstein 1978: 112). Pickard was elected as Liberal MP for Normanton in 1885 and unhesitatingly opposed Independent Labour Party (ILP) candidates who stood against Liberals, most notably at the Barnsley by-election of 1897 (Bellamy and Saville 1972: 268–70).

Pickard's colleague Thomas Ashton was from a similar mould with the important exception that his politics leaned more to Conservatism than Liberalism. In this he reflected the political characteristics of the Lancashire coalfield which he represented. In 1895 Thomas Aspinwall, a Lancashire miners' agent, told Lord Salisbury, the Conservative Prime Minister, 'I know that you have thousands in connection with the mining industry in Lancashire who are very ardent supporters of yours'; indeed Aspinwall had just lost the mining seat of Wigan to a Tory in the 1895 general election (Challinor 1972: 215).

However, unlike Pickard, Ashton did not actively promote his politics among his members. In this he may have been persuaded to caution by the heterogeneous affiliations of the Lancashire membership: in addition to Tory voters, there were supporters of the Liberal Party, the ILP and the Social-Democratic Federation (SDF), which last two appear to have gathered much of their early support from Lancashire. Ashton seems to have put Federation unity before his own politics and the Lancashire Federation's support for two Lib–Lab parliamentary candidates in the 1890s went ahead without opposition from its secretary (Challinor 1972: 216–25; Bellamy and Saville 1972: 30–2; Howell 1983: 30).

The next generation consists of two men, Robert Smillie and Herbert Smith, born in the 1850s and 1860s and up to twenty years younger than the generation represented by Pickard and Ashton. At the time of the foundation of the MFGB Smillie was 32 and Smith 27. Both moved towards the ILP, Smillie being close to Keir Hardie from an early date, Smith rejecting Liberalism when confronted by the 1893 Lock-out. At the Barnsley by-election, when Pickard gave unhesitating support to the Liberal candidate, despite the fact that he was one of the coalowners, Smillie, president of the Scottish Mineworkers since 1894, supported the ILP candidate; Smith, then a checkweigher and delegate to the Yorkshire Miners' Association, did so too (Lawson 1941: 46, 73).

Smillie had a leading place in the Socialist vanguard. He campaigned for his friend Keir Hardie from 1888 and was a founding member of the Scottish Labour Party, established in the same year. He seconded a motion at the 1897 annual conference of the MFGB favouring the nationalization of the 'instruments of wealth production'. Although this motion was overwhelmingly defeated, the proposal to nationalize land, minerals, mines and railways was overwhelmingly endorsed. It was also Smillie who moved the resolution that the MFGB should affiliate to the Labour Party in 1908. 'In his politics he was essentially a man of the ILP – warm hearted, utterly sincere and not particularly theoretical; hating injustice and burning with indignation at the social evils around him' (Bellamy and Saville 1976).

Well-read, he was pasted by newspapers as very red, which he was not. . . . He was no Liberal, and was an opponent of the system which held at the time. Quietly spoken but ruthlessly logical. Miners went to hear a revolutionary, and discovered a man who said things they felt were just sound sense. For he was practical – except to those who wanted to keep things as they were. (Lawson 1941: 71)

The nationalization issue remained uppermost on Smillie's agenda and within weeks of attaining the presidency of the MFGB in 1912 he was making moves to introduce a parliamentary Bill to bring it about. In this he was carrying on the policies of the former generation, though possibly with more commitment. But his support for the Triple Industrial Alliance, of which he became chair in 1915, took the MFGB towards a more militant position. For Smillie, trade union power was there to be used and used not only to secure advances on trade union issues: nationalization was a matter of justice and equality as well as a means of raising wages (Bellamy and Saville 1976: 165–72).

If Smillie was 'practical', Smith was 'a miner naked of book learning, and unashamed'; he was 'contemptuous of facile theorists' (Lawson 1941: 85, 148). He was stalwart in the pursuit of the policies of the Miners' Federation in the period after 1897. He thought prices must follow wages, not vice versa. 'He was uncompromising upon that. And in both the industrial and political field he stood with those forces that insisted on the Minimum Wage, Eight Hours a Day, Nationalization of Mines, Abolition of Royalties. All designed to regulate the industry and make life decent for the miner' (Lawson 1941: 90). After the First World War, this continued to be his platform. He found 'the Pool', in many interpretations the crucial issue in the 1921 Lock-out, 'too abstract' (Lawson 1941: 148) and in this period his Socialism became much less militant even while he gained, on the industrial front, a reputation as the 'Bismarck of the miners' movement' (Bellamy and Saville 1974). After 1926, as the Minority Movement attempted to make headway among the miners, he was pugnaciously hostile to the Communist Party (Bellamy and Saville 1974: 348–50; Davies 1987: 141).

The third generation, Frank Hodges, A. J. Cook, Ebby Edwards and Will Lawther, were born in the 1880s. They were in their late teens or early twenties at the time of the great flowering of the ILP in the period after 1906 and each joined the ILP between 1905 and 1907. This generation was the first to receive any formal education beyond elementary level: each attended Ruskin College and/or the Central Labour College in the 1908–12 period, and each came into contact there with Marxist and Syndicalist ideas. All attained official positions in their lodges and branches immediately before the First World War. Hodges and Cook then enjoyed a rapid, tumultuous rise to high office reaching the secretaryship of the MFGB in 1919 and in 1924 respectively and each in consequence finding themselves working with a president of the former generation, Hodges with Smillie, Cook with Smith. Edwards spent the 1920s as secretary of the Northumberland Miners, reaching the presidency of the MFGB in 1931. Lawther rose more slowly still, reaching the post of treasurer of the Durham Miners' Association (DMA) in 1933 and the presidency of the MFGB in 1939. The early rise of this generation and the failure of the succeeding generation to progress as rapidly meant that they wielded their influence over an extended period, from 1919 until 1954, when Will Lawther retired as president of the NUM (Hodges 1925; Bellamy and Saville 1976: 38–44, 1979: 79–81, 1984: 140–4; Holton 1976: 113, 168–9).

While their origins, education and early careers were similar, the paths of the third generation began to diverge before and during the First World War. Just before the War, Hodges was associated with the Unofficial Reform Committee (URC), speaking with Noah Ablett against the nationalization of the mines on the grounds familiarized by Belloc that it would lead to servility not emancipation (Belloc 1913; Kenneth O. Morgan 1975). But he rapidly distanced himself from Ablett and the URC after 1914. He was publicly pro-war and urged miners to join the forces. In 1919 he was, as MFGB secretary, arguing the MFGB case for 'the Mines for the Nation', not 'the Mines for the Miners', the Syndicalist position (Hodges 1920, 1925: 67–9, 81–9; Davies 1987: 21). In 1922 he described British Communists as 'the intellectual slaves of Moscow' (L. J. Macfarlane 1966: 99). Although retaining a reputation as a militant, there is nothing to suggest that he did not largely conform to the official programme of the ILP and the MFGB throughout the 1919–24 period. Cook had worked with Noah Ablett in the South Wales Unofficial Reform Committee and was active in another Syndicalist movement, the Industrial Democracy League, in 1913. The same year, he resigned from the Labour Party (Davies 1987: 18–19). Like Smillie, he opposed the First World War although this did not become apparent until 1916. He continued to be active in the URC movement and was arrested and imprisoned on charges of sedition in 1918. He became a member of the South Wales Socialist Society in 1919 and joined the infant CPGB in 1921. By this time Cook was describing himself as a Communist (Davies 1987: 21–32; 42–3):

Cook's communism was of an idiosyncratic form, however. It was founded on his deep-rooted desire for an egalitarian society, his acceptance of Marxist economic theory, and admiration of Lenin's achievements. On this basis Cook was able to call himself a communist all his life. But in other respects Cook was not a communist at all; he rejected the need for a political party: [communist parties] were no more than clearing-houses for the industrial movement. He supported the formation of local soviets, but these were to be based on the trades councils and fulfil the syndicalist function of co-ordinating the seizure of industry. . . . [T]he character of Cook's environment, the apparent omnipotence of trade unions – particularly the giant MFGB – inspired such syndicalist confidence; there simply wasn't any *need*, Cook would have argued, for political action – the workers had their unions, and together they could achieve revolutionary changes. The defeats of 1921 and 1926 were imminent, yet in 1920 they were unthinkable to Cook and his generation. (Davies 1987: 44)

As we have seen above, Syndicalism had little influence outside South Wales and Scotland. In the Northumberland and Durham of Ebby Edwards and Will Lawther it appears to have had almost none. Will Lawther's most important influence during his time at the Central Labour College were Karl Marx, William Morris and Bernard Shaw rather than Daniel De Leon, the leader of the Industrial Workers of the World, the American Syndicalist union. Nevertheless Lawther helped to establish Plebs League classes in Chopwell, South Shields and Consett just before the First World War. 'In these years Lawther variously described himself as a Marxist, syndicalist, anarchist and member of the ILP.' He was opposed to the First World War (Bellamy and Saville 1984: 140–4). Similarly, Ebby Edwards was greatly influenced by Marx after joining the ILP and became a close associate of Jack Williams, one of the leaders of the SDF. Because of this he was asked to resign from the ILP in 1909 but very shortly afterwards affiliated himself to the Labour Party, apparently, at least at first, out of loyalty to the politics of the MFGB which the Northumberland Miners had joined in 1909. He fought the Wansbeck by-election in May 1918 as a Labour Party candidate and supported the Labour Party's war aims programme, demanding the repudiation of secret treaties and asserting the failure of the employing classes. This marked a rejection of the SDF (Arnot 1961: 83–5; Bellamy and Saville 1979: 79–81).

By the end of the First World War, therefore, Cook was still a Syndicalist; Lawther's politics were ambiguous but he was undoubtedly on the militant left of the time; Hodges and Edwards were Labour Party supporters. With the exception of Hodges, these positions were broadly retained until after the 1926 Lock-out. Hodges gained office in the 1924 Labour government and consequently had to resign from his post with the MFGB. From about this time he seems to have moved rapidly rightward: before and during the 1926 Lock-out he supported the lengthening of the working day and in July 1927 publicly supported Spencer (obituaries of Hodges in *The Times* and *The Manchester Guardian*, 5 June 1947; Arnot 1953: 522–3). Although the extent of Hodges's apostasy was extreme, others also moved to the right. The 1926 defeat killed Syndicalism in the miners' unions: it was then all too obvious that the miners did need all the help they could get from wherever they could get it, including political parties. By 1928 Cook had abandoned not only Syndicalism but also Communism and declared: 'It is the bounden duty of all of us to put on one side disagreements or personal differences and work for a majority Labour government' (quoted in Davies 1987: 163; cf. L. J. Macfarlane 1966: 262). In this period the only real argument was between the Communists and the Labour Party. Lawther seems to have tended towards a leftist interpretation of the defeat, authoring an article called 'One Miners' Union Now' in *Plebs* in 1927 and associating himself with Arthur Horner and other Communists at the 1928 MFGB conference (Davies 1987: 153); but he had been on the Labour Party Executive Committee in 1926 and he stood for and obtained election to the House of Commons on a Labour Party ticket in 1929 (Clarke 1969: 15, 17). 'Throughout the 1930s Lawther remained on the left of the labour movement although this nevertheless represented a gradual shift away from the very militant attitudes of his early years' (Bellamy and Saville 1984). In 1969 Lawther agreed that he had moved from left to right during his career, commenting 'Well, of course, if you're not a rebel when you're young, when will you be one?' (Clarke 1969: 21). Edwards, too, had shifted his position and in the early 1930s stood on the 'right' in terms of MFGB politics, believing that the 'patient rebuilding of numbers and morale was the only way forward, and he insisted on negotiation and conciliation at a time when the Government was unhelpful and the mineowners consistently hostile' (Bellamy and Saville 1979).

The succession of the generations detailed above, although marked by readily understandable conflicts, does not suggest that established union leaders were always able to frustrate the rise of the younger generation. Smillie became president of the Scottish Federation in 1894 at the age of 37 and attained a seat on the MFGB executive the next year despite his close association with Keir Hardie. Smith became president of the YMA at the age of 44 and gained a seat on the executive committee of the MFGB two years later, despite his support for the ILP. Hodges was elected a miners' agent at 25 and was secretary of the Miners' Federation at 32. Cook was elected a miners' agent in South Wales at the age of 36 despite being an early member of the CPGB; he became secretary of the Miners' Federation at the age of 41. The only clear example of a politically right wing and industrially conciliatory union leadership successfully preventing the succession of younger, politically leftwing, and industrially more militant generation occurred in the 1920s in Fife and in the Scottish national union where some of 'the Old Gang' prevented elected Communist militants from taking up their offices and, in Fife, finally formed a rival union in an attempt to 'dish the Reds' (Arnot 1955: 167; 185–92; Campbell 1989b: 34, 1992: 92–3).

The presumption that union leaders are always more conservative and less militant than the rank and file which permeates the work of Burgess (1975) for example, is being increasingly questioned. The view was doubted by Church (1986: 697ff, 707ff) and contested by Colin P. Griffin (1987). Griffin's detailed study of conciliation board agreements in Leicestershire led him to reject the view that the institutionalization of wage bargaining enhanced the 'respectability' and nurtured the political moderation of trade union leaders, as the Syndicalists of the *Miners' Next Step* had argued. Passivity, moderation and even obstructive attitudes towards militancy he found to be more characteristic of rank and file union members rather than of their leaders (1987: 77). The lives recounted above also suggest that during and immediately after the First World War the leadership of the MFGB was considerably in advance of the membership, at least on some issues. An instance is provided by the anti-war position of Robert Smillie; as a number of historians have remarked and Mór-O'Brien (1984–5a, 1984–5b) has detailed for South Wales, rank and file miners enlisted in large numbers and it seems safe to say that the MFGB president took a stance far to the left of most of the membership on this issue. It is also remarkable, in view of the extremely low memberships recorded by Syndicalist and Communist Party organizations, that in 1924 Cook could be elected to the secretaryship of the MFGB with well over 200,000 votes (Davies 1987: 67). This widespread support suggests that many miners were prepared to vote for a union leader who was politically considerably to the left of themselves.

Finally, these careers raise a question about the relationship between political attitudes and industrial behaviour. Is it possible to attribute the strike proneness of the industry to the leftwing politics common among its workers and their leaders? Probably the most important point to make in answering this question is that the electoral history of the coalfields provides strong evidence that the politics of the great mass of miners have been in line with the politics of the great mass of British workers: Liberal and Lib-Lab (to a comparatively late date), Labour thereafter. If these political ideas were associated with militant industrial attitudes and activity we would find industrial militancy broadly spread throughout the British working class instead of concentrated in a few industries of which mining has been one of the most prominent.

The argument that miners' strike proneness is to be explained, if only partly, by their political attitudes must concern itself with the minority who were Syndicalists or Communists or sympathetic to these movements. As a general explanation this argument is clearly inconsistent with the evidence. In South Wales and Scotland, Syndicalism was most influential between about 1910 and 1926: miners' strike proneness was well established in both countries before the first date and continued after the second. It is also worth pointing out that in the peak year of the 'late Edwardian unrest', 1910, there were fewer coalmining strikes than there had been in 1894, the peak year of what has been called the 'late Victorian unrest', when miners' trade unions were firmly in the hands of Lib-Labs in England and Wales and led by pioneer ILP members in Scotland (Stead 1972–3: 342–3; Church 1987). Dating Communism's period of maximum influence is more difficult: in some respects the early 1920s formed a high point, in other respects the 'long World War' of 1936–45 was the Party's peak in Britain. In this latter period there was a sustained rise in the number of coalmining strikes. It is telling, however banal this point has become, that the dramatic change in the Party's line on the Second World War precipitated by the German invasion of the Soviet Union in June 1941 had no discernible dampening effect on strike activity in British coal mines. Although some have accused Communists after June 1941 of agitating only for greater production and, when it came to disputes and strikes, of playing the role of 'strike-breakers and blacklegs', there were more strikes and more working days lost in coal mines in 1942 than there had been in 1940 (Department of Employment and Productivity, *British Labour Statistics*, table 197; Newton 1969: 51). Although Fishman has shown that the dramatic change in the Party line had a muted effect on the actual practice of Party members, the history continues to suggest that the ability of CP activists to lead miners out on strike before 22 June 1941 or back to the coal-face after that date was very limited (Fishman 1995: chapters 10, 11).

It is historians who have been concerned with particular times and places rather than the whole history of miners' militancy who have argued for the importance of miners' politics. Perhaps the greatest claims have been made by Holton for the influence of Syndicalism. While his claims for the influence of Syndicalist activists are based on slender evidence and have been subject to cogently expressed doubts (cf. Holton 1976: 80, 1985: 273 and White 1990: 106–7), he is on more plausible but also more treacherous ground when making the case for the importance of 'proto-syndicalism'. 'Proto-syndicalism', or sometimes merely 'militancy', is used by Holton to indicate Syndicalism as 'mentality' rather than 'doctrine' (1985: 268). He quotes with approval G. D. H. Cole's 1913 statement that 'Of real syndicalism there is in England [sic] practically none; of an impulse [towards Syndicalism] which, unless we consent to the inaccuracy, we must leave nameless, there is a great deal' (Cole 1913: 33, quoted by Holton 1976: 76). But Holton's use of this concept obscures the distinction between events in which Syndicalist ideas and activists were seminal from those in which Syndicalist language and activists merely articulated, without significantly affecting, pre-existing discontents and aspirations. That the role of Syndicalism in British mining industrial relations was to provide a new language which allowed long-standing grievances to be expressed in a more coherent and, in some circumstances, more powerful way is suggested by the close correspondence between elements of Syndicalist doctrine and two enduring features of mining industrial relations. First, the tradition of job control and freedom from close supervision enjoyed by the 'independent collier' (Campbell and Reid 1978; Reid 1978: chapter 2; Campbell 1992) ensured a sympathetic hearing for the Syndicalist demand for industrial democracy as, among other things, a guarantee of freedom from 'oppression by petty bosses' (Unofficial Reform Committee 1912/1974: 30). Second, the long history, stretching far back into the nineteenth century, of local disaffection with the actions and procedures of district and county mining union officials (see for example, Burgess 1975: 189, 196; Douglass 1977: 254–82; Spaven 1978: 212–17; Baylies 1993: 142–3, 257–65), a prominent aspect of Syndicalist analysis and rhetoric (Unofficial Reform Committee 1912/1974: 20–2). In these circumstances, it would not be surprising to discover local leaders who were 'real Syndicalists', articulating traditional grievances, accepted and supported by a rank and file whose new, 'proto-syndicalist' consciousness made little difference to their industrial behaviour.

While the debate over the role of Syndicalism has not yet reached a clear conclusion, a serious debate over the role of Communism has only just begun. Fishman has made an impressive start towards a new assessment of the role of the CPGB in the 'economic struggle'. Her detailed account of the 1933–45 period focuses on the 'daily mass work' of CP cadres who performed the usually routine tasks of shop steward and lodge official. They were sustained in this time consuming, thankless, and sometimes dispiriting routine by the belief that a repeatedly postponed Communist Utopia would, one day, emerge out of the twists and turns of 'Life Itself' (1995: 7–10). This endowed them, according to Fishman, with more stamina and a greater willingness to face the deprivations and risks that went with the life of a Communist dedicated to the 'economic struggle' (336–7).

Although Fishman's account of the distinctive features of CP activists seems to discount unduly the hard work, high risks and deep privations endured by earlier generations of activists and of 'unbelieving' contemporaries, her history does suggest a riposte to Hyman's suggestion (1972: 57) that 'agitators' are merely the 'instruments' of deeper 'causes'. It is that the ready availability of effective 'instruments' may have encouraged workers to strike in collieries where they knew they could count on the leadership of politically advanced industrial militants. Even this limited explanatory role for political militancy is doubtful, however. If Hicks's theory of strikes (Hicks 1932) has some substance to it, the presence of more effective 'instruments' on the miners' side should have resulted in better wages and conditions for miners, rather than more strikes. Colliery managers should have been able to see the nature of the opposition and have avoided strikes by making higher offers in the settlement of disputes. One would see a 'militant calm' rather than belligerent agitation. Whether this theory is merely a figment of a fine imagination or a useful guide to the reality of inter-war Britain has yet to be assessed.

The complexity of social and political structures, political ideologies and events, 'Life Itself', prevents any easy association between political leftism and strike activity. The biographies of some of the most prominent leftists in the industry offer prominent warnings against such glib assumptions. It has been written of Arthur Horner, the allegedly *Incorrigible Rebel*, that after his election to the presidency of the SWMF

he was soon boasting of his moderation. 'Let the "rights" sneer . . . let the "lefts" . . . jeer,' he [Horner] wrote in 1937, apparently regarding fully paid-up membership of the Communist Party as entirely compatible with a 'centre' industrial position; and he issued stern instructions that agreements with the employers were to be fully honoured and unofficial strikes relentlessly stamped upon. (Jenkins 1960)

During the 1926 Lock-out it was A. J. Cook, the 'raving, tearing Communist' (Fred Bramley, the TUC Secretary, quoted by Citrine 1964: 77), who was looking for a negotiated settlement and Herbert Smith, the steady, no-nonsense Labour Party man, who retreated into a stubborn refusal to consider compromise while the Federation collapsed around him (Davies 1987: 121–3).

5   Configurations of strike activity

From Nine Mile Point to Bothwell Castle: dimensions, concentration and prevalence of coalmining strikes

The development of the industry, the evolution of coalowners' associations and miners' trade unions, and the changing institutions and character of industrial relations have been the subject of chapters 2, 3 and 4. While in later chapters we shall refer back to those aspects which have a particular relevance to the history of strikes in the industry, we here consider the statistical evidence on strike activity which we have assembled from the archival sources introduced in chapter 1. In this chapter we consider important issues which historians and other scholars have explored either within a very partial, chronological or spatial context, or by using aggregate statistics, or by focusing exclusively on national strikes. The key questions which require consideration are whether the industry's reputation for being uniformly strike-prone is consistent with the evidence, and whether solidarity among miners was a prevailing feature of strikes at district and local levels. There are two justifications for focusing on district and local levels. The first is that the overwhelming proportion of strikes which occurred were limited to localities; they represented, therefore, the 'ordinary' characteristics of mining strikes and the 'normal' experience of miners and colliery owners in conflict. The second is that we know that in modern manufacturing strikes are far from being a widespread experience: they are concentrated in a small number of highly strike-prone plants (Department of Employment, *Strikes in Britain*). We need to see whether strikes have been similarly concentrated in British collieries or whether coalmining is indeed a 'special case' (Turner 1963: 7), with a high propensity to strike widely distributed across the generality of collieries.

Somewhat earlier than the study by the Department of Employment into manufacturing industry, McCormick (1969) found evidence on strikes in the Yorkshire coalfield between 1949 and 1963 which indicated the existence of substantial inter-colliery differences in strike activity. McCormick's regional study, however, is exceptional and even for the limited period encompassed by his research has received no imitators. Nobody has attempted to apply his methods to test his tentative conclusions, either in other regions or in the national industry overall. In the absence of such research, the high profile of coalmining in the aggregate statistics has tended to reinforce contemporaries' impressions of the industry's strike record and of miners' contributions to it, such as those which we quoted at the start of chapter 1.

Clearly there are dangers in assuming that the characteristics of the industry in which a plant or colliery is located will be the major influence on its strike record. Research on strikes in manufacturing industry prompted Edwards to point out that only a small part of the variation in strike experience in manufacturing could be explained in this way: 'the mere fact of being in a certain industry does not make a plant strike-prone or strike-free' (P. K. Edwards 1981b: 148). Yet this assumption underlies the literature on conflict in the coal industry. This again raises the question of whether mining strikes, too, were concentrated in a few exceptionally strike-prone collieries. For if that should be the case, then the analyses of coalfield militancy which have been devised to explain *generally* pervasive strike activity will have been formulated to explain a phenomenon which may not have existed; or if it did exist, industrial behaviour which may have varied over time. The absence of answers to such questions points to the need for a detailed analysis of the shape of coalmining strikes over the long term and on a national scale.

Such an analysis is possible for the period 1893 to 1963 because of the existence of the uniquely rich data provided by the official records of strikes (which we discussed in chapter 1 and of which more details are available in the general appendix). By using a source such as this, which contains disaggregated strike statistics, we are freed from the constraints hitherto imposed on historians by their reliance on aggregative measures of strikes or case studies at local or regional level. The remainder of this chapter considers the number, size and 'shape' of coalmining strikes before documenting the regional diversity of strike activity in Britain. This investigation confirms that the overwhelming majority of colliery strikes affected only a single colliery, a finding which leads us to the question rehearsed above: to what extent were colliery strikes a general feature of the industry and to what extent were they, like modern British strikes in manu- facturing, concentrated in a small number of very strike-prone collieries? The long time span covered by our data and our construction of strike histories for individual collieries allow us to ask and answer a further question: were collieries struck persistently, year after year? Or did struck collieries quickly revert to a peaceful state?

Figure 5.1 shows the number of officially recorded strikes in the industry from the beginning of reliable statistical data in 1893. While there are year-to-year variations of some short-term importance the main feature of this series of data is the enormous increase in the number of strikes after about 1936. This increase was sustained without interruption through the outbreak of the Second World War and through the nationalization of the industry in 1947. By the 1950s there were several thousand strikes instead of the several hundred that had been usual from the 1890s to the 1930s.

Before the First World War the vast majority of British coalmining strikes

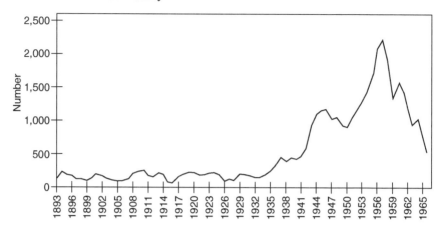

Figure 5.1.   *The number of strikes in coalmining (Great Britain and Northern Ireland 1893–1966)*
Note: strikes beginning in the year shown.
Source: Department of Employment and Productivity, *British Labour Statistics*, table 197.

affected only a single locality; only 5 per cent of strikes extended beyond the locality and most of these remained small. Big and widespread strikes, even on very generous definitions of these terms, were rarities (table 5.1). In the turbulent years during and after the First World War, miners overcame their parochialism more often than before, and in the 1914–20 period perhaps as many as 10 per cent of strikes could be regarded as widespread. In addition the national strike in 1920 there were fourteen regional or sub-regional strikes in these seven years. But after 1921 the local character of British mining strikes became re-established in an even more extreme form: in this period only 2 per cent of strikes were not confined to a single locality.

The true frequency of purely local strikes was even higher than the assembled figures indicate. One reason for this is the intentional and unintentional omission from the official records of very small strikes which we noted in chapter 1. It is likely that the overwhelming majority of those strikes affected only a single colliery. Another arises from the ambiguity in the meaning of records which place a strike in, for example, 'Lanarkshire'. The intention may have been to refer to a strike affecting all or most of the county, or, in contrast, to a stoppage which affected a particular place somewhere in Lanarkshire. We have avoided making *ad hoc* judgements, interpreting the records to indicate a strike of the widest extent compatible with the wording in each case. The effect of this is that table 5.1 provides the maximum possible measure of widespread strike activity and the minimum possible measure of local stoppages. We have, however, also distinguished those non-local strikes which were large scale and we suggest that these figures would be adopted as central estimates of the number of officially

Table 5.1. *The geographical extent of coalmining strikes (number of strikes, Great Britain 1893–1940)*

	Period					
	1893–1913[b]		1914–1920		1921–1940	
Extent[a]	Small[c]	Large[c]	Small[c]	Large[c]	Small[c]	Large[c]
Local	2,597	49	868	61	3,851	95
(% of all strikes)	(94)	(2)	(85)	(6)	(96)	(2)
District	54 [d]	20	41	24	24	14
County	26 [e]	6	9	7	9	6
Sub-regional	1	8	0	3	0	5
Regional	1	8	0	11	1	5
National	0	1	0	1	0	2
Total non-local	82	43	50	46	34	32
(% of all strikes)	(3)	(2)	(5)	(5)	(1)	(1)
Total	2,679	92	918	107	3,885	127
(% of all strikes)	(97)	(3)	(90)	(10)	(97)	(3)

Notes:
[a] 'Local' strikes are those that are located at a single village, town or city by the source, e.g. 'Walbottle', 'West Boldon, Co. Durham', 'Gateshead (near)'. 'District' strikes are those located by the source at more than one village, town or city and those that are located in an area which is not a village, town or city but which is not as extensive as a county, as defined below, e.g. 'Ruabon & Wrexham'; 'Rhondda', 'Swansea Valley', 'Cumnock District', 'South Lancs'. 'County' strikes are those located in a county or in one of the sub-county colliery districts recognized in the industry. These include South Yorkshire, West Yorkshire, North Staffordshire, Cannock Chase, South Staffordshire, South Derbyshire, and the Forest of Dean. 'Yorkshire', 'Lancashire' and 'Lancashire and Cheshire' are treated as regions not counties. 'Sub-regional' strikes are those located in aggregations of counties, as defined above, which are not as extensive as a region, or aggregation of regions, as defined below, e.g. 'Derbys, Notts, Staffs, and Warwickshire'. 'Regional' strikes are those placed by the source in South Wales, South Wales and Monmouthshire, Scotland, the North East, Yorkshire, Lancashire, Lancashire and Cheshire, the East Midlands (Derbyshire, Nottinghamshire and Leicestershire), the West Midlands (Warwickshire and Staffordshire), and aggregations of these regions falling short of Great Britain. This class therefore includes the 1893 Lock-out. 'National' strikes are those affecting England, Scotland and Wales.
[b] Data for January 1901 to January 1902 are incomplete and for February–December 1902 are missing.
[c] Large strikes are defined as those directly involving more than 2,000 workers.
[d] Includes one strike of unknown size.
[e] Includes three strikes of unknown size.
Sources: 1893–1900: Board of Trade, *Reports on Strikes and Lock-outs*; 1901–2: Board of Trade, *Gazette*; 1903–40: Board of Trade (later, Ministry of Labour), *Trade Disputes: . . . Strikes and Lock-outs in 1903* and subsequent volumes, PRO LAB 34/3–20 and 39–55.

Table 5.2. *The number of collieries affected by coalmining strikes (Great Britain 1927–40)*

Number of collieries affected	Strikes	
	Number	%
1	2,849	92
2	54	
3–5	35	
6+	0	
Total known to have affected more than one colliery	*89*	*3*
Unknown[a]	173	6
Total	3,111	100

Note:
[a] Of the 173 strikes which affected an unknown number of collieries, 36 involved more than 2,000 workers and almost certainly involved more than one colliery; including these with the strikes known to have affected more than one colliery raises the proportion of multi-colliery strikes to 4 per cent.
Sources: as for table 5.1.

recorded strikes which were definitely not local. These central estimates imply that, depending on the sub-period chosen, between 1 and 5 per cent of strikes were truly widespread and that therefore 95 and 99 per cent of all colliery strikes were strictly local.

In the period 1927–40, for which we have information on the colliery as well as the place that was affected by the strike, we know that at least 92 per cent of strikes were purely 'domestic' affairs affecting only a single colliery (table 5.2). This table gives some limited support for the view that industrial solidarity, while rarely extending beyond the locality, more frequently extended beyond the pit. While at least 95 per cent of strikes in this period were confined to a single locality, 'only' 92 per cent of strikes were definitely confined to a single colliery. Detailed analysis of the multi-colliery disputes falling short of county-wide stoppages shows that the circumstances most frequently generating inter-colliery solidarity were where a small number of collieries in close proximity were owned by the same company. Outstanding examples include Amalgamated Anthracite's East, Steer and Mardy pits, all at Gwaun-cae-Gurwen near Ammanford in South Wales, which struck together on a number of occasions in the 1930s. However, it was only in the anthracite district of South Wales that company-wide strikes were at all frequent. Elsewhere, despite the fact that the majority of collieries in this period were owned by companies operating more than a single colliery, only one firm, the Shotts Iron Company which operated in Lanarkshire and Midlothian, routinely faced strikes involving more than one of its collieries.

Our conclusion that the great majority of strikes were local and domestic must, of course, be read in conjunction with the recognition that widespread strikes occurred. Such strikes were relatively frequent in the mid-1890s (although there were only a handful of any great size) and in the period from 1908 to 1920, particularly during the First World War itself and its immediate aftermath. Moreover, in the 1908–20 period, widespread strikes affected not only the enduringly strike-prone areas of Scotland and South Wales but also the Midlands, Yorkshire and the North East. Especially in this period, therefore, the experience of strike action at district, regional or national level was common. The fact that at certain moments of crisis the miners and their employers were able to mount sustained and intense national campaigns suggests that the limited spatial and organizational extent of the great majority of stoppages cannot be attributed solely to either organizational deficiencies or to the small-scale, widely dispersed nature of mining activity.

British coalmining strikes were not only limited in extent, they also became very short and have been relatively small at least since the 1890s. Table 5.3 shows that before 1907 the median duration of stoppages was between six and eight days, falling by the late 1930s to no more than one day. Before the First World War the median strike directly involved between 125 and 184 workers, and was thus a minor event. The war brought a rise in this figure to 430, but the inter-war period saw a gradual return to pre-war levels. The relative brevity of coalmining strikes deserves more detailed comment. Not only did the median strike duration fall after about 1907 but so did the durations of strikes at the 75th and 95th percentiles. Before the First World War the 95th percentile stood at well over 100 days; by the late 1920s and early 1930s this had shrunk to 30; by the late 1930s to 11 days. Although it is conceivable that these changes are a result of an improvement in the coverage of small-scale strikes there is no evidence, either internal or external, to support this hypothesis. What seems to be happening here is what Shorter and Tilly have described in another context as the replacement of 'tests of endurance' by 'shows of strength' (1974: 67).

Shorter and Tilly assumed the 'modern' strike to be merely a 'show of strength'; short in duration, large in scale and relatively high in frequency. These characteristics were already becoming evident in French mining strikes in the 1915–35 period and provide a point of comparison for British coalmining strikes. The contrast is clear, for the British strikes reveal neither an 'early' nor a 'modern' shape. Before the First World War, British mining strikes were typically small and a little longer than the typical length of a strike in early industrial France, though they were thoroughly 'modern' in their high frequency, often more than twice as frequent as the French strikes, which Shorter and Tilly considered fully satisfied their criteria of modernity. During and immediately after the First World War, British coalmining strikes became bigger and shorter and it is in this period that the 'shape' of the British strikes approximates most closely to Shorter and Tilly's idea of a 'modern' strike. After 1926, however, elements of the 'early' strike re-emerge as the size of the median strike dwindles.

Table 5.3. *The shape of coalmining strikes[a] (Great Britain 1893–1940)*

Period	Duration (calendar days) Percentiles of distribution					Nos. directly involved Percentiles of distribution					Strike rate[b]	Total no. of strikes
	25	50	75	95	N	25	50	75	95	N		
1893–7	3	8	22	125	680	60	140	400	1,500	768	234	810
1898–1902[c]	2	6	15	113	317	48	125	341	1,200	485	179[d]	677[d]
1903–7	2	8	33	134	411	41	130	408	1,581	460	107	460
1908–13	2	5	15	114	980	59	184	560	1,906	1,015	163	1,015
1914–20	2	4	9	50	1,014	100	430	1,016	4,672	1,024	137	1,024
1921–6	1	3	7	61	879	92	327	700	2,138	899	131	899
1927–31	1	2	6	30	632	59	211	520	1,802	656	142	656
1932–5	1	2	4	31	574	64	235	524	1,550	583	188	583
1936–40	1	1	3	11	1,859	44	160	439	1,250	1,872	490	1,872

Notes:

[a] Data exclude the national strikes and lock-outs of 1912, 1920, 1921 and 1926.

[b] Average annual number of strikes per million workers.

[c] Data for January 1901 to January 1902 are incomplete and for February–December 1902 are missing.

[d] The strike rate is based on the 677 strikes recorded by the Board of Trade from January 1898 to December 1902 (Department of Employment and Productivity, *British Labour Statistics*, table 197). All other results for this period are based on the number of strikes shown and relate to the period January 1898 to January 1902.

Sources: strike numbers as for table 5.1. Employment: 1893–6: Home Office, *Summaries of Statistics Relating to Mines . . .* ; 1897–1919: Home Office, *Mines and Quarries: General Report . . ., Part III. Output*; 1920–38: Mines Department, *Annual Report of the Secretary of Mines*, statistical appendices; 1939–40: Ministry of Fuel and Power, *Statistical Digest 1944.*

We have to conclude that Shorter and Tilly's summary of the changing shape of French strikes has only limited applicability in the context of British coalmining; in particular, the idea that there is a unidirectional trajectory for the shape of strikes is misleading.

The observation that the industry's unusual strike-proneness has been more characteristic of some regions than others is a commonplace but it has rarely been precisely delineated. As we anticipated in chapter 3, two regions, South Wales and Scotland, have always accounted for the great majority of coalmining strikes. Table 5.4 shows that South Wales was pre-eminent in the 1903–26 period and in the years 1903–7 accounted for almost half the strikes in the entire industry. From the late 1920s onward, however, the proportion of Scottish strikes increased and by the late 1930s Scotland had assumed the position taken earlier by South Wales when almost half the British strikes took place in this region. The only other regions to have experienced more than 10 per cent of the industry's strikes were the North East and Yorkshire. Neither region achieved the degree of pre-eminence of South Wales or Scotland before 1940, although each generated substantial shares of the industry's conflicts from time to time, the North East becoming especially prominent in the 1908–13 period and Yorkshire in the 1890s and the 1930s. At other times these regions gave the appearance of relative tranquillity.

Naturally, one of the reasons why South Wales and Scotland generated so many strikes was that they were each very large fields. To allow for this factor we computed the strike rate, or the number of strikes per million workers, in each of the regions. In order to reveal the relative strike propensities of the regions we also expressed each strike rate as a percentage of the mean for Britain as a whole. The results are in table 5.5. On this measure, South Wales and Scotland emerge as consistently more strike-prone than the industry in the country as a whole. That the majority of British coalmining strikes have frequently occurred in these two areas is therefore not simply the result of their size. Every major English region showed a strike propensity which was less than average with the exceptions of the North East just before the First World War and Yorkshire in the 1890s. So-called quiescent areas such as Lancashire and the East Midlands would appear to have been rather more strike-prone than is sometimes suggested. Each of the minor regions has at one time or another exhibited a strike propensity in excess, in some cases far in excess, of the norm. In part this is a statistical artefact caused by the small size of the minor regions. Kent is the most extreme example of this. For most of our period there were only four working collieries in Kent and at times these experienced very high numbers of strikes. But it would be easy, as we shall see below, to pick out of many of the larger regions four collieries which were as strike-prone as those in Kent. Too much weight, therefore, should not be put on the contrast between some of the minor regions and some of the major regions.

Over time, the relatively strike-prone regions became more strike-prone while the relatively quiescent became more peaceful. While in the periods before the

Table 5.4. *The regional distribution of colliery strikes (numbers and percentages Great Britain 1893–1940)*

Period		Major regions							Minor regions				
		Scotland	South Wales	North East	Yorkshire	Lancashire and Cheshire	East Midlands	West Midlands	Cumberland	North Wales	South West	Kent[a]	Great Britain[b]
1893–7	no.	231	153	78	136	76	51	30	23	16	14	1	810
	%	29	19	10	17	9	6	4	3	2	2	0	100
1898–1902[c]	no.	118	149	36	71	33	31	17	13	8	9	0	485
	%	24	31	7	15	7	6	4	3	2	2	0	100
1903–1907	no.	98	222	46	27	12	17	14	7	13	2	0	460
	%	21	48	10	6	3	4	3	2	3	1	0	100
1908–13	no.	132	318	226	84	76	72	59	19	16	13	0	1,015
	%	13	31	22	8	7	7	6	2	2	1	0	100
1914–20	no.	168	444	106	88	24	91	43	36	6	10	5	1,024
	%	16	43	10	9	2	9	4	4	1	1	0	100
1921–6	no.	248	354	80	64	44	22	45	23	3	7	9	899
	%	28	39	9	7	5	2	5	3	0	1	1	100
1927–31	no.	196	195	110	58	21	8	23	39	1	1	4	656
	%	30	30	17	9	3	1	4	6	0	0	1	100
1932–5	no.	203	188	55	68	22	19	5	14	6	2	1	583
	%	35	32	9	12	4	3	1	2	1	0	0	100
1936–40	no.	920	400	98	285	50	44	35	12	12	3	13	1,872
	%	49	21	5	15	3	2	2	1	1	0	1	100

Notes:

[a] Coal was not produced from the Kent field until 1912 but exploratory borings started in 1882; the strike in 1893–7 was of sinkers working in such exploratory shafts (Jevons 1915/1969, ch. 6).

[b] Excluding the national strikes and lock-outs of 1912, 1920, 1921 and 1926; including one cross-regional strike in 1893–7 (the Federated Districts Lock-out of 1893) and 1903–7 and three in 1914–20.

[c] Data for January 1901 to January 1902 are incomplete and for February–December 1902 are missing. Department of Employment and Productivity, *British Labour Statistics*, table 197, records 677 strikes in British coalmining for 1898–1902. There is no reason to suspect that the regional distribution has been distorted by these omissions.

Sources: as for table 5.3.

Table 5.5. Annual numbers of strikes per million employees (regional relatives, Great Britain 1893–1940)

Period	Major regions							Minor regions				
	Scotland	South Wales	North East	Yorkshire	Lancashire and Cheshire	East Midlands	West Midlands	Cumberland	North Wales	South West	Kent	Great Britain
1893–7	216	105	49	130	75	60	45	249	113	99	n.a.	100
1898–1902[a]	192	159	38	111	55	59	42	224	112	109	–	100
1903–7	166	243	50	44	23	35	38	142	183	42	–	100
1908–13	102	150	109	58	74	69	77	187	107	89	–	100
1914–20[b]	136	186	55	59	25	83	51	n.a.	n.a.	n.a.	–	100
1921–6	237	194	47	44	55	21	63	255	21	61	588	100
1927–31	287	160	89	48	38	9	43	556	109	13	135	100
1932–5	333	181	50	63	47	24	10	284	74	28	20	100
1936–40	419	126	26	83	36	18	22	81	52	14	80	100

Notes:

[a] Data for January 1901 to January 1902 are incomplete and for February–December 1902 are missing. Department of Employment and Productivity, British Labour Statistics, table 197 records 677 disputes in British coalmining for 1898–1902. There is no reason to suspect that the regional relativities have been distorted by these omissions.

[b] A complete regional breakdown of employment data is not available for 1914–20 and these results are based on estimated employment in the major regions. Helpful estimates of employment in the minor regions could not be computed.

Sources: as for table 5.3.

Table 5.6. *The concentration of domestic^a coalmining strikes by colliery (Great Britain 1921–1940)*

	1921–6	1927–31	1932–5	1936–40
Percentage of strikes in the *n* most strike-prone collieries^b				
n = 5	4–7	8–9	8–9	9–10
n = 10	7–12	13–15	14–15	16–17
n = 20	11–20	21–3	24–7	25–6
n = 35	16–29	29–33	38–40	35–7
Gini coefficient^b	0.514–0.844	0.801–0.816	0.868–0.881	0.845–0.869
No. of mines at work^c	2,846	2,395	2,102	2,105
No. of collieries struck^d	314–701	242–318	245–73	507–74
Strike prevalence^e (%)	11–25	10–13	12–13	24–7
No. of domestic strikes at identified collieries	512	580	555	1,805
No. of strikes at unidentified collieries^f	387	76	28	67
(and the percentages they form of all strikes)	(43)	(12)	(5)	(4)

Notes:

^a 'Domestic' strikes are those confined to a single colliery.

^b The lower figures in the ranges are computed on the assumption that the strikes at unidentified collieries were completely unconcentrated; the upper figures are computed on the assumption that the strikes at unidentified collieries were as concentrated as the strikes at identified collieries. Both computations assume that all strikes at unidentified collieries were domestic strikes.

^c Mines at work under the Coal Mines Act at the midpoint of the period. A small number of mines, mainly of ironstone, in Cleveland, Lincolnshire and Northamptonshire have been excluded.

^d Here the lower figure is the number of identified collieries at which a strike was recorded; the upper figure is the lower *plus* the number of strikes at unidentified collieries.

^e The proportion of mines at work struck at least once in a domestic strike.

^f Including non-domestic strikes.

Sources: Ministry of Labour, *Trade Disputes: . . . Strikes and Lock-outs of 1921* and subsequent volumes, PRO LAB 34/39–55; Mines Department, *Annual Report of the Secretary for Mines*, 1921–38, e.g. 1938, table 45.

First World War, especially between 1908 and 1913 during the 'late Edwardian unrest', regional differences were not so pronounced, by the 1930s the regional diversity of the industry's strike record was quite extraordinary. By the outbreak of the Second World War, Scotland was more than ten times as strike-prone as Lancashire, more than fifteen times as strike-prone as the North East and about twenty times as strike-prone as the East and West Midlands.

'Back up pit' in Shotts and Barnsley: persistent strike locations

Thus far, our analysis of the strike statistics has confirmed in rather more detail and temporal scope than existing studies the generally small scale of strikes in coalmining and the existence of enduring regional variations in miners' militancy. As Krieger's study (1984) of coalfield industrial relations has shown, the disparate experiences and traditions of the regions have proved remarkably persistent and have continued to influence labour relations in the modern coal industry. Yet if the detailed case studies of historians and other researchers into the history of coalfield industrial relations have demonstrated anything, it is the existence of distinctive experiences and traditions at sub-regional level, that is at individual collieries and in the communities that grew up around them (Dennis et al. 1956; Campbell 1978, 1979; Spaven 1978; Macintyre 1980a; Goffee 1981; Krieger 1984; Waller 1983). Our data can now be used to draw a much more detailed picture of the shape of coalfield militancy at this level than has been available before.

Earlier we pointed out that modern studies of manufacturing industry have found that strike activity is concentrated in a small number of highly strike-prone plants. To assess the level of concentration by colliery it is necessary to know which collieries were affected by strikes. Beginning in 1921 the official data make it possible to say what proportion of strikes occurred in the most strike-prone plants and, unlike previous analyses of strike concentration (e.g. Department of Employment, *Strikes in Britain*), over a relatively long period. Before 1921 the records do not pin down the whereabouts of each strike so exactly, but they do give the geographical location and this has enabled us to compute measures of strike concentration by place. These allow us to assess the changes and continuities in strike concentration over the entire period from 1893. In these exercises we have restricted our attention to 'domestic' strikes, affecting single collieries and 'local' and 'district' strikes, affecting one or a few neighbouring localities. Other strikes we term 'widespread'. The existence of very large-scale and widespread strikes and lock-outs involving entire regions or the entire country, is, of course, an important feature of the industry; but they were rare, as we have shown in table 5.1, and have distracted the attention of historians from the study of more typical domestic and local strikes.

Table 5.6 presents our measurements of the concentration of domestic strikes. They show the proportion of domestic strikes which occurred in the most strike-prone five, ten, twenty and thirty-five collieries. The table also shows

Table 5.7. *The concentration of local and district[a] coalmining strikes by place (Great Britain 1893–1940)*

	1893–7	1898–1902[b]	1903–7	1908–13	1914–20	1921–6	1927–31	1932–5	1936–40
Percentage of strikes in the n most strike-prone places[c]									
$n=5$	11	13	15	13	17	14	14	14	17
$n=10$	19	21	23	24	27	23	24	22	26
$n=20$	30	32	36	37	41	35	35	35	39
$n=35$	42	46	49	49	53	46	46	49	49
Gini coefficient[c, d]	0.819	0.880	0.878	0.738	0.869	0.817	0.848	0.873	0.882
No. of places at which strikes were recorded	311	206	187	290	271	302	262	222	371
No. of local and district[a] strikes	790	478	455	997	994	893	643	581	1,867
No. of widespread[a] strikes	20	7	5	19	31	8	13	2	5

Notes:

[a] 'Local and district' strikes are defined as for table 5.1; these data include a small number of strikes at unidentified places. 'Widespread' strikes are county, sub-regional, regional and national strikes and lock-outs as defined for table 5.1.

[b] Data for January 1901 to January 1902 are incomplete and for February–December 1902 are missing. Department of Employment and Productivity, *British Labour Statistics*, table 197, records 677 disputes in British coalmining for 1898–1902. These omissions bias the measures of concentration upwards.

[c] Strikes at unidentified places are assumed to be as concentrated as strikes at identified places. The small number of strikes at unidentified places implies that alternative assumptions make little difference to the results.

[d] Computed on the assumption that there were 1,531 places 'at risk' of a strike in each period. This is the number of separate 'situations' at which mines were listed in the 1913 Home Office, *List of Mines*.

Sources: strike numbers as for table 5.1; places: Home Office, *List of Mines*, 1913.

the degree of inequality of the distribution of domestic strikes as a whole, as indicated by the Gini coefficient. Finally, it records the number of identified collieries which experienced at least one domestic strike. The fact that some strikes in the records happened at collieries which the statisticians failed to identify lends some uncertainty to our estimates, so for each measure we have computed a range of values between which the true figure lies. These ranges are quite wide for the period 1921–6 but are narrow thereafter and negligible by 1932–5.

The table shows that after 1926 between 8 and 10 per cent of all officially recorded strikes occurred in only five strike-prone collieries; that one-fifth or one-quarter of such strikes took place in just twenty collieries, and that the thirty-five most strike-prone collieries accounted for between 30 and 40 per cent of recorded stoppages in the industry. The Gini coefficient tells a similar story, indicating very high levels of concentration in the period after 1927. Strike prevalence, or the number of collieries at which at least one strike was recorded, seems to have fallen after 1926 to as low as 10 to 13 per cent of all mines at work, before rising to about double those figures in the late 1930s when the frequency of strikes rose. The results for 1921–6 are less clear. While the proportion of strikes which took place in the highly strike-prone collieries was high, the level may have been rather lower than in the period following the 1926 Lock-out.

Table 5.7 presents alternative measures of concentration, concentration by place. The data on which this table is based are not entirely satisfactory and it should be treated with caution. The 'places' that appear in the source data vary from colliery villages to major conurbations. Moreover, there is some inconsistency in the use of place names in the sources; strikes at a particular colliery are sometimes 'placed' at the local pit village and sometimes at or near one or other of the nearby towns. This kind of ambiguity in the place data inevitably limits the validity of measures of concentration based upon them.

Despite these deficiencies in the data, table 5.7 reveals a picture that is surprisingly consistent over time. In every period, between 42 and 53 per cent of officially recorded local and district strikes occurred in only thirty-five places. The Gini coefficients also suggest that the overall degree of concentration by place was remarkably high and fairly stable, with only the coefficient for 1908–13, the years of the 'late Edwardian unrest', being markedly out of line. They also tend to confirm the shift to somewhat higher levels of concentration in the period after 1927 which was apparent in table 5.6. In short, tables 5.6 and 5.7 suggest that the dense concentration of domestic and local colliery strikes in a relatively small number of collieries and places has been a feature of the industry since reliable records began.

The above comments all relate to officially recorded strikes. As we remarked in chapter 1, the coverage of the official record is not complete and small strikes in particular are likely to be under-recorded. The effect of this coverage failure on the measure of concentration is unclear: it all depends on the concentration of unrecorded strikes. Small strikes could be highly concentrated, indicative

Table 5.8. *The prevalence of domestic[a] coalmining strikes (Great Britain and regions 1921–40)*

	Major regions							Minor regions				Great Britain
	Scotland	South Wales	North East	Yorkshire	Lancashire and Cheshire	East Midlands	West Midlands	Cumberland	North Wales	South West	Kent	
1 No. of mines at work 1921[b]	535	663	389	350	286	217	373	38	44	89	4	2,988
2 No. of mines at work 1938[b]	426	424	349	237	155	181	231	25	28	45	4	2,105
3 No. of identified collieries struck 1921–40	273	254	120	105	56	39	39	9	9	8	4	916
4 No. of strikes at unidentified collieries 1921–40	165	214	63	35	21	15	29	11	1	3	1	558
Prevalence of strikes (%)												
5 Upper estimate[c]	90	86	49	47	35	27	22	57	28	13	100	57
6 Lower estimate[d]	57	47	33	36	25	20	13	29	25	12	100	36

Notes:

[a] 'Domestic' strikes are those confined to a single colliery.

[b] Mines at work under the Coal Mines Act. A small number of mines, mainly of ironstone, in Cleveland, Lincolnshire and Northamptonshire have been excluded.

[c] The upper estimate is [(row 3 + row 4) / (mean of rows 1 and 2)] ×100% or 100% if this is lower.

[d] Lower estimate is [row 3 / (mean of rows 1 and 2)] ×100%.

Sources: strike numbers as for table 5.6; number of mines: Mines Department, *Annual Reports of the Secretary for Mines*, 1921–38, e.g. 1921, table 35.

perhaps of a particular 'style' of industrial relations or of highly fragmented work-forces at particular collieries or places (see Goffee 1981). On the other hand, such strikes could be very unconcentrated, a typical feature of the industry as a whole.

Table 5.8 attempts to measure the prevalence of domestic strikes. Did most collieries experience domestic strikes in the inter-war years, or was the experience of such strikes much less prevalent? In an attempt to answer this question, the table contrasts the number of coal mines struck in domestic strikes with the number of mines at work between 1921 and 1938. The mean number of mines at work are our estimates of the number of collieries 'at risk' of a strike in the period 1921–40. This estimate is not ideal because the number of mines at work includes some that produced a mineral other than coal, for instance iron-stone or fireclay. We have been able to exclude mines in the iron-stone districts where these are separate from colliery districts, but this still leaves perhaps about 8 per cent of mines at work which did not mine coal. This biases our measure of prevalence downwards by about the same proportion for Great Britain as a whole.

A further problem arises from the missing data on colliery names which badly affect the records at the start of the inter-war period. Indeed, the number of strikes at unidentified collieries is quite high in relation to the total number of collieries at risk for much of the inter-war period. For this reason we have computed two extreme measures of prevalence between which, bearing in mind our other caveats, the true figure must lie. The lower estimate is based on the assumption that all strikes not at identified collieries were in fact at collieries among those already known to have experienced at least one strike. The upper estimate is based on the assumption that none of the unidentified struck collieries were among those already identified. These upper and lower estimates are quite far apart for Scotland and South Wales and, because of the size of these regions, for Great Britain as a whole. We have therefore taken an alternative approach and computed prevalence estimates for Scotland, South Wales and Great Britain for the shorter 1927–40 period, for which the data are more complete. These estimates are given in table 5.9 . They show that in this period between 33 and 43 per cent of collieries were struck in a domestic strike in the country as a whole. In short, according to official records, the typical colliery was free of domestic strikes in this period. Strike prevalence in South Wales was at about the British average but was significantly higher in Scotland, where probably more than half of the collieries were struck at least once during these years.

Returning now to the longer period covered by table 5.8 we see that strike prevalence may well have been higher in Britain as a whole with somewhere between 36 and 57 per cent of all collieries in Britain affected by one or more domestic strikes large enough to engage the attention of the Ministry of Labour. The picture was not uniform over the country, however. Strikes were much more prevalent, as well as normally more frequent, in Scotland and South Wales than in the British industry as a whole. Conversely, in Lancashire and Cheshire and in the Midlands among the major regions, and in North Wales and the

Table 5.9. *The prevalence of domestic[a] coalmining strikes (Scotland, South Wales and Great Britain 1927–40)*

	Scotland	South Wales	Great Britain
1 No. of mines at work 1927[b]	506	639	2,831
2 No. of mines at work 1938[b]	426	424	2,105
3 No. of identified collieries struck 1927–40	225	195	809
4 No. of strikes at unidentified collieries 1927–40	59	22	260
Prevalence of strikes (%)			
5 Upper estimate[c]	61	41	43
6 Lower estimate[d]	48	37	33

Notes: as for table 5.8.
Sources: as for table 5.8.

South West among the minor, strikes were less prevalent than in the country as a whole, and in these regions, with the exception of North Wales, strikes were also usually less frequent.

Domestic and local colliery strikes were concentrated in a relatively small number of collieries and places and, in the inter-war period at least, many collieries experienced no officially detected strike activity beyond participation in the small number of widespread strikes. Conversely, a few collieries and places were very strike-prone. Did these collieries strike persistently, year after year, or did they quickly return to peaceable industrial relations? Table 5.10 identifies the ten most strike-prone collieries in each of the four periods for which data exist. Logically, at least ten collieries must appear in this table and as many as forty could appear and these numbers provide some parameters for judgement. Thirty-two separate collieries are listed in table 5.10, indicating a high degree of turnover in the population of highly struck collieries. No colliery appears more than twice and only five (Bothwell Castle in Lanarkshire; Brynamman in Glamorgan; Brynhenllys Slant in Carmarthen; Dewshill and Duntilland in Lanarkshire; Whitburn Nos. 1 and 2 in Durham) appear as frequently as that. In other words, highly strike-prone collieries typically emerged and disappeared within relatively short spans of time.

A similar exercise has been conducted with the place data for each of our nine periods from 1893 to 1940 though we have not reproduced a tabulation of these data here. At least ten places must appear in such a tabulation and up to ninety could do so. In the event, fifty separate places appeared in these rankings. Among these, twenty-five places appeared only once, sixteen appeared twice, and five appeared three times. Rotherham in Yorkshire, Burnley in Lancashire and Shotts in Lanarkshire appeared four times while Barnsley was ranked six times. No place appeared in the lists in all nine periods. These results justify the conclusion that the typical strike-prone place, like the typical strike-prone colliery of the inter-war period, was not strike-prone year after year. Much more typical was a dramatic upsurge of strike activity which subsided equally rapidly. Fence Houses in Durham exemplified this pattern clearly. After first appearing in the records with a strike in December 1908, followed by twenty-four more ending in January 1913, Fence Houses disappeared from the record books until the 1930s.

Another fairly frequent pattern was that of an area achieving prominence for a more extended period, preceded and/or followed by periods of relative quiescence. Port Talbot exemplified this experience, small numbers of strikes occurring in the 1890s followed by six during 1903–7, fifteen during 1908–13 and an extraordinary fifty-five between 1914 and 1926. After 1926 no strikes were recorded there until two in 1932–5 and nine during 1936–40. The pattern exemplified by Barnsley, Shotts, Burnley and Rotherham (and no where else) was rare but remarkable. Barnsley was the most strike-prone colliery locality in the country in the 1890s and while it was surpassed by many other places in the next twenty-five years, in the late 1920s and the late 1930s it once again took a place near the head of the lists. Similarly, Burnley and Rotherham experienced an alternation of very troubled and relatively quiet periods. Shotts came to prominence in the early 1920s: nineteen strikes were recorded there between 1921 and 1926, eighteen between 1927 and 1931, twenty-one between 1932 and 1935, when the village was the most strike-prone place in all the British coalfields, and a remarkable 147 between 1936 and 1940. Its pre-eminence remained unchallenged throughout the Second World War and in the post-war period until the last collieries in the area were closed down in the 1960s. However, these four places, and especially the unremitting militancy seen in Shotts, were exceptional. With the caveat that our analysis includes recorded strikes only, it appears that before the Second World War extreme strike proneness at both place and colliery level was a transient experience.

To summarize, our statistical analysis reveals the typical British coalmining strike to have been localized and short-lived, confined to a single colliery, and involving a few hundred workers for a little over a week before the First World War, or no more than a day thirty years later. The 'shape' of these strikes conformed neither to that posited for 'early' nor for 'modern' strikes by Shorter and Tilly. Regardless of period, recorded domestic and local strikes have been heavily concentrated in a small number of highly strike-prone collieries and highly strike-prone places. The obverse of this feature is that many collieries in inter-war Britain, possibly more than half, experienced no domestic strike large enough to come to the attention of the Ministry of Labour. In other words, the prevalence of domestic strikes was far from total. Although widespread strikes took place, they were few in number and not all of them were large in scale. Those which were of a significant scale were concentrated in the years of the 'late Edwardian unrest' and the First World War.

It would be a mistake, therefore, to assume that the strike proneness of particular collieries or particular places was as enduring as the regional charac-

Table 5.10. *The ten most strike-prone collieries in each of four periods (Great Britain 1921–1940)*

Rank	1921–6	1927–31	1932–5	1936–40
1	Nine Mile Point Cy [a], Burnyeat Brown & Co. Ltd *Monmouthshire* (11)	Whitehaven Haig & Wellington Cy, Whitehaven Cy Co. Ltd *Cumberland* (15)	Gwaun-cae-Gurwen Maerdy Cy (A), Amalgamated Anthracite Cies Ltd *Glamorgan* (13)	Blantyre Cy, Wm Dixon Ltd *Lanarkshire* (47)
2	Brynamman Level (A), Brynamman Cy Ltd *Glamorgan* (7)	Whitehaven Ladysmith Cy, Whitehaven Cy Co. Ltd *Cumberland* (11)	Gwaun-cae-Gurwen Steer Cy (A), Amalgamated Anthracite Cies Ltd *Glamorgan* (13)	Gartshore Nos. 1, 3 and 12 Cy, Wm Baird & Co. Ltd *Dumbartonshire* (35)
3	Dewshill & Duntilland Cy [b], Coltness Iron Co. Ltd *Lanarkshire* (7)	Brynhenllys Slant (A), Brynhenllys Anthracite Cy Co. Ltd *Carmarthen* (10)	Brynhenllys Slant (A), Brynhenllys Anthracite Cy Co. Ltd *Carmarthen* (10)	Dewshill Cy ++ Duntilland Cy [b], Coltness Iron Co. Ltd *Lanarkshire* (34)
4	Towneley Demesne Cy ++ Towneley Drift Cy, Brooks and Brooks Cies Ltd *Lancashire* (6)	Hassockrigg Cy, Coltness Iron Co. Ltd *Lanarkshire* (10)	Whitburn No. 1 + Whitburn No. 2 Cy, Harton Coal Co. Ltd *Co. Durham* (10)	Bothwell Castle Nos. 3 and 4 Cy, Wm Baird & Co. Ltd *Lanarkshire* (33)
5	Brownieside Cy, Brownieside Coal Co. Ltd *Lanarkshire* (6)	Brynamman Slant [c] (A), Pwllbach, Tirbach and Brynamman Anthracite Cies Ltd *Glamorgan* (8)	Auchengeich Cy, James Nimmo & Co. Ltd *Lanarkshire* (9)	Cardowan Nos. 1 and 2 Cy, James Dunlop & Co. Ltd *Lanarkshire* (27)
6	Gellyceidrim Cy (A), Gellyceidrim Cies Co. Ltd *Carmarthen* (6)	Houghton Main Cy, Houghton Main Cy Co. Ltd *South Yorkshire* (8)	Bothwell Castle Nos. 3 & 4 Cy, Wm Baird & Co. Ltd *Lanarkshire* (9)	Calderhead Nos. 3 & 4 Cy, James Dunlop & Co. Ltd *Lanarkshire* (26)

7	Ardenrigg No. 5 Cy, Ardenrigg Coal Co. Ltd *Lanarkshire* (5)	Abercrave Slant (A), Welsh Anthracite Cies Ltd *Brecon* (7)	Barnborough Main Cy, Manvers Main Cies Ltd *South Yorkshire* (8)	Castlehill No. 6 Cy, Shotts Iron Co. Ltd *Lanarkshire* (25)
8	Broomrigg Nos. 2 & 3 and Knowhead Cy, Banknock Coal Co. Ltd *Stirlingshire* (5)	International Slant (A), Welsh Anthracite Cies Ltd *Brecon* (7)	Gwaun-cae-Gurwen East Cy (A), Amalgamated Anthracite Cies Ltd *Glamorgan* (8)	Kinneil Cy, Kinneil Cannel & Coking Coal Co. Ltd *West Lothian* (25)
9	Reedley Cy, Executors of John Hargreaves Ltd *Lancashire* (5) [d]	Whitburn No. 1 + Whitburn No. 2 Cy, Harton Coal Co. Ltd *Co. Durham* (7) [e]	Hickleton Main Cy, Hickleton Main Cy Co. Ltd *South Yorkshire* (8)	Gleison+Tareni Nos. 1 & 2 Cy (A), Tareni Cy Co. Ltd *Glamorgan* (23)
10	[d]	[e]	Yniscedwyn Slant (A), Amalgamated Anthracite Cies Ltd *Brecon* (8)	[f]

Notes:

See the general appendix for our conventions for defining and naming collieries. Figures in brackets are the number of domestic strikes recorded at that colliery. 'A' indicates an anthracite Colliery; 'Cy' colliery and 'Cies', Collieries.

[a] Nine Mile Point East Cy++ Nine Mile Point West Cy + Nine Mile Point Rock Vein Cy according to our conventions.

[b] Dewshill and Duntilland Colliery was treated as two separate collieries in the *List of Mines* in the 1930s; in accordance with our conventions we have treated it as a single colliery throughout the inter-war period.

[c] Formerly Brynamman Level.

[d] There were fifteen collieries with a rank of 10= in this period, with four strikes each.

[e] There were two collieries with a rank of 10= in this period, with six strikes each.

[f] There were two collieries with a rank of 10= in this period, with twenty-two strikes each.

Sources: as for table 5.6.

teristics of the industry, or indeed as the strike proneness of the industry as a whole. Although in each of our periods it is possible to identify extremely strike-prone collieries and places, the identity of these collieries and places generally changed rapidly over time. Although the industry in Britain has been marked by turbulent industrial relations since reliable records began, and some regions have consistently experienced more strikes than others, the turbulence at the level of colliery and community has shifted from colliery to colliery and from place to place.

The conclusion that, typically, strikes were confined to colliery or locality, may seem surprising because of the preoccupation of historians of the industry with extensive county or regional strikes, such as those involving the Durham miners in 1892, 1902, 1908 and 1910, the massive stoppage across the inland coalfields in England in 1893, the Scottish miners' strike in 1894 and the strike and lock-out in South Wales in 1898 and 1910. Most attention of all has been given to the history of the national coal strikes beginning in 1912. In addition to diverting attention away from one of the essential characteristics of mining strikes as localized, brief and, typically, not recurrent, the preoccupation in the literature with major strikes at regional or national levels has encouraged the stereotypical perception of the 'militant miner', based largely on the social solidarity which was certainly a special feature of each of the national strikes and lock-outs. In the following chapters, the extent of miners' participation in strikes is measured and the notion of miners' solidarity explored.

6   Strike participation and solidarity before 1912

One enduring assertion in the literature concerned with coalfield conflict is the association of coalmining strikes with solidarity:

A strike with small beginnings in a section of a face in a pit usually spreads quickly to involve the whole pit and evokes responses from the various sections of the neighbourhood. Adjoining pits tend to respond to each other's difficulties. Miners assume that there should be solidarity over whatever area relates to their dispute. They, therefore, expect sympathetic action from other Areas [of the National Union of Mineworkers] and other unions. When it does not occur they ask why and set out to get it. (Allen 1981: 182)

Yet the notion that British miners' strike behaviour has always been solidaristic is a myth.

We saw in the last chapter that strikes rarely extended beyond the confines of a single locality and a single colliery (tables 5.1 and 5.2). 'Sympathetic strikes' were rare: of the 4,000 strikes recorded in the 1921–40 period, only 60 (1.5 per cent) were classed as 'sympathetic' by the Ministry of Labour. The day-to-day experience of the industry was of small-scale strike action taken by people who all worked in the same pit or lived in the same community or were employed by the same company. But even within the pit the scope of solidary behaviour appears to have been much more restricted than myth would allow. This chapter documents this assertion as a prelude to a re-examination of miners' solidarity at national and local level during the period up to the first national strike in 1912. In chapter 7 we consider the subsequent period which saw triumphs of working-class solidarity rapidly succeeded by division and a subsequent, painful reproduction of solidary structures.

'We band of brothers': the limits of solidarity

By linking the Ministry of Labour data on strike activity to Mines Department data on colliery employment we have been able to compute the proportion of colliery employees who were classed as 'directly affected' in domestic strikes. This proportion is the 'participation rate' and we have assumed that the distinction between workers who were, in the official parlance, 'directly affected' by the strike and those who were 'indirectly affected' corresponds to the distinction between those who were participants in the strike and those who were laid off by

Table 6.1. *Colliery strike participation rates[a] by size of colliery (domestic strikes,[b] Great Britain coalmining 1927–38)*

Colliery size class[c]	Number of strikes	Number of strikes for which the participation rate is known	Mean participation rate (%)
0–99	150	125	62
100–199	149	138	54
200–499	566	543	60
500–999	604	586	48
1,000–1,999	421	417	37
2,000+	238	237	26
All above	2,128	2,046	48
Unknown	201[d]	0	na

Notes:
[a] The participation rate (*PR*) is the percentage of a colliery's work-force directly involved in a strike. Workers 'indirectly involved' are 'those workers who are . . . thrown out of work at the establishments where the disputes occur although not themselves parties to the disputes' (Department of Employment and Productivity, *British Labour Statistics*, 19). Discrepancies of definition and timing between the sources of the data for the size of the work-force and the numbers directly involved and inaccuracies in both sources sometimes give rise to calculated participation rates in excess of 100 per cent. Calculated participation rates in excess of 140 per cent have been excluded; calculated participation rates $100 < PR < 140$ have been retained to avoid unduly biasing the data. The cut-off point of 140 per cent was chosen after inspecting the distribution of participation rates.
[b] Strikes confined to a single colliery.
[c] Employment above and below ground.
[d] The 201 strikes at collieries of unknown size comprise two distinct classes. The first are strikes which were not restricted to a single colliery and for which the allocation to a colliery size class makes no sense; these strikes often involved large numbers. The second class consists of domestic strikes at collieries which could not be identified.
Sources: Ministry of Labour, *Trade Disputes: . . . Strikes and Lock-outs of 1927* and subsequent volumes, PRO LAB 34/45–53; Mines Department, *Lists of Mines*, 1927–38.

the management because of the effects of the strike on the colliery's operations. The great majority of coalmining strikes were domestic strikes and we have been able to compute participation rates for the great majority of domestic strikes that occurred in the industry in the 1927–38 period. The mean participation rate in these strikes was 48 per cent (table 6.1). These data provide evidence which rejects the notion entertained by Kerr and Siegel (1954: 192) that mass walkout strikes were typical of the industry's labour history: the walkouts were frequently walkouts of *sections* of the work-force, not the work-force *en masse*. Further

Table 6.2. *Distribution of domestic strike participation rates by size of colliery (Great Britain coalmining 1927–38)*

Colliery size class	N	Percentages of strikes falling in each class Participation rate (%)						Total
		0–	20–	40–	60–	80–	100–140	
0-99	125	6	18	26	24	16	11	100
100–199	138	21	17	20	14	20	8	100
200–499	543	22	12	11	19	24	12	100
500–999	586	36	12	10	15	21	6	100
1,000–1,999	417	50	13	9	10	12	7	100
2,000+	237	62	15	3	7	13	0	100
All	2,046	35	13	11	15	19	8	100

Note: For definitions and explanations see the notes to table 6.1.
Sources: as for table 6.1.

investigation revealed significant variations in the participation rate by colliery size and table 6.1 shows that participation rates were roughly constant at around 60 per cent until colliery size reached 500 employees, then fell with size, declining to 26 per cent in collieries which employed over 2,000 workers.

The decline in the average strike participation rate with increasing size of colliery indicated by table 6.1 masks a process of differentiation in the pattern of strikes in the larger collieries. Table 6.2 shows the distribution of strike participation rates for each of the colliery size classes. This table shows that in the smallest two colliery size classes the distribution is single peaked with a modal value in the range 40–60 per cent. As colliery size increases a bi-modal pattern emerges, with peaks at participation rates in the 0–20 and 80–100 per cent ranges. While in collieries of between 200 and 499 employees the number of collieries in these modal ranges is about equal, as colliery size increases the lower modal range steadily becomes more dominant so that in the very largest collieries we can see that three-fifths of strikes gained the participation of fewer than 20 per cent of the work-force.

When participation rates are analysed by region and county for the period 1921–40 (table 6.3) they suggest a rough correlation between strike frequency or strike prevalence and strike participation rates. In none of the districts were more than 30 per cent of strikes joined by more than 90 per cent of employees. But the median strike in the militant coalfields of South Wales and Scotland involved between 70 and 80 per cent of employees in the former and between 50 and 60 per cent in the latter, both of which could be regarded as indicative of solidaristic behaviour. By contrast in Northumberland and Durham, largely quiescent in this period, the median strike involved between 20 and 30 per cent of employees and in Yorkshire (not at this point the byword for militancy it was to become),

Table 6.3. *Domestic strike participation rates by selected regions and counties (Great Britain coalmining 1921–40)*

Strike participation rate (%)	Regions and counties: per cent of strikes					
	South Wales	Scotland	North-umber-land	Durham	York-shire	Nottinghamshire and North Derbyshire
0–	17	28	43	41	53*	55*
20–	7	13	18*	16*	16	10
40–	14	11*	10	8	6	9
60–	21*	15	8	10	10	20
80–100	24	22	12	18	10	2
>100	16	10	10	7	4	4
All	100	100	100	100	100	100
N	739	939	51	192	348	56

Notes: For definitions and explanations see the notes to table 6.1. Participation rates could not be established for 674 (17%) of strikes. The group in which the median strike lies is distinguished by an asterisk.
Sources: as for table 6.1.

Nottinghamshire and Derbyshire the median lay between only 10 and 20 per cent.

These low rates of participation should not be assumed to represent, necessarily, some kind of failure. It is possible that participation rates were low because these very small strikes were none the less effective or, at least, no less effective than strikes in which relatively large numbers participated. Table 6.4 suggests that this hypothesis has some plausibility. It indicates that as long as the participation rate was above 20 per cent, increases in participation did not increase the probability of winning the strike.

However, the assumption that domestic colliery strikes had definable objects may be misplaced. As we indicated in chapter 1, at least some strikes may have been spontaneous walkouts resulting from the 'accumulated tensions' of the job. In such cases, a low participation rate and a 'failure' of the strike to achieve an improvement in the terms or conditions of employment may be quite beside the point. The strike would have achieved a temporary respite from work and this may be all that was wanted.

The data we have reviewed so far are consistent with at least two patterns of behaviour: participation rates may have been more or less constant from strike to strike in any given colliery, suggesting a structural explanation for this behaviour, or participation rates may have varied from strike to strike within any given colliery, suggesting that a structural explanation would be insufficient. The data show that it is the latter pattern which is more typical. Table 6.5 illustrates the pattern found in the data. It gives the distribution of participation rates for large

Table 6.4. *Domestic strike participation rates[a] by result of strike (Great Britain coalmining 1921–40)*

Participation rate (%)	Result: per cent of strikes[b]				N
	Won	Compromised	Lost	Total	
0–	16	28	56	100	1,101
20–	23	30	47	100	423
40–	24	34	42	100	357
60–	23	31	46	100	490
80–100	24	30	46	100	631
>100	21	34	45	100	334
All	20.7	30.3	48.9	100.0	3,336
N	692	1,012	1,632	3,336	

Notes: For definitions and explanations see the notes to table 6.1. Participation rates could not be established for 674 (17%) of strikes. Results are described from the workers' point of view.
Sources: as for table 6.1.

collieries which experienced seven or more local strikes during 1927–38. All but one of these collieries occasionally achieved very high participation rates but much more frequently they failed to do so and strikes often gained the participation of less than 20 per cent of the work-force.

The data we have presented in this chapter throw serious doubt on the validity of the traditional view of miners' solidarity. Solidary behaviour was normally limited to workers in the same locality, company and colliery. Even within the colliery solidary behaviour in the 1927–38 period rarely extended across the entire colliery work-force and, especially in the very largest collieries, sectional behaviour was the norm rather than the exception. Regional differences can be identified. In Scotland and South Wales most strikes were actively supported by most of the work-force of a colliery, but elsewhere this limited extension of solidarity was absent. There is, however, some support from the data for the view that a minority of the recorded strikes, but possibly a substantial minority, were 'protests', resulting from the 'accumulated tensions of the job', rather than in pursuit of clearly defined ends beyond the strike itself. For such strikes, solidarity is not an issue.

Are these conclusions, derived as they are from evidence from the period immediately following the miners' defeat in 1926, historically specific? It is true that the momentum on the industrial and political front established in 1912 during the first national strike and strengthened by the war and dual control was lost in 1926. But before 1912 fragmentation and sectionalism were the historic characteristics of the industry and of labour relations between coalowners and mineworkers (Church 1986: 668–9, 701, 746). Moreover, during the Second

Table 6.5. *Distributions of domestic colliery strikes by strike participation rate (large colliery with seven or more strikes, number of strikes, Great Britain 1927–38)*

| Colliery | Participation rate (%) | | | | | |
	0–	20–	40–	60–	80 and over	N
Barnborough Main	6	2	0	1	1	10
Betteshanger	3	0	0	0	4	7
Bullcroft Main	6	4	0	0	0	10
Frickley	3	2	0	0	3	8
Grimethorpe	11	2	0	2	3	18
Hickleton Main	15	3	1	1	2	22
Roundwood & Silverwood	9	4	0	0	1	14
South Kirkby	7	1	0	1	1	10
Thorne	3	2	0	1	1	7
Whitburn	4	0	1	0	2	7
Total	67	20	2	6	18	113

Notes:
Large collieries are defined as those employing over 2,000 workers at the time of the strikes. Given the poor coverage of very small strikes in the official records these data are likely to underestimate the true number of strikes with low participation rates.
Sources: as for table 6.1.

World War and until at least the 1960s, the small-scale, short duration and low participation rates of colliery strikes which we have seen in the inter-war period became more, not less, marked characteristics of domestic coalfield industrial relations (see chapter 13). This suggests that the domestic sectionalism indicated by low strike participation rates was the long-term historic norm in the industry and 'solidarity' was reserved for the occasional district, regional and national strikes organized beyond the confines of pit and village. The disparity between domestic sectionalism and industrial solidarity renders the latter newly problematic. The solidarity so evident in the major regional and national strikes cannot be explained as a natural geographical extension of behaviour common in every colliery and every pit village. In the remainder of this chapter we examine afresh the circumstances in which, and the means by which, solidarity was achieved at national, regional and district levels before returning to a re-examination of strikes in the locality.

'Stop the wheels': generating solidarity before the 1912 national strike

The massive national strikes and lock-outs which are the major source of the British coalminer's reputation for solidary action were initiated, co-ordinated and eventually terminated by national organizations of coalminers normally in conflict with national organizations of coalowners. While each has spawned an extensive literature no attempt has been made to link these to theoretical approaches, no attempt has been made to define the circumstances under which solidary action was generated and sustained, and no attempt has been made to consider the methods and procedures by which the miners' trade unions achieved and maintained solidary behaviour at county and national levels. The intention of this chapter is to begin the process of filling these lacunae.

The creation of organizational forms which could extend support to miners in dispute with their employers without jeopardizing their own survival was a process marked by many initial failures. The practices and institutions which eventually emerged generated a form of solidary action which we shall argue showed significant differences from that which one would expect from a reading of the theoretical literature. To provide a full account of that history is a task beyond the resources and space available to us. Instead, we have selected a number of episodes in this history which are designed to elucidate the structural constraints on trans-local organization, the ways in which these constraints were understood by significant personalities, and the consequences of these for the nature and forms of the solidary action observed at county and national level.

Our approach derives from both Durkheim's theory of social solidarity and from more recent accounts of the provision of mutual social support in terms of exchanges taking place in networks of social relationships. Durkheim's use of the term 'solidarity' was more general both in conception and application than our use of the term in this book. Whereas in this book we are largely concerned with strike solidarity, operationalized in terms of the strike participation rate, solidarity in Durkheim's thought refers to the coherence between the actions of a set of individuals which allows us to treat that set as a society rather than a mere agglomeration of individuals. Solidary relations in Durkheim's analysis have, he suggested, the characteristics of stability, duration and frequency of contact, are associated with feelings of attachment and are symbolized by law (Durkheim 1893/1984: 21, 24, 26). Durkheim famously distinguished 'mechanical' and 'organic' solidarity: the former was based on similarities and the latter on complementarities arising through the 'division of labour in society'. Durkheim's search for observable 'social facts' corresponding to these two forms led him to link mechanical solidarity with laws providing for 'repressive' sanctions against rule breakers and organic solidarity with laws providing for 'restitutive' sanctions. Repressive sanctions result from insults to collectively held values, 'are administered in a diffuse way by everybody without distinction' and consist of inflicting some harm on the wrongdoer. Restitutive sanctions 'do not necessarily imply any suffering on the part of the perpetrator, but merely consist in *restoring the previous state of affairs*, re-establishing relationships that have been disturbed'. Restitutive legal sanctions are administered by specialized legal institutions (Durkheim 1893/1984: 16–29; quotations from p. 29, emphasis in the original).

Economists have frequently emphasized the necessary and reciprocal connection between the division of labour in the economy and exchange, and it is therefore unsurprising that sociologists have sought to extend this notion to the connections between the social division of labour and the nature of the relationships observed in socially specialized societies. That such relations may be understood as relationships of exchange is the underlying thesis of theories of 'social exchange'. In applications of such theories, the processes by which community-level 'informal social support' are provided are conceptualized as a set of exchanges between individuals located in social 'networks'. The relationships within which exchanges take place are of two types. The first, corresponding closely to the economic model, are relationships of *restricted exchange* in which the reciprocation marking exchange takes place within a dyad. The second, unrecognized by orthodox economics but subject to a long history of investigation by anthropologists, are relationships of *generalized exchange* in which reciprocation is expected not from within the dyad of giver and receiver but from elsewhere in the social group: A helps B expecting no recompense from B in particular but fully expecting that A will be helped in appropriate circumstances by other members of the group.

The level of support provided by members to each other is supposed to be dependent on the structure of the network of relationships linking group members together. Different features are emphasized by different analysts but possibly the most frequently cited features of social networks are their 'density', or the proportion of all possible links which actually exist, their 'multiplexity', or the diversity of the types of relationship linking given pairs of network members, and their 'closure', or the degree to which identifiable sub-networks are isolated from wider networks. People who are located in networks which are dense, multiplex and closed are hypothesized to provide high levels of support to each other. These network characteristics are precisely the characteristics that a long tradition of research on mining communities would lead one to expect to find in a typical mining village and recent work in the study of mining communities has been based explicitly, in part at least, on these ideas (Bulmer 1975a, 1975b; Gilbert 1992; Warwick and Littlejohn 1992).

Miners' solidarity, or at least the myth of it, can be cast easily into such theoretical frameworks. The social homogeneity of mining communities leads us to expect any solidarity within them to be 'mechanical', to use Durkheim's categorization, and, turning to theories of social exchange, for behaviour within those communities to be marked by 'generalized reciprocities'. And, indeed, there are certainly aspects of, and episodes in, the historical record which are consistent with each of these theoretizations. Perhaps the clearest behaviours consistent with the concept of mechanical solidarity have been the treatments of strike-breakers by striking miners. The history of miners' industrial relations in Britain is replete with instances of the verbal abuse of strike-breakers (and sometimes non-unionists), their ostracization and physical attacks upon them (see, for example, Jevons 1915/1969: 135; Welbourne 1923: 152–3, 217; Holton 1976:

81; MacFarlane 1976a: 79, 82–4; Francis and Smith 1980: 59–69; Macintyre 1980a: 56; Gilbert 1992: 104–5; Beynon and Austrin 1994: 248), and there is no difficulty in interpreting these incidents as 'repressive sanctions resulting from insults to collectively held values' in line with Durkheim's theory of mechanical solidarity. However, as we saw in the first part of this chapter, the limited level of participation in domestic coalmining strikes raises questions about the truthfulness of this picture and suggests that county, regional and national solidarities cannot be explained as simple geographical extensions of established local practices. Accordingly we now turn to a re-examination of the history of such solidarities, starting with the establishment of two of the earliest 'permanent' trade unions in the British industry, the Northumberland Miners' Mutual Confident Association and the Durham Miners' Association.

The immediate progenitor of the permanent unions in the North East was the so-called 'Third Union' of the miners of Northumberland and Durham founded in 1862. A year later 15,000 Durham miners had become members. It was, however, in Durham that the Third Union was destroyed. The occasion was a local strike at Love's collieries beginning in October 1863, shortly after the Durham men were admitted. They received aid from the union which organized a membership levy from those still at work. As the strike continued into January 1864, men subject to heavy and long-lasting levies began to desert the union. Although the miners at Love's collieries gained some concessions, the union collapsed (Welbourne 1923: 115–23).

This experience was formative. The union was re-established in 1864 as the Northumberland Miners' Mutual Confident Association which embarked on a policy of high subscriptions, strike avoidance and the pursuit of recognition from the coalowners (Welbourne 1923: 125–6; Cousins and Davis 1974: 290). A union was not established in Durham until 1869, leading a precarious existence until 1872 when William Crawford became General Secretary (Beynon and Austrin 1994: chapter 3; Webb 1921: 61–2). Crawford's views on the Third Union were publicly known and unequivocal: 'the Willington strike [at Love's collieries] gave union its death blow. Of the 15,000 new members who joined from Durham, 14,000 were at once on strike' (*Durham Chronicle*, 12 February 1864, quoted in Welbourne 1923: 123).

In Durham, too, the union sought to preserve its funds and its existence and also to increase its legitimacy in the eyes of the coalowners by controlling local strike activity. The 1870 rules of the Durham Miners' Association prohibited any colliery from striking without the approval of the Association's central committee or delegate meeting and denied the Association's support to any colliery striking in an 'unconstitutional manner' (Beynon and Austrin 1994: 62–3; Burgess 1975: 181). The rules governing local strike action were even more stringent in Northumberland (Cousins and Davis 1974: 290). The rules on financial support to strikers were the key elements in the new policy, for in practice, of course, neither the Northumberland nor the Durham Association could stop local strikes.

These rules, which institutionalized the practice of solidary behaviour at county level in the North East, were widely adopted throughout the industry. The rules sanctioned the provision of material support by the county union to members on strike or locked out, but the circumstances and extent of that support were defined within strict limits and were rigidly subordinated to the objective of maintaining the survival of the union both financially and as a recognized and legitimate bargaining agent. The rules represented an attempt to control the conflict between local and general interests within the union. In the eyes of its leaders the unbridled pursuit of local interests by sections of the membership, if supported by the union, would prevent the attainment of the general interests of the membership: so, at least the Durham leaders interpreted the experience of the Third Union's demise. Hence, trans-local solidarity was achieved by the *denial* of support to local groups pursuing local interests. This structural conflict is one key to understanding the nature of miners' industrial solidarity at trans-local levels. Because of it, solidary actions at these levels cannot be seen as automatic responses to appeals for aid reflecting shared experiences and shared values, as *Wertrational* or 'sympathetic' (Weber 1922/1968: 24–5). Instead, the desire to improve miners' wages and conditions on the one hand, and the need to maintain the union in existence and its bargaining relationship with the coalowners' association on the other, introduced a conflict of objectives and a degree, at least, of *Zweckrational*, or 'calculatedness', in solidary behaviour.

The formation of the Miners' Federation of Great Britain (MFGB) in 1888–9, which we narrated in chapter 3, was preceded by a long period in which, though the advantages of national organization were clearly perceived, no effective national union or federation of unions was achieved. In the 1870s discussions foundered on issues which county as well as previous national experience had demonstrated to be all too real: 'the majority feared that the weaker districts would drain away the strength of the better organized' (Arnot 1949: 82). The short-lived and geographically limited Amalgamated Association of Miners, formed in 1868, which failed to achieve a national membership, had experienced this process (Church 1986: 686–7). In the 1887 discussions on national union, Thomas Burt, founder of the Northumberland Miners' Mutual Confident Association and president of the ineffectual Miners' National Union since 1881, stated that he had

found that two things were essential in order to carry out any general federation to support strikes and lock-outs, and that was a large amount of central control and a large amount of funds. . . . What they found in their various districts was often this – that those who cried out loudest for federation were those who stood out most strongly for what he might call . . . the principle of Home Rule, and to that principle they would adhere. They found that the districts would not be controlled, that they would not be advised. They would go out on strike opportunely or inopportunely, and then they asked the central body to put on levies to support them after they did come out. That came to an end because it was an irrational principle. (Thomas Burt, address to the 1887 conference of the miners of England, Scotland and Wales at Edinburgh, quoted by Arnot 1949: 84)

The 1889 debates at the founding of the MFGB resulted in rules on the support of strikes which were based on highly 'rational' principles (Arnot 1949: 101–7). Two circumstances were distinguished: the first was where strikes arising out of decisions taken by the MFGB conference arose in some but not all collieries; the second was where constituent federations or districts were attacked on 'the general wages question' or on actions arising out of conference decisions. In the first case support by levy of the membership was envisaged; in the second, covered by 'Rule 20', support by joint strike action. In both circumstances support was not automatic but depended on the approval of a special conference of the MFGB. These rules were amended in 1911 when the possibility of support in the form of joint strike action was extended to cover attacks on the 'conditions of labour' and attempts to secure improvements in wages or conditions. The requirement for prior approval by the MFGB conference remained. The later history of the Federation gave considerable prominence to the rules on 'support' and their provisions became well known (Arnot 1949: 107–8, 1953: 81, 87–9). The circumstances in which support by joint strike action could be mobilized were limited by these rules to those in which the support of the majority of the conference delegates could be secured. Prior to 1911, the Federation effectively ruled out support to those engaged in local or sectional movements for improvements in wages or conditions. Subsequent to 1911, constituent unions seeking improvements had some hope of MFGB support. But in every circumstance and in each period mobilizing support necessitated arguing a case at an MFGB conference.

In practice, mobilizing support involved mobilizing not only the conference delegates but also the membership of the federated unions. Although the final decision on joint strike action lay with the conference, the practice of balloting the membership on such questions grew from a very early date in the history of the Federation. At a conference in October 1889, immediately prior to the founding of the MFGB, it was resolved to press for an eight-hour day through strike action but it was also decided to put this question to a ballot of the membership of the federating unions. The results of this ballot, though revealing enthusiasm for strike action in some areas, were regarded as insufficiently unanimous by the conference delegates to warrant a strike. Membership ballots became normal practice in subsequent years both at county and Federation level. Ballots were organized in Durham over the lock-out of 1892 in that county, at Federation level over the 1893 Lock-out of the federated districts, over the Cambrian Combine strike of 1910–11, and prior to the minimum wage strike of 1912 (Arnot 1949: 213–16, 229, 283, 1953: 57–60, 86). It was at this point that the requirement of a two-thirds majority for strike action was first introduced. The rules of some constituents of the Federation already contained such requirements, prompting a fear of legal repercussions should they join a strike without the support required. The introduction of a similar rule in the affairs of MFGB was at first taken in response to these fears in an *ad hoc* manner in 1911, but after a 1913 membership ballot had shown only a narrow majority in favour of strike action to gain a five-day working week, the twin requirements of a ballot and a two-thirds majority were codified in an MFGB conference resolution.

The MFGB's rules on support clearly replicated the essential features of the practice of the early North East county unions. The MFGB was not an organization designed to provide support for the pursuit of sectional interests; only actions in the pursuit of general interests of the membership or the general values of the membership could win support among the membership and at conference. Just as at the county level in the North East, so too at national level, solidary action should not be seen as an automatic response to an appeal for aid, reflecting shared experiences and values and expressive of mechanical solidarity.

Because the MFGB was a formal, rule-bound association we might expect to be able to interpret it as an expression of Durkheim's 'organic solidarity'. But it seems impossible to interpret the rules or the practices of the MFGB in contractual terms as the theory of organic solidarity would lead us to expect. The rules and practices of the MFGB gave no grounds for a member to expect the automatic support of the Federation even in the pursuit of Federation policy: the MFGB conference had no duty to support MFGB members in any circumstances. Members disappointed by a conference decision not to extend support had neither legal nor moral right of redress against the MFGB since there was no agreement or understanding to provide support that could be interpreted as having been breached. If this was an example of Durkheim's 'organic solidarity', it was an example in which the element of restitutive law was absent. All a dissatisfied constituent union could do was withdraw from the Federation. All a dissatisfied MFGB could do to a recalcitrant member was to expel it from the Federation. The sanction in this form of solidarity was neither retribution nor restitution, but expulsion.

For a long time, the MFGB was something less than a national organization. To summarize a complex history of affiliation, disaffiliation, admission and suspension, continuing differences between the county unions prevented the final entry into the Federation by South Wales until 1899, Northumberland until 1907 and Durham until 1908 (Arnot 1949: 189, 190–203, 216, 228–30, 233, 286–98, 369). These differences are traditionally represented as being largely ideological. The representatives of the old unionism in Northumberland, Durham and South Wales (accommodative, ideologically rather than pragmatically opposed to strike action, politically Liberal or Conservative) were fighting a losing battle with the representatives of the new unionism (combative, uninhibited in the use of strike action, politically 'advanced') in Lancashire, Yorkshire, the Midlands and Scotland (Ness Edwards 1938: chs. 1 and 2; Arnot 1949). However, the differences in ideology correlated with differences of interest which emerged in the two areas of policy which divided the federated from the non-federated districts in the 1889–1908 period: the eight-hour day and the sliding scale.

Despite a resolution during the conferences leading up to the formation of the MFGB to secure an eight-hour day by industrial action, the MFGB's strategy was largely legislative. In 1891 MFGB leaders accused the miners' unions of Northumberland and Durham of forming the major stumbling block on the road to the eight-hour day. This accusation was reinforced in 1892 when Thomas Burt of the Northumberland miners took an active part in the parliamentary opposition to renewed attempts to pass an Eight Hours Bill through the Commons. Although the Northumberland and Durham leaders claimed to be opposed to legislative intervention on principle, few were in doubt that a more powerful reason lay in the existing pattern of shift working in Northumberland and Durham. This combined short hours for the hewers but long hours for other classes of workpeople, rendering the prospect of a uniform eight hours for all unattractive to the hewers who were the most powerful section of the membership (Arnot 1949: 131–90). The opposition of Northumberland and Durham to the eight-hour day never wavered, leaders of both unions continuing to speak out against renewed attempts at legislation well into the Edwardian period. Eventually, however, a bill was passed and the eight-hour day came into effect by law in July 1909 (Arnot 1949: 330–5). Although this was a defeat for Northumberland and Durham, it removed the basis of their differences with the Federation and shortly after the bill was passed both unions had affiliated to the Federation.

The differences, largely with South Wales, over the 'sliding scale', followed a somewhat different course. As we have seen in chapter 3, from its foundation the MFGB opposed sliding scales. This position reflected to some extent the circumstances of the inland districts which formed the majority of the affiliated membership of the MFGB in this period. These districts sold the bulk of their coal on domestic markets which were much more stable than the export markets supplied by the North East, South Wales and, to a lesser extent, Scotland. As such the unionists in the inland coalfields were largely oblivious to the survival risks that would be faced by a union forced to negotiate frequently on a rapidly falling market without a clear framework for reaching an agreement and avoiding potentially disastrous strikes and lock-outs.

MFGB policy enunciated from the chair at the 1892 conference was 'that so long as our organisation exists we shall have nothing to do with sliding scales' (Arnot 1949: 205). The concern to retain, or inability to throw off, the sliding scale therefore kept the South Wales miners outside the Federation until, in 1897, they determined to end the scale, appealing for aid from the MFGB in the lock-out which followed in 1898 (Arnot 1967: 44–5). In return for a substantial weekly grant the MFGB demanded changes in policy designed to aid the formation of a single union organization with a central fund covering the whole of the collieries in South Wales and Monmouthshire. The MFGB also called for a public declaration of intent to abolish the sliding scale. Acceptance of these demands led to the re-foundation of the South Wales Miners' Federation (SWMF) in 1898 and its admission to the MFGB as a partial affiliate in 1899. Even so, a sliding scale was reimposed in South Wales, surviving until 1902 (Ness Edwards 1938: 9–12, 21; Arnot 1967: 49, 67–70, 76–94).

These two episodes indicate that for twenty years differences of policy between the county unions reflecting differences in interests, experience and ideology stood in the way of solidary action at national level, despite the common class position defined by the broadly similar standards of life and working experiences of miners throughout the nation. This much may not be surprising. Of greater interest is the way in which these differences were overcome. In the case of South Wales, the MFGB was able to reinforce its ideological campaign against the sliding scale with an exercise of its financial power in bargaining with a weak union. But by the time of the MFGB's foundation the unions in the North East were among the best-organized and wealthiest unions in the country. The MFGB was comparatively powerless. Joining the MFGB may have helped the North East secure wage advances or avoid wage reductions but would have required giving up their hewers' short hours for which a 10 per cent wage advance had been sacrificed in Durham in 1890 (Arnot 1949: 186). The issue, therefore, could not be resolved by negotiation between the parties. Instead, success in unifying the industry was a consequence of the introduction of a legislated eight-hour day, itself the result of political campaigning.

The processes described above cannot be interpreted easily within existing understandings of the sources of miners' solidarity. Superficially, the common class position of the British coalminers, and the comparability of their standards of life and work experiences, lead us to expect that the solidarity between miners was rooted in these similarities; in short, that miners' solidarity at national as well as local levels was mechanical and marked by strongly developed and shared values (Durkheim's *conscience collective*). But we have seen that serious, fracturing divisions existed, despite the strong commonalities in miners' lives, and that these divisions were overcome, partly, it is true, by ideological campaigning designed to establish and reinforce common values and understandings, but partly also by the exercise of power, financial in the case of South Wales, political in the North East case. This exercise of power was necessitated by conflicts of interests and conflicts of codes.

The history of solidary behaviour at the local or colliery level is much more difficult to analyse. The reason for this is the lack of research on purely local strikes. Crucial data and information, particularly relating to the meanings attached to particular disputes by their participants, are inaccessible, rendering an analysis of local strikes in similar terms to those we have adopted in our analysis of the national and some regional strikes impossible. In many ways historians' neglect of local strikes is understandable. The available sources refer to them only in passing and usually with perfunctoriness, while oral history techniques encounter insurmountable problems in attempting to stimulate memories of events which are all but forgotten even by their participants. Moreover, few indeed of the many thousands of local strikes have had an identifiable impact on matters of general historical concern. More surprisingly, there are few historical studies which examine the union branch or lodge with any thoroughness; certainly nothing that can compare, even allowing for the difficulties of historical research, with the studies of NUM lodges in the 1970s

and 1980s by Christine Edwards (1978) and Rigg (1987). Gilbert's study
(1992) of the contrasting histories of Ynysybwl and Hucknall Torkard ignores
local strike activity; K. Brown's study (1987) of the lodges of the DMA before
1926 has nothing of significance to say about their role, if any, in local strikes;
Baylies's history of the Yorkshire miners in the 1881–1914 period is the one of
the few studies of which we are aware that treats local strikes as significant in
their own right. Along with the studies of a previous generation of historians, her
account of the 1902 'bag-dirt' strike at Denaby Main in South Yorkshire, often
discussed solely in terms of what it demonstrated about the impact of the Taff
Vale decision of 1901, is sufficiently detailed for us to re-examine this strike for
what it can tell us about the nature of miners' solidarity.

Denaby Main took four years to sink, reaching the Barnsley seam in 1867. As
the colliery was sunk, the company added substantially to the original small,
farming settlement of Denaby, which lies about seven miles west of Doncaster.
In the mid-1880s it was said that the company owned virtually the whole of the
village (MacFarlane 1976b: 109, 112–13). It has been described as a classic
company town in which the 'company wielded a paternalistic hand . . . in an
unambiguous attempt to control the workforce as comprehensively as possible'
(Baylies 1993: 302). Houses, schools and the parish church were built by the
company. The schools were for many years run by the company, and so was the
village store until the ownership was transferred, on the initiative of the colliery
manager, to a co-operative society (MacFarlane 1976b: 113). The Miners'
Institute in Denaby was built by the company in commemoration of the corona-
tion of King Edward VII and the company supported 'cricket and football clubs,
ambulance, mining and other educational classes, [a] rifle club, [a] choral
society, brass and orchestral bands and numerous other institutions' (*Mexborough and Swinton Times*, 7 November 1902, quoted by Neville 1976: 147).
The resulting village culture was not uniformly favourable to or compliant with
the company, however. Instead, the village was split between 'company' and
'union' men and the colliery, alongside the neighbouring Cadeby colliery,
gained a reputation for a 'dogged militancy' (MacFarlane 1972: 100; Neville
1976: 147).

The original grievances which led to the strike were over 'excessive' deductions from wages for 'bag dirt' (dirt mixed with the coal) and fines from wages.
The 'bag dirt', or 'bag muck', issue had been a prominent grievance among face
workers for some years and remained without a satisfactory resolution. One
weekend in June 1902 a particularly severe set of deductions from the pay of
some Denaby miners triggered a chain of events which soon led to a strike. A
rapidly organized and well attended mass meeting of miners from the Denaby
and Cadeby collieries resolved that the 'only thing that is left for us to do is to
stop the wheels at both collieries' (*Mexborough and Swinton Times*, 4 July 1902,
quoted by Baylies 1993: 311). Most miners stayed away from work that evening
and the strike appears to have received the support of the great majority of the
employees of the two pits. But a full set of grievances was not specified until the

third day of the stoppage and only at this point was a deputation sent to management. The list of grievances formulated at this time reads like a catalogue of the unresolved disputes from the previous several years. It included the abolition of fines for petty infractions, full implementation of an 1898 agreement on pit lads' wages, a 'fair day's wage' for men employed in difficult places and the fixing of a price list for contractors (Baylies 1993: 311). Little substantive negotiation took place on these issues between the men's representatives and Chambers, the Denaby manager. When the men returned to work in the middle of July in order to tender their notices in accordance with their contracts and thereby render their strike legal, they were presented with new contracts by the Denaby management. The majority refused to sign these and were accordingly not allowed to work. This transformed what had been a strike in breach of contract into a lock-out. The issue was no longer the long list of grievances that had been drawn up at the beginning of the month but the terms of the new contract. The strikers drew up a new price list of their own as a basis for negotiations. The issues in dispute were thus widened from specific grievances affecting particular groups of workers from time to time at the Denaby colliery to the whole gamut of terms and conditions of employment affecting all those paid according to the price list in both Denaby and Cadeby (Baylies 1993: 314–15).

The strikers were initially denied support from the Yorkshire Miners' Association (YMA). The YMA executive committee directed the men to return to work, insisting it could not support a strike in breach of contract, certainly not after the Taff Vale judgment. However, the transformation of the strike into a lock-out also transformed the willingness of the YMA to support the Denaby–Cadeby miners. Strike pay was authorized from the date of the lock-out and the YMA also suggested that other YMA branches should contribute funds to the Denaby–Cadeby miners on a voluntary basis in lieu of the strike pay which had been denied them for the two weeks before this. The strike – and strike pay – continued into 1903 when a legal injunction was granted which threatened to end the YMA's payments. The action had been brought by a YMA member called Howden and was financed by the owners. The appeal by the YMA was rejected, strike pay stopped, and the YMA executive committee recommended a return to work. By the time this advice was finally accepted the lock-out had lasted eight months.

Despite the attempts of the owners to prevent it, the Denaby–Cadeby miners' formal organization, their local branch of the YMA and its central executive committee, succeeded in providing miners with material support almost throughout the lock-out. Informal support was also organized. Large numbers of children were fed breakfast at the Baptist church in Denaby Main. Collections were held at other YMA branches to aid the strikers (Baylies 1993: 318). By far the greatest pressure on local support networks came from the company's decision, implemented on 6 January 1903, to evict strikers living in the company's houses. Accommodation for miners and their families was found in churches, chapels, the Primitive Methodist schoolroom, the urban district council's smallpox hospital, in the homes of friends and relations, and in tents erected in the open fields. A local cleric, the Reverend Jesse Wilson, much involved in organizing the community's support, later wrote: 'These people have a rough and ready way of believing in the immortality of small kindnesses. They believe goodness survives, that evil dies' (Jesse Wilson 1904: 28, quoted by Baylies 1993: 324).

The solidarity evoked by the lock-out was not entirely complete. Some miners continued to work during the strike and later, after the evictions had freed accommodation, the company introduced strike-breakers into Denaby. Attempts to obtain a complete cessation of work at the colliery 'in some cases led to a degree of barracking' (Baylies 1993: 315). At one stage only sixty men were at work at Cadeby and twelve at Denaby (ibid.). Bricks were thrown, while the people who congregated at the pithead who had earlier merely stared in silence, now howled and booed and carried sheep's heads in reference to the local term for the strike-breakers: the 'blacksheep' (Neville 1976: 150). Howden, the 'handle for the Coalowners' Association and the company' in the later legal actions over the strike, claimed to have been 'hooted out' by strikers as he continued to report for work (Baylies 1993: 319). He ceased to do so in late August shortly before the company closed down the pits completely and indefinitely. By mid-December, the company was trying to work the Denaby pit again. Women led a pithead protest against the strike-breakers, local and strangers alike, in which one woman shouted to the scabs: 'You ought to be ashamed to show your dirty faces' (Baylies 1993: 320). Police protection for the 'strangers' 'did not prevent women and children throwing stones, or whatever else they could find, at the strike-breakers' (Baylies 1993: 324). Although incomplete, the solidarity shown by the Denaby and Cadeby community was powerful and impressive and the courage shown in the face of hardship, moving. Nevertheless, as Neville bluntly points out, the miners were defeated and the principal reason for their defeat was the cancellation of the union's strike pay brought about by Howden and his sponsors (1976: 152–3). Community was no substitute for organization.

Beyond this point the main interest of the 'bag muck' strike lies in two texts which emerged from the conflict. One is the Reverend Jesse Wilson's comment on the local belief in the 'immortality of small kindnesses'; the other is the abuse shouted at scabs by the anonymous woman at the pithead demonstration of December 1902. Wilson's comment is a succinct description, in theological terms, of what is meant by 'generalized reciprocity'. The woman's abuse is perhaps less obviously interpreted. The reference to 'dirty faces' is ambiguous: the women were confronting men coming off their shift and the abuse might have meant only 'You ought to be ashamed to show you have been working (by showing faces covered with the grime of the pit)'. However, dirt also has connotations of defilement and dishonour. The reference to shame is much less ambiguous. Shame may be defined as an emotion brought about by a transgression of a code of behaviour or values to which the transgressor is him or herself committed. The abuse assumed a set of commonly held values and was hurled because these were being transgressed. The anonymous woman, one of a crowd, without distinction, was administering a repressive punishment to those who had insulted the local *conscience collective* exactly in line with Durkheim's model of mechanical solidarity. Here, at local level, we find clear evidence of social solidarity as generalized reciprocity operating in a context of mechanical solidarity.

The episodes in the history of the unions of the North East and of the MFGB we recounted earlier in this chapter reveal the complexity of solidary behaviour at county and national level. However, one key feature stands out: the control of action. Solidary action by the unions of the North East and the MFGB was controlled by rule, by membership ballot and by council or conference decision: each functioned to limit solidary action not to encourage it. The paradox that organizations which by their existence were expressive of solidarity should seek to limit solidary action is only apparent. The formative experiences of those most prominent in their foundation had been of organizations which by failing to control solidary action had been destroyed. Destruction came from defeat in major strikes or lock-outs which sapped the union's funds and left the union deserted by its membership. Avoiding destruction meant avoiding defeat, and to strike on an issue where the membership was divided by interest or value was to court defeat. Hence the membership ballots seen in the episodes recounted above. Hence also the very high participation rates that have marked the national strikes and lock-outs since their beginning until 1984–5 and hence also, their rarity.

The final federation of all the major miners' unions in 1908 was soon followed by a sequence of events which, originating in purely local disputes, eventually culminated in the first national coalminers' strike in 1912. The processes through which this was achieved are of special interest since the problems faced in securing united action in 1912 were potentially more difficult than any faced by British miners' unions before the strike of 1984–85. For this reason the episode receives detailed examination in chapter 7.

7　Strikes, organization and consciousness in 1912 and after

The solidaristic basis of the first national coal strike

The origins of the first national miners' strike can be traced back to 1908. In that year a legal ruling established that miners paid on piece-rates, as most face workers were, had no legal rights to the customary payments received for working in abnormal conditions or in recompense for other difficulties encountered in reaching normal earnings, unless these were expressly provided for in piece-rate price lists. The case, which concerned a collier employed at the Lady Windsor colliery of the Ocean Coal Company in South Wales, had been supported by the South Wales Miners' Federation (SWMF), and its loss appeared to open the way for a general attack by the coalowners on the payment of allowances. The issue was one of particular concern in South Wales because the geological conditions in the coalfield made the issue more salient than in some other districts (Ness Edwards 1938: 51–2; Arnot 1953: 68; Gilbert 1992: ch. 4).

However, the response to the ruling from the SWMF developed only slowly. Eventually, in 1909, the SWMF annual conference instructed its leaders to 'take steps' through the established collective bargaining machinery in South Wales to secure a minimum fall-back wage of 4s 9d per day for colliers working in abnormal places (Ness Edwards 1938: 52). This proposal was duly included as part of a package of measures tabled for inclusion in a new agreement with the coalowners set for negotiation in 1910 at the termination of the then existing agreement. For their part, the owners tabled amendments to the conciliation board agreement which would have led to cuts in earnings, in effect frustrating negotiations. The initial steps towards a coalfield strike to begin in March were put in motion (Ness Edwards 1938: 26–7). The SWMF executive committee reported the situation to a special conference of the Miners' Federation of Great Britain (MFGB), which sent three members of its executive committee to South Wales to 'assist' the negotiations. However, this largely symbolic act of support did nothing to bring the South Wales owners closer to agreement (Ness Edwards 1938: 27; Arnot 1967: 157).

The SWMF delegate conference, meeting towards the end of March, resolved to call for stronger support from the MFGB, appealing specifically for joint strike action under rule 20, the rule designed to prevent a piece-meal attack on wages. Understandably, the MFGB executive was unimpressed, as was the special MFGB conference called to discuss the SWMF proposal (Arnot 1967: 159–61). Solidary action was clearly not available simply for the asking, as one might have expected from Durkheim's model of mechanical solidarity. In the face of these rebuffs, the SWMF executive's recommendation of agreement to the owners' terms was accepted by a large majority in a ballot vote. The terms did not include provision for an individual minimum wage (Ness Edwards 1938: 27–9; Arnot 1967: 161–2).

Until this point, the efforts of the South Wales miners to secure MFGB support had been an appeal for aid in their own struggle, repeating, in this respect, the history of the 1898 lock-out (chapter 6). Now that the SWMF was firmly inside the MFGB, however, the basis for a transaction similar to that seen in 1898 no longer existed. Instead, the South Wales miners' leaders now set about making their struggle the MFGB's struggle. The first step was taken almost immediately, at the SWMF's annual conference in May 1910. There it was decided to ask the MFGB to 'demand a fair living wage to be paid to all colliers working in abnormal places, failing to get which, that a National Conference be called with the view of further dealing with the matter' (Ness Edwards 1938: 53). To this the October 1910 annual MFGB conference agreed (Arnot 1967: 241, 274). The consent of the conference may well have been prompted by the start of the big, long, bitter and well-publicized strike over the minimum wage issue at the Cambrian Combine collieries. Although initially only affecting a single section of a single colliery in the Combine, by the time of the 1910 MFGB annual conference the entire Combine work-force of 12,000 miners were preparing to strike, strengthened by a ballot of the coalfield which had agreed a weekly levy for their support (Ness Edwards 1938: 36; Arnot 1967: chs. 7–8).

The limited progress of negotiations to secure a 'fair living wage' by the constituent unions was reported to an MFGB special conference in June 1911 when militant SWMF resolutions to the conference were ruled out of order and the issue postponed (Arnot 1953: 77–8, 1967: 263–4). Apparently stung into action by their disappointments at this conference, the SWMF embarked on a publicity campaign, sending speakers all over the coalfields to press the SWMF's case (Ness Edwards 1938: 54; Arnot 1967: 262). By the time of the adjourned conference in July 1911, Lancashire and Yorkshire had been converted to the SWMF position and urged an immediate strike ballot. Other districts were still not ready to move, however, and it was decided only to change negotiating tactics, by abandoning district-level negotiations and seeking a joint meeting between the MFGB and representatives of all the owners. The owners proved willing to meet the MFGB but insisted that the issue was one for district, rather than national, negotiation (Arnot 1953: 78–9, 1967: 264). After further hesitations and further fruitless attempts to open national negotiations the MFGB conference finally, in December 1911, resolved to ballot the membership on strike action. The ballot resulted in a four to one majority in favour and the first national miners' strike began on 26 February 1912 (Board of Trade, *Report on Strikes and Lock-outs in 1912*, xxi–xxx; Arnot 1953: 80–6, 90–1, 1967: 274–5).

The strike lasted for seven weeks. The government intervened, passing an Act of Parliament at the end of March to put the principle of the minimum wage in the mines on a statutory footing. But the Act stipulated no figure for the minimum and the MFGB conference declared it unacceptable. A ballot of the membership taken subsequent to the Act revealed only a narrow majority for continuing the strike, however, and the conference voted to advise a resumption of work, South Wales voting with the majority, Lancashire and Yorkshire with the minority (Arnot 1953: 85–110).

In the episodes discussed above the appropriate economic analogy would appear to be not with *exchange,* in which support is given at a present cost in the expectation of receiving from others a future benefit, but with *production,* in which a group undertakes to co-operate in a joint project in which all accept present costs in order to achieve future benefits. For the most part, the forms of solidarity exemplified by the history of the MFGB involved not the *transfer* of resources but the *pooling* of resources. If solidarity is to be produced in this way, those proposing it must demonstrate that benefits will or may flow and will or may flow to all concerned in it. With the exception of South Wales in 1898 and, until the error was realized, in 1910, those seeking support of the MFGB did not argue explicitly, nor could they be understood to be saying implicitly, 'Support us now in this our struggle and we shall support you later in your struggle'; rather they argued 'Support us now in this our struggle because it is your struggle too'. Those districts which, in the early years of the MFGB, refused participation were punished, if punishment it was, by exclusion from the collectivity, not by retributive or restitutive measures.

Social exchange theory is useful in this context not in itself but because it provokes the formulation of an antithesis: that social solidarity is to be understood here as social production or *construction,* not as a set of social exchanges. Constructed social solidarity is generated by the purposive action of individuals who co-operate in activities designed to further the interests or values of group members. It involves not transfers of resources from givers to receivers but a pooling of the resources of the group's members. The construction of solidarity may be aided by the use of social capital, an established set of organizations, institutions, relationships, activities and values. The construction of social solidarity takes time, just as does the production of commodities. Individuals or sub-groups refusing to co-operate are punished not by the imposition of retributive or restitutive sanctions but by expulsion and exclusion.

These, we suggest, are general characteristics of constructed solidary behaviour. The particular history with which we are concerned here shows additional features. Perhaps the most interesting is the control and restriction of solidary actions arising from the desire to maintain and preserve the social capital with which solidary behaviour has been constructed in the British mining industry at county and national level. The social capital concerned has been the organizational structures and material resources of the county unions and their national federation. Hence the restricted support given to local strikers by the county unions of the North East which we saw in the last chapter; hence the elaborate apparatus of rule, membership ballot and conference decision established by the MFGB in its early years. The major 'work' involved in constructing solidarity was the transformation of sectional issues into general issues. The clearest instance of this in the history of the MFGB occurred in the genesis of the 1912 strike. What had started as a dispute involving a single collier in the Lady Windsor Colliery was widened by a legal ruling to one affecting the interests of an entire region. By transforming the issue into one affecting all miners (the individual minimum wage) the regional union succeeded in constructing through its own organization and that of the MFGB much more: solidary behaviour across the entire industry.

At local level, we have much less evidence on which to base an understanding. The 'bag muck' strike, which we examined in chapter 6, demonstrated the existence of solidary behaviour in the locality which conformed closely to Durkheim's model of mechanical solidarity and in which behaviour consistent with practices of generalized reciprocity was discernible. But the strike also demonstrated a number of features now familiar from the history of trans-local solidarity: the concertation of interests, there inadvertently assisted by the company's lock-out, and the importance of formal organizations, especially the YMA, capable of channelling material support towards the strikers. So far, our history suggests that while solidary behaviour at the local level can be understood largely in terms of traditional ideas of communal solidarity emerging out of the dense network of social relationships tying together the members of a socially homogeneous community, solidary behaviours at the county and national levels are different phenomena which are more readily understood by applying to them the new concept of constructed social solidarity.

The concept enables us to suggest why solidary behaviour among miners has sometimes not emerged as well as why substantial levels of solidarity have sometimes occurred. The successful creation of solidarity requires first, appropriate social capital; second, time for its construction; and third, a concertation of interests where this does not already exist, typically by the transformation of an issue affecting one section to one affecting all sections. Given these conditions it become possible to envisage several reasons why grievances affecting a small group of miners may fail to gain support, a frequent occurrence at colliery level (chapter 6). One possible reason is that appropriate social capital may not exist, possibly as a result of managerial actions taken to frustrate trade union organization. The issue may 'die' before there has been sufficient time to create solidary behaviour. Sectional interests may prove incapable of transformation into general interests, perhaps because the interests of one section are directly opposed to those of others, as were those of the North East hewers and of other classes of workpeople before the passage of the Eight Hours Act. Sections may choose not to use the available social capital to generate solidarity, possibly because the section does not wish to lose control of the dispute to the wider membership, or possibly because the section's members calculate that they are more likely to be successful in pursuit of concessions if such concessions are demanded for the benefit of the section alone. This is not an exhaustive list, but sufficient to signal that if we use the concept of constructed social solidarity the enormous variations in strike participation rates at local level cease to be such a puzzle. If, on the other hand, we continue to utilize theories of mechanical solidarity or generalized reciprocity to comprehend miners' solidarity we cannot begin to interpret the co-existence of sectional strikes, unsupported by the great majority of colliery work-forces, and the impressive displays of unity and solidary behaviour frequently seen in the major national strikes and lock-outs of the twentieth century.

Ideas consonant with those that we have expressed here have been put forward by a number of researchers. Beynon and Austrin's account of Durham mining communities has stressed, as we have, that 'solidarity had to be *built*' (1994: 364, original emphasis) and has argued that the solidarity shown by mining villages was created out of social relations which may have been originally neither trusting nor 'brotherly' but conflictual. In this process Beynon and Austrin emphasized the role of organization, specifically the Primitive Methodist chapels and the trade union, in establishing a new moral code and extending a new social discipline throughout the county.

Our concept of constructed solidarity is easily related to Warwick and Littlejohn's concept of 'local cultural capital' which they created to aid the understanding of modern mining communities. They defined this in the following terms:

The local culture is the outcome of the sharing of knowledge about the place, its history as a mining locality and the social networks and institutions which have developed. Further it is the sharing of skills, particularly those of communication which help to maintain, confer and renew identities and membership among them. Finally, it is the set of dominant values which characterise relationships and activities in the locality.
. . .
[I]t is possible to sense that the dominant local culture is held as a kind of capital which is transmitted and sometimes modified from generation to generation. It then forms benchmarks around which individuals and households can trace their identity and interests.
. . .
It would seem possible too that in each generation there are key people who become significant reproducers of this local cultural capital, who define its limits and to some extent create modifications. (1992: 84–5)

However, our concept of 'social capital' is broader than this; it includes institutions and organizations themselves as well as knowledge about them and the skills required to create, maintain and modify them. Moreover, our concept is not confined to the locality; indeed the most prominent and impressive examples of social capital are remarkable precisely because they transcend the limitations of face-to-face interaction within the locality and extend to interactions between office holders and others who may be strangers to each other, who may reside in localities widely separated in space and may be divergent in culture.

In some respects our concept of the construction of solidarity through the use of social capital resembles Tilly's 'resource mobilization' theory of social movements and social change. Tilly has studied 'popular collective action' in a wide variety of manifestations and a variety of nation states (notably France, USA and Britain) but usually in the eighteenth and nineteenth centuries. The popular collective actions in which he is interested are those that are in some way 'contentious' of the existing distribution of power: he is interested in riots, not sporting events. He evolved a series of key concepts with which to analyse such actions. For Tilly, a formal analysis of popular collective actions

would consist of mapping the interests of the participants, estimating the current state of opportunity and threat with respect to those interests, checking their mobilization levels, gauging their power positions, then seeing to what extent these variables account for the intensity and character of their collective action. One step back from that formalization we would find ourselves examining the prevailing system of repression and facilitation, the impact of the various groups' organization on their mobilization and on their interests, the effect of coalitions with other contenders on their current power positions, and so on. (Tilly 1978: 227)

Tilly's analysis is clearly designed to encompass a wider range of social action than we are concerned with here, and his conceptual armoury is correspondingly both more abstract and more complex. Tilly uses these concepts and propositions to consider a number of questions about long-run changes in popular collective action. But each of these applications is a mere sketch and Tilly's treatment is limited to producing a programme rather than a performance. In Tilly's major work, *Popular Contention in Great Britain 1758–1834*, the concept of a 'repertoire' of actions remains at the fore of his writing (see, for example, 1995: 281–3) but the concept of 'resource mobilization', despite Tilly's claim to 'accent' it (1995: 36), turns out to have been all but retired: the word is used simply as a denotation.

Tilly has remarked that the 'hard part' (1978: 228) of understanding history is applying a conceptual schema to the historical record. But the 'hard part' also helps to refine and elaborate the concepts and advance understanding. Tilly's concepts, approach and propositions have important similarities to our own but are too skeletal to give us much insight into our subject matter; our research has led us to a more specialized but also complex set of concepts. At the local level, we have found the concepts of mechanical solidarity and generalized reciprocity useful. Lurking in the shadows, rarely in plain view, we find hints of dense and multiplex social networks. Also at the local level, but much more obviously at the trans-local level, formal, rule-bound associations (trade unions) played a large part in strike activity. These associations may be seen not merely as pools of resources, knowledge and skills but as purposefully created structures, blocks of social capital, which aid the construction of solidarity. The 'mobilization' which created these organizations was in itself a complex process, involving a long period of trial, error, learning, negotiation, and the orchestration of disparate interests into a united association. The organizational forms which eventually arose regulated solidary behaviour according to practices which became established almost to the point of habituation: observance of rule, debate in a conference of representatives, conference vote and membership ballot.

'Everybody out': the national lock-outs of 1921 and 1926

During and after the First World War state control of the industry acted as a powerful force for solidarity among the county unions in the MFGB. The state's treatment of the industry as a national entity, described briefly in chapter 3, served to consolidate the interests of the once disparate regions and helped to generate the national solidarity which culminated in the 1926 Lock-out. These instances are remarkable, therefore, not for what they tell us about the concertation of interests but in other ways which allow us to enrich our understanding of solidary behaviour. First, the collapse of solidarity in 1926 in the face of the owners' and government's divisive strategy reminds us that solidarity is constructed for the purposes of pursuing conflicts and that the actions of opponents may have decisive effects on the levels of solidarity achieved. Second, the well-documented local conduct of the lock-outs of 1921 and 1926 enables us to examine the forms and mechanisms of solidarity seen at local level.

Gilbert's work on the 1921 and 1926 lock-outs in Ynysybwl in South Wales recounts a history which would seem representative of much of that region. Both lock-outs in Ynysybwl were fought with the aid of rapidly established local organizations, which in 1921 included committees of the miners' lodge charged with communications, publicity, organization, relief and picketing. The lodge served as a focus of community pressure: it organized deputations to the colliery management; it urged the local authority director of education to feed children and local teachers to keep a 'vigilant eye' upon them (Gilbert 1992: 133). The miners' distress fund was initiated by the lodge and a communal kitchen was set up at the Miners' Institute; a village distress fund was also established which incorporated the few members of the local middle class: shopkeepers, teachers and the local doctor who chaired the first few meetings. In 1926, a similar repertoire of organizational activity was performed by the local miners' lodges with the participation of the local branch of the National Union of Railwaymen during the General Strike itself. This time relief monies were issued in the form of vouchers, redeemable 'for all necessities except intoxicants' at the local shopkeepers' premises (Lady Windsor Lodge, *Minutes*, 4 June 1926, quoted by Gilbert 1992: 135). Local churchmen were in prominent roles on the relief committee. The committee solicited contributions from those of the local community who could afford a donation: 'the few who remained employed in

Ynysybwl proved very generous under collective pressure, as did those miners and mining families better placed to survive the hardship. In all, the committee collected an astounding total of £2,204 from the local population during the nine-month strike' (1992: 136).

This history of organizational creativity and collective pressure appears to have been not unusual in South Wales (Francis and Smith 1980: ch. 2) but in some other parts of the country the level of organizational creativity in 1921 and 1926 appears to have been considerably less. In some parts of Nottinghamshire funds were established to feed strikers and their families and a soup kitchen was opened in Mansfield Woodhouse but the general scene was one of 'quietude and considerable apathy' (Gilbert 1992: 187). In this area many strikers appear to have concentrated on private pursuits such as gardening or public pursuits not associated with the Lock-out: 'in the Hucknall and Annesley district there was hardly a church or a chapel which had not been redecorated by voluntary labour during the lockout' (Alan R. Griffin 1962: 96). Garside, too, remarks on the beneficial effect which the 1921 Lock-out had on horticulture in Durham and the efflorescence of sporting activity seen there. But in Durham the local lodges seemed to have run with the local enthusiasms, not against them, and organized concerts and sports matches as fund-raising events (Garside 1971: 148; Beynon and Austrin 1994: 239). Nevertheless, as so often, the regional variations in miners' behaviour are notable.

From July 1926 onwards the Ynysybwl lodge committee was more and more concerned with picketing and other measures to prevent individuals returning to work. A mass meeting was held in a neighbouring village after some had started work at the next colliery up the valley. The lodge was able to identify men who had restarted work through the networks of village society and 'waited upon' a number of those. One who 'declined to give an assurance not to continue working' was shortly after waylaid and assaulted; the lodge encouraged not only its members but also local traders to ostracize all who returned to work before the end of the Lock-out. In an act of ritual humiliation, 'The names of these faint-hearted heroes . . . [were] duly enshrined in the records of the Lodge' (John E. Morgan 1956: 29, quoted by Gilbert 1992: 139).

Personal reminiscences of the 1921 and 1926 lock-outs, especially of the latter, emphasize the extent of unorganized activity. Bill Carr, a miner from Millfield, near Newcastle, recalled the attempts made to deprive a local steel works of coal and incidentally redirect it to miners' benefit during the 1926 Lock-out. Picketing had failed and the works were guarded by special con-stables.

Night after night, raids on coal-stocks took place within 100 yards of where the specials were stationed. Coal wagons were raided on their way to the yard; many arrived empty, the drop floor of the wagon expertly released. Some of the men were caught and fined, but most were not. This was entirely unorganised. (Carr 1976: 346)

In Mapperley, near Derby,

One . . . woman's mother organised a local soup kitchen. 'She and grandmother used to light the old brick copper in the big kitchen, and made coppers full of pea-soup. She also made jam pasties, and boiled great big iron saucepans of potatoes. At dinner times there used to be a queue of miners' children with jugs . . . my mother used to do this for free.' ('Mrs M. B.', letter to Peter Wyncoll, quoted in Wyncoll 1976: 184)

This was not an isolated instance; the son of a safety official at Silverdale colliery near Hanley in North Staffordshire, remembering the 1921 Lock-out, wrote:

My father's odd day of safety duty saved me from the depths of starvation. . . . But, regular meals as such had ceased. When once I complained, my mother turned and gave me a stern look and addressed me with sterner words, 'Hast forgotten that we are *all* fighting this together? Because thy father does an odd day's work does not mean that his bit of money is used *only* for this hearth. Hast forgotten those empty bellies in Earl Street? Think of them with nothing coming into the house next time thou feelst like complaining.' There were plenty of empty bellies in Silverdale at this time. My mother sent me with a large jug of hot soup each day to a very poor family in Earl Street, a family where there was no father; this was only one case where my mother's compassion was too strong for her. The womenfolk were wonderful, their sacrifice too varied to be enumerated; Christian spirit carried out to the last letter. (Harold Brown 1981: 100–1)

Similarly, the treatment of strike-breakers was often meted out by individuals and small groups of miners and their families in an unorganized way. Bill Carr remembered the first strike-breaker in his village, escorted by what seemed an army of special constables.

The younger element, having agreed that he should not enjoy any of the spoils of his treachery, decided to extract the concessionary coal delivered to him. This was done in the middle of the night by the simple act of taking his coal-house door off its hinges, and removing the coal in bags. The cat-calls as he returned from his daily work must have made his life wretched. (1976: 347–8)

The history of solidary action at local level during the 1921 and 1926 lock-outs presents a mixed picture. On the one hand the activities of the miners' lodge at Ynysybwl present a cameo illustrative of Warwick and Littlejohn's concept of local cultural capital, where key individuals operated and modified local organizations and made creative use of their relationships with friends, comrades, relations and other contacts in the local social network to pursue their conflict with the coalowners. In this way local miners' leaders were able to generate solidary activities involving many hundreds of people: mass meetings, demonstrations and pickets. Such activities conform to the concept of solidarity as a constructed activity based on a pooling, rather than an exchange of resources. But much local solidary behaviour was unorganized and this, and some organized activity, corresponded closely to Durkheim's concept of mechanical solidarity and to later conceptions of solidarity as a generalized reciprocity. The verbal assaults, ostracization and personal violence offered to strike-breakers are clear examples of punishments, 'administered in a diffuse way by everybody without distinction' to those who outraged collectively held values. The resource sharing, sometimes organized through lodge committees and sometimes resulting from purely individual initiative as recounted in the reminiscences of Bill Carr, 'Mrs B.' and Harold Brown are clear examples of generalized reciprocity which could only take place within the social networks characteristic of many mining villages. The history of the 1921 and 1926 lock-outs suggests therefore that the history of miners' solidarity is complex: at national and regional levels solidarity was constructed but so, too, were some solidary behaviours at local level. Moreover these activities took place on a foundation of local-level mechanical solidarity and generalized reciprocity. Major instances of this are described in the next section, followed by a review of that and previous evidence and conclusions to be drawn therefrom.

Local exemplifications: the Ammanford anthracite strike of 1925 and the Harworth strike of 1936–7

So far we have emphasized the differences between nationally constructed solidarity and locally based solidarity. We suggested that the latter could be understood largely in terms of traditional ideas of communal solidarity but that the latter was a different phenomenon which we tried to understand in terms of the concept of constructed solidarity. However, in our examination of local activities during the national lock-outs of 1921 and 1926 we found elements of both types of solidarity. This raises the question of whether it is possible or sensible to make a rigid distinction between the forms of solidarity observed in the local and national arenas. The first of the case studies, of the strike in the anthracite district of South Wales in 1925, suggests that such a distinction is valid – indeed necessary. From the detailed studies of the strike it is possible to discern a real break between local solidarity, dependent on the mobilization of local social capital and 'repressive law' to preserve its values and discipline recalcitrants, and trans-local solidarity based on the concertation of interests and the mobilization of organizational resources in arenas in which there is no sanction to wield except exclusion.

The relatively buoyant market for anthracite during the 1920s underwrote exceptionally favourable conditions in the South Wales anthracite district. In the estimate of one local union leader the anthracite miners had 'good conditions, good price lists and allowances and general customs' and a high degree of job control exercised by the lodge committee (Ianto Evans, *Daily Worker*, 17 June 1932, quoted by Francis 1973: 16). The immediate background to the 1925 strike was a rapid centralization of local colliery ownership during the early 1920s. The two combines, Amalgamated Anthracite (AA), sometimes known as 'the Mond group' after the chairman of the company, and United Anthracite (UA), dominated the district after their formations in 1923 and 1924. These were not merely changes in ownership. The combines were intent on rationalizing production methods and at the Ammanford No. 1 Colliery, where the 1925 anthracite strike started, UA immediately put in a new manager to achieve this.

A combine committee of the union lodges was formed within six months of the UA amalgamation, securing official recognition under the relevant rule of the South Wales Miners' Federation (Francis 1973: 16–17; Arnot 1975: 265–7; Francis and Smith 1980: 87).

There is disagreement and some inconsistency in the accounts of what the original strike issues actually were, Francis referring to the sacking of a man named Wilson in a dispute about the allocation of working places, Arnot to the dismissal of more than a hundred workers a month later in breach of a seniority rule (Francis 1973: 17; Arnot 1975: 265–7). But both Francis and Arnot refer to the dispute as a victimization dispute, since in each interpretation the issue involved management's rights to dismiss workers as they saw fit. However, what 'the' issue was does not lie in the nature of the case but in how the events leading up to the strike were defined socially. The management is likely to have seen the dispute over Wilson as one involving 'the' issue of an employee's obedience to lawful instructions from management; the lodge saw the dispute as over 'the' issue of protecting custom and practice and resisting all possible precedents for victimization; rank and file miners may have perceived 'the' issue entirely differently from either constituency.

Initial attempts by the Ammanford lodge to broaden the definition of the strike issue were highly ambitious. A mass meeting was held at Ammanford Park on 25 May 1925, when a resolution was passed protesting 'against the action of the Mine Owners in placing pressure upon the Workers and attempting to again reduce their standard of living, and call[ing] upon the Trades Union Congress General Council to press for unity of all classes of workers internationally' (Arnot 1975: 268). This conjunction of a presentation of the issue in very broad terms and an extremely broad appeal for solidarity from the international working class was not coincidental. But the appeal was clearly over-ambitious and nothing more was heard of it. Instead, local miners' leaders stressed the seniority rule and protection against victimization. The preservation of existing wages and conditions in the final settlement, after the owners had proposed sending the seniority rule to arbitration, allowed it to be hailed as a victory by the miners and by later commentators (Ness Edwards 1938: 137; Francis 1973: 21).

The leaders of the 1925 anthracite strike therefore fought on very limited terrain. They made no attempt to broaden the issues out beyond the restoration of local lodge customs and practices; there was no demand for joint control over employment, no demand for a closed shop or for enhanced union facilities. Support, therefore, could only be expected from other collieries with similar customs expecting similar threats, in other words from elsewhere in the AA and UA combines; solidarity from the steam coal areas of the field, let alone the 'international working class' was not likely to occur. It is little wonder that, despite the majority vote of the anthracite district for the strike, anthracite miners in the Dulais Valley employed not by the AA or UA combines but by Evan Evans Bevan, an independent concern, did not join the strike voluntarily but had to be picketed out by a large force of strikers. The limited relevance of the struggle may also explain the less than staunch support given to the strikers by the SWMF. When a deputation from the Ammanford combine committee addressed the executive council of the SWMF in August their reception was such that they were forced to reconsider previously rejected proposals from the owners. Issues of district autonomy may also have been a factor here. In early August the anthracite district meeting had resolved 'that the executive council of the South Wales Miners be consulted, but that the District Meeting control the dispute'; in mid-August the executive council rode roughshod over such niceties and resolved to 'take over the District with power to settle' (Arnot 1975: 273). In achieving the level of support that was achieved the strike leaders were undoubtedly aided by the existence of the AA and UA combines and the aggressive policies which they appeared to be following. On the basis of an interview with an Abercraf miner in 1969, Francis observed that 'it was widely believed that an attack on the Seniority Rule in Ammanford could quite easily lead to a similar attack in all other parts of the Anthracite Coalfield', and this is one part of the explanation of why five local pits struck in sympathy with Ammanford (Francis 1973: 18). But the detailed history of the strike indicates that the local communities and local organization were also of major importance in the construction of the solidarity seen in this strike.

The first step in generating a response to the crisis at Ammanford No. 1 was to ensure the solidarity of the Ammanford miners themselves, the mass meeting in Ammanford Park at the end of May forming part of this process. Resolutions were passed in support of the Ammanford strikers at successively higher levels of the union hierarchy: lodge, district agent and the UA combine committee, and the SWMF executive council. A ballot vote of the anthracite district on a district-wide strike, that is, a declaration of mandates set by lodge meetings, was announced on 11 July. The results were 9,918 for and 5,795 against with 1,399 not represented; of those represented, 63 per cent favoured strike action. At this meeting delegates representing 2,006 or another 13 per cent of those represented agreed to 'fall in with the majority'. A district-wide strike of the anthracite miners accordingly began on 13 July 1925; according to the Ministry of Labour it involved 20,000 miners (Ministry of Labour, *Trade Disputes: . . . Strikes and Lock-outs of 1925*, PRO LAB 34/43; Arnot 1975: 269).

The strike was remarkable for a series of demonstrations, marches, disturbances and riots which brought national attention to the strike and has ensured the continuing interest of historians. The major object of each of these actions was to make the strike 'solid' by stopping the few working pits and preventing the few miners who had continued working from doing so. Early in the strike, at Cwmamman on 14 July, a mass meeting took place at which news arrived from a 'contact' that some collieries in the Neath Valley were still working and, following a lead from the platform, a decision was made to march that night to picket those going to work the following morning. It was then about six o'clock in the evening and 'a rush was made to Ammanford to get a crowd together, as no prior arrangements had been made' (Ianto Evans, *Daily Worker*, 17 June 1932, quoted by Francis 1973: 18). Led by the village band, the march started at Ammanford at 10.40 pm and picked up further contingents, each headed by their own bands, as it moved up the Amman Valley and over the moors into the Swansea Valley and then to Crynant in the Dulais Valley. At this stage between 15,000 or 20,000 people, in the estimate of one observer, had joined the march. When the marchers confronted miners coming off trains from Neath on their way to work, 'the foreigners' (as the men from Neath were thought to be) drew knives and a skirmish ensued. None the less, the Ammanford picket stopped all the Dulais Valley pits. Two days later a demonstration at the remaining mine at work, Rock Colliery at the head of the Vale of Neath, succeeded in persuading the workers there to join the strike too. It was here that the first major disturbance took place. A short riot occurred after police made a baton charge against the 700 strikers who formed the picket (Francis 1973: 18–19; Arnot 1975: 270–1).

Lodge delegates now voted for the withdrawal of safety men from the collieries; the majority had themselves already decided to come out. The attempt to get out the remainder and to make strike-breaking 'volunteers' join the strike led to further riots and disturbances. On 28 July there were disturbances at five collieries; gun shots were fired at one and explosives discharged at two. There were six separate disturbances on 30 July. The disorder culminated in the 'Battle of Ammanford' on 5 August. It was claimed that an electrician had gone into Ammanford No. 2 Colliery and a crowd demanded that the electrician cease work. Soon the crowd and the police were locked in a riot which lasted most of the night; notably, police reinforcements were ambushed on the way to the scene after being spotted by a motorcyclist delegated to monitor police activities. This was not the first time that the strikers had made effective use of information about police activities: the strikers had 'unusual friends' on the inside (Francis 1973: 19–20; Arnot 1975: 271).

This narrative of the anthracite strike of 1925 acquires greater meaning when it is placed in the context of the 'local social capital' approach to understanding solidaristic behaviour. Francis has claimed that Ammanford was 'still very much a frontier town in the 1920s' (1973: 16). Despite this, strike leaders showed great skill in mobilizing the area's resources. They had 'contacts' to tell them whether collieries two valleys away were on strike or at work; they heard rapidly if anyone so much as an electrician went to work during the strike; they had 'unusual friends' in Ammanford police station; they were able to mobilize mass meetings; they could organize a twenty-mile over-night march from Ammanford to Crynant in a matter of hours and persuade 15,000 to 20,000 to join in. None of this would have been possible unless the strike leaders were deeply enmeshed in a dense network of local social contacts.

An attempt to construct solidarity by a *local* orchestration of interests is also evident, achieved partly by impressing on people a particular interpretation of the original issues. The initial attempt to portray UA's actions as an attack on the standard of living of 'the Workers' was soon dropped, but the focus on the seniority rule which succeeded this was consistently maintained thereafter. The attack on the seniority rule at Ammanford was presented by the local leaderships not as an attack on job security or on individual's acquired job rights but as an attack on the union itself resulting from the actions of the new combines and thus of relevance to all lodge members. The then recent and partly successful attempts to form a monopoly in the South Welsh anthracite district by AA and UA no doubt helped to produce an understanding of common interests throughout the area. But the concertation of interests was only local in scope. While the interpretation of the strike as a seniority or victimization dispute would have helped persuade those employed in the combines to participate in the strike, it simultaneously proclaimed the irrelevance of the strike to the material interests of those outside the AA and UA combines. Despite this, a number of anthracite miners or their representatives did decide to 'fall in with the majority' as happened when the results of the strike vote were declared and as happened in the Dulais Valley where, once miners had been picketed out of work, they stayed out until the strike was called off: there was no need for the strikers to follow the 'March on Crynant' with an enduring occupation of the Dulais Valley.

The respect for the views of the majority whether expressed through the ballot box or by a mass picket is an important aspect of mechanical solidarity. This, and the frank exertion of repressive sanctions by the local community, remind us of the two faces of mechanical solidarity: support to those on one side, antagonism to the point of assault to those on the other side; kindness to familiars, harshness to strangers. That the Ammanford strikers considered men from Neath to be not only strike-breakers but 'foreigners' also suggests that definitions of familiars were sometimes very parochial, contrasting with the appeal to international working-class solidarity early in the strike.

While the strike leaders demonstrated much skill in the use of local social capital they fumbled in manipulating the existing trans-local organizational resources. The initial appeal to the TUC General Council to press for international unity was little short of fatuous; the approaches to the SWMF yielded no extension of the strike and little moral support. The strategy pursued by the strike leaders in the search for local solidarity was based partly on 'shows of strength', intimidation and violence; the strategy was clearly widely supported by the anthracite miners and their communities but because of its reliance on massive forces was incapable of extension over an area wider than three close-running river valleys. In this local context, however the construction of solidarity through these mechanisms was a much faster process than we have seen so far at national level; from the first mass meeting in Ammanford Park to the start of the district-wide strike was a period of only seven weeks.

The anthracite strike of 1925 confirms the picture of mechanical solidarity we developed in the last chapter but also emphasizes its repressive aspects and suggests the presence of some limits to community-based solidarity enforced by repressive sanctions. The strike was extended from the Ammanford No. 1 Colliery to the anthracite district as a whole through the combine committees and the district organization of the SWMF including a ballot on the issue. But the failure of the strike leaders to find an issue in which every miner of the anthracite district had an interest made them fall back on community-based repressive mechanisms of generating solidarity: the mass meeting and the mass picket. Aided as they were by the existence and actions of the two big combines, the strike leaders were able to extend the strike until it involved 20,000 miners and to maintain it in collieries scattered along the floors of three valleys. A wider extension brought about by the same means would have over-stretched the resources available to the strikers, while the strikers failed to achieve a wider solidarity by other means, for instance by using the available 'social capital' embodied in the SWMF and the MFGB and combining interests over a wider arena as had been done during the build up to the 1912 national strike. In short, the 1925 anthracite strike shows us the limits to community-based, mechanical solidarity based on similarities of experience and attitude and on the disciplining of recalcitrants by repressive sanctions. It persuades us of the necessity of distinguishing community-based solidary processes from those seen in wider arenas.

As we saw briefly in chapter 3, the 1926 Lock-out saw the almost immediate re-emergence of divergent interests, marked most notably by the early return to work in the Midlands and the formation of 'Spencer' and company unions outside the MFGB. This collapse of inter-regional solidarity was not repaired until the mid-1930s. The events in the process by which this was achieved bear comparison with the events leading up to the first national strike in 1912. Again a domestic strike over local issues, this time at Harworth colliery in North Nottinghamshire, developed into a national strike over a general issue, the recognition of MFGB-affiliated unions in place of the unaffiliated 'Spencer' company unions. In many ways these events follow a now familiar pattern and a detailed narrative of this episode (for which see Arnot 1961; Alan R. Griffin 1962; Fishman 1995) would add little to our understanding. However, some aspects of these events give us a useful warning, suggesting that the roles of mechanical solidarity and generalized reciprocity in trans-local strike action, which we have argued were limited, should not be dismissed completely.

The recognition issue at Harworth led eventually to a negotiated outcome, but only after an MFGB special conference and a national strike ballot. The MFGB's leaflet urging a 'Yes' vote argued that 'principles are at stake of outstanding importance to every mineworker in the country'; that 'the future welfare of the whole of the mineworkers of the country' was 'deeply involved'; referred to the division of forces represented by Spencer's union, the Notting-hamshire Miners' Industrial Union (NMIU) as a 'fatal weakness'; declared that 'this [latter issue] overshadows them all'; and that 'the whole future of the mineworkers is at stake' (MFGB, *The Issues in the Nottinghamshire Dispute: A Message to the Miners of Britain*, quoted in Alan R. Griffin 1962: 271; Fishman 1995: 188). The ballot secured an enormous seven-to-one majority for strike action, including particularly large majorities in Lancashire and Yorkshire neither of which had been significantly affected by Spencer unions (Arnot 1961: 221).

The MFGB's ballot leaflet appealed to self-interest but it also appealed for aid for the miners at Harworth who had been victimized for their membership of the MFGB-affiliated Nottinghamshire Miners' Association (NMA) and for support for general values and 'rights which are of the very essence of our liberties': freedom of representation; free citizenship; peace and justice; free trade unionism. These appeals are consistent with a model which sees the ballot result as an example of 'generalized reciprocity' in a context of mechanical solidarity. Another aspect of the Harworth dispute also accords with such an interpretation. The MFGB was clearly looking for a concrete grievance with which to mobilize support: 'The flame which is the result of the spark at Harworth is going to spread' (Arthur Horner to MFGB special conference, 20 January 1937, quoted by Arnot 1961: 213). In other words, the general interest in eliminating the NMIU, which had existed for a decade, was not regarded as sufficient to mobilize national support on the issue. One way to interpret this in line with the mechanical solidarity perspective is that a specific 'outrage' of collective values had to be awaited before effective solidary action could be generated on the issue; though this is not to deny that the recovery from the slump of the early 1930s and the renewed self-confidence of the MFGB after its successful wages campaign in 1935–6 were also important factors explaining the timing of the dispute and the strike. In short, the Harworth dispute suggests that one cannot dismiss entirely the role of mechanical solidarity as a basis for national strike action.

At the beginning of chapter 6 we showed that the industrial solidarity for which British miners have a widespread reputation was, in some respects, a myth. While in national-level strikes and lock-outs solidarity was often impressive, in domestic strikes it was often all but absent; the prevailing picture in many districts before and after the Second World War was one of sectionalism rather than solidarity. This raised questions about the nature and origins of miners' strike solidarity; the sectionalism of many domestic strikes suggested that strike solidarity could not be understood as a cultural norm emerging out of the shared class position, the shared hardships and dangers of the miners' lives and their co-residence in isolated mining villages. Nor could the impressive solidarity seen in the national strikes and lock-outs be explained as a simple geographical extension of the behavioural norms seen in every mining community. These traditional interpretations of miners' solidarity are closely related to Durkheim's concept of mechanical solidarity and to later conceptualizations of social support as a set of generalized reciprocities between people linked by dense and multiplex social networks. While these interpretations, therefore, have a long-standing and sometimes illuminating theoretical grounding, they are insufficient as explanations of the historical record.

Our re-examination of the early unions in the North East revealed the difficulties that stood in the way of any effective, trans-local organization of miners; not

only were coalowners frequently and powerfully antagonistic to such organizations but there were structural conflicts among mineworkers between the desire
to act sympathetically in the support of local strikes and the painfully learned
necessity of acting in a calculated fashion and denying trans-local support on
sectional issues in order to keep the union in being and recognized as a legitimate
bargaining agent. Our reconsideration of the origins of solidary action at county
and national level before 1912 led us to emphasize the serious, fracturing
divisions of interests and institutions between the county unions that stood in
the way of an effective national federation of miners' unions for many years.
Those divisions of interest were eventually overcome partly by ideological campaigning but also partly by the exercise of financial and political power by the
MFGB leadership; in these ways the shared values and understandings of British
miners were to a significant extent *created* by their leaders.

Inevitably, the structural conflict of interests between section and generality
remained. Comparable with developments in the regional arena of the North
East, in the national arena of the MFGB we saw that leaders recognized the
necessity of limiting the level of support to affiliates and we traced the evolution
of the complex of rules and practices which served to control solidary action at
national level: the rules on 'support', the delegate conference and the strike
ballot. These rules and practices made it incumbent on those seeking support
from the MFGB to find common ground and common interests between
themselves and the generality of MFGB affiliates and their members. Our prime
illustration of the influence of these structures and processes was the sequence of
events leading up to the first national miners' strike in 1912.

This reconsideration of the regional and national history led us to suggest that
miners' solidarity at these levels should be regarded not as a phenomenon that
'emerged' out of the commonalities of miners' lives but as an achievement of
purposive social action. We suggested that, at these levels, solidarity was *constructed*. The term is intended to draw attention to a number of features of the
concept. Constructed solidarity is the result of purposive action (it does not
spontaneously 'emerge'); it is a co-operative venture involving the joint activity
of individuals who pool resources and seek to further their shared or concerted
interests or values (it is not a form of social exchange); individuals or groups
refusing their co-operation may be expelled or excluded from the solidary group
but are not subject to further punishment (sectionalism, at this level, attracts
neither repressive nor restitutive sanction); it is aided by the use of social capital:
established organizations, institutions, relationships, activities and values (at
this level, only sectionalism is spontaneous); it takes time to construct (and
where there is no time there is, at this level, no solidarity).

Nevertheless we do not wish to deny the role of shared experience and shared
values in the genesis of solidarity at the national level completely. We saw that
the history of the Harworth strike was in many ways consistent with the traditional view of miners' solidarity. The intervention in the dispute by the MFGB
can be interpreted consistently with the evidence as an example of mechanical

solidarity and as marked by generalized reciprocities. The victimization of the members of the NMA at Harworth can be interpreted consistently and legitimately as an outrage of collectively held values, and the overwhelming 'Yes' vote in the strike ballot on the issue can be seen as an offer of support by the national membership in the assertion of those values, support for which no immediate return from Nottinghamshire could be expected: in short, as a transaction of generalized exchange.

However, it is at the local level, whether in domestic or district strikes like the 'bag muck' strike in 1902 and the anthracite strike of 1925, or in the local conduct of national strikes and lock-outs, that strike solidarity, where it existed, most obviously and most closely conformed to the traditional picture. But even in the 'bag muck' strike we saw features of local solidarity familiar from the regional and national history: the concertation of interests, sometimes aided by the inadvertent words or actions of the company; the importance, sometimes crucial, of formal organizations such as the county unions. However, there is a great paucity of evidence on local strikes and the histories that have been written have been more concerned to celebrate working-class solidarity than investigate the reasons for its presence and absence. This means that we can only speculate on the reasons why sectionalism was often more apparent in domestic strikes than solidarity.

Where local social capital was poorly developed or absent, or where social networks had failed to develop in density and multiplexity, perhaps because the local village or neighbourhood was of recent origin, housing an unstable population of transients, or perhaps because of divisions of religion, ethnicity, language, nation or ideology, we would expect mechanical solidarity to have been a rare achievement and generalized reciprocities to be largely absent. Mechanical solidarity depends on shared values; generalized reciprocity flourishes only where people are tightly linked together by relationships of different kinds. It is the absence of shared values that makes us unsurprised to find communities like the mid-nineteenth-century Lanarkshire town of Coatbridge, butchered by religious and nationalist divisions, incapable of industrial unity (Campbell 1978: 82–97). Where the local social capital was in the control of coalowners or others hostile to the achievement of working-class solidarity, as in the 'company towns' to which some colliery villages approximated, we would also expect difficulties to have dogged the path of any seeking to achieve economic, social or political objectives through solidary action.

These conditions might suffice to explain long-term absences of social solidarity but in many collieries that struck frequently strike solidarity fluctuated rapidly over time (table 6.5). It is difficult to pinpoint the reasons for this in the current state of research but it does imply that traditional explanations for miners' strike solidarity are inadequate not only at the national and county level but also at the domestic level. We have seen that solidary behaviour which conforms to the theoretical picture of mechanical solidarity and generalized reciprocity is discernible in the historical record but that there was also much sectionalism. One way of reconciling these facts is by the imputation of social values which are rather more subtle and differentiated than is usually suggested in the historical and sociological literature. Whatever values were shared by the typical colliery work-force they did not include the view that if one struck all should strike. The records show strike after strike in which very few miners were directly involved and none were indirectly involved; the majority of the colliery work-force carried on working. 'One out, all out' was a myth. With equal confidence we can say that in some strikes and lock-outs, most obviously the national strikes and lock-outs of the 1912–26 period, working while others were striking or locked out was widely and greatly deprecated. It is possible that miners viewed sectional and general conflicts in different ways. Possibly it was felt that sections might pursue their own 'private' struggles but could not expect active, general support; that active, general support was accorded only to general actions. Views similar to these have been attributed to Tyneside shipbuilding workers to account for the predominantly sectional character of their conflicts with their employer (R. K. Brown et al. 1972: 39). Another possibility is that miners' values attached great importance to conforming to or 'falling in' with the majority. Once a ballot or a show of hands had indicated that a majority were for strike action, solidarity was expected and obtained; where these conditions were absent, sections were not supported by the generality. The history of the anthracite strike of 1925 is suggestive of such values. These hypotheses are consistent with colliery histories of domestic strike activity in which, as we have demonstrated (chapter 6), strike solidarity waxes and wanes. They also help to explain why the construction of strike solidarity was necessary in local and domestic strikes and account for the most common process to be observed in that construction process, the transformation of the issues in dispute from the parochial towards the universal.

Miners' strike solidarity was a much more complex phenomenon than has been supposed. Impressive solidarities at national level occurred almost simultaneously with a remarkable sectionalism in many domestic strikes. It is true that an important element in the explanation of miners' solidarity at local level, where it existed, and sometimes at national level, was the background of shared experience that lay behind miners' view of themselves as a special and clearly defined group. But miners' solidarity cannot be understood solely in these structural terms. Instead, we also need to understand that strike solidarity was, most obviously at the national level but also at the local level, the creation of sustained and purposive social action by generations of local and national leaders of the mining work-force.

8 Conflictual context? The 'isolated mass' revisited

Locality and community: illustrations, models and critiques

The background of shared experience which lay behind miners' view of themselves and influenced their actions was formed partly by the workplace and partly by the locality. In this chapter we examine the influence of the structures of the colliery locality on strike activity, before returning to the impact of the structures of the workplace in chapter 9. Structures are frequently more amenable to measurement than the sometimes transient elements of consciousness and action. Accordingly this chapter and the next two use statistical methodologies to investigate the variations in miners' strike activity. A technical account of our procedures is provided in the appendices to these chapters; the text gives a less formal exposition of our investigations.

In chapter 2 we were concerned to stress, in contrast to much recent writing, the modernity of many aspects of the British mining industry. However, in one respect it is undeniable that the industry remained traditional and that 'modernity' passed it by. This was in its pattern of settlement and in the communities that established themselves in those localities. The 'modern' locality strictly segregates work and leisure, production and consumption. Workplace and residence are geographically separated, often by considerable distances, and are separate also in the structures of ownership: employers and landlords are distinct people or organizations with few or no links each to the other, formal or informal; workers who own none of the means of production may nevertheless own the house which is their major asset and the basis of their consumption. In these respects the degree to which the British coalmining industry modernized was limited. During the 1984–5 coal strike contemporary rhetoric and affirmation was predicated on the widely shared belief that destruction of the industry implied destruction of colliery communities and settlements (Samuel *et al.* 1986). Before this, at the beginning of the nationalization period, the National Coal Board had acquired 140,000 houses thereby becoming a major landlord; in 1925 colliery companies owned about 171,000 houses and in 1890 perhaps 140,000. Most of these had been built by colliery companies which were both employer and landlord and most were sited within walking distance of, if not in sight of, the pit which provided the miners with work (Church 1986: 599; Supple 1987: 458).

At least some coalowners felt it was important to provide colliery housing either to enable them to compete for 'reliable' and 'steady' workmen (particularly colliery officials and hewers during the long nineteenth century when such workers were in growing demand (Daunton 1980)) or to retain such men, discourage mobility, and preserve a settled colliery community. To help achieve this latter objective some colliery owners promoted savings clubs and the purchase of houses built by the company (Church 1986: 282–7). Others were selective in their choice of tenants. A Cumberland pit manager explained in 1913 that 'By having men in Colliery houses the Manager is able to get a better class of men and to keep them. They will sacrifice a great deal rather than move, they are more dependent on their work, one can enforce strict discipline in the Colliery, they are content with a rather less rate of wages, no inducement need be given' (quoted by Wood 1988: 183). An outspoken trustee of the Dowlais Iron Company expressed the view that home ownership produced peaceful relations between employers and workers, describing the typical strike-prone worker as young, lacking savings, and a worker who 'at worst' could migrate. He suggested that 'older, steadier householders' were more prepared to wait for an upturn in trade (Church 1986: 286).

The provision by colliery owners of day and Sunday schools, welfare services, halls, institutes, libraries and reading rooms, chapels, sports grounds, allotments and other recreational facilities was common in colliery villages; these measures were intended to cultivate respectable and especially sober behaviour on the part of the inhabitants. In a leading textbook on colliery management published in 1896, reprinted several times in the next forty years, the authors underlined the difficulties colliery managers faced when they found themselves implementing policy decisions which would be unpopular with the men. For this reason, managers were advised to 'cultivate relationships with them . . . by taking a personal interest in their reading rooms and institutes, their athletic clubs, their musical bands, or in some of the various institutions which usually exist in colliery villages' (Bulman and Redmayne 1896: 65). In practice, these 'paternalistic' policies were accompanied by either hostility to, or grudging acceptance of, miners' trade unions (Church 1986: 290).

It is evident that the rapid growth of the industry between the 1890s and 1914 (a period of labour shortage in the industry) did not diminish the localized nature of coalmining as an occupation. In some coalfields the urban-dwelling miner was by no means a rarity. In Lancashire in 1931 over a third of the county's miners lived in the cities and towns of Ashton-under-Lyne, Bolton, Burnley, Manchester and Salford, Wigan and St Helens, and in Staffordshire over a third lived in the cities or towns, the great majority in the county town of Stoke-on-Trent. Yet from 1900 especially, the kind of isolated colliery villages which had long been characteristic in parts of the North East and South Wales, spread to the sparsely populated, expanding fields of Yorkshire and the East Midlands, which in employment and production by the 1930s rivalled the coalfields of the North East, Scotland and South Wales. By 1921, some 50 per cent of all miners in England and Wales lived in census districts where more than one-half of all adult male workers were employed in coal mines (Supple 1987: 479). These districts were away from the major conurbations and the big towns. Only about one in six miners counted by the English and Welsh censuses from 1911 to 1951 lived in a large city or town. There was no detectable tendency for this proportion to rise and the traditional rural character of the industry seems to have been impervious to change before the mid-century.

While far from being universally valid, the popular image of the British coalminer as a villager is nevertheless not seriously misleading. Companies sinking large pits in rural areas risked perennial labour shortages unless they built adjacent housing and social infrastructure. Out of this necessity emerged the opportunity for a company to use its control over the physical basis of the colliery settlement in an effort to create a disciplined, compliant and captive work-force. Such labour management strategies which extended beyond the colliery gates into localities clearly have a potential significance for the study of differential levels of conflict and for this reason warrant our consideration.

Colliery and 'company' villages have long attracted scholars' attention, especially since the 1984–5 miners' strike and the associated campaigns to save coalfield communities from economic and social collapse as the industry contracted (J. E. Williams 1962b; Waller 1983; Samuel *et al.* 1986; Baylies 1993). This attention has not yielded a consensus on how one might portray a 'typical' colliery village; instead the available studies have revealed significant differences which warn us against attempting any such description. These differences are exemplified by contrasting two well-documented histories of pit villages: Creswell in Derbyshire and Mardy in South Wales.

Creswell had its origins in the pit sunk by the owners of the Bolsover Company, who included Emerson Bainbridge, a leading mining engineer whose anti-union stance earned him a national reputation. Built in the 1890s, the 'model' village consisted of 280 houses constructed 'on modern and hygienic lines', many with flower gardens, in a landscaped environment including a playground, rustic seats and a bandstand. Rent was stopped from employees' wages, while less than acceptable behaviour met with eviction (Downing and Gore 1983: 21, 24). Working and living were inseparable in Creswell. A comprehensive battery of social amenities was intended to achieve Bainbridge's aim to create 'a village where three things could exist successfully . . . the absence of drunkenness, the absence of gambling and the absence of bad language' (Bainbridge, quoted by Downing and Gore 1983: 22). Joint committees comprising officials and workmen managed the Workmen's Institute, which formed the centre for the activities of the various colliery sports organizations, the dramatic society and the colliery band. Joint participation characterized the dances, social evenings and dinners held at the Drill Hall. There the colliery manager led the Boys' Brigade, his wife captained the Girls' Bugle Brigade while other colliery officials filled adjutant roles. Drilling, parades and bugle playing, seaside camping, gymnastics and team sports amounted to a strategy for discipline. One ex-miner recalled 'kids wouldn't answer you back. When that Brigade finished, this village had finished' (Hayhoe, quoted by Downing and Gore 1983: 23). Alternative organizations, such as the 'Comrades' Club' were suppressed. Creswell residents

daren't do as they'd a mind. You were absolutely under t'control of Bolsover Company. You were working for them and you were controlled by them. . . . What that manager or that under-manager said, that were law. You worked under them and they were your masters. At one time a day, it were a white-collar village, this was. You'd got to go down this street dressed proper . (Hayhoe, quoted by Downing and Gore 1983: 22–3)

'Position and status were everything' (Green, quoted by Downing and Gore 1983: 24). The residents perceived the manager, rather than the owners, as determining the character and tone of life and labour in Creswell. Whether attendance at church outnumbered that at chapel was significantly affected by the denomination favoured by the colliery manager. To him, or to a deputy, would be carried reports of malingering or improper dress and, while away from the pit on social or sporting occasions managers were approachable and affable, once the colliery wheels were rolling 'you had to be more or less servile' (Lowther, quoted by Downing and Gore 1983: 26).

'Servile' was not a word associated with the village of Mardy, one of the earliest proving grounds of Arthur Horner, the 'incorrigible rebel' and the first Communist secretary of the Miners' Federation of Great Britain (Horner 1960). Situated high up in the valley of the Rhondda Fach in South Wales, Mardy, or Maerdy, exemplifies the geographical isolation often thought typical of mining settlements. The first of the Mardy collieries was sunk in 1875. The collieries were run by Lockett's Merthyr Steam Coal Company from 1894 until they were taken over by Bwllfa and Cwmamman Collieries and then the Powell Duffryn combine in the 1930s. The site of the village boasted nothing but a farmhouse before the first pit was sunk but grew rapidly to a place of 880 dwellings housing 7,000 people in 1914, at which time the Mardy collieries employed 2,700 men. About half these houses were owner occupied, the remainder being owned by landlords apparently independent of the coal company. By the First World War the village also contained shops, public houses, a church, six chapels, a school and a police station. The constricted valley floor provided little enough room for these buildings but somehow space was found for allotments, a recreation ground and a football field. The village appeared remote and isolated in that it lay at the head of the valley; beyond the pits lay only mountain and moorland. But the village was served by a railway and, from 1912, a tramline; two miles down the valley lay the rather bigger colliery village of Ferndale and ten miles further lay the town of Pontypridd, twenty-five miles away from Cardiff (Francis and Smith 1980: 155–60; Macintyre 1980a: 24–6, 36). Social and recreational activities were centred on the Workmen's Institute, the nucleus of which had been provided by a director of the company in 1881. A large meeting hall serving as cinema, theatre, dance hall and sports arena; it also contained a gymnasium, a billiards room, a library and two reading rooms.

Overwhelmingly, the people of Mardy were members of households dependent on the Mardy collieries for work, for no other significant source of employment existed. The middle class was represented by perhaps a hundred shopkeepers and tradespeople; the professions by the colliery agent, a doctor who was also a Justice of the Peace, and small numbers of less prominent doctors, clerics and teachers. So far this picture is little different from that presented by many of the smaller villages of the South Wales coalfield (Macintyre 1980a: 23–6). However, in the 1920s Mardy was to gain a reputation as a 'Little Moscow': a village hot bed of Communist activity. The historian of the 'Little Moscows' of inter-war Britain has sought to explain this in terms of the villages' geographical, social and industrial characteristics. Yet it is apparent that prior to the 1920s these characteristics of Mardy were not unusual features of mining villages. While the Mardy miners' lodge underwent a significant radicalization in the first twenty years of the twentieth century, so did many others in other villages. The history of confrontation between the coal company and the lodge indicates that the lodge was able to mobilize the support of men and women in the community in the prosecution of the large-scale national strikes and lock-outs of the 1920s. A food riot involving some 1,500 residents early in 1918 again suggests that the community, rather than simply the union, was militant in its pursuit and protection of its local interests. These rapid mobilizations of people to demonstrate, to riot and, more quietly, to establish mechanisms for mutual support such as the communal kitchens set up during the 1926 Lock-out can only have been aided by the compact form of the settlement, the homogeneity of the economic circumstances of its population and the absence of tied housing. Yet it is clear that divisions existed even within this community. Conflicts occurred between ex-servicemen and anti-war campaigners during the First World War and shortly afterwards, skirmishes and more substantial struggles took place over non-unionism in the Mardy collieries, while divisions existed between Welsh speakers, the English-speaking Welsh and English immigrants (Francis and Smith 1980: 163; Macintyre 1980a: 33).

Apart from the colliery company itself, the most significant organization in the village was the local lodge of the miners' union. Macintyre has described how during the strikes and lock-outs of the early 1920s the lodge incorporated representatives of the churches, shopkeepers and teachers on to its committees and commanded the support of local traders who were aware of the importance of good relations with the lodge for their business. In contrast the colliery manager, although supported by the colliery doctor and many colliery officials, and despite the earlier philanthropy of the company, had lost the allegiance of the rest of village society by the early 1920s, when he and his associates found themselves marginalized in the local Conservative Club. The resignation of the colliery manager as a trustee of the Workmen's Institute in June 1926 symbolized this change. While the company necessarily dominated the economy of the village, the miners' lodge dominated its society (Macintyre 1980a: 33–4).

This domination was broken after the 1926 Lock-out. As leftwing sectarianism took hold, village organizations divided and re-formed into competing factions based around the Communist Party on the one hand and the Labour Party on the other. The miners' lodge was expelled from the South Wales Miners' Federation (SWMF) in 1930 for supporting the Communist Arthur Horner in the general election of the preceding year. A new lodge was formed which supported the Labour Party in conformity with SWMF rules. The colliery company supported a local branch of a company union, the South Wales Miners' Industrial Union, to which the few miners who secured work at the Mardy collieries between 1927 and the liquidation of Lockett's Merthyr in 1931 belonged. The distress committee which had been led by the miners' lodge found itself in competition with a better funded committee linked to the Lord Mayor of London's relief organization set up in 1928 (Francis and Smith 1980: 165–7; Macintyre 1980a: 36–8). Unemployment became a long-term feature of the village where no more than 500 miners were at work between 1926 and the Second World War. The pits were put on a maintenance-only basis in 1940 and were not redeveloped until after nationalization.

The contrast between Creswell and Mardy is stark. Both the economy and the society of Creswell were dominated and manipulated by the Bolsover Colliery Company. In Mardy, Lockett's Merthyr dominated the village economy and pursued confrontational policies in the pits but only ever made half-hearted and unsuccessful attempts to influence the society of Mardy. The absence of company domination of village social life, and especially the absence of company-owned housing, undoubtedly aided the attempt by the miners' lodge and the Communist militants of Mardy in their attempt to create and lead a 'counter community', a 'little Moscow' (Francis and Smith 1980: 161; Macintyre 1980a: 44).

The contrast between these villages raises questions concerning the implication of a number of historians' studies which suggest that industrial or political militancy and its absence can be explained by the structures of colliery communities. At a structural level, the only clear differences between Creswell and Mardy are the presence of colliery-owned housing in Creswell and its absence in Mardy, and high unemployment in Mardy after 1926 and (presumably) relatively high employment in Creswell. Differences in housing tenure are of importance and give us some understanding of the moderation shown by the miners in Creswell which was evident in labour relations. However, the nature of this moderation cannot be interpreted, as historians have been inclined to do, simply as evidence of a subservience typical of members of a 'boss's union' (J. E. Williams 1962b: 51; Waller 1983: 121). The minutes of the Rufford Workers' 'independent pit committee', subsequently the Rufford branch of the Nottinghamshire Miners' Industrial Union, which organized miners in Rainwell, a village that shared many of the characteristics of Creswell, reveal branch officials pursuing members' grievances with vigour, and suggest that pragmatism, rather than either submissiveness or ideology, explains conduct in those organizations (Colin P. Griffin 1990: 11–12). Similarities and differences between the experience of those villages are of little help in explaining the rebelliousness of Mardy; many villages were free of colliery housing but only a few became 'little Moscows'. Again, the high unemployment suffered by Mardy after 1926 may have exacerbated the divisions brought about by the political factionalism of the period but, in general, we would associate high rather than low unemployment with the apparent 'servility' of Creswell miners. Such considerations reinforce our suggestion in chapter 1 that purely structural explanations of strike activity are likely to be insufficient and that matters of organization, consciousness and action must be explored.

Nevertheless the attempt to explain British miners' strike proneness in terms of the characteristics of the localities and communities in which they lived has a long history, stretching back at least as far as the First World War. Since that time an implicit or explicit sociology of place has formed an important part of the conceptual framework adopted by the scholars and observers of many kinds who have had an interest in the social and political aspects of the coal industry. The culmination of this approach was the classic ethnography of a colliery community provided by Dennis et al. (1956) which formed an important point of reference for much later theorizing on the nature of working-class communities and the sources of working-class social and political attitudes (Lockwood 1966; Bulmer 1975b; Warwick and Littlejohn 1992: ch. 2). But the scepticism of other scholars of the possibility of explaining particular social phenomena solely in terms of social relationships specific to the communities involved (for example, Stacey 1969) temporarily halted this search for a sociology of place in the late 1960s. Since the mid-1980s a renewed interest in the spatial dimensions of social and economic change has led to a revival of research on localities (Massey 1984; Gregory and Urry 1985; Lancaster Regionalism Group 1985; Rees et al. 1985). This renewed attention is from an 'older and wiser' viewpoint which distinguishes 'community' from 'locality'. A 'community' has been very variously defined but would usually be thought of as a network of social relationships with connotations of stability, durability and 'social health', of social introversion, of isolation from outsiders, and of high levels of interaction among insiders ('The mark of a community is that one's life may be lived wholly within it' (MacIver and Page 1950: 9)). The term 'locality' is meant to be devoid of such connotations and to refer simply to the set of social relations obtaining between people present in a small-scale geographical space. There may or may not be a community or communities in a locality. It is because we have often wished to avoid the raft of connotations with which the word 'community' has been loaded that we, in common with most recent writers, frequently refer to 'localities' rather than 'communities' (Cooke 1989).

Bulmer (1975a) distinguished three general sociological models of mining communities: the 'archetypal proletarian' in which mineworkers are seen as a group of workers who experience capitalist exploitation in an extreme form and respond with an unusual degree of solidarity; the 'isolated mass' model in which the segregation of mineworkers in internally undifferentiated masses is seen as the key feature, and the theory of the 'occupational community' in which the totality of mineworkers' social relationships, whether of kinship, neighbourhood or voluntary association, and miners' subjective orientations to those relations, are permeated by and only understandable in terms of mineworkers' relationships in the workplace (Blauner 1960).

Only one of these models, however, offers a general explanatory framework concerning (and predicting) the relationship between aspects of community and industrial conflict: the 'isolated mass' hypothesis first advanced by Kerr and Siegel in 1954. Although subjected to damaging criticism on theoretical grounds and despite claims that it is empirically falsifiable, the Kerr and Siegel hypothesis continues to influence attempts to explain either the strike-prone nature of coalmining (McCormick 1979; Pitt 1979: 22; Barnett 1986: 69–70; Trevor Wilson 1986: 223; Colls 1987), the broader nature of miners' militancy (Allen 1981; Beynon 1985; Samuel et al. 1986; Seddon 1986; Winterton and Winterton 1989), or the spatial dynamics of labour markets (Massey 1984: ch. 5). Like many others we consider the hypothesis crude and over-simple but still of sufficient attractiveness to warrant detailed consideration and systematic empirical testing.

Kerr and Siegel (1954) argued that the high strike propensity of coalminers could be explained by the tendency of their industry to direct its workers into isolated and homogeneous industrial communities. Shared grievances – industrial hazards, a tendency to severe economic depression, unemployment, bad living conditions, low wages and/or intermittent work – lead workers to develop a 'habit of solidarity'. Largely separate from other industrial workers and with occupational, geographic and social mobility severely curtailed, miners find it hard to 'exit' from the mass. Their grievances are likely to be expressed in bitter industrial conflict. Hence the strike takes the form of a 'protest' rather than that of a 'modern' strike as described by Shorter and Tilly (1974) and discussed by us in chapter 5. Strikes in an isolated mass are 'a kind of colonial revolt against far-removed authority, an outlet for accumulated tensions, and a substitute for occupational and social mobility' (Kerr and Siegel 1954: 191–3). To this Kerr and Siegel added a further argument, that the sort of workers attracted to difficult and dangerous jobs such as coalmining were likely to be 'tough' and combative and more likely to strike than those in less arduous occupations.

Although Kerr and Siegel were the first to elaborate these ideas into an explicit hypothesis, some of the suggestions it incorporated were by no means novel either in the USA or in the UK. When the 1917 government Commission of Enquiry into Industrial Unrest turned to Wales and Monmouthshire and came to investigate the 'reasons for the greater discontent manifested by miners as compared with other classes of workers', it was impressed by the social consequences of geology and geography. It suggested that the very high density of colliery employment in some areas induced 'an exaggerated view of their [miners'] indispensability to the employers and to the nation' and also a high degree of commitment to the miners' union, and that the location of the industry away from large towns precluded 'intercourse with the inhabitants of such towns and participation in their public life and activities' (Commission of Enquiry into Industrial Unrest, *Report on No. 7 Division (Wales and Monmouthshire)*: 21). Both G. D. H. Cole (1923) and W. H. B. Court (1951) expressed similar views in their influential studies of the industry in wartime conditions.

Each of these studies sees social and industrial solidarity as an unproblematic outcome of social, economic and occupational homogeneity. That divisions based on ethnicity, language, nationality or religion existed has been admitted and researched, sometimes admirably, in the more modern literature (Campbell 1978; Francis 1980: 170–7). But there were other divisions. Different miners pursued different 'livelihood strategies' and sometimes these differences led to deep divisions and bitter antagonisms, for example, when some decided to join a 'non-political' union and others did not. While this particular example has been explored in some detail (chapter 3), other, less dramatic, differences have not. We saw in our account of the village of Creswell earlier in this chapter that there were divisions between churchgoers and chapel attenders, the religious affiliation of the colliery manager being a determining factor for some. Some villagers were prepared to act as informers, reporting misdemeanours to colliery officials, presumably in the hope of some preferment. Vernon has given a vivid account of similar divisions in the South Yorkshire colliery village of Thurcroft where he worked from 1937 until 1949:

[The under-manager Mr] Robinson ruled the pit with an iron hand. Both deputies and colliers used to scuttle like rabbits on the scent of a ferret when he came through the pit. He had his yarddogs (spies) in every section of the pit. An old collier, once told me 'Every telephone installed in a pit, had a yarddog to go with it'. When Robinson went in the miners' club the 'leeches' would fall over one another to buy his drink. On one occasion one of the 'leeches' told him he'd won the raffle prize, a basket of fruit. Robinson said, 'How can I have won the raffle, I haven't bought any tickets'. 'I've bought them for you!' the leech replied. (Vernon 1984: 20)

Other villagers have explained that, just as in Creswell, religious worship was replete with social meaning and economic implication. A Wesleyan chapel was built in 1930 and in 1939 the colliery owners built the Church of St Simon and St Jude, affiliated to the Church of England.

These churches represented the section of the village that considered themselves most respectable, and as such enjoyed the patronage of the powerful: . . . 'They used to call them sky pilots, those that went to church or chapel. . . . [If you had passed the deputies' examination and if but only] if you said 'I'm going to start going to church', you'd get a deputy's job.' (Mr 'JJ', president of the local branch of the Yorkshire Miners' Association in the 1940s, quoted in The People of Thurcroft 1986: 21–2; for a similar account see Beynon and Austrin 1994: 192)

The result was 'an uncrystallised hostility toward the Chapel and Church folk' among the other villagers. 'Tensions were symbolised regularly every Sunday morning. The congregation of St Simon and St Jude's would be just dispersing . . . as the plebs waited for the . . . club to open. Neither acknowledged the other' (The People of Thurcroft 1986: 22; cf. Beynon and Austrin 1994: 187). The impact of such 'tensions' on the community is difficult to assess. Speaking in the 1980s it was asserted that there had been no shortage of 'comradeship' in Thurcroft:

Anyone in trouble was not on their own for long before somebody would knock on the back door offering help of some kind, either food for the family or to do the washing or look after the children or supply some coal – anyway that help was needed. Often someone in need would find a rabbit hanging on the back door. (Mr 'R', a third generation branch officer and committeeman, quoted in The People of Thurcroft 1986: 22)

But quite how the differences between the Thurcroft 'yarddogs', 'leeches', 'sky pilots' and 'plebs' would affect 'comradeship' in the possibly more divisive circumstances of a strike remains unclear. All one can say with assurance is that there were few strikes of any significance at Thurcroft Main in the 1920s and 1930s.

The subtleties of meaning, strategy and action and the imponderable impact they might or might not have had on strike activity find no place in the account of the 'isolated mass' provided by Kerr and Siegel. Their virtue was to bring the clarity of an explicit sociological hypothesis to the study of industrial conflict; but with this they also brought along the pre-conceptions of 1950s' structuralist sociology. In this view of the social world actions were supposedly directly explained by particular aspects of social structure (Hyman 1984: 69ff). To accuse Kerr and Siegel of this variety of reductionism is a little (though only a little) unfair, for Kerr and Siegel did attach some importance to 'cohesion' or organization (1954: 193) which may be construed as a variable mediating the otherwise ineluctable force of structure on action. Nevertheless it is true to say that 'organization' receives much less stress in their treatment than do the structural characteristics of isolation and massness. More importantly, Kerr and Siegel appear to be defenceless against modern critiques of structure–action duality (for example, Giddens 1979). The isolated massness of mining communities is presented as an unavoidable consequence of natural, techno-logical and economic imperatives and their social characteristics as direct con-sequences of massed isolation. Quite how the collection of mutual strangers who first come to work at a new pit from diverse backgrounds, for varied motives and with different modes of thought and expectation knit themselves into a coherent mass (if they do) Kerr and Siegel did not explain. Nor did they explore the process by which the isolated mass reproduced itself socially over time (Calhoun 1978: 370–1).

What seems to have been overlooked by those critics who have pointed to the 'structuralist' aspects of Kerr and Siegel's contribution is that it should also be seen in the context of inter-war attempts to establish a 'social ecology' (Park 1952) or a sociology of the city (Wirth 1938; Saunders 1981). Wirth's classic attempt at a 'sociologically significant' definition of the city was paralleled by Kerr and Siegel's attempt to define the 'industrial environment' of the strike-prone worker. For Wirth a city was a 'relatively large, dense, and permanent settlement of socially heterogeneous individuals (1938: 8). For Kerr and Siegel an isolated mass was a large or small, dense and not so permanent settlement of socially homogeneous individuals. Similarly for Redfield (1947) the antithesis of the city was the folk society: although intended primarily to characterize 'traditional' societies its description is faithfully echoed at many points in Kerr and Siegel's paper:

> The folk society is an isolated society. . . . [It is] made up of people who have little communication with outsiders . . . . This isolation is one half of a whole of which the other half is intimate communication among the members of the society. . . . [O]ral tradition has no check or competitor. . . . The people who make up a folk society are much alike. . . . Since the people communicate with one another and with no others, one man's learned ways of doing and thinking are the same as another's. . . . The members of a folk society have a strong sense of belonging together. . . . Communicating intimately with each other, each has a strong claim on the sympathies of the others. . . . [T]hey emphasize their own mutual likeness and value themselves as compared with others. They say of themselves 'we' as against all others, who are 'they'. . . . [I]n the folk society conventional behavior is strongly patterned: it tends to conform to a type or a norm. . . . Men act with reference to each other by understandings which are tacit and traditional. There are no formal contracts or other agreements. . . . [Members of the folk society behave towards other members as persons, not as things with no claim upon their sympathies.] . . . [But it is not only that] relations in such a society are personal; it is also that they are familial. (Redfield 1947: 296–301)

In this light, the innovation of Kerr and Siegel was to suggest that social conflict in the form of the strike was to be found not in the supposed anomic void of the city but in tightly integrated communities with 'their own codes, myths, heroes and social standards' (Kerr and Siegel 1954: 191).

As a sociological account of miners' propensity for high levels of strike activity, however, Kerr and Siegel's hypothesis did not survive unqualified for very long. Rimlinger (1959) directly challenged the Kerr–Siegel thesis on empirical grounds and pointed in particular to the relatively pacific industrial relations in coalmining in the Saar Territory and more generally to the contrast between the strike-proneness of Anglo-American miners and the peacefulness of their continental European counterparts. Nevertheless, building on the work of Wellisz (1953), Rimlinger agreed that 'the conduct of miners everywhere reflects the impact of a peculiar environment' arguing only that 'the inherent environmental tendency towards strike proneness may be counteracted or reinforced by sociocultural factors' (1959: 405). Using language reminiscent of a psychological or a 'human relations' approach to the problem rather than a purely sociological one, Rimlinger suggested that the harsh and dangerous mining environment constituted 'a source of discontent and tension' and also helped mould the miners' response to their feelings. The 'separateness' of miners' communities and miners' need to co-operate closely at work to ensure their own safety gave a natural tendency towards labour solidarity. Solidary action often acquired 'aggressive characteristics' because of the tension inherent in the work, 'forceful work habits' and the miners' sense of separateness.

Rimlinger also argued, however, that 'under appropriate historical circumstances' miners' separateness and cohesion could also become a 'major support of disciplined industrial conduct' which could make it possible for management to rely on the resulting inclination of miners to conform to group values as an indirect form of control. In other historical circumstances, however, where the 'effective organisation and expression of protest are inhibited', the tension and frustration generated by the work environment could result in aggressive individualism manifesting itself in 'friction between workers, refusals to co-operate, heavy absenteeism, the rise of informal or secret organisations, mutual recriminations, and acts of violence' (Rimlinger 1959: 395). In a series of historical sketches Rimlinger illustrated the diversity of historical circumstances, the most prominent determining factors being the pattern of mine ownership, differences in management strategies, notably in relation to the presence or absence of paternalism, the development of trade unionism, the nature of the state's involvement in industrial relations and in its attitude towards the mining environment, and the political traditions of the country concerned.

Rimlinger's approach combined a distinct theoretical orientation with a regard for the specifics of the historical record in a way which successfully avoided some of the deficiencies of the structuralist account of miners' strike activity offered by Kerr and Siegel (P. K. Edwards 1977). Nevertheless, his work has had few modern imitators, possibly because of a suspicion among historians that Rimlinger's method obscured detail of the particular and a suspicion among sociologists that his approach implicitly denies the possibility of finding a succinct, generally applicable, model of miners' strikes.

Rimlinger, like Kerr and Siegel, accepted the importance of social isolation, and drew attention to the impact of occupational experience in the life of the mining community. In doing so, these authors anticipated the concept of the 'occupational community' later formulated by Blauner (1960) and promoted by Bulmer as an important component of his 'ideal type' model of a mining community. Blauner specified three defining features of the occupational community: workers in their leisure hours socialize more with persons in their own line of work than with a cross-section of occupational types; workers talk 'shop' outside working hours; and the occupation is a reference group, whose standards of behaviour and system of status and rank guide conduct. As Bulmer noted, the emphasis on systems of meaning in the concept of the occupational community marks a helpful move away from the blunt confrontation of structure and action characteristic of Kerr and Siegel (Bulmer 1975a). However, the definition of an occupational community is so broad as to apply equally to many of the professions and even to the police and armed forces as well as to groups of industrial workers. Moreover, a definition which relegates the importance of control over resources and the geographical propinquity which is necessary if the 'occupational community' is to provide active support for workers in dispute, affords limited analytical assistance to the student of strikes, however useful it may be as a shorthand description of mining communities.

Since Rimlinger's and Blauner's contributions were published, the catalogue of 'exceptions' to the Kerr and Siegel thesis has been gradually extended. In the 1960s Eldridge observed that British steel workers often lived in isolated communities, performed work that was arduous and dangerous and yet were notably peaceable in their industrial relations (1968: ch. 5). P. K. Edwards (1988: 203) pointed out that the once strike-prone British car workers did not live in isolated masses; indeed Kerr and Siegel themselves noted that US automobile workers did not conform to their theory's predictions. However, neither Eldridge nor Edwards have shared Rimlinger's interest in not only identifying the weaknesses of the thesis but also modifying it and developing a more convincing model. Rather than examining the exceptional cases in detail, Kerr and Siegel's critics have focused on a number of theoretical and methodological points (which we shall discuss shortly) rather than empirical testing, referring almost casually to specific cases as if they completely invalidated the Kerr and Siegel hypothesis.

The main sources of dissatisfaction expressed with regard to the original, 'strong' form of the thesis put forward by Kerr and Siegel are conceptual and methodological. P. K. Edwards's unqualified critique (1977) concluded that the lack of satisfactory definitions, notably the failure to explain adequately the nature of an 'isolated mass', the methodological weaknesses in the measurements employed in making international comparisons, and the preoccupation with the typologies of polar cases – the integrated individual and integrated group contrasted with the isolated mass – undermined the validity of Kerr and Siegel's otherwise helpful attempt to analyse strike activity within a wider social context. Edwards concluded that so far as British miners were concerned the isolated mass hypothesis had little to commend it: 'Mass isolation is simply not a very useful concept in the explanation of interesting aspects of miners' behaviour: it describes certain features of their situation but in itself adds nothing to an explanation of their strike propensity' (P. K. Edwards 1977: 564; see also his reiteration of this critique in P. K. Edwards 1988: 202–10). For Edwards, Kerr and Siegel merely formed a suitable subject for a study in 'the falsification of sociological knowledge'.

Even before Edwards's attempt at terminal damage, positive references to the Kerr–Siegel hypothesis in its strong form have been rare (among these rarities are Petras and Zeitlin 1967 and Lincoln 1978). Nevertheless, in a less stark and less thorough-going 'weak' form the hypothesis survives in a diversity of mainly (though not exclusively) historical writings which continue to stress the relationship between coalminers' industrial conflict and the characteristics of their settlements, not as an exclusive explanation but as one factor among many (McCormick 1979; Pitt 1979: 22; Barnett 1986: 69–70; Trevor Wilson 1986: 223; Colls 1987). Possibly, the survival of the Kerr–Siegel hypothesis, even in a weak form, in such writings indicates nothing more than the traditional disdain of some historians for sociological research and their equally traditional reliance on contemporary material. However, this would not explain the numerous studies of the 1984–5 miners' strike which, by focusing on the strike in pit village or coal town, gave particular importance to local social institutions in its conduct (Beynon 1985; Samuel *et al.* 1986; Seddon 1986; Waddington *et al.* 1991). While the authors of one of the most closely researched studies of the strike (Winterton and Winterton 1989) explicitly distance themselves from the Kerr–Siegel hypothesis, they nevertheless offer evidence to suggest that the 'important determinant [of active strike involvement was] . . . the existence of a cohesive mining community' (1989: 105, 107). Notwithstanding Edwards's penetrating critique of Kerr and Siegel, therefore, both because the claims to have falsified the thesis at the empirical level are insubstantial and inadequate and because the thesis, in modified forms, continues to be applied in scholarly research into the history and sociology of industrial conflict, empirical testing of the relation between miners' location in isolated masses and their strike propensity seems to be amply justified. It is to this that we now turn.

Although Kerr and Siegel's hypothesis was advanced as an explanation of inter-industry variations in strike propensity, we accept P. K. Edwards's view that the appropriate level at which to test theories of this kind is the individual workplace (1983: 227). For this reason we examine here how far inter-colliery variations in strike activity can be explained by variations in the characteristics of their immediate localities highlighted by the isolated mass theory. Data limitations restrict our investigations to England and Wales in the inter-war years. Although this period was one of almost unrelieved depression for the British coal industry, it continued to experience strike activity at levels which were high in comparison with those recorded in other industries (table 1.1).

Meaning and measurement of the 'isolated mass'

Any attempt to test Kerr and Siegel's ideas is confronted at once by the lack of a succinct definition of an isolated mass. Their descriptions of massness and isolation include comments on social stratification, working-class organization and culture, and the symbolism of the 'actions' taken by workers (Kerr and Siegel 1954: 191–3). Faced with such a multi-dimensional picture, the researcher might pursue two different strategies. One strategy is to investigate a smaller number of cases intensively in an attempt to capture the local detail of social structures, organizations, culture and action. The other is to investigate a large number of cases extensively in an attempt to acquire the power of a large sample. These strategies are not exclusive but, in our view, complementary. In this chapter, we pursue an extensive approach, analysing a large sample of mining localities and the strike activity that occurred in them. After further statistical analysis we turn in chapter 11 to a more intensive study of a small sample of collieries in an attempt to extend and enrich the statistical results. In outline, the method we used in the work reported in this chapter was to take a large sample of small-scale administrative areas in the mining districts of England and Wales. For each area in our sample we established indices of isolated massness from the Census and other sources, and indices of strike activity from the official Ministry of Labour records of strikes and lock-outs which we discussed in chapter 1. We then correlated these two sets of data in an effort to discover whether high values of the indices of isolated massness were associated with high values of the indices of strike activity as Kerr and Siegel's theory predicts.

The concept of massness had a number of separate dimensions for Kerr and Siegel. First, a 'mass' was internally undifferentiated and homogeneous in terms of occupations within the industry, work and experiences (Kerr and Siegel 1954: 192). Second, it was 'undiluted' by workers in other industries and 'undiluted' by a significant resident middle class (1954: 191). Third, the industry had large-scale 'employing units' (1954: 194). The assertion that mineworkers were undifferentiated and homogeneous can, of course, be contested: divisions between face workers and other underground workers, between underground and surface workers, between apprenticed trades people and others and between occupations such as winding enginemen, supervisory grades and others certainly existed and were expressed in organizational forms (J. E. Williams 1962b; Garside 1971; Bulmer 1975a: 83). Nevertheless, colliery-to-colliery variations in such differentiation are unlikely to have been large, and for our purposes may be treated as a constant in the industry. The remaining two features ('dilution' and 'employing units') were subject to substantial colliery-to-colliery variation however. We have measured the extent of 'dilution' in terms of two variables: the number of adult males in mining and quarrying occupations and the total adult male population of the area in which the colliery was located, both as recorded by the 1931 *Census of England and Wales*, and their ratio, which we call 'occupational density'. We measured the scale of the 'employing units' by colliery employment both underground and surface as recorded in the Mines Department *List of Mines* for 1931. That Kerr and Siegel's concept of massness includes massness within the workplace as well as in the community means that their theory encompasses a 'size effect' theory of industrial conflict. This point, which has been little noticed, emerges as one of some importance in the light of the data, as we shall see below.

The difficulties in measuring isolation are much greater than those involved in measuring massness. With respect to 'coal towns', Kerr and Siegel referred to 'geographical isolation' (1954: 191, note 5) and some contributors to the literature have interpreted isolation in this way wholly or in part (Benson 1980: 82–4; Bulmer 1975a: 85). Nevertheless the bulk of the literature subsequent to Kerr and Siegel has been concerned to interpret isolation as a limited level of social interaction between the residents of the colliery settlement and the wider society. More recently geographers have been concerned to emphasize the subjective interpretation of distance and space by social actors and to question the relevance of 'objective' measures (Sack 1980). In this view, which many sociologists will share, 'isolation' becomes an attitude or a socially constructed meaning or an aspect of local culture rather than a physical feature or an aspect of behaviour.

While we have sympathy with these developments the difficulties of measuring isolation conceived as behaviour, or as culture or as subjectivity are obvious. Although we expected little to emerge from the geographical measurement of isolation we felt it incumbent upon us, in fairness to Kerr and Siegel, to do what was possible in this area. Thus we measured the distance from each colliery to the nearest large urban centre. In selecting these centres we looked first to the major regional centres, such as Newcastle, Cardiff and Manchester, and then, where communications between such centres and the colliery districts seemed extended or indirect, to regional sub-centres such as Nottingham and Swansea. We also experimented with another measure, defined as the distance from the colliery to the nearest town or city with a population of 50,000 or over at the 1931 Census. To use the North East as an example, this had the effect of bringing into the definition of 'large urban centre' such towns as Darlington, Gateshead, Sunderland, Tynemouth and West Hartlepool, as well as New-castle. It was possible, however, to supplement these measures of geographical isolation by classifying mining districts as rural or urban. Beynon and Austrin have emphasized the rurality of colliery villages in the Durham coalfield (1994: ch. 5) and this may have been one aspect of isolation, subjectively conceived. Our measure of 'isolation' therefore consists of two components: distance and a measure of rurality as administratively defined.

Kerr and Siegel stress the limited opportunities for occupational mobility within the isolated mass: 'It is hard to get out of this mass. The jobs are specialized, and the workers come to be also. . . . Protest is less likely to take the form of moving to another industry and more the character of the mass walkout' (1954: 192). Although we have no measure for opportunities for occupational mobility, the logic of Kerr and Siegel's argument applies to the opportunities for mobility from one workplace to another. We accordingly measured the number of separate collieries in each of our sample areas. If grievances were related to the conduct or characteristics of the mine owner rather than the mine management, then the number of companies operating collieries in the area should also have been of significance. Similarly, though less plausibly, it is possible that griev-ances may have been related to the colliery settlement itself: the 'bad living conditions (which seem additionally evil because they are supplied by the employer)' (Kerr and Siegel 1954: 192). If this was the case then the opportunity presented by a plurality of settlements should have reduced the likelihood of a 'mass walkout', and we therefore counted the number of separate 'situations' at which collieries were located in the area according to our sources.

The measures referred to above represent an attempt to capture both the ideas of massness and isolation as Kerr and Siegel conceptualized them al-though not, perhaps, as some later researchers would prefer in the case of isolation. The absence of 'neutrals' we consider to be part and parcel of the concept of massness, but the actual character of class relations in colliery settlements, the level of unionization, and the forms and contents of local cultures, as they have been documented in, for example, the cases of Creswell and Mardy, are left unmeasured by any of our proxies. Such measurement problems do not necessarily render a quantitative approach uninformative but they do indicate the desirability of supplementing quantitative information by qualitative data wherever possible. The approach adopted in subsequent chapters reflects this conviction.

Kerr and Siegel measured strike propensity by the number of working days lost in relation to employment. They noted that this choice implied that an industry which had frequent small strikes of short duration could be measured as less strike-prone than an industry with a few big strikes of substantial length. They accepted this possibility with the comment 'We are more concerned here with the significance of strikes than with their numerical occurrence' (1954: 189, note 1). Significance, of course, depends on standpoint, and a large number of strikes, even if they be small and short, may well be of significance to their participants. Moreover, statistics of working days lost, however useful in economic terms, are a sociological dog's dinner. As P. K. Edwards has noted, an isolated mass according to Kerr and Siegel may, because of the force of workers' solidarity, produce large strikes which are long because of the absence in the homogeneous mass of middle groups able to mediate the dispute. To confound these separate aspects to a single measure is not likely to be helpful (1977: 554). Here, we consider both working days lost and the number of strikes; the former because we wish to give the fairest possible test of Kerr and Siegel's hypothesis, the latter because we wish to see whether their hypothesis applies to any of the components of working days lost, or only to that measure.

We have already discussed some aspects of these strike statistics in chapter 1 and further details are available in the general appendix. Nevertheless, it is perhaps worth reiterating here that the incomplete coverage, both intentional and unintentional, of the official data, which is perhaps their most frequently noted shortcoming, affects the measurement of the number of strikes more seriously than the measurement of the number of working days lost. The coverage of the larger strikes which give rise to the bulk of the working days lost is likely to be very much higher than the coverage of the small strikes. This indeed provides a pragmatic argument for utilizing the days lost data. The most important point to make here though is that the adequacy of the data can only be judged in the light of the uses to which they are put. In the final analyses which we present below we require the data only to distinguish between the very strike-prone collieries and the rest, and a degree of 'fuzziness' in this distinction is quite acceptable, given our statistical techniques. In our judgement the data are adequate to our tasks.

The statistical procedures we followed in testing the Kerr–Siegel hypothesis are described in detail in the appendix to this chapter. Our first approach was to perform a conventional regression analysis. This allowed us to see whether increases in our indices of massness and isolation were associated with increases in strike propensity as Kerr and Siegel would predict. The answer was that they were, with the exceptions of our indices of mobility opportunities (the number of collieries, colliery companies and settlements in the locality). In view of the divergence between these last measures and the phenomena we were trying to measure this is perhaps not surprising. Nevertheless, the results of this analysis confirm that whether measured by the number of strikes or the number of working days lost, the level of strike activity was higher, other things being equal, in areas where miners formed a higher proportion of the population, where collieries were bigger, in areas which were distant from large urban centres and in areas which were rural.

Were it the case that every rise in each of the indices of massness or isolation was always associated with the same rise in the level of strike activity, not just on average but exactly, the association between isolation and massness on the one hand, and strike activity on the other would be 'perfect' and in such a situation statisticians would say that variations in isolation and massness 'explained' 100 per cent of the variation in strike activity. Were there to be no association at all between the isolation and massness variables and strike activity, so that increases in isolation or massness had no measurable effect on levels of strike activity, we would say that isolation and massness 'explained' none of the variation in strike activity. In practice, a set of variables explains between zero and 100 per cent of the variation in the variable one is trying to understand. This gives us a way of measuring the 'explanatory success' of the isolation and massness variables we have measured. These statements clearly use the word 'explain' in a rather special and much weaker sense than is normal. But if this is borne in mind this language allows us to say something with meaning and use. For, of course, the association between isolation, massness and strike activity is not perfect. In fact, the explanatory success of the isolation and massness variables achieved here is not very high at 19 per cent in the case of the number of working days lost and 18 per cent in the case of the number of strikes. This means that there was a great deal of variation in strike activity between different areas in inter-war England and Wales that cannot be accounted for by variations in the isolation or massness of the localities concerned.

However, we found that the association between strike activity and some of the variables measuring isolated masses could be brought out in a more illuminating and more informative way by alternative techniques of analysis. Table 8.1 shows that, while collieries with one or no strikes and collieries with fewer than 10,000 working days lost were distributed across the full range of areas, seemingly regardless of occupational density, highly strike-prone collieries were more likely to have been located in areas of high occupational density. In the appendix we show that this perception is not a figment of our imagination and is very unlikely to have occurred by chance.

The relatively small numbers of collieries which experienced high levels of strike activity are more significant than they may appear at first sight. Although in one sense these collieries are all statistical 'outliers', they accounted for a very high proportion of all local recorded strike activity. The 121 collieries in table 8.1 which experienced more than two local recorded strikes formed only 30 per cent of the 405 collieries in the sample areas but accounted for 92 per cent of the strikes. The 52 collieries in the sample areas which lost more than 10,000 working days due to recorded local strikes accounted for 91 per cent of the total of days lost.

Table 8.1. *Cross-tabulations of the number of strikes and the number of working days lost against occupational density (local strikes, area sample, Great Britain coalmining 1921–40)*

A. Number of local strikes at colliery 1921–40	Occupational density[a] 1931		
	<50%	≥50%	Total
0 or 1	168	116	284
≥2	47	74	121
Total	215	190	405

B. Number of working days lost at colliery in local strikes 1921–40	Occupational density[a] 1931		
	<50%	≥50%	Total
0–10,0000	202	151	353
>10,000	13	39	52
Total	215	190	405

Note:
[a] 'Occupational density' is the proportion of the adult male population of the administrative area in which the colliery was located whose occupations were in the mining and quarrying industries on Census night 1931.
Sources: number of strikes and working days lost: Ministry of Labour, *Trade Disputes: . . . Strikes and Lock-outs of 1921* and subsequent volumes, PRO LAB 34/39–55; occupational density: *Census of England and Wales 1931*, occupation tables.

Similar results to those reported in table 8.1 can also be obtained from cross tabulations of measures of strike activity against colliery employment. This led us to construct table 8.2 which allows us to examine the degree of association between occupational density, colliery employment and strike activity simultaneously. The table shows the percentage of collieries experiencing substantial local recorded strike activity as measured by the number of strikes in part A of the table and by working days lost in part B of the table for each combination of colliery size and occupational density. Only 19.8 per cent of the 126 collieries which were both small and in areas with low densities of mineworkers experienced at least two recorded local strikes; where these conditions were negated the figure rises to 46.5 per cent. Turning to the number of working days lost, the table shows that only 7 of the 126 collieries (5.6 per cent) which were both small and in areas with low densities of mineworkers experienced substantial strike activity on this measure. At the other end of the table, 32 of the 114 collieries (28.1 per cent) which were both large and in areas of high occupational density experienced such activity.

Nevertheless, it is important to note that even in the high employment and high density group of collieries, the majority of collieries experienced only very limited levels of strike activity. Thus neither large scale nor high occupational density nor both were sufficient conditions for high levels of strike activity.

Table 8.2. *Cross-tabulations of the number of strikes and the number of working days lost against colliery employment and occupational density (local strikes, area sample, Great Britain coalmining 1921–40)*

	Occupational density[a] 1931				
	<50%		≥50%		
	Colliery employment		Colliery employment		
A. Number of local strikes at colliery 1921–40	<650	≥650	<650	≥650	Total
0 or 1	101	67	55	61	284
	80.2%	*75.3%*	*72.4%*	*53.5%*	*70.1%*
≥2	25	22	21	53	121
	19.8%	*24.7%*	*27.6%*	*46.5%*	*29.9%*
Total	126	89	76	114	405
	100.0%	*100.0%*	*100.0%*	*100.0%*	*100.0%*

	Occupational density[a] 1931				
	<50%		≥50%		
	Colliery employment		Colliery employment		
B. Number of working days lost at colliery in local strikes 1921–40	<650	≥650	<650	≥650	Total
≤10,000	119	83	69	82	353
	94.4%	*93.3%*	*90.8%*	*71.9%*	*87.2%*
>10,000	7	6	7	32	52
	5.6%	*6.7%*	*9.2%*	*28.1%*	*12.8%*
Total	126	89	76	114	405
	100.0%	*100.0%*	*100.0%*	*100.0%*	*100.0%*

Note and sources: as for table 8.1.

Strikes were rare, even in British coalmining; high levels of strike activity were even more rare; but large-scale collieries and dense concentrations of miners were relatively common: it inevitably follows that these features could not be sufficient conditions for high levels of strike activity. It does not follow, however, that there is no connection of any sort between these phenomena.

Our formal analysis, details of which appear in the appendix to this chapter, confirms that colliery size and the massing together of mineworkers in the area of colliery do indeed have significant effects on strike activity, whether this is defined in terms of working days lost or in terms of the number of strikes. The working days lost data, but not the strike numbers data, also suggest the presence of an 'interaction effect', i.e. that the effect of occupational density is greater at the bigger collieries or, equivalently in our analysis, that the size effect is greater in the areas with a greater density of miners.

The scale of these effects is expressed in terms of a deviation from an overall mean. Taking the working days lost data first, the mean proportion of collieries which experienced significant strike activity on this measure was 12.4 per cent. This proportion rose or fell 6.2 points as occupational density was high or low. The size effect was marginally smaller, at plus or minus 5.0 points. The inter-action effect is quite strong and adds a further 4.4 points where density was high *and* collieries were large. The symmetry of these results, it should be noted, is a feature imposed by our model, not the data: it is an assumption, not a result. The overall mean proportion of collieries experiencing significant strike activity according to the numbers of strikes was 30.2 per cent. Location in an area with a high density of mineworkers added 7.2 points while large colliery size added 5.3 points. As before, the results are estimated by methods which impose symmetry. Here, though, there is no evidence of any interaction between occupational density and colliery size.

To sum up the foregoing analysis, a two-fold, binary classification of collieries by the occupational density of their localities and by their size defines four groups of collieries which had statistically significantly different degrees of strike activity. The group of large-scale collieries in areas of high occupational density experi-enced notably higher levels of strike activity than the other groups of collieries. Each of the two classifying variables had distinguishable effects of roughly similar magnitude. Nevertheless, even in the most strike-prone group of collieries, high levels of strike activity affected only a minority of the collieries in the group.

Our two analyses using regression analysis and cross-tabulations invite two rather different interpretations of the data. The regression analysis tells us that, on average, where collieries were large, where they were located in areas with a large proportion of miners in the population, where they were located in rural districts far away from large urban centres, strike activity was high. The low 'explanatory success' of these variables warns us that deviations about this average were very large, however. The analysis of the cross-tabulations tells us something slightly different: where collieries were large and where they were located in areas where there was a dense population of miners, the proportion of collieries that experienced high levels of strike activity was higher than average. Importantly, however, it also makes it clear that this proportion was low which-ever group of collieries is examined.

In short, Kerr and Siegel's hypothesis does help to explain inter-colliery variations in strike activity in inter-war England and Wales. Nevertheless our results demonstrate that massed isolation by no means guaranteed high levels of strike activity: massed isolation appears to have 'facilitated' strike activity or 'predisposed' a colliery to high levels of strike activity but did not ensure such activity. Even where mineworkers were massed in both workplace and locality, the majority of such collieries in inter-war England and Wales lost fewer than 10,000 working days due to local industrial disputes; the majority experienced no more than a single recorded dispute at local level.

The massed isolation of many British mining communities is by no means a complete answer to the puzzle of miners' strike propensity. The low explanatory success of our measures of isolation and massness suggests strongly that other factors are at work and we shall turn to alternative hypotheses in subsequent chapters. However, before we do so we need to examine one aspect of massness in more detail. We noted earlier in this chapter that the empirical results suggested that an important component of massness was massness, not in the locality, but in the workplace. Kerr and Siegel's hypothesis is normally seen as a theory of how aspects of community can influence aspects of workplace behaviour. Yet we have seen that insofar as Kerr and Siegel's theory has some explanatory success in the present case it is in large part due to the fact that bigger collieries were more strike-prone than smaller collieries. Kerr and Siegel's hypothesis incorporated the idea that there was an effect of workplace size on workplace industrial relations and in doing so makes a point of contact with another very long-standing idea in industrial sociology: that there is a 'size effect' on workplace behaviour and that large-scale industry is productive of poor industrial relations. It is to this question which we turn in the next chapter.

Appendix: the area sample and statistical procedures

THE AREA SAMPLE

We sought a sample of small-scale administrative areas with a non-negligible mining presence in the 1931 Census of England and Wales. Scotland was excluded because of the lack of adequate data in the 1931 Census of Scotland. Large-scale areas (urban districts and municipal boroughs with populations over 50,000, all county boroughs and the administrative county of London) were excluded because of potential problems in detecting 'isolated masses' of mineworkers in such large areas. Areas with a 'non-negligible mining presence' are those areas in which 100 or more adult males with occupations in mining and quarrying were enumerated in the 1931 Census.

For small-scale areas data are only available on the number of people with occupations in 'mining and quarrying'. This category covers, *inter alia*, slate and stone quarry workers, iron-stone mine and quarry workers and tin miners, each of whom were quite numerous in particular areas. We therefore excluded from the sampling frame all administrative areas in counties which the Mines Department *List of Mines* for 1931 showed had no coal mine. The sampling frame thus derived consisted of 412 administrative areas.

We took a simple unstratified random 1–in–2 sample from our sample frame to yield an initial sample of 206 administrative areas. The sample included both parts of Tamworth Rural District which straddled a county boundary; the two parts were merged in our sample, so that at this stage it consisted of 205 administrative areas.

DATA LINKAGE

Collieries were linked to administrative areas via the 'situation' of the colliery given in the Mines Department *List of Mines* for 1931. The general appendix discusses the problems involved in defining collieries and our solutions to them. We ignored the following listed mines: mines which were not coal mines but mines of some other mineral, e.g. fireclay, iron-stone; mines of coal which were not producing coal, mines at which work had been suspended, or which were used solely for pumping or ventilation purposes; and mines employing fewer than fifty people in total. The reason for the last exclusion is that it is relatively unlikely that strikes at such mines would feature in the Ministry of Labour strike records because of their likely small scale (see the general appendix).

In 80 areas, containing 35,438 workers in mining and quarrying occupations, no colliery could be attached to the area. The reasons for this include: the exclusion of various categories of mines and quarries from our list of sample collieries; the existence of miners who worked in one administrative area but lived in another; the existence of unemployed and retired miners living in an area no longer containing a sample colliery. These 80 areas were excluded from our sample leaving us with 125 areas in the final sample.

DATA DEFINITIONS AND SOURCES

Strike frequency (*STRIKES*): the number of local strikes affecting each sample colliery between 1921 and 1940. Widespread strikes were excluded from our analysis. Widespread strikes were rare (see table 4.1). (Source: Ministry of Labour, *Trade Disputes: . . . Strikes and Lock-outs of 1921* and subsequent volumes, PRO LAB 34/39–55).

Working days lost (*WDL*): the total 'working days lost' in the local strikes and lock-outs affecting each sample colliery between 1921 and 1940. Working days lost in multi-colliery strikes were allocated to the collieries involved according to their employment in the year of the strike. (Source: as for *STRIKES*).

Logarithms of strike frequency and working days lost (*LSTRIKES* and *LWDL*): the common logarithms of (*STRIKES*+1) and (*WDL*+1). The logarithm of zero is undefined: hence the unit addition to *STRIKES* and *WDL*. (Sources: as for *STRIKES*).

Mining population (*CSM&Q*): the number of adult males (14 years and over) in mining and quarrying occupations on census night 1931 in the administrative area to which the colliery was linked. (Source: *Census of England and Wales 1931*, occupation tables).

Population (*CSMPOP*): the number of adult males (14 years and over) enumerated on Census night 1931 in the administrative area to which the colliery was linked. (Source: as for *CSM&Q*).

Occupational density (*OCCDENS*): (*CSM&Q* / *CSMPOP*).100.

Colliery employment (*EMPT*): the numbers employed at the colliery (underground and surface) in 1931. (Source: Mines Department, *List of Mines*, 1931).

Distance (*MILES1*): the distance in miles by rail from the colliery's nearest railway station to the appropriate large city. The 'appropriate large city' is for Northumberland and Durham, Newcastle-upon-Tyne; for Cumberland, Manchester; for Lancashire and Cheshire, the nearer of Manchester and Liverpool; for Yorkshire, the nearer of Leeds and Sheffield; for the East Midlands, the nearest of Sheffield, Derby, Nottingham and Leicester; for the West Midlands, Birmingham; for the South West, Bristol; for Kent, London; for North Wales, Liverpool; for South Wales, the nearest of Swansea, Cardiff and Newport. (Sources: colliery's nearest station: *Colliery Year Book and Coal Trades Directory 1931*; mileages: *Bradshaw's April 1910 Railway Guide*).

Distance (*MILES2*): the distance by rail in miles from the colliery's nearest railway station to the nearest town or city of 50,000 or more according to the 1931 Census. (Sources: as for *MILES1* together with *Census of England and Wales 1931*, occupation tables).

Rurality (*AREADUM*): *AREADUM* = 0 for collieries linked to urban districts and municipal boroughs; *AREADUM* = 1 for collieries linked to rural districts. (Source: *Census of England and Wales 1931*).

Numbers of collieries, companies and situations (*NCIES, NCOS, NSITS*): the number of sample collieries, separate owners of sample collieries, and separate 'situations' at which sample collieries were located respectively, in the administrative area to which the colliery was linked. (Source: Mines Department, *List of Mines*, 1931).

STATISTICAL PROCEDURES: REGRESSION

Both *STRIKES* and *WDL* are highly skewed but the independent variables, with the exception of *MILES1*, are only moderately skewed. These data attributes imply that there is little hope of finding well-fitting linear equations expressing *WDL* and *STRIKES* in terms of our measures of massness and isolation. To solve this problem we formed a logarithmic transformation of the dependent variables giving us *LWDL* and *LSTRIKES*.

The best linear regression equations we could find to explain our dependent variables are reported in table 8.3. These and all other statistical results reported in this appendix were computed using the SAS package (SAS Institute Inc. 1985). We assessed equations by the R^2 adjusted for the number of regressors statistic, subject to the constraint that the estimated coefficients were each of the 'correct' sign. The variables *NCIES, NCOS*, and *NSITS* were eliminated from the equations because when entered together *NCOS* took the 'wrong' sign and when entered in sub-sets at least one of the coefficients on the variables in each subset was always incorrectly signed. We found that the adjusted R^2 statistics could be raised slightly by replacing *CSMPOP* and *CSM&Q* by their ratio, *OCCDENS*. The variables remaining in the equations are all well determined by conventional criteria and all have the 'correct' sign as posited by the Kerr–Siegel model.

Table 8.3. *Regression results*

$LWDL=$	-0.171	$+0.126OCCDENS$	$+0.000793EMPT$
	(-0.68)	(2.71)	(6.84)
	$+0.0141MILES1$	$+0.424AREADUM$	
	(3.91)	(2.50)	

F=23.0   Prob>F=0.0001 $R^2 = 0.19$ Adjusted $R^2 = 0.18$ $n = 405$

$LSTRIKES=$	−0.0891	$+0.00311OCCDENS$	$+0.000139EMPT$
	(-1.81)	(3.38)	(6.07)
	$+0.00294MILES1$	$+0.0876AREADUM$	
	(4.16)	(2.63)	

F=22.2   Prob>F = 0.0001 $R^2 = 0.18$ Adjusted $R^2 = 0.17$ $n = 405$

Notes:
Figures in brackets are 't'-statistics; 'Prob $>$F' gives the probability of observing the computed F statistic under the null hypothesis of no association.

Table 8.4. *The saturated additive model for working days lost*

A   Analysis of variation

Source	df	Chi²	Probability
M	1	61.54	0.0001
$OCCDENS$	1	15.63	0.0001
$EMPT$	1	10.06	0.0015
$OCCDENS.EMPT$	1	7.82	0.0052
Residual	0	0.00	1.0000

B   Estimated parameters

Effect	Estimate	Standard error
Mean	0.124	0.016
$OCCDENS$	−0.062	0.016
$EMPT$	−0.050	0.016
$OCCDENS.EMPT$	0.044	0.016

Notes:
Degrees of freedom are given under 'df'; 'Chi²' is the Neyman chi² statistic; the probability of observing the computed chi² statistic if the null hypothesis is true is given under 'Probability'.

Table 8.5. *The additive model for the number of strikes*

A   Analysis of variation

Source	df	Chi²	Probability
Model	2	19.06	0.0001
OCCDENS	1	10.26	0.0014
EMPT	1	5.71	0.0169
Residual	1	2.39	0.1218
Total	3	21.45	0.0001

B   Estimated parameters

Effect	Estimate	Standard Error
Mean	0.302	0.022
OCCDENS	−0.072	0.023
EMPT	−0.053	0.022

For notes see table 8.4.

STATISTICAL PROCEDURES: TESTS OF ASSOCIATION IN CROSS-TABULATIONS

Chi² tests of association between the variables defining the cross-tabulations reported in table 8.1 yielded test statistics of 14.1 ($p < 0.001$) for the tabulation given in part A of the table (1 degree of freedom) and 18.9 ($p < 0.001$) for that given in part B (1 degree of freedom).

STATISTICAL PROCEDURES: CATEGORICAL DATA ANALYSIS

The cross-classification of collieries in terms of the two binary variables *EMPT* and *OCCDENS* yields four groups of collieries. The proportion of each group which experienced a high level of strike activity is the 'response proportion'. The four response proportions are denoted q_{ij} where $i = 1, 2$ indexes the value taken by *EMPT* and $j = 1, 2$ indexes the value taken by *OCCDENS*. The formal analysis attempts to discover whether there are statistically significant differences between the q_{ij}. This is achieved by estimating a statistical model for the q_{ij} of the form:

$$q_{ij} = M + EMPT_i + OCCDENS_j + EMPT.OCCDENS_{ij}$$

where:

$i = 1, 2; j = 1, 2$
M is the overall mean response proportion
$EMPT_i$ is the employment effect
$OCCDENS_j$ is the density effect
$EMPT.OCCDENS_{ij}$ is the joint effect of the two variables.

The model assumes these effects are additive (Freeman 1987: 113).

The model as given writes four equations as functions of nine parameters. The model therefore has an infinity of solutions and some method of selecting from this infinity must be found. The conventional solution, which we have followed here, is to impose a symmetry requirement on the solution. Specifically we require that:

$$EMPT_1 = -EMPT_2 = -EMPT;$$
$$OCCDENS_1 = -OCCDENS_2 = -OCCDENS$$

and

$$EMPT.OCCDENS_{ij} = -EMPT.OCCDENS \text{ for all } i, j.$$

The model can now be written:

$$q_{11} = M + EMPT + OCCDENS + EMPT.OCCDENS$$
$$q_{12} = M + EMPT - OCCDENS - EMPT.OCCDENS$$
$$q_{21} = M - EMPT + OCCDENS - EMPT.OCCDENS$$
$$q_{22} = M - EMPT - OCCDENS + EMPT.OCCDENS$$

which is a model of four equations in four unknowns. The solution of this model, the 'saturated model' is exact, given the 'response' proportions q_{ij}, requiring only algebra to solve it (Freeman 1987: 115). Often in applications it is possible to show that the interaction terms such as $EMPT.OCCDENS$ can be eliminated to give a simpler model still, which nevertheless provides an acceptable fit to the data. The solution of such models is no longer exact because the number of equations is now greater than the number of unknowns and solutions are computed using statistical techniques. Table 8.4 shows, in part A, the results of testing the null hypotheses that the true parameters M, $EMPT$, $OCCDENS$ and $EMPT.OCCDENS$ are each zero against the working days lost data. These hypotheses are all rejected, including that pertaining to $EMPT.OCCDENS$. Hence our inability to reject the saturated model with this data. Part B of the table sets out the computed parameters of the model with their standard errors, as reported in the text.

Table 8.5 shows the results of applying our techniques to the data on the number of strikes. Here the saturated model can be dispensed with in favour of a simpler model consisting of the 'main effects' of $OCCDENS$ and $EMPT$ and a residual. Part A of table 8.5 again shows the results of testing various null hypotheses. The line labelled 'Total' gives the result of a test of the hypothesis of homogeneity i.e. that $q_{11} = q_{12} = q_{21} = q_{22}$. This hypothesis can be rejected safely. The line labelled 'Residual' shows the result of testing the hypothesis that the data fit the model specified for the q_{ij}: this hypothesis can be accepted safely. The remaining lines give the results of tests that $EMPT$ and $OCCDENS$ are separately and jointly equal to zero. These hypotheses are all rejected. Part B of the table sets out the estimated parameters as reported in the main text.

9 Mining and modernity: size, sectionalism and solidarity

Consequences of size: ideas and hypotheses

The colliery- and plant-based analyses of industrial conflict, which form part of the industrial relations literature referred to in chapter 5, have been confined to a handful of studies restricted to short periods during the post-nationalization era (see Scott *et al.* 1963; McCormick 1969; Christine Edwards 1978; Christine Edwards and Heery 1985; Rigg 1987). While it is only relatively recently that such approaches have incorporated explicit concepts relating to size, and have involved quantification and the formal testing of hypotheses, the interest in workplace scale in relation to labour relations and human behaviour is not new. Before examining the potential of colliery size for explaining the history of strikes in the industry, therefore, we provide a context in the form of a survey of the social comment and analysis provoked by the emergence of large-scale workplaces.

Three traditions are discernible in the economics and sociology of size. The first is that introduced by Charles Babbage, who in 1832 was the first to link Adam Smith's concept of the division of labour with large-scale industry. Size of factory, he thought, both facilitated and advanced the technical division of labour (Babbage 1832/1989: ch. 19, section 263; compare with Adam Smith 1776/1976: ch. 1). The economic advantages of the division of labour were stressed, but the consequences for the social relations of production were addressed only in passing, if at all. Writers in the second tradition, originating with Marx, expanded the concept of scale to encompass large-scale organizations as well as large-scale workplaces, both in part the result of division of labour and the application of large-scale machinery. Writers in the third tradition, associated with Weber, have been impressed by the 'impersonality' of 'big capitalist enterprises' and the bureaucratization of their internal social relations (Weber 1922/1968: 980).

Marx emphasized that a necessary condition for 'the development of the social productivity of labour' was 'co-operation on a large scale' involving the 'concentration on a vast scale' of capital in large industrial plants (Marx 1867/1976: 775 (ch. 25.2); cf. 929 (ch. 32)). The concentration of capital led to the combination of workers. 'Large-scale industry concentrates in one place a crowd of people unknown to one another. Competition divides their interests.

But the maintenance of wages, this common interest which they have against their boss, unites them in a common thought of resistance – *combination*' (Marx 1847/1976: 210). In this interpretation large-scale industry forms a prominent site for the class struggle, not because of abnormally severe exploitation but because it is a location for exceptionally intense solidarity among workers. A rather different, Liberal, assessment can be found in the 1894 *Majority Report* of the Royal Commission on Labour:

> The growth and development of large industrial establishments during the present century has necessarily resulted in the creation of considerable bodies of workmen more or less separated in their lives and pursuits from those under whom they work. In those manufactures, which in modern times have been carried on upon a great scale with costly machinery, there cannot exist the intimate relation between the workman and his work which is to be found in some small industries where the workman owns, or may hope some day to own . . . his tools, workshop, and material. The mutual ignorance arising from this separation is, we believe, a main reason why so many conflicts take place . . . (*Majority Report*: 112)

Among the few Marxist scholars and the wider circle of Marxist polemicists who continued Marx and Engels's research into the concentration and centralization of capital, the work of D. J. Williams is of special interest in relation to the history of industrial relations in the coal industry. He was a miner, a lodge secretary in the anthracite area of South Wales (Francis and Smith 1980: 109, note 47), and the author of *Capitalist Combinations in the Coal Industry*, published in 1924, a history of the rise of combines in the coalfields of South Wales, the North East and Scotland after the First World War.

Echoing the Marx and Engels of *The Communist Manifesto*, Williams emphasized the effect of large-scale organizations in uprooting 'the old personal relations of master and men', while the concentration of production in fewer and larger companies through the process of combination meant that workers became unaware of the identities of their employers. Quoting from the 1918 *Report* of the Committee on Trusts, he stressed 'The tendency of these large aggregates . . . to become impersonal and to make the worker feel that he is dealing with a vast machine. . . . From a social point of view, the bigger the employers the more detached they are from the men they employ' (Committee on Trusts, *Report*: 7). As this process intensified, so too did the opposition of labour and capital which struggled 'not only for a greater share in the proceeds of the industry, but also for its eventual control' (D. J. Williams 1924: 171–2).

A warning of the significance of the trend towards monopolization was also contained in the 50,000 copies of the manifesto of the Lanarkshire Miners' Reform Committee which it circulated in 1917 (Campbell 1992: 91). Awareness of the rapidly changing structure of the industry in certain parts of the coalfield thereby entered into the consciousness of leading trade unionists, and mineworkers' industrial and political actions and organization may have been influenced as a consequence. Campbell has suggested that the Minority Movement, the Communist Party's industrial arm, may have had greater success in

Scotland's larger collieries because it was there that Marx's predictions about the increasing concentration of capital were being made manifest, although there is no indication that the Minority Movement was particularly successful in larger *firms* (Campbell 1992: 98).

Williams's emphasis on the 'impersonality' of relations between labour and capital in colliery combines, although expressed in a style unmistakably influenced by Marx and Engels, is nevertheless distinct from Marx's emphasis on the crowding together of workers in large-scale plants. Indeed, the idea that the important aspect of size is impersonality, although present in the *Communist Manifesto,* is one we would now normally associate with Weber rather than Marx. But the idea Williams chose to emphasize, though under the different title of alienation, became the main means of understanding the impact of large-scale industry on workers' attitudes and behaviour by the 1960s.

In the hands of investigators such as Blauner, Marx's concept of alienation came to mean a combination of powerlessness, meaninglessness, isolation and 'self-estrangement' or 'detachment' in the work process (Blauner 1964: 26, 32–3). For others, such as Gallie, it came to mean little more than an absence of 'deep satisfaction' with work (1978: 86–7). The most intense levels of dissatisfaction were, it was thought, generated by mass production technologies; here, it was assumed, would be found the most strike-prone workers. In the UK Woodward advanced a similar argument, that size was just a concomitant of assembly-line manufacture and that the empirical relationship between strikes and plant size obtained simply because assembly-line plants tended to be big (Ministry of Technology, *Management and Technology*: 29–30; Woodward 1965: 61).

However, when Woodward's survey work, carried out in the 1950s, is disaggregated a more complicated picture emerges which is relevant to an understanding of the relation between size, technology and social action. Among her sample firms using mass production technology she encountered some employing fewer than 250 workers, while some firms adopting 'unit' production methods employed more than a thousand workers (Ministry of Technology, *Management and Technology*: 20). Eisele's later investigation of plant size, technology and strike frequency (1974) also suggested that the high strike activity of large plants could not be explained entirely by the type of technology employed.

The early attempts by Marx and Engels to relate emergent large-scale structures and organizations to social action have yet to result in a precise analysis. Instead, a wide variety of hypotheses remain current: that large-scale industry differs from industry on a more 'human' scale because of the extent to which work is divided, or because it involves the use of 'instruments of labour' which can only be used by large collections of workers, or because it crowds workers together and gives them a common interest, or because it 'alienates' workers to an extreme degree; large-scale companies and combines (which may comprise several plants of relatively small size) may differ from smaller organizations because of their 'impersonality' and the bureaucratization of their internal social relations.

The third, Weberian, tradition in the history of comment and concern with large-scale industry focuses on the bureaucracy required and facilitated by production on a mass scale. Most of Weber's discussion of bureaucracy was directed towards state, rather than corporate, bureaucracies and is, therefore, relevant to our concern with the relations between size, organization and social conduct only after 1946. Corporate bureaucratization and its effects on industrial relations have been explored most persuasively by Marginson and Ingham. Marginson emphasized the replacement of direct forms of management by hierarchical systems in large organizations, the increasing standardization and formalization of management procedures and relations with workers and a growing impersonality which results from these developments: 'Longer chains of communication enhance the scope for systematic distortion of information passed through the hierarchy and hence the scope for friction between top managers and workers. One consequence is to make large organizations more conflict prone' (Marginson 1984: 2). However, Marginson also points out that bureaucratization is a heterogeneous phenomenon, the various aspects lacking a uniform relation to size, and that the degree of bureaucratization is a matter of choice for managers – managers who may consider the impact of their management structures on future industrial relations.

Ingham's empirical study into a small number of Bradford engineering firms in the mid-1960s confirmed the greater extension of the division of labour in large plants, attested to the great unpleasantness of work associated with mass production technologies, and identified bureaucratization as peculiar to large firms. The novelty of his findings was the absence of grievance among workers in large plants compared with small-plant employees. Workers in large-scale plants seemed to be prepared to accept a trade-off in which higher pay offset the possibly greater satisfactions of employment in small firms. Workers in small firms valued shopfloor social relations and non-economic aspects of their work; workers in large firms had values which were the reverse of these (Ingham 1970: tables 8.7–8.10).

Ingham was cautious in drawing implications from his research for the relation between size and strike activity, and specifically between corporate scale and bureaucratization and the development of a solidaristic and anti-management outlook among workers. He rejected the view that such tendencies were direct and automatic consequences of intra-organizational factors: 'large scale will tend to inhibit the identification of the worker with the plant; but antagonism and conflict do not necessarily flow from a lack of such identification'. The reason for this he saw as the 'individualistic and calculative attitudes of many of the large-plant workers' who defined their work activity in an economistic way (Ingham 1970: 116–17). In other words, it was not and is not possible to read off workers' attitudes or behaviour from the nature of structures in which they work; their orientations to, and the meanings they attach to, those structures are essential to an understanding of their actions.

The modern development of the insights contained in the work of Marx and Weber is at once discouraging to anyone interested in the history of industrial conflict. Long-established concepts continue to exercise social scientists and others, but their research has emphasized variety and heterogeneity in the differences between large- and small-scale workplaces and work organizations. Technology, the organization of work tasks through the division of labour and specialization, and bureaucratization have been discovered to stand in an indeterminate relationship to scale as measured by employment, and researchers have come to realize that the interrelations between these variables are complex.

Comment on the effects of colliery and coal company size on mining industrial relations has had a long history, as we have seeen. But for long after the Sankey Commission hearings in 1919 the size question in the coal industry was dominated by arguments that mines were too small and colliery companies too many for economic efficiency (Kirby 1977: 39). As the pioneer investigators of the 'size effect' wrote in the 1950s: 'In the first half of the present century all the emphasis in industrial management was on centralisation and the build up of large-scale organisation' (Acton Society Trust 1953: 7). But after this movement reached its high point during the nationalizations of the Attlee government a reaction set in, partly as a result of the failure of some of those nationalized industries to demonstrate a 'transforming improvement' in the relations between worker and management (*ibid.*: 9). The 1953 investigation carried out by the Acton Society Trust, published as *Size and Morale*, was the first of many research inquiries into the consequences of large-scale industry for the efficiency of labour relations; they included investigations into productivity, flexibility, mobility, turnover, absenteeism, accidents and strikes (Baldwin 1955). The drift of the Trust's findings on absenteeism, based partly on research in eighteen National Coal Board (NCB) collieries, was that a major contributory factor to poor 'morale' was the reduction in face-to-face contact and the resulting depersonalization and formalization of communications between management and workers and between different groups of workers: the bureaucratization of the workplace (Acton Society Trust 1953, 1957).

Of even greater relevance for our study was the outcome of the simultaneous research carried out by Revans, whose use of data from the coal industry led him to become the first to assert a positive correlation between size and strike activity (Revans 1955, 1956, 1958). This thesis, known as the 'size effect' thesis, was the seminal contribution which generated the subsequent literature on size in manufacturing industry. Revans was concerned with 'industrial morale', which he defined as 'the willingness of men and managements to work together'. He diagnosed poor morale from 'withdrawal, for any reason, from the working situation'; absence from work, industrial accidents and strikes were all regarded by Revans as manifestations of low 'morale' (Revans 1956: 304). While emphasizing that 'size alone is only one factor in determining the level of morale', none the less on the basis of his research on Welsh and Yorkshire collieries, he claimed that there was 'a regular progression of coal lost per man in stoppages throughout the size range' (Revans 1956: 307). Furthermore, within collieries of given size the least strike-prone were those which had a higher ratio of supervisors to operatives and therefore smaller working groups (Revans 1956: 307–9). These findings and subsequent research led him to conclude that the evidence showed 'beyond doubt that the willingness of the individual miner to join, and to remain out with, his mates in a strike goes up steadily with the size of the mine' (Revans 1958: 200–1).

However, the picture was considerably more complex than this conclusion allowed. Revans's conclusions were based on data for 1949–53 and covered two of the three most highly strike-prone regions, South Wales and Yorkshire. Revans omitted the highly strike-prone Scottish region, on the grounds that 'many of the strikes in the smaller mines of Lanarkshire may be a rearguard action against the total closure of the coalfield' (Revans 1958: 200). However, Paterson's contemporaneous work showed a *negative* effect of colliery size on the number of strikes per thousand employees in the Scottish collieries (Paterson 1956). And a study by Wellisz, which was based on data from the more quiescent Manchester, Wigan, and North Wales districts for 1947–50, reported only moderately high correlation coefficients between colliery employment and the percentage of tonnage lost from strikes (Wellisz 1953). These studies suggest that Revans's results may have been particular to the two regions he considered and/or dependent on the measure of strike activity used. Revans himself could find no 'regular progression' in the number of strikes per thousand employees, the second measure of strike activity which he considered. His results revealed that while in Yorkshire this measure clearly differentiated the very large collieries (2,500 or more workers) from the small (500 or fewer workers), no clear progression could be discerned in the collieries of intermediate scales; in South Wales this measure showed no association with size at all (Revans 1958: 201). In the light of Revans's own data and the somewhat large 'exception' he made of Scotland, together with the evidence presented by Wellisz and Paterson, Revans's conclusion must be regarded as exaggerated.

Applying regression techniques to Yorkshire colliery data for the period 1947–63, McCormick produced evidence which also indicated an effect of size on colliery strike activity measured as the number of strikes per hundred face workers. This size effect persisted even when mechanization and levels of supervision ('technology' and 'bureaucracy') among other factors were controlled for (McCormick 1969). However, McCormick's result is unusual. Typical results for British manufacturing are that the *number* of strikes per plant or, equivalently, the probability of a strike in any given plant, rises with plant size but the number of strikes *per head* is often found to be roughly constant or to show no consistent relationship with plant size (Department of Employment, *Strikes in Britain*, table FF, 60; P. K. Edwards 1980: 153). These results indicate the importance of clarity in defining how strike activity is measured.

To summarize, the notion that workplace size is important in some way to the explanation of strike activity has a long history: Kerr and Siegel's inclusion of this factor in their concept of the strike-prone 'isolated mass' was no novelty. While the literature on the industry after nationalization has supported the view that a size effect on strike activity existed, it has never progressed beyond this to answer such questions as which particular dimensions of strike activity have been critical and by what mechanisms size contributed to strike propensity in the coalfields. Furthermore, the existing literature on the industry before nationalization has not even posed the basic empirical question of whether large collieries were in some sense more strike-prone than small collieries.

While the historiography of the industry emphasizes the large number of small collieries that managed to survive in the inter-war period, our discussion in the first section of chapter 2 underlined the large size of the typical miner's colliery. By 1938 no less than 55 per cent of all miners were employed in collieries with more than a thousand workers; in the rest of British industry in 1935 only in vehicle manufacture was the median worker an employee in a larger plant. It follows, therefore, that had there been a size effect in coalmining between the wars, that might have accounted for at least part of its relative strike proneness. What follows is an empirical investigation of the size effect in relation to strike propensity in collieries under private ownership.

The 'size effect' in coalmining

The statistical basis of our investigation of the size effect is a sample of collieries drawn randomly from the 1921 population of collieries and observed until the end of 1938. The level of strike activity at these collieries was established by linking them to the Ministry of Labour records of strikes. In practice we encountered particularly severe problems in linking strikes with collieries in the period up to 1925. This, and the existence of the seven month lock-out in the industry in 1926 following the General Strike, led us to discard our observations for the period before 1927. Although a number of collieries closed in the 1921–6 period, very few opened and it is therefore legitimate to treat our sample as if it had been drawn from the 1927 population. This 'colliery sample' is described in more detail in the first section of the appendix to this chapter.

The 166 collieries in our colliery sample were in production for up to twelve years between 1927 and 1938. We might have measured their average strike activity and other characteristics over this twelve-year period, or we could have made single 'colliery-years' our units of analysis, relating the strike activity in each year to colliery size in that year. The 'colliery-years' procedure has the advantage that it easily generates a large sample of colliery-years, which is desirable for statistical reasons. However, because strikes are rare events it is not helpful to relate measures of strike activity to colliery characteristics over periods as short as a single year. We decided on a compromise between our desire for a large sample and our desire to examine strike activity over moderately long periods, and made our unit of analysis a colliery over a four-year period. This means that we shall be relating the strike activity of a colliery in the periods 1927–30, 1931–4 and 1935–8 to the colliery's size and other characteristics during those periods. For all practical purposes, colliery X in 1927–30 is treated as a separate colliery from colliery X in 1931–4. With 166 collieries appearing up

Table 9.1. *Number of strikes by colliery size (colliery sample, Great Britain 1927–38)*

Colliery size class[a]	Number of sample collieries	Mean employment at sample collieries	Number (and %) of collieries struck at least once	Mean annual number of strikes per colliery	Mean annual number of strikes per thousand employees
0-99	41	57	0 (0.0)	0.00	0.00
100–199	52	143	5 (9.6)	0.06	0.57
200–499	107	331	19 (17.8)	0.11	0.39
500–999	77	707	20 (26.0)	0.20	0.28
1,000–1,999	54	1,398	16 (29.6)	0.20	0.14
2,000+	22	2,515	6 (27.3)	0.31	0.13
All	353	653	66 (18.7)	0.14	0.29

Notes:
Observations of strike activity are of collieries X, Y, Z, etc. over the period 1927–30, of collieries X, Y, Z, etc. in 1931–4 and of collieries X, Y, Z, etc. in 1935–8. These observations are pooled. In this way the 166 collieries in the sample give rise to 353 observations.
[a] Size is measured by mean employment, above and below ground, over 1927–30, 1931–4 or 1935–8.
Sources: Ministry of Labour, *Trade Disputes: . . . Strikes and Lock-outs of 1927* and subsequent volumes, PRO LAB 34/45–53; Mines Department, *Lists of Mines,* 1927–38.

to three times we would have 498 sample points were it not for the closure of collieries during the period, which reduces the number of sample points to 353. This explains why the number of observations in many of this chapter's tables is given as 353 even though the colliery sample contains only 166 collieries.

Table 9.1 classifies the sample collieries by size (measured by the number of workers including both underground and surface workers). It shows that the number of strikes per colliery rose with colliery size; that the proportion of collieries struck at least once rose with size but the number of strikes per thousand workers was roughly constant with respect to size. The second section of the Appendix presents statistical confirmation that the latter perception is not a figment of our imaginations.

Table 9.2 reveals that the number of working days lost per colliery and per thousand employees rose and rose particularly rapidly in the middle size ranges, but fell back in the largest collieries. In all these respects coalmining conformed to the characteristics associated with modern manufacturing industry.

The increase in the number of working days lost per thousand workers shown in table 9.2 could in principle result from an increase in the number of strikes per thousand workers, an increase in the average numbers involved, or an increase in

Table 9.2. *Working days lost by colliery size (colliery sample, Great Britain 1927–38)*

Colliery size class[a]	Number of sample collieries	Mean annual working days lost per colliery	Mean annual working days lost per thousand employees
0-99	41	0	0
100–199	52	14	131
200–499	107	88	294
500–999	77	709	904
1,000–1,999	54	2,052	2,847
2,000+	22	531	1,199
All	353	694	653

For notes and sources see table 9.1.

the average duration of strikes since, in principle, the number of working days lost per thousand workers is the product of these three terms. We have already seen that the number of strikes per thousand workers is a constant in our sample; it follows that either the numbers involved or the duration of strikes or both must increase with size. Table 9.3, which uses the complete file of officially recorded strikes, shows that the average strike duration fell somewhat with colliery size. Therefore the increase in the average number of working days lost with colliery size must have resulted solely from an increase in the numbers involved. Table 9.4 provides confirmation of this. The increase in the numbers involved is apparent in both the numbers directly and indirectly involved. Workers indirectly involved in a strike have been officially defined as 'those workers . . . thrown out of work at the establishments where the disputes occur although not themselves parties to the disputes' (Department of Employment and Productivity, *Strikes in Britain*: 19). That the numbers indirectly involved increased with size is indicative of a degree of technical interdependence between work groups in a colliery. That the sum of those directly and indirectly involved did not exhaust the complete colliery work-force, at least in the larger collieries, indicates that some degree of technical independence also existed: it was possible for some to continue at work while others struck.

These results are open to more than one interpretation. It is possible to interpret the rise in the number of strikes per colliery and the number of working days lost per thousand workers (for collieries employing up to two thousand workers) as evidence that a size effect was present. But it is also possible to conclude from the observation that the number of strikes per thousand employees was invariant to size that there was no size effect: large collieries were

Table 9.3. *The length of strikes and the number of working days lost by the size of colliery (all officially recorded strikes, Great Britain 1927–38)*

Colliery size class[a]	Number of strikes	Number of strikes of known duration	Mean duration (days)	Mean working days lost per strike
0-99	150	142	8	339
100-199	149	146	7	1,571
200-499	566	561	6	1,431
500-999	604	598	5	2,073
1,000-1,999	421	417	5	4,182
2,000+	238	233	6	7,130
Unknown	201	193	7	22,924

Notes:
National strikes and lock-outs are excluded. The 201 strikes at collieries of unknown size comprise two distinct classes. The first are strikes which were not restricted to a single colliery and for which the allocation to a colliery size class makes no sense; these strikes often involved large numbers. The second consists of strikes at single collieries which could not be identified; these strikes often involved small numbers.
[a] Size is measured by employment, above and below ground, in the year in which the strike occurred.
Sources: as for table 9.1.

struck more often merely because they were bigger collieries. Behind these conflicting conclusions lie two different views about the nature of domestic strike activity: one which regards the whole colliery work-force to be the appropriate unit of analysis, the other which regards the work group as the appropriate unit.

In the first view, the 'solidarity model', the work-force is seen as a unit and strikes are assumed to involve the whole work-force, however big that might be. Strikes are supposed to result from grievances which affect the whole work-force, for example rises in the cost of living. For simplicity, we can suppose that grievances are events that occur at a given rate per year per colliery. This rate is unrelated to colliery size. Again for simplicity, we can assume that a fixed proportion of grievances turn into strikes. In the second view, the 'sectionalism model', it is a 'production team' that experiences grievances and the work-force is simply an agglomeration of production teams. Strikes involve only particular production teams. Grievances arise at the production team level and occur at a given rate per year per team. This rate is unrelated to colliery or team size. The kind of grievances most easily visualized in this context are grievances to do with working arrangements or work discipline, for example, an issue over payments to be paid in an 'abnormal place'. For simplicity we can assume that production teams are all the same size so that a colliery twice as big as another has twice as many production teams working in it. Suppose again that a fixed proportion of grievances turn into strikes. In both models, strike duration is unrelated to colliery size.

If we assume the 'solidarity model' to be broadly correct, we would expect the number of strikes to be constant with respect to colliery size (because workers in bigger collieries experience grievances no more frequently that do workers in smaller collieries). Because one expects strikes to involve the whole work-force and strike durations to be constant, one would expect the number of working days lost per thousand employees to be a constant with respect to colliery size. Therefore, when one sees that, according to the data, the number of strikes rises with colliery size and also the number of working days lost per thousand employees rises with size, one is surprised and concludes that there is, indeed, a size effect. With the 'sectionalism model' in mind, however, we would expect the number of strikes to be proportional to the number of production teams, i.e. proportional to employment, because the frequency of grievances varies directly with the number of production teams. When the data confirm this expectation, we are not surprised and we conclude that there is no size effect: bigger collieries struck more often simply because they employed more production teams. This is all there is to it: bigger collieries did not predispose miners, or managements, to become more easily aggrieved, more belligerent or worse at resolving disputes before they turned into strikes; bigger collieries were struck more frequently merely because they were bigger.

The first conclusion, therefore, is that the existence of a size effect on strike activity is partly a question of perception and that different assumptions about whether domestic strikes usually involved the whole work-force or only particular work groups lie behind these different perceptions. In order to decide which perception is correct we consider the data on strike morphology and ask whether the units typically involved in mining strikes consisted of work teams or the entire colliery work-force.

Clegg defined a 'work group' as a group of workers 'who act together to make or influence rules affecting their employment' and as a 'group of employees whose jobs bring them into such close contact that they form a cohesive social unit' (Clegg 1976: 7, 1979: 42). This suggests a group of people working in close physical proximity; the size and composition of the group will therefore reflect the organization of work and the technology in use. As most strikes originated in the grievances of face workers, a re-examination of face technology should yield some clues. The inter-war trend towards longwall mechanization was accompanied by significant increases in the size of coal-face work groups; the available sources suggest longwall 'cycle groups' were of between twenty and one hundred men, though forty or fifty was typical. However, cycle groups were normally divided over three shifts and would not have been in day-to-day, face-to-face contact at work, though they may well have been acquainted through a miners' institute or other social activities (Manley 1947: 12, 16; Zweig 1948: 22; Handy 1981: 50; Tailby 1990: 217–25). In unmechanized mines, typical coal-face work groups would have been considerably smaller. Table 9.4 showed that except in

Table 9.4. *The scale of strikes by the size of colliery (all officially recorded strikes, Great Britain 1927–38)*

Colliery size class[a]	Number of strikes	Mean numbers involved per strike					
		Directly		Indirectly		Total	
		N	(%)	N	(%)	N	(%)
0-99	150	47	(84)	9	(16)	56	(100)
100–199	149	120	(73)	44	(27)	164	(100)
200–499	566	240	(81)	58	(19)	298	(100)
500–999	604	368	(76)	114	(24)	482	(100)
1,000–1,999	421	537	(73)	196	(27)	733	(100)
2,000+	238	705	(62)	441	(38)	1,146	(100)
Unknown	201	2,790	(80)	702	(20)	3,492	(100)

For notes see table 9.3. For sources see table 9.1.

the smallest collieries the average number of workers directly involved in strikes was a multiple of these group sizes. Yet the whole pit was not normally directly involved as the data we discussed in chapter 6 made abundantly clear (see especially table 6.1). Thus, neither the 'sectionalism model' nor the 'solidarity model' is an accurate reflection of reality. Instead, it would appear that work groups typically persuaded some others to strike with them, but that the extension of solidarity did not keep pace with the extension of colliery size.

This conclusion leads us to suggest that the size effect on colliery strike activity can be understood in terms of a model of sectionalism *and* solidarity. The following suppositions define a model consistent with the evidence. Grievances affected work groups and occurred at a rate that was invariant to colliery size. A constant proportion of those grievances led to strikes. So, as in the 'sectionalism model', the number of strikes per colliery, and the proportion of collieries struck, rose with size but the number of strikes per thousand workers was a constant. Striking work groups typically secured the support of other work groups. In the bigger collieries support was secured from a larger number but a lower proportion of the work-force so that the numbers directly involved rose but the strike participation rate fell with colliery size. As collieries increased in size more workers became indirectly involved, possibly as a result of technical interdependencies in the production process, and this added to the scale of strikes as collieries increased in size. The increased numbers involved led to a larger number of working days lost per thousand workers in the larger collieries than in the smaller.

If this model is correct, then the explanation of the size effect lies in solidary rather than conflictual behaviour. The latter has usually been assumed: the tenor of much of the literature suggests that for either social, technological or organizational reasons (bureaucracy, mass production, the detailed division of labour) work is more unpleasant in larger plants. Thus workers in larger plants experience more grievances than workers in smaller plants; management and union are no better at preventing these grievances erupting into strikes at larger plants than smaller; consequently more strikes occur in larger plants. This interpretation is consistent with the data so far. But this explanation also implies that the number of strikes per thousand workers increases with size, whether one assumes that grievances affect the whole colliery or only individual work groups, and we know that the number of strikes per thousand workers did not increase with size.

An alternative view, which avoids this conflict with the data, suggests that the problem with larger collieries was not the level of grievances but the management of grievances: more of the grievances led to strikes in the larger collieries and/or those strikes took longer to settle. But this, too, implies a counterfactual proposition: that the number of strikes per thousand workers increased with size and/or that strikes were longer in larger collieries. Instead, the data suggest that the size effect existed because when grievances did turn into strikes the aggrieved work groups were supported by other parts or the whole of the work-force and this work-force was bigger in the bigger collieries. Here, then, the size effect is to be explained by technology, bureaucracy, and so forth only in so far as these factors influenced solidarity, rather than the production and processing of grievances. The colliery size effect is best explained not by Weber but by Marx.

When considered in conjunction with our evidence from previous chapters on the spatial aspects of strike activity, therefore, our confirmation of the connections between size and conflict points to the conclusion that, in some form, 'massness', both in the community outside the colliery gates and down the pit, has contributed to a high strike proneness: 'massness' in the community made strikes more frequent and bigger as measured by the number of working days lost; massness in the mine made strikes bigger still. Once again, the processes governing strike solidarity appear crucial.

Appendix: the colliery sample and statistical procedure

THE COLLIERY SAMPLE

The initial sample frame consists of the Mines Department, *List of Mines in Great Britain and Ireland, and the Isle of Man, for the Year 1921*. A simple random sample from such a frame gives each colliery that operated in 1921 an equal chance of inclusion in the sample. This generates a 'panel' of collieries which was 'observed' through the available sources until its closure or to 1938 if this was later. This panel is not quite the same as a random sample of collieries operating in the 1921–38 period, since such a sample would include collieries which opened after 1921. However, the number of newly opened collieries was so small in this period that this distinction is of little significance here.

We discarded from the initial frame all mines which were not coal mines but mines of some other mineral such as iron-stone and fireclay and all mines which employed fewer than fifty employees in 1921. The collieries remaining in the frame after these exclusions and discards we called the final sample frame. We took a simple, systematic, unstratified sample of every tenth colliery from the frame. Our procedures generated a sample of 166 collieries. As explained in the text, we discarded our observations for the period before 1927. Because of colliery closures in the 1921–6 period our sample was effectively reduced to 138 collieries.

STATISTICAL PROCEDURE: THE CONSTANCY OF THE NUMBER OF STRIKES PER THOUSAND WORKERS WITH RESPECT TO COLLIERY SIZE

Table 9.1 appeared to show that the number of strikes per thousand workers was roughly constant with respect to colliery size. We tested this perception by regressing the number of strikes per thousand workers (*RELFREQ*) on a constant and colliery employment (*EMPLOYT*). The calculations were performed using the SAS package (SAS Institute 1985). Using the data underlying table 9.1 rather than the grouped data shown there, we obtained the following results:

$$RELFREQ = 0.368 - 0.000117 \ EMPLOYT \qquad n = 353$$
$$(3.592) \ (-1.075)$$

The *t*-statistic on the employment coefficient indicates that the hypothesis that the true coefficient is zero cannot be rejected at any conventional level of significance. Hence we cannot reject the hypothesis that *RELFREQ* is a constant with respect to colliery size.

10   The foundations of strike propensity

Alternative models of coalfield conflict

Only two strong quantitative hypotheses have been formulated to explain the high level of strike propensity among coalminers: the Kerr–Siegel hypothesis and Revans's 'size effect' idea (chapters 8 and 9). In chapter 8 we found that insofar as Kerr and Siegel's hypothesis was successful, its incorporation of massness in the workplace was as important as its treatment of massness in the locality. These two hypotheses are therefore closely linked. We were critical of both, yet we also concluded that each possessed some potential to contribute towards clarifying which were the key factors. We investigated the collieries contained in a random sample of English and Welsh colliery areas in the inter-war period, and found that of large-scale collieries in areas dominated by mineworkers more than a quarter were strike-prone as measured by the number of working days lost and almost half as measured by the number of strikes (table 8.2). Our investigation of the size effect in a sample of British collieries in the same period confirmed the importance of colliery size, indicated the importance of understanding solidarity in understanding strikes and enabled us to put forward an explanation of why colliery size was associated with strike activity.

Although the insights we have gained from these two hypotheses are very useful the fact remains that their joint explanatory power remains disappointingly low. Some collieries that were neither isolated nor large were nevertheless strike-prone; a much larger number of collieries were isolated and large but not at all strike-prone. Therefore some factor or factors other than isolation and massness must have been involved in creating a strike-prone pit. In this chapter we survey a number of the more qualitative explanations for colliery strike proneness, recast them in quantitative form and proceed to evaluate them using statistical techniques.

In the general industrial sociology of the 1950s and 1960s to which Kerr, Siegel and Revans made their contributions, workplace size was seen as a concomitant of technology. Yet contemporary specialist sociological studies of the interrelationships between workplace technology and industrial behaviour in coalmining could not help but notice that working methods and technical organization showed little variation with colliery size. Instead the focus of these

Table 10.1. *Strike activity in hand-got and mechanized collieries (colliery sample, Great Britain 1927–38)*

Technology[a]	Number of collieries in sample	Number (and %) of collieries struck at least once	Mean annual number of strikes per colliery	Mean annual number of strikes per thousand workers
Hand-got	85	9 *(11)*	0.04	0.31
Mechanizing	23	7 *(30)*	0.16	0.17
Mechanized	245	50 *(20)*	0.17	0.29

Note:
Observations of strike activity are of collieries *X, Y, Z*, etc. over the period 1927–30, of collieries *X, Y, Z*, etc. in 1931–4 and of collieries *X, Y, Z*, etc. in 1935–8. These observations are pooled. In this way the 166 collieries in the sample give rise to 353 observations.
[a] 'Mechanized' mines are those listed as having coal cutters at work in the *List of Mines* throughout the period of observation; 'mechanizing' mines are those where coal cutters were introduced during the period of observation; 'hand-got' mines are the remainder.
Sources: Ministry of Labour, *Trade Disputes: . . . Strikes and Lock-outs of 1927* and subsequent volumes, PRO LAB 34/45–53; Mines Department, *Lists of Mines*, 1927–38.

studies was on the implications for worker behaviour of different methods of working otherwise similar collieries. In a series of studies we discussed in chapter 2, members of the Tavistock Institute and others suggested that collieries or faces worked on the 'hand-got' system, on 'conventional longwall' systems, and on the 'fully mechanized' system, would experience different forms of worker behaviour; specifically that the conventional longwall system could 'give rise to a variety of situations in which it could be said that supervisor-worker conflict is inherent' (Goldthorpe 1959: 222).

The Tavistock Institute used a case study approach for their investigations of the impact of technology on industrial relations. Whatever may have happened in the particular collieries studied by the Tavistock in the 1950s, the general experience of the 1920s and 1930s does not support their case. Table 10.1 shows, indeed, that a higher proportion of mechanizing and of mechanized than of hand-got collieries were struck and that the frequency of strikes was higher in mechanizing and mechanized collieries. However, the differences in the frequency of strikes disappears when colliery size is controlled for: the average annual number of strikes per thousand workers was almost identical in the hand-got and the mechanized collieries. Strikes in hand-got collieries tended to be somewhat smaller than in mechanized collieries, involving an average of 404 workers in the hand-got and 582 in the mechanized; but the bulk of this difference is accounted for by the lower number of workers indirectly involved in the hand-got collieries, 60, compared with the mechanized collieries where the average was 185. This suggests that there was indeed a technological effect on strike activity but it was a simple one: the lower levels of technical interdependence in hand-got collieries led to fewer workers becoming indirectly involved. Apart from this point, the evidence of the inter-war years does not suggest that the reason for miners' strike proneness lies in the nature of the technology used to dig the coal. Miners working in hand-got collieries were as strike-prone as those working in mechanized collieries. The hand-got era was not a golden age of peace at work.

More useful work has been undertaken by a small number of historians who have developed an approach to coalfield industrial relations in which worker and employer organization, the institutions of collective bargaining, and changes in management practice are acknowledged to have played an active role alongside other features of the industry. Two themes appear repeatedly in this literature. One consists of the tensions between the colliery rank and file on the one hand and the union branch leadership on the other and similar tensions between branch leaderships and union head offices; the other concerns differences between, and changes in, management strategies which are sometimes related to broader changes in industrial and market structure. Almost all of this literature relates to the nineteenth century. While the focus of our study is principally on the twentieth century, the literature concerned with the earlier period offers several clues deserving further consideration, for it is by no means obvious that nineteenth-century management practices were superseded by more modern approaches and methods in the pre-nationalization period.

Spaven's systematic analysis of strikes in the South Yorkshire coalfield in the nineteenth century suggested the importance of internal union politics, among other factors, for strike activity. He concluded that differences in strike proneness could be explained by differences in the 'independence' of a work-force from the district union and from its employer (Spaven 1978: 211). Spaven assessed the degree of independence from the union by examining branch histories for instances of disaffiliations from the district union arising out of dissatisfaction with union policy; for strikes against the district union's directives; and for traces of Republican or Independent Labour Party political activities, both of which were contrary to the political stance taken by the district union in this period (Spaven 1978: 213–14). By 'independence from the employer' Spaven meant a number of different facets in the relationship between employer and worker: an absence of tied colliery housing and company built villages; an absence of, or 'half-heartedness' in, employer intervention in miners' lives beyond the colliery gates; and an absence of the 'residential presence of the "coalowner-squire" '. The latter characteristic, Spaven suggested, became increasingly marked as colliery capital came more and more to be held in outside hands and absentee ownership became the norm (Spaven 1978: 205–7). It is absentee ownership which Spaven emphasized most strongly as a causal factor behind the relatively high levels of strike incidence found in some South Yorkshire collieries. However, Spaven was unable to offer a clear analysis of the nature of this link, suggesting only a gradual elimination of paternalism as an employer strategy and a change in employer motivations towards a greater emphasis on profitability (1978: 222). Campbell, however, in work from the same mould on the contrasts in strike activity between two Lanarkshire mining communities (1978, 1979), suggests that in one community the large scale of the local coal and iron companies and the competitive product market in which they operated led to persistent attempts by management to undermine custom and practice in the struggle to maintain profits. It is possible that this underlies Spaven's observations too.

The literature on colliery-level labour management strategies has two interrelated themes; one is the struggle for control at the point of production, the other is the attempt by some coalowners to exert control over the lives of their workers beyond the pit gates. The former theme has generated a number of fascinating ethnographic studies, some of which we discussed in chapter 2 (Goodrich 1920/1975; Krieger 1984; Hopper et al. 1986). But these works have given no clear explanation of if, how and when managerial attempts to gain greater control over the production process lead to strikes. Nor has there been much attempt to locate the circumstances in which managements find it in their interests to push back the workplace 'frontier of control'. We have already noted that Campbell attributes the persistent attacks on custom and practice documented in his study to large company size and competitive product market conditions. Francis, in his study of the anthracite strike of 1925 which we discussed in chapter 7, attributed the attacks on custom and practice to the contemporary 'rationalisation and centralisation of ownership and control' in the anthracite coalfield of West Wales (1973: 16).

The latter theme, concerning employer control over workers' lives outside working hours, has been conducted in the context of debates among historians and sociologists over industrial 'paternalism' and the related context of the history and significance of 'company welfare' in the eras before the welfare state (Melling 1979, 1981; Joyce 1980; Fitzgerald, 1988). In both cases, scholars have been oriented to wider debates about the sources of social stability in nineteenth-century England. Hence, while there has been considerable interest in whether or not industrial paternalism and company welfare policies functioned to contain large-scale social conflict, little interest has been shown in the links between such managerial strategies and the level of 'routine' industrial conflicts of the kind under examination here. Church's review of a number of local studies confirms that practices consistent with a policy of paternalism were by no means unknown on the coalfields in the nineteenth century, though he also drew attention to the anti-union policies which often accompanied welfare provision (1986: 281–99). Fitzgerald's brief review of labour management strategies (1988: 158–64) confirms that paternalistic welfare policies continued to exist during the inter-war period, while Waller (1983) provides extensive documentation of the paternalistic policies pursued by colliery companies operating in the Dukeries in the 1920s and 1930s.

Dintenfass's study of four colliery concerns during that period is one of few studies which have asked whether or not welfarist policies actually served to reduce strike activity. Of the three companies studied for which adequate documentary evidence survives, one (the Ashington Coal Company) implemented almost the entire gamut of welfarist policies, at another (the Throckley Coal Company) such policies were notable by their absence, while Henry Briggs, Son and Company adopted an intermediate position (Dintenfass 1985: 251–78, 292–302, 311–13). Dintenfass remarks that evaluated in terms of strike activity, neither Ashington's nor Throckley's policies were notably successful in avoiding strike activity. Both companies experienced levels of strike activity about average for their coalfield in the 1920s and 1930s, whereas Briggs was apparently immune from local strike activity during this period (Dintenfass 1985: 288, 304, 320).

There is some suggestion in the literature that family-controlled firms were more likely to implement paternalist labour management policies than others. It seems possible that such policies might also have had an effect on levels of strike activity, although Dintenfass's case studies warn us not to accept this proposition uncritically and Gospel, for one, is careful to limit the application of this hypothesis to 'traditional paternalism', in contradistinction to the 'bureaucratic paternalism' characteristic of, for example, Victorian railway companies (Gospel 1992: 26). Church has also remarked on the combination of paternalistic policies with high levels of strike activity at pits owned by Henry Briggs and Son, Butterley, Clay Cross, Newton Chambers, Pope and Pearson (later Denaby Main), and the Staveley Coal and Iron Company (1986: 296–7). With the exception of Staveley, each of those companies was under family control and management. Supple, on the other hand, has argued that the conjunction of family control and poor labour relations was not accidental. Writing of the inter-war years, he suggested that family and other 'closely' controlled firms were characterized by 'an extreme sensitivity on the issue of managerial control' and an 'unyielding opposition to the sharing of managerial responsibilities or even of information with the work-force' (Supple 1987: 402). In the face of such militant stances on work control issues, workers may have been more likely to strike. However, for our purposes the implications of these studies of managerial strategy are limited. While there is a widespread presumption among historians that variations in colliery managerial strategies were causally connected with variations in the level of strike activity, the nature and strength of that link remains obscure.

One notable omission in the literature on organization and strategy is a consideration of district and local levels of union membership. For while figures and estimates of trade union density have been or can be produced for the late nineteenth and early twentieth centuries (table 3.1) there is virtually no sustained discussion of this topic at the local level, except in the context of the

Table 10.2. *Strike activity by union membership density (colliery sample, Great Britain 1928–37)*

Union membership density[a]	Number of collieries in sample[b]	Number (and %) of collieries struck at least once[b]	Mean annual number of strikes per colliery[b]	Mean annual number of strikes per thousand employees
Low	30	4*(13)*	0.04	0.06
Medium	38	7*(18)*	0.12	0.18
High	40	15*(38)*	0.25	0.25
All	108	26*(24)*	0.14	0.17

Notes:

[a] Membership of unions affiliated to the Miners' Federation of Great Britain, only. Union membership density is the percentage of the workers in the branch or lodge 'catchment area' who were members of that branch or lodge. Normally, the catchment area was a single colliery but it sometimes contained two or more collieries; in these cases membership density at the sample colliery was estimated as the average for the catchment area. Low, medium and high union membership densities are respectively less than 33.3 per cent, more than 33.3 but less than 66.7, and more than 66.7 per cent.

[b] The observations underlying the table are of strike activity in collieries X, Y, Z, etc. over the period 1928–32 and of collieries X, Y, Z, etc. in 1933–7. These observations are pooled so each row refers to a mixture of observations, some for 1928–32 and some for 1933–7. The years 1928–32 and 1933–7 are centred on 1930 and 1935, which are the years for which we have computed estimates of union density. With 166 collieries in the colliery sample observed twice, there are a potential 332 data points; colliery closures reduce this to 239 and missing data on union membership to 108.

Sources: archives of the affiliates of the Miners' Federation of Great Britain: see appendix under *PRTUDENS* for details; Mines Department, *Lists of Mines*, 1928–37.

growth and eradication of 'Spencer' and 'company' unionism after the 1926 Lock-out (David Smith 1972–3; Alan R. Griffin 1977; Waller 1983; Colin P. Griffin 1984, 1990; the one discussion we have found is Andrew J. Taylor 1984a). Yet it would appear to deserve a central place in any discussion of mining industrial relations. The data indicate that without union organization, strike activity was so rare in the collieries of inter-war Britain that talk of strategy is otiose. Table 10.2 gives the relevant data. For this exercise the data were reorganized into five-year periods centred on 1930 and 1935: 1927–32 and 1933–7. In the same way as before, colliery X in 1927–32 is treated for all intents and purposes as distinct from colliery X in 1933–7. The 166 collieries in the sample yield 239 such 'collieries', after closures are taken into account. Of the thirty collieries in which union membership density was 'low', with union

Table 10.3. *Union membership density by colliery size (colliery sample, Great Britain 1930 and 1935)*

Colliery size class[a]	Number of collieries in sample	Number of collieries for which union membership density is known	Mean union membership density (%)
0–199	67	17	67
200–499	70	32	58
500–999	52	24	55
1,000+	50	35	57
All	239	108	59

Notes:
[a] Size is measured by the mean employment, above and below ground, over the period 1928–32 and 1933–7.
See also notes to table 10.2.
Sources: as for table 10.2.

members forming less than a third of the work-force, only four were struck at all in the 1928–32 or 1933–7 periods and they were each struck only once. Trade union organization was plainly an important means to the securing of the solidaristic basis of strike activity.

The results of research into the determinants of union membership in British manufacturing in the post-war period lead us to expect the bigger collieries to have been the better organized (Bain 1983: 27–8). Table 10.3 compares trade union membership density in 1930 and 1935 in our sample collieries with colliery size. Surprisingly, the data show that union density was no greater at the biggest collieries than at the smallest: indeed, it was somewhat lower. The 'size effect' we examined in the last chapter, although closely related to strike solidarity, cannot be explained as a consequence of the better organization of the bigger collieries.

The interplay of organization and the forces of the market is one of the recurrent topics in the historiography of the industry but one which has normally been discussed at the level of the industry as a whole. However, both the historiography of the inter-war coal industry and some theoretical work by economists suggests that colliery to colliery variations in the type of coal mined may have had indirect effects on the industrial relations of the period. Different types of coal were sold in different markets, commanded different prices and were differentially affected by the inter-war slump (Supple 1987: 182). There appear, however to have been only minor differences in mining technology for the various coal types, consequently it seems legitimate to treat inter-colliery variations in the coal type mined as a direct indicator of inter-colliery variations in product market conditions. Economists have suggested that strikes should be concentrated in firms whose 'ability to pay', is low, possibly because of adverse product market conditions (Hayes 1984). Analyses of the post-war period have also concluded that changes in product market conditions have had a major impact on the temporal variations in coalmining strikes (Handy 1981: 216–26; Winterton 1981: 161). Both these strands of work, one limited to the historiography of a particular industry, the other based on general theories and empirical observation of strike activity in industry as a whole, suggest that variations in strike activity are to be understood largely in terms of product market conditions. But the most obvious market impact on strike activity is through the labour market: unemployment has long been presumed, by employers, workers and researchers, to have a restraining impact on strike activity.

The background to many of the studies reviewed above has been provided by the peculiar work environment of a mine in which difficult and potentially dangerous conditions of work are inevitable (Douglass gives a particularly emphatic account, 1977: 207–12). The views that such an environment would necessarily generate tensions and difficulties that, in appropriate conditions, would result in industrial conflict, or that particularly bad conditions would generate a particularly high level of grievances some of which would erupt into strikes, have a long history. The former is an element of Kerr and Siegel's thesis, and one that was accepted by Rimlinger in his comparison of international differences in coalminers' strike activity which we reviewed in chapter 8 (Rimlinger 1959). The latter is a pre-theoretical idea which, although largely ignored in the historical and social science literature, has sometimes featured prominently in the views of those who worked in the industry (Douglass 1972) or outside observers. Such a view was also implicit in the report of the Samuel Commission, for example, which argued that the strike proneness of the industry could be reduced by removing 'well-founded' grievances (Royal Commission on the Coal Industry (1925), *Report*: 113).

This brief review demonstrates the diversity of thought on coalmining industrial relations. In addition to the models propounded by Kerr and Siegel, and by Revans, it is possible to formulate at least four models of colliery strike behaviour. The first, the 'technical organization model', sees high levels of strike activity as resulting from the use of 'conventional longwall' techniques of production. The second, which we call the 'union and management' model, relates strike activity to the characteristics of the organizations involved in collective bargaining. The third explains strike activity in terms of the markets on which coal was sold and labour purchased, the 'markets' model. Finally, the 'grievances' model explains the high level of strike activity in coalmining as a simple reflection of the high level of grievances generated by the poor working conditions found in the industry. None of these models is mutually exclusive and each may be able to add some explanatory power to the models put forward by Kerr, Siegel and Revans.

Testing the models: the basis of strike propensity in coalmining

To see which, if any, of these models has some explanatory power we used a form of regression analysis; a technical account of which is given in the appendix to this chapter. This approach requires us to express our models in quantitative terms and find relevant data to measure the variables highlighted by them. On the basis of such an exercise it is possible to determine objectively whether a model, as quantified, is capable of adding significantly to the explanation of strike activity. The strength of this procedure is its objectivity; the weakness is its appetite for valid data on our sample of collieries. As with most other quantitative analyses related to this subject, it has been necessary to settle for a series of proxy measures in place of the variables which, ideally, we would have wanted to measure. Briefly, the main proxies employed were as follows.

The Kerr–Siegel isolated mass model

In chapter 8 we saw that the most powerful variables in this explanation of miners' strike proneness were a measure of occupational density in the colliery locality and the scale of the colliery itself. Here we wish to distinguish massness in the mine from massness in the locality and use a measure of the latter, solely, to quantify this aspect of Kerr and Siegel's model. The quantifier chosen, therefore, was the percentage of the adult male population in the colliery locality who were employed in the mining and quarrying industries according to the *Census of Population*.

The Revans size-effect model

'Size' we have defined, following Revans, as colliery employment. But in view of the importance of *company* size suggested by some of the more modern literature we also counted the number of collieries owned by the company and we measured the total employment of the company across all its collieries.

The technical organization model

The shift from pillar and stall to longwall working is difficult to date for individual collieries from the surviving sources. However, we can date the shift from hand-got methods to mechanized methods because the sources tell us the year in which coal cutters were first introduced into a colliery. We have used the presence of coal cutters as a proxy for the presence of conventional longwall extraction methods. While the use of coal cutters indicates a longwall method of extraction with a high degree of certainty, the absence of coal cutters was compatible with hand-got longwall working and with hand-got pillar and stall working. The proxy is therefore by no means ideal.

The union and management model

We attempted to capture the potential role of trade unions by measuring membership density at colliery and district level using the archives of unions affiliated to the Miners' Federation of Great Britain (MFGB). The difficulty of finding such detailed information at colliery level required us to use statistical techniques of data replacement for some collieries (see the appendix). However, more complete estimates were possible of the district-wide membership of the relevant trade unions and we have treated these as an indicator of the power of the district unions. While colliery-level union membership data was difficult to find, data on the membership of the district coalowners' associations was too imperfect to be used at all. As we gained the clear impression from the archives we searched that most large firms tended to be members whereas few of the smaller enterprises belonged to the associations, we regard company size as a proxy for membership. The available data allow us to infer the presence or absence of family control over the colliery company, although only in a rough and ready way. The identity of the boards of directors of the colliery companies in this period can be established through contemporary trade publications. We inspected the list of board members for the presence of directors with family names in common and scored the colliery company according to the number of such directors we found. The same sources were used to give a proxy for 'owner-absenteeism', emphasized in Spaven's work. We scored colliery companies according to whether their registered office was near or far from its collieries. A London registration was regarded as indicative of 'owner-absentee-ism'; a registration at or near one or other of the company's collieries was taken to indicate the local presence of higher management personnel.

The markets model

The survival of no more than a few complete series of colliery accounts, other than for the large publicly quoted joint stock companies, undermined the feasibility of assessing the relative strengths of collieries' product markets and profitability for the companies in our sample. Instead we used the type of coal mined as a proxy. Labour market conditions were measured by the officially calculated mean rate of unemployment among coalminers for the unemployment districts in which each of the sample collieries was located.

The grievances model

The bad working conditions which may have given rise to grievances in collieries in our period were many and varied: heat, water, dust, cramped seams, soft floors, soft roofs and irregularities in the seam are often mentioned (for example by Douglass 1977: 207–12). Many of these conditions would change from day to day and such changes and variations are now, of course, lost to history.

Nevertheless, some endured and we saw in chapter 3 that the high levels of strike activity recorded in the anthracite district of West Wales have been attributed largely to the exceptionally poor working conditions found there. However, only estimates of average seam heights and average depths of workings can be constructed, from data compiled for the 1925 Royal Commission on the Coal Industry. The impact of seam thickness on working conditions will be clear. Deep mines tended to be hot and so great depth tended to affect working conditions adversely. These estimates fail to capture the full range of factors affecting working conditions but, in the absence of anything better, we have used them as proxies for the working conditions which have been supposed to lie behind miners' more manifest grievances.

Finally, we had to decide how to measure strike activity itself. We experimented with the average annual number of strikes recorded for each colliery over the 1927–38 period. We found that this measure gave results very little different from those given by a simple binary measure indicating whether or not each colliery was struck at all between 1927 and 1938 and in what follows we largely confine our discussion to our results for the struck/not struck dichotomy.

The outcome of the modelling exercise was that only the Revans 'size effect' model and the 'union and management' models contributed significantly to the explanation of why some collieries were struck and some were not. The proxies used in quantifying these models were able to correctly predict whether or not a colliery was struck in almost 80 per cent of cases. The remaining models were unable to make any significant improvement over this figure. The positive aspects of these results are more interesting than the negative aspects. Someone impressed by the worth of any of the specific models we have eliminated could reasonably argue that had our quantification of these models been less hampered by data limitations, or had our statistical strategy or tactics been different, we might well have reached different conclusions on the worth of an eliminated model. We do not dissent from this view. Indeed, we have argued, on the basis of different statistical techniques and using English and Welsh data rather than the British data used here, that one of the eliminated models, the Kerr–Siegel hypothesis, has much to recommend it (chapter 8 above). Yet the positive aspects of our results are of considerably more significance. These are, first, that in line with numerous previous investigators we have found a significant size effect on strike activity and, second, we have found that variables concerned with the organization of the work-force and the company also play a significant role in the determination of which collieries were struck and, if so, how often.

Our statistical techniques not only allow us to say which of the quantified models have explanatory power and which do not, but also allow us to measure the 'importance' of each variable to the explanation of variations in strike activity and to make 'predictions' of whether or not a particular colliery with given characteristics will have been struck or not. After recording the mean and standard deviation of each variable in the colliery sample, table 10.4 gives the

Table 10.4. *Indicators of the 'importance' of the variables involved in determining strike activity (Great Britain coalmining 1927–38)*

Variable	Mean	Standard deviation	Direction of impact	Variable 'importance'[a]
Colliery employment	620	649	Positive	0.193
Trade union membership density:				
At colliery	60.3%	29.8%	Positive	0.224
In district	56.8%	20.4%	Negative	0.242
Score for:				
Employer presence[b]	3.07	1.00	Negative	0.158
Family control of company[c]	0.636	0.692	Positive	0.134

Notes:

[a] For explanation, see text.

[b] The score runs from 1, indicating that the company's registered offices were in London, to 4, indicating that they were in a small town or village, almost always adjacent to a company colliery.

[c] The score runs from 0, indicating no apparent family control, to 2, indicating that at least three colliery company directors shared the same family name, and 3, indicating a sole proprietorship.

direction of impact of each variable on the probability that a colliery was struck at least once during the 1927–38 period. As expected, colliery employment has a positive impact indicating that bigger collieries were more likely to be struck as the Revans 'size effect' hypothesis suggests. It also shows that the more effective was the organization at colliery level – and the weaker the organization at district level – the greater the strike activity. This is consistent with Spaven's interpretation of the role and activities of the district union in the South Yorkshire area during the nineteenth century. His conclusion, that a local manager's presence was conducive to more harmonious labour relations, is also supported by our research which shows that strike action was less likely at those collieries which were owned by companies with local headquarters as indicated by the location of their registered office. However, when we turn to the colliery owners responsible for overall company policy and to Supple's judgement that family-owned firms were more likely to adopt a militant stance over issues of work control, we can add that they were also more likely to be struck. These results prevent simple answers to simple questions. If we ask 'What impact did rising trade union membership have on strike activity?' the answer must begin by distinguishing rising membership at the lodge from rising membership in the district as a whole. If we ask 'What impact did the supersession of family controlled and locally managed firms by anonymous corporations based in the metropolis have on strike activity?' the answer must begin by distinguishing family control from local management.

Table 10.5. *Estimated probability of strike activity[a] at various hypothetical collieries (Great Britain 1927–38)*

| | Values assumed | | | | | |
| | | Trade union membership density | | Score for employer | Score for family | Estimated strike |
Case	Employ-ment	At colliery	In district	presence	control	probability
Central Case	620	60	55	3	1	0.465
Little Pit	100	60	55	3	1	0.290
Big Mine	1,270	60	55	3	1	0.689
Independent Colliery	620	90	35	3	1	0.903
Dependent Colliery	620	30	75	3	1	0.070
Family Colliery	620	60	55	4	3	0.725
Capitalist Colliery	620	60	55	1	0	0.776
Traditional Pit	100	90	35	4	3	0.936
Modern Mine	1,270	30	75	1	0	0.300

Notes:
[a] The estimated probability that a colliery with the given characteristics would experience at least one officially recorded local strike during 1927–38.
See also notes to table 10.4.

Table 10.4 also gives a numerical estimate of the 'importance' of each variable. This estimate gives the effect of a one standard deviation change in the variable on the estimated probability of at least one strike occurring during the 1927–38 period, assuming that all variables initially take their mean values. The standard deviation is taken as the unit of variation since what counts as a significant variation differs for each variable. Use of the standard deviation avoids the absurdity of comparing the impact of, say, one extra employee (a trivial change of no conceivable consequence) with an increase of one in the score for family control (a fairly big change, possibly of some significance). The table shows that all variables were of comparable importance for strike activity with the measure of 'importance' lying in the range 0.12 to 0.25 for all variables. However, without wishing to exaggerate the differences in the 'importance' of each variable, it is clear that trade union membership variables were foremost, followed by colliery size and, lastly, company characteristics.

Table 10.5 presents several 'predictions' of strike activity in a number of hypothetical cases designed to show the estimated impact of the variables and proxies we have identified. In the Central Case the value of each of the variables has been set at a figure near its mean or its mode. Such a colliery had an estimated probability of experiencing at least one strike in the 1927–38 period of 0.465. In other words the 'average' colliery was more likely to be peaceable than not in this period but the odds were fairly even. In the next pair of cases the colliery retains its average characteristics in every respect except size: 'Big Mine' is bigger than the Central Case by about one standard deviation, or 650, employing 1,270 people; 'Little Pit' would not employ anyone if it were smaller than the Central Case by one standard deviation, so we have set its employment at 100 people. The estimated strike probability rises to 0.689 in Big Mine and falls to 0.290 in Little Pit, showing the substantial impact of colliery size on the chances of strike activity.

The next pair of cases shows the powerful but surprising impact of trade union membership on a colliery which, in other respects, has average characteristics. 'Independent Colliery' has a very high level of union membership at the colliery branch level (90 per cent of employees) but is in a district where generally trade union organization is weak (membership density at district level is 35 per cent). The estimated strike probability of 0.903 shows that this was not quite a 'sure fire' recipe for strike activity but approached that point. 'Dependent Colliery' is, by contrast, a weak branch but in a strongly organized district: in such collieries strike activity was highly unlikely. This finding suggests that Spaven's explanation of differential strike activity in nineteenth-century South Yorkshire in terms of differences in the 'independence' of the work-force from its district union may have a wider relevance.

The 'Family Colliery' and the 'Capitalist Colliery' differ in two more of the respects emphasized by Spaven. The Capitalist Colliery is owned by a company managed from the metropolis (scoring a minimal 1 for employer presence) and has no trace of family control on its board of directors (so it scores a minimal 0 on this measure); the 'Family Colliery' is a sole proprietorship, which we regard as the acme of family control, and is owned by a company managed from the locality (therefore scoring a maximal 4 for employer presence). *Each* of these collieries was quite likely to experience some strike activity (the probability was about three-quarters in each case) but for different reasons: family control in the one case and employer absenteeism in the other. This gives another reason, if another reason is needed, to doubt the existence of a 'golden age' in colliery industrial relations in which family-owned and locally managed enterprises achieved harmonious industrial relations with a contented work-force. The reality would appear to have been more accurately perceived by Supple who, as we mentioned above, was impressed by the aggressive approach to labour management in 'closely owned' collieries. Our results suggest that this militancy, or some other characteristic of family-controlled colliery companies, led to poor industrial relations and also to strikes. The take-over of a family firm by an anonymous corporation could be expected, therefore, to have led to an improvement of industrial relations rather than a deterioration unless, that is, the corporation simultaneously removed local management to a regional or national metropolis.

In the final two examples we have tried to specify two collieries which embody the conception of 'tradition' and 'modernity' in the industry. The 'Traditional Pit' is small-scale, family-controlled, and locally managed; the 'Modern Mine' is large-scale, anonymously controlled and managed from the national metropolis. These specifications of 'tradition' and 'modernity' are straightforward. Setting values for the trade union membership variables is more difficult. Some conceptions of 'tradition' would be antithetical to any unionism whatsoever; some conceptions of 'modernity' would identify it with 'one hundred per cent unionism' at all levels. Here, we have specified the 'traditional' as a combination of strong workplace unionism combined with weak district-level unionism; the 'modern' possesses the reverse in the form of centralized, bureaucratic unions which are powerful at the centre but weak in the workplace. The results are interesting because they are the reverse of what one might expect. Strike activity is estimated at a near certainty (0.936) in the Traditional Pit despite its small scale and local management, but at no more than a one in three chance (0.300) in the Modern Mine despite its large-scale and metropolitan management. What lies behind this reversal of expectations is the role of trade unionism. Our results suggest that the traditional, family-owned pit possessed a high potentiality for strike action. If a high proportion of the work-force could be unionized then strike activity would very likely occur, unless the district union was strong enough to prevent it.

Our results identify several characteristics which were associated with colliery strike proneness, but they do not explain the transmission mechanisms by which those underlying characteristics were linked to the outbreak of strikes. It is possible, for example, that family and other 'closely' controlled companies were under-capitalized or poorly managed and that the difficulties which these features led to, rather than the militant attitudes of their owners which Supple emphasized, lay behind the poor industrial relations in these collieries. Our analysis does, however, exclude other possibilities: family-controlled companies were more strike-prone regardless of company or colliery size and independently of the levels of trade union membership.

This chapter has considered the reasons why some collieries were more strike-prone than others. Although it has focused on the inter-war period, we can see no obvious reason why our analysis should not be broadly valid for a considerably lengthier period before nationalization. Indeed, Spaven's analysis, which we have found much to support, was originally put forward as an explanation of inter-colliery strike variations in South Yorkshire from 1858, the foundation year of the South Yorkshire Miners' Association, until the 1890s. Whether or not the conclusions reached here have any force for the era after nationalization is a question we take up in chapter 12. First, however, chapter 11 reverts to an investigation at local and colliery level, reconstructing the strike histories from archival and oral sources of a number of pairs of collieries matched, as far as possible, for their structural characteristics but displaying contrasting histories of strike activity.

Appendix: statistical procedures

DATA DEFINITIONS AND SOURCES

The following variables were measured for each case in the colliery sample (appendix to chapter 9).

STRUCK: a binary variable indicating whether the sample colliery was (*STRUCK* = 1) or was not (*STRUCK* = 0) struck in a local strike during the 1927–38 period. (Sources: Ministry of Labour, *Trade Disputes: . . . Strikes and Lock-outs of 1927* and subsequent volumes, PRO LAB 34/45–53).

'Exposure time' (*WINDYRS*): the number of years the colliery wound coal in the 1927–38 period. (Sources: Mines Department, *Lists of Mines*, 1927–38).

Occupational density (*OCCDENS*): the proportion of the adult male population which was occupied in mining or quarrying on census night 1931 in the administrative area linked to the sample colliery. The administrative areas are rural districts, urban districts and county boroughs in England and Wales and, in Scotland, 'large burghs' or counties after the exclusion of the populations of the 'large burghs' and any city in the county. (Sources: *Census of England and Wales 1931*, occupation tables; *Census of Scotland 1931*, occupations and industries tables).

Colliery employment (*MEANAGUG*): mean employment at the sample colliery during its years of production in the period 1927–38. (Sources: Mines Department, *Lists of Mines*, 1927–38).

Company size (number of employees) (*MNCOEMP*): mean employment at the collieries owned by the owner of the sample colliery during its years of production in the period 1927–38 estimated by forming an appropriately weighted average of company colliery employment in 1930 and 1935. (Sources: Mines Department, *Lists of Mines*, 1930 and 1935).

Company size (number of collieries) (*MEANNCY*): the mean number of collieries owned by the owner of the sample colliery during its years of production in the period 1927–38, estimated by an appropriately weighted average of data for 1930 and 1935. (Sources: Mines Department, *Lists of Mines*, 1930 and 1935).

Trade union membership density at colliery level (*PRTUDENS; FORE*): mean actual or predicted trade union membership density at the colliery during its years of coal production in the period 1927–38 as estimated by an appropriately weighted average of data for 1930 and 1935. Note: Data on trade union membership could not be found for a large number of sample collieries. Where data were unavailable the predicted mean trade union density derived from a regression equation was used instead. This equation was estimated on the available sample data. It is reported more fully later in this appendix. Where the density predicted by the regression equation was used we set the value of the binary dummy *FORE* to 1 (and otherwise to zero); this gave us a check on the validity of our method of data replacement. (Sources: Derbyshire Miners' Association, *Minutes*, DeRO N3; Durham Miners' Association, *Records of Membership*, DuRO D/DMA 1–30; Lanarkshire Mine Workers'

Union, *Statements of Dues and Funeral Claims*, National Library of Scotland Dep. 227/45a; Lancashire and Cheshire Miners' Federation, *Monthly Statements of Accounts*, Salford Mining Museum; North Staffordshire Miners' Federation, *Official Statements of Accounts*, National Union of Mineworkers (NUM), North Staffordshire District, Library, Stoke-on-Trent; North Wales Miners' Association, later North Wales and Border Counties Mineworkers' Association, *Statements of Accounts*, CRO, D/NM/66 and D/NM/79–97; Northumberland Miners' Mutual Confident Association, *Balance Sheets*, NuRO, NRO 759/68; Nottinghamshire Miners' Association, *General Fund Receipts and Payments Accounts*, NoRO; South Wales Miners' Federation, *Average Membership and Vote Entitlement of SWMF Lodges 1933–40*, South Wales Coalfield Archive, SWMF/NUM Misc. Office Papers F(22); Yorkshire Mine Workers' Association, *Balance Sheets and General Statements*, NUM, Yorkshire Area, Library).

Trade union membership density at district level (*MFGBDENS*): the mean proportion of the district colliery work-force organized by the relevant MFGB affiliate in the district in which the sample colliery was situated as estimated by an appropriately weighted average of data for 1930 and 1935. (Sources: MFGB, *Minutes of Proceedings*, 1931 and 1936, NUM Library; Mines Department, *Annual Reports of the Secretary for Mines*, 1930, table 14; 1935, table 15).

Score for employer presence (*MEANRO*): an appropriately weighted mean of 1930 and 1935 scores for the location of the colliery company's registered office.

Scores
1   London
2   Birmingham, Bristol, Cardiff, Edinburgh, Glasgow, Liverpool, Manchester, Newcastle, or Sheffield
3   A large town not scored as 2, above, e.g. Nottingham, Swansea
4   A small town or village, e.g. Leven, Wigan

(Sources: *Colliery Year Book and Coal Trades Directories*, 1931 and 1936).

Score for family control (*MEANFAM*): an appropriately weighted mean of 1930 and 1935 scores for the degree of family control of the sample colliery's owning firm.

Scores
0   All directors have different family names
1   Two directors share the same family name
2   Three or more directors share the same family name
3   Sole proprietorship.

(Sources: as for *MEANRO*).

Technical organization (*CCPERC*): the percentage of the *WINDYRS* during which coal cutters were in use at the sample colliery. (Sources: Mines Department, *Lists of Mines*, 1927–38).

Type of coal (*ACG*, *HMS* and *MIX*): binary dummies indicating whether or not the colliery mined at least one of anthracite, coking coal or gas coal and no other type (*ACG*), at least one of household, manufacturing or steam coal and no other type (*HMS*), and mined types of coal from both these triples (*MIX*). (Source: Mines Department, *List of Mines*, 1921).

Unemployment (*MEANUEMP*): the mean over the sample colliery's years of operation of the mean annual percentage rate of unemployment amongst coalminers in the sample colliery's unemployment district. (Sources: computed from Ministry of Labour, *Gazette*, 1927–38, e.g. February 1927: 60).

Depth of workings (*DEPTH*) and coal seam height (*THICK*): the mean depth (yards) and thickness of coal (feet) worked in the sample colliery's district, weighted by the output of the reporting collieries. (Source: computed from Mines Department, *Royal Commission on the Coal Industry (1925): Minutes & Appendices*: appendix 18).

TESTING SIX MODELS OF STRIKE PROBABILITY

The text identifies six separate models of colliery strike probability. In addition to the independent variables identified in the text the tested models incorporate a constant and a measure of 'exposure time', *WINDYRS*. Using the variable names defined above, the models are:

Kerr–Siegel: $STRUCK = f_1(WINDYRS, OCCDENS)$

Revans: $STRUCK = f_2(WINDYRS, MEANAGUG, MNCOEMP, MEANNCY)$

Technical organization: $STRUCK = f_3(WINDYRS, CCPERC)$

Union and management: $STRUCK = f_4(WINDYRS, PRTUDENS, FORE, MFGBDENS, MNCOEMP, MEANNCY, MEANFAM, MEANRO)$

Markets: $STRUCK = f_5(WINDYRS, ACG, HMS, MIX, MEANUEMP)$

Grievances: $STRUCK = f_6(WINDYRS, DEPTH, THICK)$

The explanatory power of the six models was assessed by means of a general-to-specific modelling strategy (see, e.g. Charemza and Deadman 1992). This requires us to estimate a general model of *STRUCK* consisting of the six models combined:

General: $STRUCK = f_g(WINDYRS, OCCDENS, MEANAGUG, MNCOEMP, MEANNCY, CCPERC, PRTUDENS, FORE, MFGBDENS, MEANFAM, MEANRO, ACG, HMS, MIX, MEANUEMP, DEPTH, THICK)$

Table 10.6. *Probit model of STRUCK: general model*

Log-likelihood	−49.099	Restricted (slopes = 0) log-likelihood	−75.275
Chi^2 (16)	52.351	Significance level	0.00001
Number of observations	119		

Specific model and *variable*	Coefficient	Standard error	*t*-ratio	Mean of x
All				
Constant	0.0416	2.05	0.020	
WINDYRS	0.0572	0.0552	1.037	9.765
Kerr-Siegel				
OCCDENS	−0.00409	0.0107	−0.383	35.61
Revans				
MEANAGUG	0.00130	0.000399	3.264	603.0
Revans and Union & Management				
MNCOEMP	−0.0000308	0.000105	−0.293	3,116
MEANNCY	−0.000343	0.0723	−0.005	5.206
Union & Management				
PRTUDENS	0.0151	0.00860	1.751	59.81
FORE	−0.525	0.346	−1.516	0.4706
MFGBDENS	−0.0354	0.0127	−2.778	56.63
MEANRO	−0.185	0.195	−0.946	3.050
MEANFAM	0.648	0.251	2.586	0.6303
Technical Organization				
CCPERC	−0.00193	0.00441	−0.439	74.34
Markets				
HMS	0.0135	0.414	0.033	0.5210
ACG	0.387	0.641	0.603	0.09244
MEANUEMP	0.127	0.0532	2.393	22.73
Grievances				
DEPTH	−0.00552	0.00361	−1.528	336.5
THICK	−0.312	0.694	−0.450	4.012

Frequencies of actual and predicted outcomes

	Predicted		
Actual	0	1	TOTAL
0	72	8	80
1	16	23	39
TOTAL	88	31	119

Proportion of correct predictions: 80%.

Table 10.7. *Probit model of STRUCK: effects of eliminating specific models*

Model	Number of restrictions imposed	LR test statistic	Substantial changes to remaining parameters?	Proportion of correct predictions (%)
Kerr–Siegel	1	0.148	No	80
Revans	3	16.234	Yes	72
Union & Management	7	21.726	No	77
Technical Organization	1	0.192	No	80
Markets	3	6.734	No	80
Grievances	2	8.740	Yes	79

Notes: LR test critical value (5%, 1 df) = 3.84. LR test critical value (5%, 7 df) = 14.07. General model proportion of correct predictions: 80%.

The dependent variable *STRUCK* can only take the values zero or one and therefore violates the assumptions of the classical linear regression model. We therefore used a probit model. This technique has been used in previous analyses of strike frequency by, e.g. Blanchflower and Cubbin (1986).

There is one further estimation problem. This is the possibility of attrition bias. Of the 138 collieries in our sample, 40 closed before 1938 and the average period of observation was 9.8 years out of the 12 years covered by the study. If the probability of closure is correlated with the probability of strike activity then the techniques used here will lead to biased estimates of strike probability (Hausman and Wise 1979). We have been unable to resolve this problem, which may be serious, and our results should be read with caution in view of this.

All model estimates reported below were computed with version 6.0 of the LIMDEP package (Greene 1987–92).

Our estimates of the general model are given in table 10.6. The next step was to assess whether any specific model can be eliminated from the general model without adversely affecting the performance of the estimated equation for the general model. If it could, we concluded that the eliminated model added nothing to the explanation of variations in the dependent variable. Performance was judged by three tests: the elimination of a specific model was required to not reduce significantly the likelihood of the estimated equation as assessed by a likelihood ratio (LR) test at the 5 per cent level; to not lead to substantial changes in the remaining parameter estimates and to not substantially and adversely affect the predictive performance of the model as assessed by the proportion of the sample for which the independent variable was correctly predicted. Whether or not there were 'substantial changes' in estimated parameter values was judged in relation to the estimated standard errors: where these

Table 10.8. *Probit model of STRUCK: final model*

Log-likelihood	−54.914	Restricted (slopes = 0) log-likelihood	-76.785
Chi² (6)	43.743	Significance level	0.00000
Number of observations 121			

Specific model and *variable*	Coefficient	Standard error	*t*-ratio	Mean of *x*
All				
Constant	−0.322	0.673	−0.478	
WINDYRS	0.0947	0.0457	2.073	9.769
Revans				
MEANAGUG	0.000893	0.000254	3.512	620.1
Union & Management				
PRTUDENS	0.0225	0.00669	3.369	60.29
MFGBDENS	−0.0356	0.0105	−3.380	56.84
MEANRO	−0.477	0.148	−3.217	3.066
MEANFAM	0.582	0.225	2.592	0.6364

Frequencies of actual and predicted outcomes
Predicted

Actual	0	1	TOTAL
0	72 (89%)	9 (11%)	81 (100%)
1	17 (43%)	23 (58%)	40 (100%)
TOTAL	89	32	121

Proportion of correct predictions: 79%.

are large we would expect the parameter estimates to be unstable in sign and magnitude, in any case. Only where an estimated standard error indicated that the parameter was significantly different from zero at the 5 per cent level and where there was either a change in the estimated parameter's sign or at least an order of magnitude change in its value was there deemed to have been a 'substantial change' in the parameter estimate.

Before beginning the reduction process, we noted that the estimated coefficient on *FORE*, which is not statistically significantly different from zero, suggests that our method of data replacement did not introduce any bias into our results and we eliminated *FORE* from the model. The effects of eliminating each specific model in turn are given in table 10.7. These effects strongly suggest that neither the Kerr-Siegel nor the technical organization model add significantly to the general model. Because the LR test statistic was slightly lower for the Kerr–Siegel model than for the technical organization model we decided to reduce the general model at this first stage by eliminating the Kerr–Siegel model.

Table 10.9. *Regression equation used for the prediction of PRTUDENS*

Variable	Estimated parameter	t-ratio
Constant	−10.417	−0.215
WINDYRS	−1.289	−0.783
MEANAGUG	0.002	0.314
MNCOEMP	−0.001	−0.225
MEANNCY	0.049	0.020
OCCDENS	0.155	0.639
MFGBDENS	0.731	2.970
MEANRO	8.065	1.739
MEANFAM	−0.044	−0.008
HMS	−8.054	−0.867
ACG	21.707	1.578
MEANUEMP	2.420	2.394
DEPTH	−0.062	−0.774
THICK	−4.160	−0.240
CCPERC	−0.046	−0.457

F-value: 4.897	Prob > F: 0.0001	
R^2: 0.5882	Adjusted R^2: 0.4681	Number of observations: 62

The reduction process now went into round two. All the indicators were that here too, the technical organization model added nothing of significance. At this stage the elimination of the markets model became warranted, although at the cost of some minor loss of predictive power: the proportion of within sample correct predictions fell from 81 per cent to 78 per cent. We felt this was acceptable in the interests of model parsimony. In the next round the elimination of the grievances model became warranted on each of our three statistical criteria. The resulting model consisted of only the Revans and the union and management models. Our statistical tests indicated it was not possible to reduce this model further.

However, this model was still not entirely satisfactory. The coefficients on the company size variables MNCOEMP and MEANNCY were poorly determined and that on MNCOEMP had an unexpected negative sign. We investigated the effects of deleting MNCOEMP and MEANNCY separately and in combination using LR tests of the relevant parameter restrictions and investigating the impact of the deletions on the remaining parameter estimates and the within-sample predictive ability of the model. These investigations strongly suggested that neither MNCOEMP nor MEANNCY nor the two together contributed anything of value to the model. We therefore deleted them to give our final model for STRUCK which is reported in table 10.8.

THE ESTIMATION OF TRADE UNION MEMBERSHIP DENSITY AT COLLIERY LEVEL

As noted above, data on trade union membership at colliery level (*PRTUDENS*) could not be found for a large number of sample collieries. Here we report the equation we used to estimate *PRTUDENS* for those collieries.

We used the 'first-order' regression method recommended by Maddala (1977: 201–5). This is to compute the regression of the independent variable, x, for which some values are missing on the remaining independent variables in the model, z, and substitute the predicted value of x for each missing value of x. The regression equation used to find the predicted values of x is reported in table 10.9.

This is clearly not a very good equation by the usual criteria, despite the quite impressive unadjusted and adjusted R^2 values. Most of the variables are not significantly different from zero, the exceptions being *MEANRO*, *MEANUEMP* and *MFGBDENS* at 10 per cent. Nevertheless we did not eliminate the remaining variables on the grounds that this would have inevitably impaired the predictive ability of the model, however marginally, and in this context predictive ability was the only criterion on which to judge the equation.

11 Miners and management: agency and action

A close reading of the few existing studies which explore labour relations in detail at company, pit and community levels in our period tends to reinforce a scepticism to a search for a general explanation of colliery strikes, an attitude to which we alluded in chapter 3. For example, studies of two Northumberland collieries, Ashington and Throckley, by Dintenfass (1985), revealed a similar history of low strike activity over many decades, though punctuated by a brief period of labour unrest shortly after the First World War. The approach to labour management in the two collieries, however, was in the sharpest contrast. The owners and managers of Ashington colliery cultivated a harmonious community through an acceptance of trade unionism and a paternalist welfare policy which, after a period of labour unrest and under a new manager, included publication of *The Ashington Colliery Magazine*, which occasionally editorialized on the theme of 'team spirit'. Layoffs and short-time working resulting from pit closures and colliery reorganization were accepted by the union branch as a better alternative to wage cuts (Dintenfass 1985: 257–74). At Throckley a limited provision of institutional and other forms of welfare was combined with what Dintenfass has described as 'tight-fisted and hard-nosed' management methods. These included victimization of workers after strikes in 1926 and 1928, a continued preference for recruiting non-union labour, vindictive, petty deductions from wages, and non-co-operation with the union's own welfare programme. Another contrast between the two collieries was in investment and technical change. Ashington's investment programme and reorganization stood in contrast to Throckley's much slower adaptation to competition in a sagging market where traditional methods of pit working persisted (Dintenfass 1985: 290–303).

We have already commented in chapter 3 on the comparison of labour relations, communities and strike histories of four South Wales collieries explored by Zweiniger-Bargielowska (1990, 1992–3). Based on studies of Oakdale Colliery, owned by the Tredegar Iron and Coal Company, Parc and Dare Colliery, Penrikyber Colliery and Seven Sisters Colliery (1992–3: 364–79), her concluding generalizations were very broad: 'Miners' militancy at colliery level was determined by a combination of local pit conditions, the balance of power between lodge and management, the degree of lodge leaders' control over the rank-and-file membership and managerial strategies' (1992–3: 383). While few would disagree that these were relevant factors, the conclusion is so broad as to reinforce, rather than dispel, the scepticism of the possibility of generalization which have we noted.

These comparisons, drawn between collieries in Northumberland and between others in South Wales, the best available for our period, bring us back to our often repeated observation that wide variations in the strike histories of collieries have been found within the same region and even within the same district. Yet this very divergent experience offers a method of exploring the roots of this divergence more rigorously.

The first step in pursuing this method was to construct a database of matched pairs of collieries, one relatively strike-prone and one relatively strike-free for each of the coalmining regions between 1920 and 1940. The logic of our method was that by choosing neighbouring and matched collieries one could standardize many of the structural factors which affected colliery strike propensities in order to isolate other factors. We chose the most strike-prone collieries in each region and then sought pacific comparators for them. We searched for two pairs in each of the major regions and one pair in each of the minor coalmining regions. We applied two criteria in making a match. The first was the geographical proximity which we have already mentioned, which we regard partly as a proxy for geological characteristics, depth of working, width of seams and types of coal (all of which affected the underground working environment), and partly as a proxy for social characteristics of the work-force and the local institutional framework and local bargaining traditions. The second was colliery size as measured by the number of workers employed. In some cases it was not possible to find a match because there were no collieries with the required characteristics. To some extent data limitations also prevented the achievement of our aspirations. Nor can our sample of matched pairs be treated as a random sample; nevertheless we did not construct the sample to illustrate a theory but to facilitate the identification of the causes of colliery strike proneness: whatever biases the sample exhibits are unintentional. In the event, we succeeded in assembling some data for thirty-eight collieries which could be paired to our satisfaction. The number of those about which more can be learned from non-statistical sources, enabling us to flesh out their individual strike histories, is smaller. Without that evidence, however, conclusions based on the matched pairs exercise might be described as conjectural rather than convincing. To avoid this, before attempting to generalize from the results of the matched pairs exercise, we present brief commentaries, necessarily episodic rather than narrative, on the histories of those nine pairs for which supplementary evidence exists. Some details of these nine matched pairs are presented in table 11.1. Here, after the predominantly structural approach pursued in previous chapters, the principal focus is upon agency and action.

Table 11.1. *Matched pairs of frequently and infrequently struck collieries (Great Britain 1921–1940)*

Pair	Colliery name and location	Owners	Number of employees 1932	Number of strikes 1921–40
Cumberland				
1a	Whitehaven Haig & Wellington Cy, Whitehaven	Whitehaven Cy Co. Ltd *later* Cumberland Coal Co. (Whitehaven) Ltd	1,137	16
1b	Walkmill Cy, Walkmill	Moresby Coal Co. Ltd	574	2
County Durham				
2a	Hylton Cy, Sunderland	Wearmouth Coal Co. Ltd	1,941	2
2b	Whitburn Cy[a], South Shields	Harton Coal Co. Ltd	1,810	23
Northumberland				
3a	Burradon Cy[b], Dudley	Burradon and Coxlodge Coal Co. Ltd, *later* Hazlerigg & Burradon Coal Co. Ltd	785	6
3b	Dudley Cy, Dudley	Cramlington Coal Co. Ltd, *later* Hartley Main Cies Ltd	753	1
South Yorkshire				
4a	Hickleton Main Cy, Thurnscoe, Rotherham	Hickleton Main Cy Co. Ltd, *later* Doncaster Amalgamated Cies Ltd	3,177	27
4b	Rossington Main Cy, Rossington, near Doncaster	Rossington Main Cy Co. Ltd, *later* Amalgamated Denaby Cies Ltd	2,731	2
5a	Wharncliffe Silkstone Cy, Tankersley, Barnsley	Wharncliffe Silkstone Cy Co. Ltd	948	0
5.b	Mitchell Main Cy, Wombwell, Barnsley	Mitchell Main Cy Co. Ltd	1,069	12

Table 11.1. *(cont.)*

Pair	Colliery name and location	Owners	Number of employees 1932	Number of strikes 1921–40
North Staffordshire				
6a	Whitfield Cy, Norton in the Moors	Chatterley-Whitfield Cies Ltd	3,385	6
6b	Norton Cy, Norton in the Moors	Norton and Biddulph Cy Ltd	1,101	0
Lanarkshire				
7a	Hamilton Palace Cy, Bothwell	Bent Cy Co. Ltd	745	16
7b	Thankerton Cy, Holytown	John McAndrew and Co. Ltd	584	3
8a	Earnock Cy, Holytown	John Watson Ltd	869	17
8b	Cadzow Cy, Hamilton	Cadzow Coal Co. Ltd	531	2
Monmouthshire				
9a	Nine Mile Point Cy[c], Ynysddu, Sirhowy Valley	Burnyeat Brown and Co. Ltd	2,055	27
9b	Oakdale Navigation and Steam Cy[d], Blackwood, Sirhowy Valley	Oakdale Navigation Cies Ltd	1,845	6

Notes:
See the general appendix for our conventions for defining and naming collieries.
'Cy' abbreviates 'Colliery'; 'Cies', 'Collieries'.
[a] Whitburn No. 1 + Whitburn No. 2 Cy.
[b] Burradon + Weetslade Cy.
[c] Nine Mile Point East Cy++ Nine Mile Point West Cy++ Nine Mile Point Rock Vein Cy.
[d] Oakdale Navigation Steam + Waterloo Levels + Waterloo Pit Cy.
Sources: strikes: Ministry of Labour, *Trade Disputes: . . . Strikes and Lock-outs of 1921* and subsequent volumes, PRO LAB 34/39–55; names and employment: Mines Department, *Lists of Mines*, 1921–38.

'Staying down and marching out': pit strikes

One of the most strike-prone collieries in Britain for a time was the Whitehaven Colliery, which experienced sixteen strikes between 1921 and 1940. There had been a long history of poor industrial relations at this colliery before the First World War, marked by an arbitrary treatment of the men by the management, a rigid insistence on managerial prerogatives and, on the miners' side, violence and disorder (Wood 1988: 188–9). Violence of another sort was all too frequent in the Whitehaven collieries. Geological conditions were difficult and gas was a major problem. In 1910 an explosion in the Wellington Pit had killed 136 people: the report on the explosion commissioned by the Miners' Federation of Great Britain denounced the 'reckless indifference' of the colliery officials; the report by Professor Galloway stated that 'Nothing can be said in palliation of the state of affairs shown to have existed before the explosion' (Thomas Richards and Herbert Smith, *Wellington Colliery, . . . Report to the Executive Committee of the Miners' Federation of Great Britain*, quoted by Arnot 1953: 32; Home Office, *Report on the . . . Explosion . . . at the Wellington Pit . . . : 43*). Apart from serious technical deficiencies there had been managerial failings resulting in an absence of discipline underground: a 'Great laxity on the part of both the officials and workmen existed at the mine in respect of gas' (Home Office, *Report on the . . . Explosion . . . at the Wellington Pit . . . : 10*) with men preferring to continue working when gas was present rather than leave their places and sacrifice earnings. This 'culture of recklessness', shared by workers and management, appears to have survived undamaged by the shock of the 1910 catastrophe. R. A. S. Redmayne, the main author of the Home Office *Report*, was astonished to find that only six months after the explosion a man had been found in the mine in possession of matches (*ibid.*: 9).

Managerial neglect of safety seems to have been symptomatic not only of recklessness but of a wider incompetence. Following a period of unprofitability arising from inadequate ventilation, inefficient transport and an unsuitable method of working, the lessor 'took the unusual step of compelling the company to surrender the colliery in the hope that under new management better results might be obtained' (National Coal Board (NCB), *Registration of Assets: . . . Cumberland Coal Co. (Whitehaven) Ltd., Mining Report*, PRO COAL 37/121, 1–5; quotation from Wood 1988: 249). Whatever its impact on profits, liquidation brought to an end four years of almost perpetual strikes. It also brought to an end the sequence of explosions. This is one of several collieries we have identified where evidence of poor management and lack of investment was accompanied by high levels of strike activity. The question arises of whether 'the culture of recklessness' was part of the mechanism that linked these factors with both accidents and strikes (cf. Fitzpatrick 1980). Little information of relevance to the contrast between labour relations at Whitehaven and the Walkmill colliery of the Moresby Coal Company has been found. Walkmill was 'for many years' a profitable colliery and after its purchase by the United Steel Companies in 1924 saw a substantial increase in output. It survived until 1961 by which time its seams had been exhausted (NCB, *Registration of Assets: . . . Moresby Coal Co. Ltd.*, PRO COAL 37/265; Wood 1988: 160, 261). As in the case of most of the quiescent pits, little more than these bare details are known but this little suffices to show that poor industrial relations were not an inevitable counterpart of Cumberland circumstances.

Industrial relations in the North East coalfield were relatively peaceful during the period under review. At Hylton Colliery (two strikes) situated in the Northumberland village of Castleton, membership of what was one of the longest established unions was high and the union strong, partly as a consequence of the policy of the owning company, Wearmouth Coal, in recruiting only union members (Timson interview, 12 March 1990). The opinion of a former chairman of Hylton lodge was that Hylton miners 'knew when to come out on strike' but also that 'they had a manager who they could go over and speak to', a person whom another contemporary union official described as 'a real gentleman' (Errington interview, 12 March 1990). Another piece in the jigsaw was an under-manager who imposed strict discipline in a framework which nonetheless provided a predictable working environment (Errington interview, 12 March 1990; Timson interview, 12 March 1990).

The highly strike-prone Durham colliery of Whitburn (twenty-three strikes), owned by the Harton Coal Company with which Hylton was paired, differed from Hylton in several respects. The departure in 1929 of an under-manager who was well-regarded by the workers was followed by a replacement who proved to be less approachable. This change in personnel coincided with a transition from board and pillar working to longwall. The 'lightning strikes' at the colliery in the 1930s have been attributed to changes in working methods imposed by management and involving reduced manning levels, alterations to shifts, delays and an increase in idle time (Ellwood interview, 28 May 1990), all of which produced loss of earnings and frustration among the workers. Whitburn's reputation as a strike-prone pit was confirmed by a contemporary who considered that industrial action was also a consequence of the strong union presence at the colliery, the ability of union officials to present a strong case and to the inability of managers to deal with the balance of power (Timson interview, 12 March 1990).

Nowhere were pit lodges potentially more powerful than in Northumberland and Durham where, at least until the 1930s, the practice of 'cavilling' (sharing out working places down the pit) was controlled by lodge officials (K. Brown 1987: 144). This long-established custom presented difficulties to managers during the 1930s, when they sought to gain greater control as part of colliery reorganization, mechanization and changes in working methods. In 1931, the branch minutes of the Burradon Colliery recorded the management's insistence on a 'manager's right to select men as he wanted', an indication that the union's control over recruitment was also an issue (Northumberland Miners' Mutual Confident Association (NMMCA), *Burradon Colliery Branch Minutes*, NuRO

NRO 3013/1, 22 October 1931). The possibility that the social cohesion engendered by the lodge, which played a social as well as a union role, might pose a threat to employers' power to manage did not go unnoticed. The owners of some large collieries favoured the splitting of lodges (K. Brown 1987: 141–2), an acknowledgement that they regarded massness to be an important factor affecting labour relations, and that the division of a lodge might encourage new loyalties and perhaps diminish union influence.

The extent to which lodge practice could depart from central union policy depended on the constitution of each branch, particularly on its financial organization; much, too, rested on the personality and inclinations of the elected lodge officials and of lodge members. That each particular situation might produce different outcomes is suggested by the ability of a clique of activist members of the Whitburn lodge to mount frequent and successful strikes regardless of official union policy (Whitburn colliery in the matched sample struck twenty-three times) (Ellwood interview, 28 May 1990). At Burradon colliery (six strikes) lodge officials drew a motion of censure for failing to press the miners' case, either with the union or with management (NMMCA, *Burradon Colliery Branch Minutes*, NuRO NRO 3013/1, July 1931 – August 1934).

The action taken by lodge members of Burradon Colliery was one of the consequences of an amalgamation between the Burradon and Coxlodge Coal Company with Hazlerigg to form the Hazlerigg and Burradon Coal Company. This involved the closure of the Burradon pit before reopening and the re-engagement, at lower rates, of former employees selected after medical examination (NMMCA, *Burradon . . . Minutes*, NuRO NRO 759/21, 18 March 1929). Minutes taken at a special meeting of the lodge in 1931 referred to the secretary's detection of a 'bitter feeling' in the village concerning the new company's hiring methods and rate cutting (*ibid.*, 1 November 1931). Closure, reopening and the selection of those re-engaged was part of the management's tactic to reduce cavilling by allowing it only on each single face rather than throughout a whole district within a colliery, as had been the traditional practice. The introduction of conveyors also prompted the managers to insist on special teams to remain specialist operators rather than to 'cavil' the work in rotation which the union, customarily controlling the process, preferred (*ibid.*, 4 January, 17 July, 2 October 1932). Contrary to the men's wishes, the company also resisted submitting the rates for conveyor work to the joint committee; the branch minutes recorded the management's threat to 'close the conveyor down and probably the pit' (*ibid.*, 10 November 1932). These developments were followed by a period when Burradon emerged as relatively strike-prone by comparison with other collieries in the North East, with six strikes between 1927 and 1938.

Surviving evidence on labour relations at Dudley colliery (one strike), Burradon's comparator, is sparse. Owned by the Cramlington Coal Company, Dudley benefited from the company's substantial programme of investment and reorganization following a consultant's report on the collieries in 1926, yet despite the changes and disruption of existing custom and practice which we would expect to follow this only one local strike was recorded at Dudley between 1921 and 1940 (Northumberland Coal Owners' Association, *Cramlington Colliery Co. Ltd.*, *Report of Directors*, NuRO NCB 1274/49, 14 January 1927). In this instance, change appears to have been achieved without external evidence of deteriorating labour relations.

The first of the two matched pairs in Yorkshire consists of Hickleton Main Colliery (twenty-seven strikes), owned by the Hickleton Main Colliery Company (a subsidiary of the Staveley Coal and Iron Company), and Rossington Main (two strikes), owned by the Rossington Main Colliery Company (a subsidiary of the Sheepbridge Iron and Coal Company). Both were located in South Yorkshire, where since 1890 the Yorkshire Miners' Association (YMA) and the coalowners' associations of South and West Yorkshire practised collective bargaining through joint conciliation committees (Baylies 1993: ch. 7). In 1906, Parker Rhodes, secretary of the South Yorkshire Coal Owners' Association (SYCOA), recorded his appreciation of the transformation in the YMA's approach to industrial relations:

They express their claims with vigour, and they sometimes support, very likely against their own better judgement, claims which are not reasonable in themselves, but no one can help observing that they do now rely much more on the strength of their case and on their reasoning powers with reference to it rather than on a policy of threats and bluster as often used to be the case. (SYCOA, *Minutes*, 25 April 1906, Sheffield City Archives, MD 2699/1–25)

Baylies's study of the YMA has shown that most grievances which were potential sources of strikes were dealt with not only outside the joint committee but also outside the district committee, by the union branch (Baylies 1993: 169–71). Assisting this process of local resolution was the existence of joint colliery committees at some collieries. One such committee was formed at Hickleton Main in 1900. It consisted of representatives from management and union members who worked in the pit, who met frequently to discuss issues of concern to either side. The emphasis was upon the need for local settlement of local disputes (if possible without reporting to branch officials), an approach approved by both sides. In 1912, for example, managers convened a meeting of the committee to discuss the recent national minimum wage agreement in order to consider possible ambiguities with a view to reaching local agreement on interpretation and to avoid future differences (Doncaster Amalgamated Collieries (DAC), *Hickleton . . . Deputations Book*, Sheffield City Archives, NCB 1137–9, 28 May 1912). Negotiations over eight-hour shifts in 1912 between the company and the surface workers who belonged to the National Amalgamated Union of Labour prompted a resolution:

That the best thanks of the meeting be given to the management for the courteous manner in which they met the deputation, and seeing that under a competitive system it is essential that both employers and employed should work together we trust that the friendly feeling which has existed in the past will still continue in the future [which] is the wish of this branch of surface workers. (DAC, *Hickleton . . . Deputations Book*, Sheffield City Archives, NCB 1137, 28 October 1912)

Perceived by trade unionists to have been organized 'up to the hilt' (*ibid.*, 10 June 1913), Hickleton Main was peaceful during the early years of the twentieth century. After the war, however, the arrival of new managers and the recruitment of unskilled workers prompted one of the new members of the joint committee to describe the pit as a 'seething mass of discontent', the result of overcrowded faces which had the effect of reducing individual's earnings to unreasonable levels. Management's view was that the discontent was limited to the sixty miners who attended branch meetings (*ibid.*, 11 May 1922, 3 August 1922). It was not until the General Strike, however, that Hickleton Main's record of strike-free labour relations was broken. When it ended, the company adopted the traditional policy of even-handedness towards union and non-union labour, co-operating with the union but refusing to sack non-union employees. For the men's part, a meeting of their representatives on the joint committee in 1927 supported the view, reiterated by the Hickleton Main checkweighman, that district union officers should not become involved in disputes and that the joint committee of management and union within the colliery should continue to 'settle between ourselves' (*ibid.*, 18 March 1927). However, the issue raised by the emergence of the Spencer union, which succeeded in gaining strength in one of the colliery's pits, proved too divisive. This development culminated in unofficial stoppages and the eventual sacking of Spencerist workers for breach of contract (*ibid.*, 3 September 1928; cf. Andrew J. Taylor 1984a: 50).

The degree of trust between the lodges, the company and the pit representatives is suggested by the sanction given by branch officials to the colliery joint committee to negotiate a provisional mutual agreement on piece-rates when cutting machines were introduced in 1930 (*ibid.*, 30 October 1930). However, the appointment of a new colliery manager responsible for organizing the new machine face added to the difficulty of agreeing a list of rates and resolving differences over demarcation and caused wildcat strikes, some lasting less than a day. The manager's list provided for rate differences for each category of worker, one effect of which was to cause disagreement between rippers, who were responsible for setting up, moving and maintaining the machines, and the gummers, whose job included clearing coal removed by the machine. Rippers required skill, whereas gummers, it was alleged, needed only the physical stamina to sustain long hours of work in order to approach the level of earnings available to rippers (DAC, *Hickleton Main Colliery, Reports to Directors*, Sheffield City Archives, NCB 1820, 2 October, 4 November 1933; 23 August 1934).

Friction occurred over allegations that managers were creating shortages of timber to justify the introduction of steel pit props, to which the men objected. The introduction of conveyors led to further disputes affecting fillers who were transferred from day wage to piece-rates. In 1936 strikes were related to that dispute and to the mixing of contract workers (whom the Yorkshire Mine Workers' Association (YMWA) claimed had priority for the work) and 'market men'. These casual workers were hired for specific projects or for a specified period, usually accepting lower standards of wages and conditions (*ibid.*, 7 March, 16 April 1935; 20, 21 March 1936; 5 May 1936). An unofficial strike on this issue led to the issue of summonses by the company, withdrawal after a return to work, and a threat to proceed regardless should unofficial action take place in future. The YMWA officials accepted that action had been contrary to agreed procedure and undertook to ensure that in future strikers involved in such action would not receive support from the union (*ibid.*, 30 March 1935). Lightning strikes took place in 1937, when they involved more than one hundred fillers, and again in 1939, when the company took out summonses against the strikers. In order to escape prosecution 'for leaving work without permission or just cause', those summonsed bought out the summonses and gave a written undertaking, signed on their behalf by the checkweighman and another member of the joint committee, that their action would not be repeated (*ibid.*, 20 October 1939). The history of labour relations at Hickleton Main reveals the complexity of the events and forces which transformed a peaceful pit into one of Britain's most strike-prone collieries. In this instance a strong union branch and firm management working co-operatively failed to prevent intra-colliery dissension over new working practices which upset the local payment structure.

Rossington Main was a younger pit than Hickleton Main, winding coal from 1916 (compared with 1894 at Hickleton Main). The most marked differences between the two collieries were Rossington's lack of mechanization until the 1940s, the persistence of a butty system until the mid-1930s, and the docile character of the union branch. New Rossington was special as a model settlement, a planned environment whose large open spaces and provision for gardens drew praise from one observer who in 1920 described it as one of the 'best modern type' of miners' villages (Bulman 1920: 278–9). A combination of several characteristics – a new sinking, rapid growth, migrant labour – makes Rossington conform to the archetypal 'cosmopolitan pit' (Storm-Clark 1971: 51–69; Neville 1974: 74, 309).

Evidence from two Communist ex-miners who worked at Rossington between the wars suggests that one of the reasons why confrontation was exceptionally low at Rossington was the willingness of the colliery manager and under-manager not only to talk to the men (as a body, not only the union representatives), but to listen to complaints and to act on them (McKenna and Wilde interviews, 5 June 1990). Despite a feeling that the workplaces allocated to them were invariably inferior with a low earning potential, and despite the occasional dismissals on the spot, faced with reason and a respect for the miners' union organization at the pit, a small, but highly active Communist clique failed to convert an essentially conservative local branch and an equally conservative work-force to an anti-capitalist posture. The Communist leaders were, however, also listened to by management, which may explain why one was elected to the branch committee in 1943. Most of the union representatives at Rossington have been described as 'the most right wing union officials that every breathed', who lived in 'a right wing bloody village', and who, it is alleged, received medals for working when other collieries in the region were on strike. These were the views of an ex-Durham miner and a Communist activist whose attempt to alter the colliery culture at Rossington and elsewhere including the circulation of propagandist literature contained in *The Rossington Ringer*, *The Thorne Butty Squasher* and *The Sylvester Rebel*, signally failed (McKenna and Wilde interviews, 5 June 1990). These were aimed at exposing 'corruption . . . in the pit and the branch officials' (McKenna to David N. Smith, 8 May 1990). With the support of a new colliery manager in 1936, the union militants succeeded in turning the pit into an all-union enterprise and ended the butty system, remarkably without affecting the colliery's peaceful history (McKenna to David N. Smith, 8 May 1990).

Of the second pair of Yorkshire collieries, both medium-sized, long-established pits located in villages near Barnsley and owned by companies dominated by mine-owning families, one, Wharncliffe Silkstone, had a record of labour relations which showed no strikes in the 1920s or 1930s. There had been an explosion at the colliery in 1914, resulting in an inquest jury's verdict that 'the whole of the Management have been very negligent, but not criminally so' and a mines inspector's report which had criticized the 'discipline of the mine' from the managing director downwards. But unlike the Whitehaven example, the explosion appears to have resulted from lapses of management rather than from an incompetent or reckless managerial culture. In 1946 a mining engineer's report submitted on behalf of the company to the Yorkshire District Valuation Board described in glowing terms the continuing investment record since the mid-nineteenth century, including the mechanization, before 1914, of cutting and conveying which, despite its small size, established the enterprise as profitable and one of the most progressive of all Yorkshire companies (Home Office, *Report on an Explosion at Wharncliffe Silkstone Colliery*, quotation from p. 9; NCB, *Registration of Assets: . . . Wharncliffe Silkstone Colliery Co. Ltd.*, *Mining Report*, PRO COAL 37/373). The colliery appears to have been well organized, with only twenty-two non-unionists out of a work-force that approached 1,500 in 1936 (Andrew J. Taylor 1984a: 47), and if there was any opposition to union membership by the colliery management it was ineffectual. This apart, the approach to labour management displayed the classic ingredients of paternalism. By the 1930s, about 40 per cent of the workers lived in houses built by the company in close proximity to the colliery. A welfare policy included the building of a Miners' Institute in the colliery yard, opened in 1886. In 1890 one of the first miners' baths in Britain was installed, replaced and modernized in 1931, and later supplemented by 'an Aerotone Therapeutic Bath'. The company was similarly in the vanguard by providing a canteen which served hot meals. Concern for safety was marked by the building of the first rescue station in Britain, long before it was required by law, and the Wharncliffe Silkstone Ambulance Brigade, the training centre for all ambulance men at the colliery, was started in 1903. *Ex gratia* pensions to elderly, retired employees and free coal to widows at Christmas completed the schemes which the mining engineer concluded had 'done a great deal to strengthen the practical co-operation and good feeling between the owners, management and employees and has been responsible for the comparative freedom from labour disputes at the colliery and lower absenteeism . . . the men being considered as generally an excellent type' (NCB, *Registration of Assets: . . . Wharncliffe Silkstone Colliery Co. Ltd.*, *Mining Report*, PRO COAL 37/373: 6).

Wharncliffe Silkstone's strike-prone comparator was Mitchell Main, owned by the Mitchell Main Colliery Company; it experienced twelve strikes between 1927 and 1938. During the 1890s managers and local trade unionists established an *ad hoc* joint committee which involved independent umpires to adjudicate on cases where settlement could not be agreed by both sides, a model which influenced the structure and organization of the conciliation board later set up by the South and West Yorkshire Coalowners' Associations in agreement with the YMA (SYCOA, *Minutes*, Sheffield City Archives, MD 2699/1–25, 14 February 1899; Baylies 1993: 170–1). As at Hickleton Main, the catalyst which transformed the record of peaceful labour relations into a strike-prone one was the extensive introduction of cutters and conveyors which began in 1931. During this period, a high turnover of technical staff and frequent changes in working policy produced 'an unstable organization and a failure to maintain satisfactory labour relations' (NCB, *Registration of Assets: . . . Mitchell Main Colliery Co. Ltd.*, *Mining Report*, PRO COAL 37/260).

There are similarities between the characteristics of Rossington Main in Yorkshire and Whitfield Colliery (six strikes) owned by the Chatterley-Whitfield Company in Staffordshire. Both were cosmopolitan pits, the term used by a former local branch secretary to describe the colliery (Whatmore interview, 28 March 1990), and at both the butty system was a source of grievance, yet by Midland standards Chatterley-Whitfield was strike-prone whereas Rossington was not. Whatmore attributed the strike-proneness of Chatterley-Whitfield to the low level of union recruitment. A combination of geographical dispersion of the work-force (collected by buses from the pottery towns) and a lack of managerial co-operation presented union officials with practical difficulties in enrolling new members and collecting union subscriptions (Whatmore interview, 28 March 1990). Norton Colliery, the completely strike-free Staffordshire pit with which we have paired Chatterley-Whitfield, was also rural and somewhat smaller in scale, employing 'wheelbarrow farmers' who continued to combine a smallholding with working down the pit (Whatmore interview, 28 March 1990). Unlike the experience of Chatterley-Whitfield, labour turnover was low, partly because physical working conditions were superior to other pits in the district and partly because, according to the ex-National Union of Mineworkers branch secretary at Norton, son of a former miner at the pit, the under-manager was regarded as 'a reasonable fellow' (Brownsword and Shaw interviews, 5 March 1990). However, union membership at that pit was low, a fact which the same sources attributed variously to a wages system which appears to have equalized pay across all workers, to the lack of alternative employment in the district, to pit lads' mothers begrudging the union subscription, and to the hostility and insensitivity of the former guards officer who owned the colliery (Brownsword and Shaw interviews, 5 March 1990). A former branch secretary of the union at Norton commented on the low level of organization in the pit as follows, 'This myth of colliers sticking together like shit to a blanket doesn't always work out. . . . They stick together if there's anything up down pit – like an explosion or anybody hurt, but I've seen blokes scream their heads off about other blokes . . .' (Brownsword interview, 5 March 1990).

This assertion of a lack of miners' solidarity was certainly true when trade unionists found themselves competing with non-unionists under a management which was hostile, or even relatively impartial, in its conduct of labour relations. Evidence to support this view is provided, for example, by the Hamilton Palace Colliery (sixteen strikes), owned by the Bent Colliery Company in Lanarkshire, and at Earnock Colliery (seventeen strikes), both among the largest Scottish coal producing enterprises and both described as 'well-managed collieries on a large scale enjoying particularly good conditions as to wages' in 1919 and 'laggards' in the 'ebullition of the masses' that took place that year (MacDougall 1927: 772). Hamilton Palace Colliery began to produce coal in 1884. One of the Scottish mines to mechanize before 1914, it was situated in the remote company village of Bothwellhaugh, where the senior managers lived and involved themselves in prominent social and industrial roles (Duncan 1986: 5). A history of the colliery and of the village described how Stewart Thompson rose from the position of secretary of the Hamilton Palace Co-operative Society, which ran the local store, to chief cashier at the colliery, giving him control over the payment of wages and the allocation of company-owned houses in the village. Together with the colliery manager, Thompson was largely responsible for the company's conduct of labour relations (Duncan 1986: 12–15). On the workers' side, the major influence was a relatively strong Communist presence within the Lanarkshire Miners' County Union (Campbell 1992: 92–5).

When miners at Hamilton Palace took unofficial action against the company in 1919 and again in the official county and nation-wide strikes of 1921 and 1926, the Bent Colliery Company brought in strike-breakers. This was despite the fact that the participation of Hamilton Palace in the 1919 strike had initially been with some reluctance: they stopped work only after 'action of a fairly rough character – it could scarcely have been called peaceful picketing' (MacDougall 1927: 772). Intimidation, violence and victimization followed the strikes, the strong company reaction resulting in the virtual destruction of union organization and the emigration of miners from Bothwellhaugh (Campbell 1992: 92–5). After the return to work in 1926, the local branch of the Lanarkshire Miners' Union disbanded. Labour relations at the pit passed into the hands of a non-union pit committee, including a newly appointed non-union check-weigher, which operated 'in collusion with management' (Campbell 1992: 14). No provision was made for channelling formal appeals over grievances to management. After the committee advised against the introduction of pithead baths in 1930, a group of workers formed a local branch of the unofficial militant, breakaway United Mineworkers of Scotland (UMS) which quickly recruited several hundred members. A new colliery manager invited the moderate Lanarkshire Miners' Union to re-form the Bothwellhaugh branch which the company undertook to recognize. Assisted by the company to recruit members, the Lanarkshire Miners' Union soon challenged the UMS as the major organization representing miners at Hamilton Palace. The inter-union competition which that involved led to disputes and stoppages, the largest of which was the 1936 unofficial strike to secure a closed shop for the Lanarkshire Union. Success was the prelude to a period of lower strike activity (Campbell 1992: 15–18).

The paired South Wales collieries for which additional information has been found are Nine Mile Point (twenty-seven strikes), until 1927 owned by Burnyeat Brown and Co., and the Oakdale Navigation Steam Colliery (six strikes), a subsidiary of the Tredegar Iron and Coal Company. Nine Mile Point was Britain's most strike-prone colliery during the 1920s before the General Strike, and continued to be relatively strike-prone during the 1930s. As in several of the cases examined above, the catalyst was the ineffective management of change. The company was taken over by the United National group of companies in 1927, and in the following year passed under the control of the Ocean Group which was among the ten largest British coal producers. Customary wage payment practices had resulted in comparatively high labour costs and company losses, which explains why in 1928 the new owners of Nine Mile Point gave notice to introduce a new basis for determining wages involving an increase of a half hour on the working day daily for hauliers, ropemen and enginemen.

Rejection was followed by a lock-out lasting ten weeks. Of the three pits affected, one resumed work by agreement with the Miners' Industrial Union, which undertook to recruit non-union labour from outside the locality. The dispute was settled through the South Wales Miners' Federation (SWMF) and arbitration, which led to work resuming on pre-stoppage terms. Both unions continued to be recognized by the company (Anthony-Jones 1959: 63–4). The next major stoppage occurred in 1935, when Nine Mile Point was one of twenty-four collieries belonging to the Ocean and Cory Combines, which resisted the SWMF's attempt to remove non-unionists from the coalfields of the region. The attitude of management was reflected in the recruitment of more non-unionists, by the decision to keep its workers locked out for longer than the period recommended by the Monmouthshire and South Wales Coal Owners' Association, and by ignoring the Association's agreement with the SWMF that when the pits reopened strikers should resume work in their former places. 'Stay down' strikes against strike-breakers followed (Anthony-Jones 1959: 63–4). During this period of industrial unrest no fewer than nine under-managers were at some time employed at Nine Mile Point.

The history of labour relations at Oakdale Navigation was unaffected by the issue of 'Spencerism', though in 1935 Oakdale miners did strike in sympathy with the Federation at Nine Mile Point. Sunk in 1911, the owners planned

Oakdale as a model village from the beginning, attracting workers from older collieries, both within the region and further afield. Like the Ocean Group, Tredegar Iron and Coal was relatively profitable and welfare provision figured in company policy (Zweiniger-Bargielowska 1990: 94–5). A major contrast, however, was the attitude of the respective owners of the two companies towards trade unionism in general and to the SWMF in particular. Membership of the SWMF lodge at Oakdale was strong and active (Thomas 1986: 15–18). Negotiation between the lodge officials and management occurred without difficulty and pickets were never victimized. Power cutting, introduced in 1933, was achieved without strikes or lock-outs. The turnover of under-managers was relatively low and relations between managers and workers so harmonious that during the Second World War it was selected as one of the training centres for 'Bevin boys', a tribute to the company's sound management and labour relations, its policy of internal training and promotion within the colliery, and to its profitable working (Thomas 1986: 18–20).

Even though a systematic analysis of the history of strikes at the nineteen matched pairs was frustrated partly by lack of information, the statistical basis was sufficient to establish an important finding. Because one in each pair was peaceful, none of the structural characteristics which each pair shared – location and geological environment (and by proxy depth of working, thickness of seam and working conditions, and composition of labour force) and size of colliery – could be regarded as the key factor in explaining strike propensity. The Ministry of Labour strike data gave quantitative support to the impression given by the strike histories that wages issues were far more significant as a cause of strikes in collieries which were not strike-prone compared with those which were, that employment issues were much less important in the peaceful pits. Among the relatively strike-free pits, only a single strike (at Oakdale Navigation) arose out of trade unionism as an issue, compared with eight at strike-prone pits (including Hamilton Palace and Nine Mile Point). Indeed, in both Scottish and Welsh strike-prone collieries, trade unionism, employment and working arrangements were more prominent recorded causes of strikes than in quiescent collieries.

By isolating structural factors the matched pairs exercise has highlighted other factors which the theory-based analysis in chapter 10 was unable to incorporate, except as indicative possibilities, notably organization and ideology, a special source of dispute in the Celtic coalfields, and labour management. Evidence offered by those whose contemporary experience has enabled them to describe contrasting colliery cultures and their significance for industrial conflict suggests that personalities, particularly of underground managers or 'overmen', or of butties, and of local lodge officials were crucial. The significance of these contrasts emerged particularly in pits and collieries which were in flux, undergoing substantial change, when the ability of managers, at all levels, was a key factor in precipitating or avoiding strikes. For those in search of less complicated explanations than those which attribute importance to the actions of individuals in explaining general tendencies, this is discomforting evidence; but it cannot be ignored. Moreover, although not entirely unambiguous, support for including this dimension as part of the 'action within structure' model towards which our exposition is moving can be found in the results of our matched pairs exercise. Data assembled from the *List of Mines* combined with the Ministry of Labour strike statistics make it possible to measure the turnover among managers employed between 1920 and 1940 in each of the sample collieries. Among the eighteen relatively strike-free collieries in the sample which were in existence throughout the twenty-year period between 1921 and 1940, only seven experienced a higher turnover of under-managers than their strike-prone comparators. However, if the pairs from the most highly strike-prone regions of Scotland and South Wales are excluded, which might be justified by the presence of exceptional ideological and organizational factors affecting strike potential, the contrast between strike-prone and strike-free collieries with regard to management history is underlined. Of the eleven English colliery pairs only in one instance was the number of changes in under-managers greater in a peaceful pit than its strike-prone comparator. The contrasts were greatest between Whitehaven and Walkmill (ten and four), Mitchell Main and Wharncliffe Silkstone (nine and four), Burradon and Dudley (thirteen and eight), Whitburn and Hylton (eight and four), Whitfield and Norton (eight and three) and, in Derbyshire, Clay Cross and Bonds Main collieries (six and three).

We conclude, therefore, that while structural factors played an important role in the development of strike propensity, it is also likely that a satisfactory explanation will have to include the attitudes and actions of mine managers, lodge officials and rank and file miners. In the final section, therefore, we explore the nature of labour management, the interaction between miners, lodge officials and managers, and the formation and significance for strike propensities of pit culture.

Pit culture: miners and managers

Our finding, in chapter 5, that high levels of colliery strike activity were normally a transient phenomenon stands in apparent contradiction to one feature of the industry which has often been noted and forms the subject of some impressive studies: the enduring nature of pit culture. This phenomenon is often linked in the literature to patterns of 'militancy' and 'moderation'. This juxtaposition of two apparently incompatible phenomena, long-lived cultures of militancy and transient episodes of strike activity, presents a paradox which requires resolution.

Evidence which indicates the degree to which the shared norms, values and customs of pit culture supported independent action comes from a contemporary observer, a miner who became a prominent Syndicalist, who declared that 'miners are all anarchists!' and reported that should there be even the slightest dissatisfaction with working conditions, miners would 'troop out to the "roadend" cursing the manager, vigorously and picturesquely, make for the pit bottom, and clamour to the bottomer to be instantly let up the "shank" out of this God-forsaken, etc., etc., hole. This is done, of course, without consulting anybody, neither union headquarters nor county agent, sometimes not even the checkweigher on the pithead' (MacDougall 1927: 764–5).

The possibility than many local strikes occurred either despite, or without consulting, the union requires some consideration of the importance of other influences on labour relations underground. Can variations in pit or village culture help to explain the differences in strike histories between one pit and another, one village and another? Krieger's extensively researched study (1984), which we noticed in chapter 2 is germane to this question, for he suggested that traditions that could be traced back to the inter-war period and earlier still had an identifiable impact on the managerial problems faced by the National Coal Board in the early 1980s. This, too, was the theme to emerge from Dave Cliff's study of the contrast between Hem Heath and Florence collieries demonstrated during the 1984–5 miners' strike. Dave Cliff, a miner at Hem Heath and then an Oxford student, was puzzled by the contrast between the militancy of Hem Heath and the miners at Florence Colliery, who were reluctant to support the strike at all. The two collieries, both in the traditionally 'moderate' district of North Staffordshire, were less than three miles apart and joined by underground roadways; they recruited their work-forces from the same area and, of course, received the same leadership from the NUM Midland Area. There were differences in conditions, pay and job security but these were all in favour of the militant Hem Heath miners. There were differences, too, in the 'management styles' at the two collieries: at Hem Heath 'management's hard-line attitude created bitterness and militancy'; at Florence the management were flexible and paternal. But these differences in the management of the two collieries left Cliff unsatisfied that he had got to the bottom of the contrast. In a postscript he offers a more convincing explanation. An old miner told him how the work-forces for the two collieries had been recruited in the years immediately after nationalization. The Florence miners were predominantly transfers from the closed Cheddle pits, elsewhere in North Staffordshire. This was an area without a tradition of militant trade unionism despite the fact that the Cheddle pits were notorious for poor working conditions, 'harsh taskmasters and poor payers'. At Florence the new recruits found better conditions, better pay and managers who were at least honest; this encouraged them to take the attitude 'things are not so bad here, we're doing all right' and confirmed them in their 'moderation'. By contrast, Hem Heath's work-force was recruited from collieries in Scotland, Durham and Wales 'all areas where the tradition of Union and unity were strong'. These contrasts had endured into the 1980s so that Hem Heath had retained the militancy more characteristic of Scotland and South Wales, while Florence had retained the traditional Midlands 'moderation' (Cliff 1986: 86–92).

There are further contrasts. A study of a village pit at Throckley revealed a community showing neither deference nor hostility towards the local paternalist owners, found opportunities for peaceful association and self-expression, and experienced a measure of fulfilment (Williamson 1982: 60–3, 230–1). In the Dukeries a form of deference has been detected among miners, which was accompanied by a repressed hostility (Downing and Gore 1983: 21–9), a consequence of an 'industrial feudalism' that inhibited their independence (Waller 1983: 292–4). At the other extreme, historians have identified 'red' villages or 'little Moscows' of the Rhondda, notably the Mardy pit (see chapter 8), Lumphinnans in the West Fife coalfield (Macintyre 1980a), and the militant pits of north Durham, at Thornley, Chopwell, Usworth, Seaham, Washington, Felling and Wardley, some of which have been portrayed as hot beds of militant activity since the third quarter of the nineteenth century (Welbourne 1923; Douglass 1972: 68–73). According to Douglass some of these 'unruly lodges' sustained 'an unbroken tradition of militancy' through the inter-war years until the mid-twentieth century (Douglass 1972: 68–73). Lodges in these pit villages struck contrary to official policy and without consultation; the degree of solidarity shown by miners and their families under those circumstances was a manifestation of the strength of the culture down the pit and in the village. Wardley colliery stands out as a notorious battleground, described in 1888 by a prosecuting counsel acting for the owners against 181 striking miners as the worst behaved colliery in the country (Douglass 1972: 78–9). In 1935, the owners, Bowes-Lyon, sacked 1,400 miners, of whom managers selected 400 and offered re-employment. This tactic was intended also to remove perceived troublemakers from the colliery, including the lodge secretary, George Harvey, the self-styled Bolshevik known as the 'Wardley Lenin', and the entire lodge committee. This action triggered a strike lasting seven weeks (Douglass 1972: 75–82).

The evidence presented from the literature offers, either directly or by implication, models of 'militant pits' and 'peaceful pits', in which culture subordinated other competing influences on miners' behaviour, particularly in relation to strikes. In contrast, our research has emphasized the transient nature of 'militancy'. One question which needs an answer, therefore, is why collieries which did warrant the label militant, even for a relatively brief period, resumed a strike-free, or relatively strike-free, existence thereafter. Answers to this question may be important in explaining inter-colliery, as well as temporal, differences in strike propensities. Here again, sources of evidence are scarce. For obvious reasons, peaceful pits left little trace in potential sources outside the company, whereas strikes generated comment both by the participants and also by the press, especially when activity involved picketing, evictions, strike-breakers, a police presence, demonstrations by the general public, or prosecutions. How representative such evidence is of most colliery strikes is questionable, however. One unambiguous explanation for the termination of a series of strikes is a clear victory or defeat for either side, particularly when the issue was 'political', occasioned by strike-breaking, victimization or, most important, the right to unionize. Otherwise, evidence is scarce indeed. Where issues were less 'political', which were the vast majority, most strike histories probably merely fizzled out, unremarked by contemporaries.

Three reasonably well-documented cases of transition from peace through a phase of militancy and back to peaceful operation are those of the Whitehaven Colliery, one of the two most strike-prone in Britain between 1927 and 1931, the collieries in the Powell Duffryn combine, and the Lady Windsor Colliery owned by the Ocean Coal Company. As we related earlier in this chapter, Whitehaven's militancy finally came to an end with the company's liquidation when the colliery passed first into the ownership of the Priestman Whitehaven Collieries Ltd, and later, in 1935, was acquired by the newly formed Cumberland Coal Company (Whitehaven) Ltd. The controlling interest in the Cumberland Coal Company was held by the Coltness Iron Company, formed in 1839, whose original activities in Lanarkshire had shifted towards coal production for sale during the later nineteenth century. Operations were extended into other Scottish coalfields and from 1902 into the English Midlands. With respect to investment, mechanization, reorganization, labour management and welfare provision, Coltness has been described, admittedly by the company biographer, as an innovative company (Carvel 1948: chs. 10–13). Labour relations in the scattered collieries owned by the company varied, however. Hassockrigg Colliery in Lanarkshire was the fourth most strike-prone in Britain between 1927 and 1931 (table 5.10), whereas Coventry Colliery, sunk in 1911, became one of Britain's most modern pits, located in a planned village environment and was noted for harmonious relations between miners and management (Carvel 1948: ch. 15), underlining once again the importance of local management as well as ownership as we showed in chapter 10. When Coltness took over the collieries at Whitehaven early in 1937, the newly recruited, ex-miner, manager at Cardowan colliery, then one of the most frequently struck collieries in the country, established a co-operative relationship with the miners' agent and with pit delegates (Carvel 1948: chapter 16). Through investment, modernization, and careful attention to labour management, the productive potential and efficiency of the pit was transformed; a comprehensive welfare programme was introduced, and safety education was set in place for workers in a colliery which possessed an appalling history of explosions (NCB, *Registration of Assets: . . . Cumberland Coal Co. (Whitehaven) Ltd.*, *Mining Report*, PRO COAL 37/121).

A change in colliery manager often made a crucial difference in affecting labour relations, as our histories of Whitburn and Hickleton Main showed. Changes in executive managers and/or colliery reorganization could also transform relations between employers and workers, notably through mergers and acquisition, as in the cases of Burradon (which merged with Coxlodge and Hazlerigg Colliery) and Nine Mile Point (acquired by the United National Group followed by Ocean Coal). In the case of Mitchell Main, rapid staff turnover was adduced as one of the reasons for poor labour relations at that colliery.

The suggestion that management decisions and behaviour, whether through policy or inadvertence, for good or ill, could have a major impact on strike activity is supported by other case study evidence. Before 1935 the history of Powell Duffryn, Britain's largest coalmining company between the wars, is one of relatively peaceful labour relations. This, it has been argued, was not a consequence of benevolent paternalism but of circumstances of high unemployment and a lack of alternative local opportunities, and immobility because of the high proportion of company housing in the valleys (Anthony-Jones 1959: 93–5). The merger with Welsh Amalgamated Collieries (WAC) in 1935 marked a change in labour relations, especially in those pits acquired through the merger. By acquiring WAC in 1935 Powell Duffryn doubled its output, accounting for nearly one-third of the coal produced in South Wales. The two main sources of dispute were the effects of mechanization on pay and grading and the introduction of double shifts. Following years of largely unsuccessful resistance against both, the SWMF had passed the responsibility for policy to the local lodges which were left to deal with individual colliery owners (Boyns 1989: 30–7). After 1926 the SWMF formally accepted management's right to introduce both mechanization and double shifts without reference to the conciliation board. The history of management at Powell Duffryn suggests that by introducing conveyors to work with the hand-getting of coal during the 1920s, the potential friction produced by the limited associated changes in working practices was minimized. In the 1930s, however, this intermediate technology was superseded by the introduction of integrated cutting and conveying systems, and a reorganization of working based on the systematic scientific principles embodied in the Bedaux system. Most of the pits formerly owned by WAC were worked by the traditional pillar and stall system, consequently the multiple changes introduced by the new parent company, which also involved pit closures as part of the rationalization process, imposed major pressures on workers and managers alike (Boyns 1992: 372–7). One consequence of a policy of both dictating working techniques and the methods of payment was to channel miners' efforts into negotiating price lists which had to accommodate the new grades of workers created. Other specific sources of grievance leading to strikes included the move towards task work, the measurement of yardage, the new basis of price lists and the movement of workers between 'stints' from one shift to the next, usually as a consequence of breakdowns.

Boyns's research suggests that the high level of disputes which these issues generated and the strikes to which they contributed were at least as much the responsibility of managers as of workers' intransigence in the face of change. In general, Powell Duffryn's managers were confrontational rather than conciliatory. Even the minority of colliery managers who were inclined towards a flexible approach were inhibited by company policy (Boyns 1992: 379–80). As in other instances described in this book, conflict often originated with underground officials, deputies, overmen and firemen. Boyns concluded that in the pits of Powell Duffryn during the period of unrest, the major area of conflict arose between the men and mining officials (who were mostly ex-miners) rather than between the men and the colliery manager, and that at whatever level it occurred 'confrontation was undoubtedly a function of the inadequate attention paid by colliery owners to the issue of management-worker relations' (Boyns 1992: 380). This failure of management down the pit he attributed to the hierarchical structure of corporate management. Planning targets were set by general managers, usually in consultation with higher management. The responsibility of individual colliery managers and their subordinates was to implement the plans. These depended critically on labour management skills in an industry which even after mechanization continued to be relatively labour intensive. The lack of skills required for effective labour management and soundly based labour relations has been seen as a serious limitation on the ability of Britain's largest coal producer to introduce changes without stoppages (Boyns 1992: 382–3).

A similar emphasis on the role of managers underground is made by John Morgan, who for forty-five years was lodge secretary at the Lady Windsor Colliery, owned by the Ocean Coal Company. He divided the history of the colliery into three phases, each corresponding to changes in managers and policy. During the first phase, between 1886 and 1903, the colliery agent in charge was efficient and straightforward in his dealings. This was a period of rapid growth based on mining a six-foot seam. Underground, the roadways were wide and high, and the timbermen took a pride in their job. During his successor's period, which ended in 1935, the six-foot seam was worked out and production came to depend on the four-foot seam which yielded more dirt. At the same time, the manager reduced extra payment to night workers who removed the waste, cleared roadways and built walls ready for the day shift. The consequent refusal by night workers to carry out these tasks resulted in a deterioration in roadways which became constricted, increased roof pressure and reduced tonnage. The resulting difficulty for miners to earn the minimum led to friction between them, the lodge officials, and management. According to Morgan, a major reason why the Lady Windsor did not become a strike-prone pit was the reversal of policy by a new manager, J. H. Jones, appointed in 1932, whose presence changed the atmosphere. There was 'no quibbling or evasion when grievances were brought forward; they were faced up to and, without proved cases of underpayment, rectified without delay'. Long overdue repairs were attended to underground and new machinery was installed during a period of 'fairly tranquil' relations between management and the local lodge (John Morgan 1956: 11–13).

This case suggests that management at local level was a stronger direct influence on the conduct of labour relations than was the board of directors, although the attitude of certain owners to trade unionism did colour labour policy, especially where coalowners' associations were powerful organizations, as in Scotland and South Wales. On the owners' side the man on the spot was more likely to be the under-manager or other supervisory employee, rather than the colliery manager. On the interpretation he placed on events and circumstances down the pit depended whether the company would allow a grievance to turn into a strike issue. In many instances even lodge officials were excluded from pit disputes, union representatives within a colliery preferring to resolve difficulties without involving 'outsiders', particularly in collieries where joint committees existed at pit level. The potential for conducting relations in this way depended partly on colliery policy determined by the colliery manager and by the implementation of policy by his subordinates.

As we remarked in the second section of chapter 2, colliery managers are a neglected group in the history of the industry, and other, lesser, supervisory staff working underground even more so, yet they were clearly crucial to the conduct of labour relations (see Tailby 1990; Ackers 1994: 386–408). It is difficult to generalize their precise roles which, notwithstanding their legal obligations regarding pit safety, varied from region to region and probably from pit to pit. The social dynamics of collieries and the problems which this presented to managers were complex. But to imply that miners determined the strike prone-ness of a colliery ignores the possibility that managers also contributed to the formation of strike behaviour and pit culture. The evidence we have presented shows that miners did acknowledge the role of managers in this process, and that managerial change, whether at executive level or more especially underground, was often followed by a change in culture. This suggests the need for a move away from the traditional emphasis on the role of trade unions and lodge officials and a militant rank and file in influencing strike propensity to an interpretation which acknowledges the importance of management in originating conflict. The evidential basis for this contention is not noticeably weaker than that which has been used to support the traditional view.

Change was inevitable in an industry in which the working environment and the capacity to earn depended so much upon natural conditions determined by geological factors. 'There is nothing standard, uniform or assured in the working of a mine. The unexpected is the ordinary, accident is the usual routine' (MacDougall 1927: 764). The industry was also one which experienced greater extremes of cyclical changes in demand than other industries. The secular decline of coal production between the wars followed a period before the First World War which saw massive growth. In both periods changes in work organization and technology in response to the pressures generated, first by expansion and later by contraction, presented managers with problems of implementation. The growth in the size of colliery companies during the pre-war period and later, the merger and reconstruction of combines were accompanied by further change which increased the potential for grievances. Whether such grievances developed into strikes depended partly on the role of trade unions and of coalowners' associations, but initially on personnel. It does seem, however, that the management of change at pit level was more successful, in the sense that strikes were avoided, when the company possessed either formal or satisfactory informal procedures, where a willingness and ability to compromise was present on both sides, and where union rivalry was absent.

Is it possible to describe a category of pits where such circumstances were more likely to be found? Previous chapters suggest that strikes were more likely to have occurred in those collieries in which several conditions were met: isolation, size and then several circumstances capable of wide interpretation. One was that a union was present and independent (though not necessarily dominant). Often vital in the circumstances of specific strikes, a history of providing collective support (even though partial in some counties, districts and lodges at times) may also be seen to have contributed to the self-confidence of miners (or groups of miners) to press and pursue grievances within their pit, regardless of the involvement of lodge or branch officials. A further facilitating factor, with a similar influence, is a capacity for workers to draw on cultural and social capital to secure solidarity. We have seen in this chapter that inept labour management has been a frequent trigger for strike action, and this may lie behind the statistical importance of absentee ownership and family control that we discovered in chapter 10. While pockets of truly militant miners possessing a strong political agenda existed, and especially in Scotland and South Wales, may have contributed at times to the unusually high levels of strike activity in the coalfields of these regions, the link between political militancy and strike activity was complex and variable as we showed in chapter 4. Indifference to labour management at boardroom level or a lack of managerial control over the conduct of supervisory officials underground may be seen as the reverse of the coin for so long the currency in debates over the 'militant miner'.

Hence the conclusions drawn in chapter 10, which stressed certain structural characteristics of the industry, particularly related to colliery size, ownership, management and trade union organization, are not inconsistent with the qualitative evidence presented in this chapter. While the models tested in the previous chapters could not be expected to provide an explanation for specific strikes or the strike experience of specific collieries, they did underline the increased potential for, and the probability of, strike action in the industry regardless of immediate causes. In this chapter, histories of local pit strikes have provided evidence that the place of work, the effects of changes in the methods and conditions of work, and relations between managers and workers were the triggers for disputes and strikes. In chapter 14 we integrate these findings into our overall conclusions concerning the high but fluctuating strike propensity evident in British coalmining. First we consider the extent to which the various limited conclusions reached in this and preceding chapters are applicable to the industry after it passed from private into public ownership; second, we attempt to make international comparisons of strike behaviour in the industry before proceeding to the concluding chapter.

12 Industrial relations and strikes after nationalization

Management, labour and government

With the ending of private ownership after the Second World War, one of the fundamental influences on strike propensity was abolished. In this chapter we explore to what extent the pattern of coalmining strikes altered as a result of nationalization. Our analysis so far has examined the statistical record of miners' local strike activity, described its characteristics, and interpreted both in an attempt to explain strikes in coalmining in Britain between 1889 and 1940. The possibility that the circumstances of industrial development and labour's experience were in some sense unusual in this period, though especially during the depression between the wars, gives special interest to the history of coalmining strikes after the Second World War when the industry was under public ownership and for the first ten years output expanded and then stabilized. Many questions regarding the history of coalmining strikes after 1940 require answers, among which are two of particular importance: did war affect the enduring character of mining strikes which we have established for the preceding period (and which survived the First World War), and did nationalization transform the record of exceptional strike activity among miners? These are the questions of immediate relevance to our study of strikes between 1940 and 1966, when centralized bargaining was adopted nationally under the National Power Loading Agreement (NPLA). However, a search for answers will be facilitated by sketching the background to nationalization and the expectations of its chief architects, and outlining the institutional changes in management and industrial relations under the newly formed National Coal Board (NCB).

The turbulent history of industrial relations in the coalmining industry before the Second World War was a major reason why, when the war ended, contemporaries who held widely differing political views agreed on the desirability of some form of state control over the industry. The precedents for, and the basis of, further government intervention extended backwards to the nineteenth century, while the conception of a nationalized coal industry as a feasible political objective originated in a meeting of the Trades Union Congress held in 1892 (Barry 1965: 109–25). A political agenda pressed by the coalminers' trade unions and by a political party dedicated to achieving the election of a Labour government was manifested in the introduction of eight nationalizing bills affecting the coal industry between 1893 and 1942.

In two respects dual control between owners and government during the Second World War moved the prospect of national ownership forward. The first was the experience of co-operation, the second was the recognition, based on that experience, by managers as well as trade unionists, that private enterprise had failed the industry between the wars. Even the Tory Reform Committee's programme outlined in *The National Policy for Coal* envisaged the need for a central authority, which was not dissimilar to that recommended by the critical Reid Committee's Report issued in 1945. Unions, owners, managers, politicians, civil servants and expert observers were in agreement that the key to solving the industry's problems was a transformation of industrial relations. High levels of absenteeism and strikes were seen to threaten the achievement of maximum production immediately, and in the longer term the restructuring and modernization of the industry (Barry 1965: 110–23). While the ideology of nationalization originated during the late nineteenth century, gathering impetus during the years immediately preceding the First World War, the basis of nationalization when it took place was essentially pragmatic (Supple 1986: 248).

Pragmatism is also evident in the structure and composition of the first National Coal Board set up in 1946. The chairman was Lord Hyndley, who before the war had been managing director of Powell Duffryn and commercial adviser to the Mines Department, and during the war, Controller-General in the Ministry of Fuel and Power. A high-ranking senior civil servant, Sir Arthur Street, was deputy chairman. The other members of the Board included two managing directors of colliery companies, an industrialist, an accountant, a scientist and two trade union leaders. These were Ebby Edwards, formerly secretary of the Miners' Federation of Great Britain (MFGB), and Walter Citrine, formerly General Secretary of the Trades Union Congress. Responsibility for manpower planning, labour relations and welfare was given to the two trade unionists; the appointment of several district officials of the National Union of Mineworkers (NUM) to the staff was another element in the new policy intended to improve coalfield industrial relations (Ashworth 1986: 122–8).

For the purpose of managing the industry eight divisional boards were set up; their chairmen possessed no special expertise. Within these divisions area managers were equivalent, in the degree of authority they held, to the production managers or colliery agents under private enterprise; as under private enterprise, most were mining engineers. Unlike the area managers, the colliery managers were markedly more limited than under private enterprise in the degree of independence and authority they could exercise. In matters relating to labour recruitment and labour relations generally, instead of enlisting the support of managing directors or company directors in the settlement of disagreements or disputes arising at colliery level, the new procedures required the colliery manager to appeal to the NCB area Labour Officer for advice and for approval of any proposed stance or action. The tendency for Labour Officers to be former mining trade unionists inevitably weakened the authority of colliery managers in their dealings with working miners. In matters concerning safety and day-to-day working, the responsibilities of certificated colliery managers remained unchanged. Thus, although the balance of power affecting colliery managers' authority with respect to the handling of disagreements and disputes had shifted towards the miners, in other respects (because of the high degree of continuity of personnel at pit, colliery and area levels) the rank and file miner, according to Cole, regarded the NCB as 'the old coalowner writ large' (Cole 1949: 15–17); 'state capitalism' replaced capitalism based on private ownership.

The machinery intended to improve industrial relations through a more effective method of resolving disputes was the structure of joint negotiating committees which operated at pit, district and national levels. At national level, the apex was the National Reference Tribunal (NRT), a permanent arbitration body set up at the outset. Until 1961 all disputes which had not been resolved by the Joint National Negotiating Committee (JNNC) had to be referred to the NRT. The NRT comprised four assessors and three part-time members, whereas the JNNC consisted of thirty-two representatives, equally divided between the union side and the NCB. District-level machinery was similarly jointly structured, though binding arbitration was compulsory in the event of a failure to agree at district level. At colliery level, the Pit Conciliation Scheme provided for any dispute to be discussed with the workers' immediate supervisor. In the event of failure to agree, the dispute was to be taken to progressively higher and higher levels of the colliery until after no more than fourteen days the dispute was to be referred to the district conciliation board and eventually to an umpire for a final and binding decision. In marked contrast to the industrial relations machinery existing under private ownership, therefore, the separation of negotiations at pit, district and national levels after 1946 marked a formally agreed prevention of the extension of mining disputes beyond their places of origin. Furthermore, by placing compulsory arbitration at the centre of the new system, and by securing the formal agreement of the National Union of Mineworkers to it, the scheme in effect ensured that all strikes were strikes in breach of procedure and hence unofficial. Only after 1961, when the procedures of the national machinery were changed, could a strike take place which was not in breach of procedure (Royal Commission on Trade Unions and Employers' Associations 1965–1968, *Disputes Procedures in Britain*: 74–5).

Just as changes in ownership, structure and organization left the fundamental dynamics of the industry almost untouched at local level, the formation of the NUM in 1945 hardly affected traditional continuities characteristic of labour relations in the coalfields. Local and county unions, which under the MFGB had been separately affiliated to the Federation, were merged into a smaller number of area unions. However, the existence of sub-entities within the NUM (including the creation of units to represent non-mining workers in collieries) meant that the problems arising from the pre-war fragmented union structure, albeit under a national umbrella, persisted (Durcan *et al.* 1983: 100–8). This was partly because financial resources continued to be retained within the areas and partly because throughout our period piece-rates were the outcome of local negotiations (McCormick 1979: 61).

Senior figures in the NUM felt a tremendous pressure to 'make a success' of nationalization and help the new Labour government. At their first meeting with the Board in August 1946 they urged 'all members of the Union to recognise the necessity of breaking with the past and accepting their responsibilities with a view to ensuring the reorganisation of the industry and the success of the new system of ownership' (quoted by Arnot 1979: 193). At the special conference immediately before Vesting Day, Arthur Horner, recently elected as secretary of the NUM, argued that 'we must take a long view, because the advancement of our members' interests lies . . . in establishing a firm and highly productive industry' (quoted by Arnot 1979: 198). This attitude was not such a wrench as it might seem. During the war, especially after the invasion of the Soviet Union, many trade unionists had become whole-hearted 'productionists' and immediately after the war, but before nationalization, had responded with alacrity to a request from the Labour Minister of Fuel and Power for their help in securing another eight million tons of output (Arnot 1979: 124). These attitudes were also evident at area level in the NUM. Soon after the 1945 election the Yorkshire Mine Workers' Association passed a resolution attacking unofficial strikers for 'sabotaging their own interests and those for which the present government has been elected' (quoted by Andrew J. Taylor 1984b: 14); in the 1950s the young Arthur Scargill led a strike at the Yorkshire colliery where he worked and was expelled from the union at local level (Scargill 1975: 5); in Durham the NUM area took a hard line against unofficial strikes, in a county where no unofficial movement and no Scargill emerged (Garside 1971: 452–6). The same attitudes were given a different rationale by Will Paynter, the Communist president of the South Wales Area of the NUM, who condemned unofficial strikes and unofficial movements in 1950s conference addresses on the grounds that they were inevitably sectional and weakened the militant organization which was the South Wales Area (Paynter 1972: 130–2).

The inevitable result of the apparent incorporation of the NUM leadership into the structures of the NCB was the growth of unofficial leaderships (Slaughter 1958: 242–50; Margaret Kahn 1984: 6–53; Fine *et al.* 1985b: 182–3). With the benefit of hindsight, the first indications of this can be seen as early as 1948 (Andrew J. Taylor 1984b: 20). There was serious concern at the continued high level of strikes and the apparent inability of the NUM to stop them at the highest level of the NCB by the end of 1948. At a meeting of the Board in November of that year 'Mr. Edwards [Ebby Edwards, the former secretary of the MFGB, by this time the member of the National Coal Board with responsibility for labour relations] said the situation was a very difficult one to deal with. Cases were continually arising where men were going on strike against their Union. The Union seemed to have lost control' (National Coal Board, *Stoppages and Restric-*

tions due to Trade Disputes: Policy, extract from the Minutes of the 239th meeting of the Board, 5 November 1948, PRO COAL 26/89). However, unofficial strike movements, as opposed to unofficial strikes, did not become generally visible until the 1950s when the phrase 'NC bloody B' became a common expression (Francis and Smith 1980: 442). In 1951 an unofficial strike against a threatened partial closure of a colliery in South Wales gained the support of 15,000 miners and in 1955 over 100,000 miners at ninety-five collieries came out on strike in Yorkshire in defiance of the area leadership (Slaughter 1958; Francis and Smith 1980: 442–5). In 1959 workers threatened by the closure of the Devon pit near Alloa in Scotland organized a stay-down strike which eventually involved 25,000 workers; Scottish area officials intervened to end the strike: its objects were contrary to union policy (Allen 1981: 68).

Nationalization did not substantially reduce the importance of pit-level negotiations between union and managers, for a substantial minority of the workforce continued to be on piece-rates. In 1955 42 per cent of the manual labour force were pieceworkers, a minority which included the great majority of face workers who continued to be the main originators of strike activity in the industry (Handy 1981: 48). In the traditional manner which had survived mechanized cutting, piece and contract workers negotiated on-the-spot prices for such special tasks as advancing a heading or attending to unforeseen difficulties in working the face. Increasing mechanization was accompanied by greater division of labour, leading to a proliferation of different types of contract work involving colliers, or machine men, or drawers-off, or rippers, or panners. One ex-miner described one of the consequences of this payment system as a '"miniaturization" of industrial struggle' (Rutledge 1977: 413). An increasingly differentiated work-force perpetuated mining strikes which 'were typically small-scale affairs in which solidarity action was frequently limited to contract workers of the same category', and typically accompanied by 'a lot of disunity' (Rutledge 1977: 414).

When in 1951 an agreement between the NCB and the NUM prohibited local price list revisions, except where there had been a substantial change in working conditions, the definition of 'substantial' was left vague, allowances continuing to be determined locally and ensuring the continuance of an important element of decentralized bargaining. By the early 1960s in Yorkshire, where upward pressure on wages had been powerful and long-standing, allowances had come to make up a high proportion of face workers' earnings. On 16 per cent of the faces operating in 1961 the workers earned more from allowances than they did from the basic contract, and allowances formed less than 20 per cent of earnings on only 13 per cent of faces (Handy 1981: 54, 60). The introduction in 1955 of the national day wage structure, which included new national minima and national additions to wages, was intended to counter decentralized bargaining, an objective shared both by the NCB and the NUM. The piece-rates wage structure, however, continued to frustrate the aims of Board and Union alike. Proposals for reform and rationalization formulated in the mid-1950s were abandoned. Instead the Board focused its energies on co-ordinating and unifying the existing local wage agreements for power-loading faces, suggesting the negotiation of a national power loading agreement at the end of 1957 (Handy 1981: 67). Whether, and to what extent, the DPLAs and the 1966 NPLA, which substituted a form of measured day work for piece-work, did reduce strike activity has been a matter of dispute (Clegg 1979: 272–3; Handy 1981: 216–25; Winterton 1981: 17–18). Handy's careful and detailed review of evidence found discrepancies between the regional pattern and timing of the introduction of DPLAs and the pattern and trends of strike activity which led him to reject 'the wage payment systems hypothesis' in favour of an emphasis on the effects of changes in the market for coal – an aspect of the 'markets' model of strike activity which we examined in chapter 10 (Handy 1981: 216–26).

Before 1966 NCB deep mined production levels fluctuated by roughly 10 per cent around 200 million tonnes, though the post-war peak of 211 million tonnes in 1957 marked the beginning of a declining trend. The number of mineworkers fell from 0.70 million to 0.52 million between 1947 and 1963, the fall accelerating during the 1960s (Church 1990: 52–4). This trend was partly owing to pit closures and partly to mechanization; between 1957 and 1963 the percentage of coal cut by power-loading machinery rose from 23 to 92 per cent (McCormick 1979: 63; Durcan et al. 1983: 252–4; Ashworth 1986: 258–80). Not until 1962 was the problem of labour redundancy perceived to be sufficiently serious for the NCB to introduce inter-divisional transfer schemes aimed at inducing the movement of redundant miners in Scotland, the North East and Lancashire to the Midlands and Yorkshire. While regional variations existed, until at least the late 1960s alternative employment opportunities softened the impact of closures and mechanization. In general, therefore, throughout most of the post-war period under review the miners' bargaining position was relatively strong.

The record of strikes at national and regional levels reinforces the perception of the period between the end of the Second World War and the mid-1960s as relatively peaceful. It is only when local strike activity is examined that it is possible to observe high strike frequencies. The trend towards the very high strike frequencies seen in the 1940s and later originated in the mid to late 1930s. By the late 1950s the number of strikes had risen to ten times the levels recorded in the industry in the period between the late nineteenth century and the mid-1930s (figure 5.1). Whatever the effects of the change in ownership, of the development of the institutional structures of collective bargaining under nationalization, and of a partial shift from piece-work to day-work beginning in the late 1950s, they did not include a reduction in the frequency of domestic and local strikes.

An explanation of this upsurge and its subsequent decline is not the concern of this chapter. In previous chapters we established patterns and characteristics of coalmining strikes within the period from 1893 to 1940, particularly in respect of inter-colliery differences. Given these continuities in local strike activity, we ask whether the characteristics of mining strikes displayed fundamental differences during the Second World War and after nationalization.

Change or continuity? The delineation and distribution of coalmining strikes 1947–66

Our analysis of strikes in coalmining before the Second World War was based on the complete file of officially recorded strikes, which for that period was a feasible, though labour-intensive, exercise. The post-war period, however, presented a major problem because of the sheer volume of strikes. This necessitated an approach based on samples of the officially recorded strikes. It was clear that a relatively small sample of strikes would yield almost as much information as might be expected of the entire population. But a simple sample of, say, 10 per cent of all coalmining strikes would not allow us to make inferences about two of our main areas of interest – the concentration of strikes by colliery and by place. For this reason we recorded basic data on every recorded strike in a sample of years, specifically every fifth year from 1943 until 1963, after which access to the records was prevented by the thirty years' rule. We also recorded additional data on a 10 per cent systematic random sample of strikes in each of the sample years.

In chapter 5 we showed that by the end of the inter-war period the median colliery strike in Britain was short and of limited extent. Based on our samples of strikes in the years shown, table 12.1 indicates that the median strike duration was no more than a day during the period 1943 to 1963. The number of workers directly involved in the median strike fell to a low of twenty-three before returning to about thirty in the 1950s and 1960s. These were, therefore, small strikes even though they often occurred at large and very large collieries. This implies that the participation rate, measured by the numbers directly involved expressed as a proportion of the number of employees, was often extremely low. In order to compute strike participation rates we compared the Ministry of Labour data showing the number of workers directly involved in strikes, with data on the number of colliery employees extracted from other sources. Precise computations are impossible because of incompatibilities in the data; however there is no reason to believe that the general picture to emerge is seriously misleading. The distribution of strike participation rates in our sample years shown in table 12.2 indicates a remarkably low level of participation. In 1943 the median participation rate was no more than 10 per cent. The fall below 5 per cent in 1948 suggests that war conditions are not the explanation. In the period 1948–63 the median participation rate remained very low. Fewer than one in five domestic colliery strikes attracted the support of more than one-half of the colliery work-force. Domestic colliery strikes which involved more than 80 per cent of colliery workers were exceptional throughout the period.

The regional strike patterns changed after the Second World War. As we saw in chapter 5, before 1940 South Wales and Scotland accounted for between one-third and two-thirds of all strikes recorded for the industry as a whole (table 5.4). In the 1890s, and again in the 1930s, Yorkshire generated roughly one-sixth of all strikes in the industry. In the post-war period two remarkable changes occurred (table 12.3). The first was the virtual withering away of strike activity in the North East, which registered no more than one-tenth of all strikes in the

Table 12.1. *The shape of British colliery strikes (Great Britain 1943–63)*

Period	Duration (days) Percentiles of sample distribution					Numbers directly involved Percentiles of sample distribution					Strike rate[a] (per million)	Total number of strikes[b]
	25	50	75	95	n	25	50	75	95	n		
1943	1	1	2	6	85	26	60	170	1,220	85	1,191	843
1948	1	1	2	7	115	15	23	87	568	115	1,540	1,109
1953	1	1	3	5	130	17	31	62	405	130	1,832	1,306
1958	1	1	2	5	196	16	30	69	431	196	2,804	1,960
1963	1	1	2	5	98	20	33	140	534	99	1,866	985

Notes:

[a] The number of strikes per million workers. Based on 708,000 'persons employed' in 1943 (Ministry of Fuel and Power, *Statistical Digest 1944*, table 1) and 720,000, 713,000, 699,000 and 528,000 'average number of wage earners (below and above ground) in deep-mined coal production' in 1948, 1953, 1958 and 1963 respectively (Ministry of Power, *Statistical Digest 1963*, table 13).

[b] Colliery strikes only; there were seven strikes recorded under 'coal mining' in 1948 not involving collieries, one in 1953, and two in 1958 and 1963 which have been excluded from this and all subsequent tables.

Sources: as indicated in the notes plus Ministry of Labour, *Trade Disputes:* . . . *Strikes and Lock-outs of 1943*, etc., PRO LAB 34/58, /63, /69, /74 and /85.

Table 12.2. *Strike participation rates (domestic strikes, Great Britain 1943–63)*

	Numbers and % of strikes by ranges of participation rate										Sample size	Participation rate %	
	0–9	10–19	20–29	30–39	40–49	50–59	60–69	70–79	80–89	90–140		Median	Mean
1943													
Number	38	9	9	5	2	5	2	6	1	2	79	10.2	24.7
%	48	11	11	6	3	6	3	8	1	3	100		
1948													
Number	77	5	4	3	4	4	2	3	5	2	109	3.4	17.1
%	71	5	4	3	4	4	2	3	5	2	100		
1953													
Number	89	11	6	5	3	5	1	5	1	2	128	3.8	14.5
%	70	9	5	4	2	4	1	4	1	2	100		
1958													
Number	138	15	8	3	6	7	7	3	0	3	190	2.9	13.3
%	73	8	4	2	3	4	4	2	0	2	100		
1963													
Number	63	7	5	5	2	4	4	5	0	1	96	3.9	17.0
%	66	7	5	5	2	4	4	5	0	1	100		

Notes: The table refers to strikes affecting a single colliery and is derived from a systematic 10 per cent sample of colliery strikes recorded in the years shown. In a small number of cases employment data could not be found or the computed participation rate exceeded 140 per cent; these strikes have been excluded from the sample.

Sources: strike data as for table 12.1. Employment data: 1943: Ministry of Fuel and Power, *List of Mines in Great Britain and the Isle of Man 1945*; data relate to December 1945 except in cases in which the mines had ceased work earlier in the year in which case data refer to the numbers 'normally' employed when the mine was at work; 1948: Ministry of Fuel and Power, *List of Mines in Great Britain 1950*, data relate to December 1948 with the same exception as before; 1953: *Guide to the Coalfields 1954*; data are 'representative' figures for 1953; 1958: *Guide to the Coalfields 1959*; internal evidence from this and other annuals in the series confirms that this provides employment data for 1958 despite the statement in the 'Explanatory Notes' which claims the data relate to 1957; 1963: *Guide to the Coalfields 1963*; the year to which the employment data in this volume refers is uncertain.

Table 12.3. *The regional distribution of colliery strikes (Great Britain 1943–1963)*

	Major regions							Minor regions:				
	Scot-land	South Wales	North East	Yorkshire	Lancashire and Cheshire	East Midlands	West Midlands	Cumber-land	North Wales	South West	Kent	Great Britain
1943												
Number	451	128	56	104	51	31	14	4	1	2	1	843
%	*53*	*15*	*7*	*12*	*6*	*4*	*2*	*0*	*0*	*0*	*0*	*100*
1948												
Number	355	247	36	260	103	55	32	8	1	0	10	1,109 [a]
%	*32*	*22*	*3*	*23*	*9*	*5*	*3*	*1*	*0*	*0*	*1*	*100*
1953												
Number	579	217	17	372	33	45	35	5	0	1	2	1,306
%	*44*	*17*	*1*	*28*	*3*	*3*	*3*	*0*	*0*	*0*	*0*	*100*
1958												
Number	801	275	46	570	112	64	72	6	1	0	13	1,960
%	*41*	*14*	*2*	*29*	*6*	*3*	*4*	*0*	*0*	*0*	*1*	*100*
1963												
Number	215	274	5	348	39	39	52	7	4	0	2	985
%	*22*	*28*	*1*	*35*	*4*	*4*	*5*	*1*	*0*	*0*	*0*	*100*

Note:
[a] Includes two cross-border strikes affecting Yorkshire and the East Midlands omitted from the previous columns.
Sources: as for table 12.1.

Table 12.4. *Numbers of coalmining strikes per million employees (regional relatives, Great Britain 1943–1963)*

Region									
	Scotland	South Wales and South West	North East and Cumberland	Yorkshire	Lancashire Cheshire and North Wales	East Midlands	West Midlands	Kent	Great Britain
1943	458	90	35	64	75	27	20	15	100
1948	281	140	18	120	111	37	35	104	100
1953	375	108	8	144	30	24	33	17	100
1958	333	94	13	148	71	22	44	64	100
1963	205	188	6	164	62	23	72	20	100

Notes: Regions are geographically defined for 1943 and based on NCB divisions and areas for 1948–63. The employment data refer to the 'average number of wage earners on colliery books'.

Sources: strike data as for table 12.1. Employment data: 1943: Ministry of Fuel and Power, *Statistical Digest 1944*, table 53 (data for Mining Industry Act areas); 1948: Ministry of Fuel and Power, *Statistical Digest for 1948 and 1949*, table 42; 1953: Ministry of Fuel and Power, *Statistical Digest 1954*, table 42; 1958: Ministry of Power, *Statistical Digest 1959*, table 31; 1963: Ministry of Power, *Statistical Digest 1963*, table 32 ('adjusted' data).

Table 12.5. *The concentration of domestic strikes by colliery (Great Britain 1938–63)*

	1938	1943	1948	1953	1958	1963
Percentage of domestic strikes in the *n* most strike-prone collieries	a-b	a-b	a-b	a-b	a-b	a-b
$n = 5$	12–12	9–9	9–9	8–8	8–8	10–10
$n = 10$	19–19	15–15	14–14	13–13	13–13	16–16
$n = 20$	30–31	25–25	23–23	22–22	21–22	25–26
$n = 35$	43–43	38–38	33–33	32–33	31–32	37–38
Gini coefficient (mines at work)[c]	0.938–0.941					
Gini coefficient (mines producing coal)[c]		0.882–0.886	0.838–0.845	0.842–0.849		
Gini coefficient (NCB mines only)			0.761–0.771	0.759–0.769	0.712–0.725	0.723–0.734
Number of mines at work[c]	2,105	1,738				
Number of mines producing coal[c]			1,491	1,337		
Number of NCB mines			980	875[d]	825	611
Number of collieries at which domestic strikes were recorded	194–201	329–341	411–430	369–391	457–485	292–306
Strike prevalence (all mines at work)[c] (%)	9–10					
Strike prevalence (all mines producing coal)[c] (%)		19–20	28–29	28–29		
Strike prevalence (all NCB mines) (%).			42–44	42–45	55–59	48–50
Number of domestic strikes at identified collieries	362	834	1,097	1,305	1,959	981
Number (*and* %) of domestic strikes at unidentified collieries	7 (2)	12 (2)	19 (2)	22 (2)	28 (1)	14 (1)

Notes: Estimates given under 'a' assume that the strikes at unidentified collieries were completely unconcentrated i.e. each occurred at a colliery which was struck only once. The base of the percentages is therefore the number of domestic strikes recorded at identified and unidentified collieries. Estimates given under 'b' assume that the strikes at unidentified collieries were as concentrated as those at identified collieries. The base of these percentages is therefore the number of domestic strikes recorded at identified collieries.

[c]'Mines at work' are mines under the Coal Mines Act with non-zero employment. 'Mines producing coal' are mines under the Coal Mines Act excluding mines which were not mines of coal but of some other mineral and also coal mines under the Coal Mines Act which did not produce coal during the year, e.g. pumping pits and new sinkings. NCB mines exclude 'licensed' and 'other' mines.

[d]1 January 1954.

Sources: Ministry of Fuel and Power, *Statistical Digest from 1938*, table 1. 1948: Ministry of Fuel and Power, *Statistical Digest 1948 and 1949*, table 42; 1953: Ministry of Fuel and Power, *Statistical Digest 1954*, table 42. Number of NCB mines producing coal 1948: National Coal Board, *Annual Report and Statement of Accounts*, 1948, chapter 1, footnotes to tables 1–8; 1953: National Coal Board, *Annual Report and Statement of Accounts*, 1954, Statistical Appendix, table 1; 1958: National Coal Board, *Report and Accounts*, table 1; 1963: National Coal Board, *Report and Accounts*, 1958, II, table 1; 1963: National Coal Board, *Report and Accounts*, 1963–4, II, table 4.

industry after 1940. One of the birthplaces of permanent trade unionism in the industry and at times a highly strike-prone area, that region experienced no more than five strikes in 1963, all of which occurred in Northumberland; not a single officially recorded strike took place in Durham. The second was the reverse transformation witnessed in Yorkshire, where South Yorkshire especially emerged as the industry's storm centre. The rise of Yorkshire to become a major concentration of strike activity is not entirely surprising. Historically, the most rapidly growing coalfields have often generated high levels of strike activity.

That many strikes took place in Scotland, South Wales and Yorkshire is partly a consequence of the size of those regions, of course. By estimating strike rates in each region we can take into account variations in the size of regions and examine, not simply the number of strikes in each region, but the number of strikes per million mineworkers in that region. When compared with national strike statistics, the strike rates for the regions reveal that, as before the Second World War, South Wales and Scotland were usually the most strike-prone of the large coalmining regions, and that the rate in Yorkshire rose relatively throughout the period (table 12.4). We saw previously that in the decade before the Second World War the variations in inter-regional strike rates were extreme (chapter 5). Inter-regional disparities persisted during and after the war, though with the regions ranked differently than hitherto. In 1963 miners in Scotland were roughly three times as strike prone than those in Lancashire and the West Midlands, about ten times more strike prone than those in the East Midlands and Kent, and more than thirty times as strike-prone as miners in the North East.

On a different basis for measuring strike proneness, that of strike prevalence (the proportion of collieries or places affected by at least one strike), generally Scotland had the worst record during both the inter-war and post-war periods, though strike prevalences as high if not higher were also recorded for Yorkshire in most of the years we have examined after the war. Strike activity in these regions made an increasing contribution to a national trend towards the higher strike prevalence which comparisons with the past and with other industries reveal. To show this rigorously required us to recompute our strike prevalence and concentration measures for the inter-war years on an annual basis for comparability with the measures for the war and post-war periods. In table 12.5 we give details for only 1938 from the inter-war period but use the results for 1928 and 1933 (not shown there) in the discussion which follows. The prevalence of strikes in 1938, when 9 or 10 per cent of all mines at work were struck, was already considerably greater than in previous years. What happened during and immediately after the Second World War is obscured by the changing methods used to count collieries (the interested reader can follow these changes in the notes to table 12.5). However, it is clear that the prevalence of strikes was higher in 1943 than in 1938: there were strikes at over 300 separate collieries, forming about 20 per cent of all mines producing coal compared with about 200 in 1938. Between 1943 and 1948, strike prevalence increased again with

Table 12.6. *Places appearing in the 'top ten' for colliery strike activity (Great Britain, every fifth year 1943–1963)*

Number of times appearing in the 'top ten'	Years appearing	Place	County	Aggregate number of strikes[a]
4	1943, 1948, 1953, 1958	Shotts	Lanarkshire	226
4	1948, 1953, 1958, 1963	Bentley, Doncaster	South Yorkshire	114
3	1953, 1958, 1963	Wombwell, nr Barnsley	South Yorkshire	68
3	1953, 1958, 1963	Woodlands, nr Doncaster	South Yorkshire	65
2	1943, 1948	Gwaun-cae-Gurwen	Glamorgan	54
2	1943, 1948	Harthill	Lanarkshire	26
2	1943, 1948	Monkton	Ayrshire	32
2	1943, 1958	Cardenden	Fife	52
2	1948, 1953	West Calder	Midlothian	32
2	1953, 1958	Stainforth, nr Doncaster	South Yorkshire	44
2	1953, 1963	Deri	Glamorgan	33
2	1953, 1963	Whitburn	West Lothian	45
2	1958, 1963	Armthorpe, nr Doncaster	South Yorkshire	58
2	1958, 1963	Denaby, nr Doncaster	South Yorkshire	49
1	1943	Annbank	Ayrshire	17
1	1943	Dalserf	Lanarkshire	19
1	1943	Denny	Stirlingshire	14
1	1943	High Blantyre	Lanarkshire	19
1	1943	Prestwick	Ayrshire	12
1	1948	Astley	Lancashire	23
1	1948	Bathgate	West Lothian	15
1	1948	Havercroft	South Yorkshire	15
1	1948	Woodlesford	West Yorkshire	11
1	1948	Worsley	Lancashire	11
1	1953	Fauldhouse	West Lothian	16
1	1953	Kelty	Fife	22
1	1953	Lochgelly	Fife	36
1	1953	Thorne, nr Doncaster	South Yorkshire	16
1	1958	East Grange	Fife	23
1	1958	Newmills	Fife	24
1	1963	Edlington, nr Doncaster	South Yorkshire	17
1	1963	Mountain Ash	Glamorgan	15
1	1963	Thrybergh, nr Rotherham	South Yorkshire	17

Note:
[a] Number of strikes in the five years 1943, 1948, 1953, 1958 and 1963 only.
Sources: as for table 12.1.

Table 12.7. Collieries appearing in the 'top ten' for domestic strike activity (Great Britain, every fifth year 1943–1963)

Number of times appearing in the 'top ten'	Years appearing	Colliery	Situation	County	Aggregate number of strikes[a]
4	1948, 1953, 1958, 1963	Bentley	Bentley nr Doncaster	South Yorkshire	116
3	1948, 1953, 1958	Kingshill[b]	Shotts	Lanarkshire	35
3	1953, 1958, 1963	Brodsworth Main	Woodlands nr Doncaster	South Yorkshire	65
2	1943, 1948	Auchincruive Nos. 4 & 5	Monkton	Ayrshire	32
2	1943, 1948	Calderhead Nos. 3 & 4	Shotts	Lanarkshire	26
2	1948, 1953	Southfield	Shotts	Lanarkshire	27
2	1953, 1958	Glencraig	Cardenden	Fife	42
2	1953, 1958	Hatfield Main	Stainforth, nr Doncaster	South Yorkshire	44
2	1953, 1963	Yorkshire Main	Edlington, nr Doncaster	South Yorkshire	29
2	1958, 1963	Markham Main	Armthorpe, nr Doncaster	South Yorkshire	58
1	1943	Ayr Nos. 1 & 2+ Ayr Nos. 9 & 10[c]	Annbank	Ayrshire	16
1	1943	Blairmuckhill	Harthill	Lanarkshire	11
1	1943	Blantyre	High Blantyre	Lanarkshire	19
1	1943	Bowhill Nos. 1 & 2	Cardenden	Fife	12
1	1943	Brynhenllys (Slant)	Upper Cwmtwrch	Glamorgan	11
1	1943	Castlehill No. 6	Carluke	Lanarkshire	11
1	1943	Herbertshire	Denny	Stirlingshire	14
1	1943	Telfer	Dalserf	Lanarkshire	10
1	1948	Baton (including Hillhouserigg)	Shotts	Lanarkshire	21
1	1948	East	Gwaun-cae-Gurwen	Glamorgan	18
1	1948	Fortissat	Shotts	Lanarkshire	11
1	1948	Loganlea	West Calder	Midlothian	11

1	1948	Nook	Astley	Lancashire	13
1	1948	Steer	Gwaun-cae-Gurwen	Glamorgan	14
1	1953	Aldwarke	Parkgate, nr Rotherham	South Yorkshire	22
1	1953	Devon	Sauchie	Clackmannan	12
1	1953	Grimethorpe	Grimethorpe, nr Barnsley	South Yorkshire	12
1	1953	Thorne	Thorne, nr Doncaster	South Yorkshire	16
1	1953	Thurcroft Main	Thurcroft, nr Rotherham	South Yorkshire	12
1	1958	Blairhall	East Grange	Fife	23
1	1958	Cadeby	Denaby, nr Doncaster	South Yorkshire	19
1	1958	Cardowan Nos. 1 & 2	Stepps, nr Glasgow	Lanarkshire	18
1	1958	Upton	Upton, nr Pontefract	West Yorkshire	18
1	1958	Valleyfield	Newmills	Fife	20
1	1963	Ackton Hall	Featherstone, nr Pontefract	West Yorkshire	12
1	1963	Dalkeith Nos. 5 & 9	Smeaton by Dalkeith	Midlothian	10
1	1963	Deep Duffryn	Mountain Ash	Glamorgan	11
1	1963	Garw	Blaengarw, Bridgend	Glamorgan	10
1	1963	Kilnhurst	Kilnhurst, nr Rotherham	South Yorkshire	10
1	1963	Polkemmet	Whitburn	West Lothian	18
1	1963	Savile	Methley, nr Leeds	West Yorkshire	11
1	1963	Silverwood	Thrybergh, nr Rotherham	South Yorkshire	17
1	1963	Whitrigg No. 5	Whitburn	West Lothian	10
1	1963	Woolley 'A' and 'B'	Darton, nr Barnsley	South Yorkshire	10

Notes:
See the general appendix for our conventions for defining and naming collieries.
[a] Number of strikes in the years the colliery appeared in the 'top ten' only.
[b] Kingshill No. 1 Colliery++ Kingshill No. 3 Colliery.
[c] Also known as Enterkine colliery.
Sources: as for table 12.1.

Table 12.8. *Persistently struck collieries (domestic strikes, Great Britain, every fifth year 1928-1963)*

	Number of struck collieries[a]	Number and % struck: 5 years subsequently		5 and 10 years subsequently		5, 10 and 15 years subsequently		Local strikes at unidentified collieries	
		N	%	N	%	N	%	N	%[b]
1928	72	12	17	9	13	7	10	18	19
1933	81	37	46	25	31	20	25	6	5
1938	194	99	51	71	37	61	31	7	2
1943	329	186	57	129	39	104	32	12	1
1948	411	218	53	171	42	102	25	19	2
1953	369	264	72	147	40	–	–	22	2
1958	457	219	48	–	–	–	–	28	1
1963	292	–	–	–	–	–	–	14	1
Mean			49		34		25		

Notes:
[a] Excluding unidentified struck collieries.
[b] Per cent of all domestic colliery strikes.
Sources: as for table 12.1 and Ministry of Labour, *Trade Disputes: . . . Strikes and Lock-outs of 1928*, and subsequent volumes, PRO LAB 34/46–.

over 400 collieries struck, nearly 30 per cent of all mines producing coal. The final increase in strike prevalence took place between 1953 and 1958 and, although there was an ebbing away after this, in both 1958 and 1960 about half of all NCB mines were affected by strike activity.

Another trend which predates nationalization, but which intensified after state ownership, was an increase in the number of locations where colliery strikes occurred. In 1938 the number of places at which colliery strikes were recorded roughly doubled compared with levels in preceding years, and almost doubled again by 1945. After 1948 colliery strikes occurred at more than 250, and sometimes over 350, separate places annually in the period to 1963. The most strike-prone locations in every fifth year between 1918 and 1938 were Notting-ham (nine strikes in 1918), Port Talbot (eleven strikes in 1923), Airdrie, Shotts and South Shields (four strikes each in 1928), South Shields again in 1933 with six strikes, and Shotts in 1938 with twenty-one strikes. Analysis of strikes in these years in the war and post-war periods reveals Shotts as the one, unique place where very high levels of strike activity persisted throughout the period (table 12.6): it appeared in the top ten strike-prone places four times. The next three most strike-prone places were all in South Yorkshire: Bentley near Don-caster, Wombwell near Barnsley, and Woodlands near Doncaster. Bentley appeared in our list four times and the others three times. Ten more places appeared twice, five of which were in Scotland, three in South Yorkshire and two in South Wales. Viewed from the perspective of local strike activity, strikes under nationalization became more prevalent than under private ownership.

With the increase in strike prevalence came some reduction in the concentra-tion of strikes both by place and by colliery. Throughout the war-time and post-war periods the thirty-five collieries experiencing the most strikes account-ed for roughly one-third of all domestic strikes, compared with about one-half during the inter-war years. The decline in the Gini coefficient of inequality (table 12.5) indicates that the distribution of domestic strikes as a whole became gradually less unequal until 1963, when a slight reversion can be detected. In 1948 and 1963 the ten most struck collieries each experienced at least ten separate strikes. In 1953 they experienced at least eleven and in 1958 at least eighteen. A few collieries in these years experienced strikes every few weeks. However, in this context it is important to note the high turnover of the population of highly strike-prone collieries, which was as true of the post-war period as of preceding decades. An analysis of the five separate years we have examined between 1943 and 1963 (table 12.7) revealed that no colliery ap-peared among the ten most highly strike-prone collieries in all five years. Only one appeared four times, two appeared three times and seven collieries regis-tered twice.

The persistence of strike activity in the generality of collieries is quantified in table 12.8. This provides data for single years at five-year intervals and shows the proportion of collieries which were struck repeatedly. It shows that persistence was relatively low in those collieries struck in 1928 with only 17 per cent of the collieries struck in 1928 struck again in 1933; 13 per cent in 1933 *and* 1938 and 10 per cent struck in 1933, *and* 1938, *and* 1943. The persistence of strike activity increased subsequently so that of the collieries struck in 1948, 53 per cent were struck again in 1953; 42 per cent in 1953 *and* 1958; and 25 per cent in 1953 *and* 1958 *and* 1963.

Of the collieries struck in any one year, some were collieries which had been struck persistently and would be struck again, others were collieries for which strike action was transient. In order to find out the size of these groups we classified the population of collieries into three categories: those which were struck in any given year *and* struck five years previously, which we categorized as 'persistently struck'; those which were *not* struck five years earlier, which we described as having been 'transiently struck'; those which experienced no strikes at all fell into the 'unstruck' category. As the details of this analysis are tedious, we indicate here only the main features of the results. In the pre-war period, the vast majority of coal mines were unstruck in any one year; of those which were struck, most were transiently struck collieries. During the war and post-war periods, the proportion of peaceful collieries in the coal mine population declined: as we have seen in 1963 only about one half of all NCB mines were strike-free. By the early 1950s the majority of struck collieries were persistent strikers on our definitions. By 1963 more than one-third of the NCB's collieries could be described as persistently struck, outnumbering those transiently struck by three to one.

The principal conclusions which emerge from this analysis must be interpreted against the background of a huge increase in the number of strikes beginning in the late 1930s and continuing through the Second World War and after. However, strikes remained short in duration; they became even smaller in scale than hitherto, and strike participation rates fell to levels below those of previous years. The annual prevalence of strike action, as measured by the proportion of collieries affected, rose sharply, and strikes became more widespread geographically. A number of other continuities in the pattern of strikes are also evident; one was the considerable regional diversity in the strike rate and strike prevalence. At local and colliery level, too, the most strike-prone places and collieries continued to account for a very high proportion of all domestic strikes, though lower than in the pre-war period. As before, the strike-prone places and collieries did not typically remain so for long, though for the post-war period it is possible to identify a few areas and a few collieries which experienced extremely high and persistent activity. A substantial minority of collieries emerged which struck not necessarily very often but did so persistently.

The intensification of strike activity beginning in the mid 1930s was none the less combined with continuing diversity in the strike frequency recorded for collieries, localities and regions. Zweiniger-Bergielowska's study (1990, 1992–3) of four collieries in South Wales between the late 1930s and 1957, where strike activity increased after nationalization, also emphasized the continuities in the history of the collieries and communities which she examined, where, she concluded, labour relations were minimally affected by the change in ownership under nationalization. The data presented here lead us to concur broadly with her conclusions and extend them to the national scene. The implication of these patterns for the post-war period, as for the inter-war years, is that we must regard purely structural explanations for the level and nature of strike activity as inadequate. The particular content of our explanation for the strike patterns in the industry undoubtedly requires modification for the war-time, post-war, and post-nationalization periods. However, the form taken by any such explanation requires a combination of structural, including organizational, factors (because the industry remained consistently strike-prone) and non-structural features, including actions and events (because of the diversity of experience). A recapitulation and further discussion of this conclusion is included in chapter 14, following an international comparison of strikes in coal-mining.

13   International perspectives

International patterns and analyses

A detailed comparison between the history of strikes in the British coalmining industry with that in the other principal coal producing countries lies far beyond the scope of our research. The focus on ordinary, local, inter-colliery strike differences which we have adopted has no parallel in research carried out on the industry in other countries, ruling out the presentation of a comparative, systematic coda with which to end our study. Indeed, since the publication of two seminal articles in the 1950s, by Kerr and Siegel (1954) and by Rimlinger (1959), who responded to their observations on international strike propensities, the subject of coalminers' strike proneness has been either marginal to historians' research on strikes, focused particularly on strike waves, whether on a national or international basis, or limited to a relatively brief period, especially before the First World War. These studies have produced valuable contributions to the history of strikes on an international level. However, the objectives of this research, ambitious though they have been, differ from our own, in part because several of the authors were interested primarily in the political dimensions and significance of strikes in general, rather than explaining the character and causes of strikes in coalmining or any other particular industry (see Shorter and Tilly 1974; Stearns 1975; Geary 1981; Cronin 1982, 1985; Boll 1985; Michel 1987, 1992).

The view against which Rimlinger reacted was Kerr and Siegel's conclusion that occupational, rather than national socio-economic, characteristics were the main explanations for the behaviour patterns of groups of workers in different countries (Kerr and Siegel 1954: 189–212). Rimlinger's conclusions were based on data series for the United States, Britain, France and Germany for various periods from 1902 to 1955. Table 13.1 summarizes his data and extends the US series back to 1881 and the British series back to 1893. While Rimlinger expressed the concerns over the comparability of the data which all researchers would share, his work remains the only substantive attempt to compare quantitative evidence on strikes in coalmining over several countries and over several decades.

The principal contrast which the data assembled by Rimlinger revealed was the very high strike propensity in British and American coalfields compared with those in continental western Europe. This contrast emerges whether one compares the relative frequency of coalmining strikes or the number of working days lost relative to employment. While it is true that strike activity in France and Germany reached a level comparable to that seen in Britain and America in 1919 and 1920, this was exceptional. The major similarity of the four nations lay in the occurrence of mass strikes of long duration. Rimlinger's explanation for similarities was in terms of common experiences of working miners. He concluded: 'the conduct of miners everywhere reflects the impact of a peculiar [working and living] environment . . . . What miners have in common is the bearing of similar psychological and physical burdens which stem from the nature of their job and the industrial environment' (Rimlinger 1959: 405). Nearly forty years later, Feldman expressed a similar view that: 'industrial conflict was endemic to mining [and] was a natural and necessary consequence of the work itself' (1990: 364). In the international context, however, while emphasizing the potential for disputes, which more than in any other industrial occupation the nature of coalmining and colliery communities created, Rimlinger regarded differential strike propensities to be explicable more in terms of differences in socio-cultural factors which transformed a high strike potential into actual strike activity (Rimlinger 1959: 405).

Rimlinger's view was that the high strike propensity of British miners relative to their continental counterparts was the result of their history, which enabled them 'to develop, even before the country's industrialization, a sense of group solidarity, a certain spirit of independence, and habits of self-defense' (Rimlinger 1959: 402); in effect the early evolution of capitalistic relationships contributed to the formation of organizations whose acknowledgement of the 'rules of the game' resulted in effective co-operative action and to formal relations with employers. Other factors which he argued reinforced the tendencies towards frequent and effective industrial action were the absence of employer paternalism, either in the form of discipline or interference in miners' private lives, and the rejection, both by the employers and the state, of responsibility for their welfare. Miners' militancy in Britain was seen as a product of nineteenth-century liberalism, the outcome of a rational learning process: 'The miners' struggle established legacies of conflict, and of distrust and independence toward authority' (Rimlinger 1959: 403). Our conclusion that in the pre-nationalization period owner-controlled firms figured prominently among the most strike-prone collieries suggests that Rimlinger may have been incorrect in his perception of the unimportance of paternalistic policies by colliery owners and miners. Yet the view that paternalistic policies were instrumental in limiting strike activity in other European countries has continued to be a persistent theme since Rimlinger first articulated the thesis; so too, has the inhibiting effects of the state on a perceived inclination of miners to strike.

One major problem presented by Rimlinger's analysis is the absence of any distinction between what we have termed 'ordinary' domestic and local strikes, which typically were partial, of short duration, and involved few workers, and the regional and national strikes which, when measured by working days lost, he took to indicate the presence of both organizational capability and solidaristic

Table 13.1. *Measures of strike propensity (Great Britain, USA, France, Germany and the Saar Territory, various periods 1881–1955)*

Period	Average annual number of strikes per 10,000 workers				Average annual number of working days lost per worker				
	GB	USA[k]	France	Germany	GB	USA[k]	France	Germany	Saar
1881–5	na	4.58	na	na	na	na	na	na	na
1886–90	na	3.50	na	na	na	na	na	na	na
1891–5[a]	2.68	3.06	na	na	17.89	na	na	na	na
1896–1900[b]	1.75	4.36	na	na	4.51	na	na	na	na
1901–5[c]	1.60	3.14	0.98	0.36	1.77	13.05	0.21	na	na
1906–10[d]	3.53	na	0.89	0.58	2.08	19.18	0.88	na	na
1911–15[e]	1.35	0.81	0.98	0.96	8.10	8.11	4.55	na	na
1916–20[f]	1.40	3.19	0.50	5.97	4.71	7.25	0.65	4.29	na
1921–5[g]	1.48	1.41	0.66	0.92	14.37	24.82	0.55	1.55	na
1926–30	1.20	1.05	0.58	0.13	26.97	10.48	0.15	0.37	0.94
1931–5[h]	1.87	1.63	0.34	na	1.31	6.28	na	0.25	0.03
1936–40	4.86	1.08	na	na	1.06	4.15	na	na	na
1941–5	12.39	1.32	na	na	1.46	10.08	na	na	na
1946–50[i]	14.75	10.78	na	na	0.84	26.32	7.30	0.03	na
1951–5[j]	18.63	12.26	na	na	0.84	2.74	1.72	0.18	na

Notes:

[a] GB: 1893–5 only; USA: 1891–4 only.

[b] USA: 1894–1900.

[c] USA working days lost: 1902, 1904–5 only; France: 1902–5 only; Germany: 1904–5 only.

[d] USA: 1906, 1909–10 only; France working days lost: 1910 only.

[e] USA: strike numbers: 1914–15 only.

[f] Germany strike numbers: 1919 only; working days lost: 1919–20 only.

[g] Germany strike numbers: 1921–2, 1924–5 only.

[h] Germany working days lost: 1931 only; Saar: 1931–3 only.

[i] France: 1947–50 only; Germany: 1949–50 only.

[j] Germany: 1951–3 and 1955 only.

[k] US 'coalmining strikes' are: (1881–6) strikes and lock-outs listed under 'mining' when the occupations of those involved indicate the mining of coal; (1886–93) strikes and lock-outs listed under 'coal and coke' which are stated to involve 'miners'; (1894–1905) all strikes and lock-outs listed under 'coal and coke' (the data for previous periods suggest that the great majority of 'coal and coke' strikes were strikes of coalminers); (1914–28) strikes and lock-outs in 'coalmining'. Employment data refer to coalmining throughout.

Sources: Rimlinger (1959), tables 1 and 2 except GB 1893–1909 and 1926 and USA strike numbers 1881–1926 and working days lost 1902–9. GB strike numbers and working days lost: Department of Employment and Productivity, *British Labour Statistics: Historical Abstract 1886–1968*, table 197; GB employment 1893–1909, Church (1986), table 3.11, 1926, Mines Department, *Annual Report of the Secretary for Mines*, 1926, table 16. USA strike numbers: Commissioner of Labor, *Third, Tenth, Sixteenth and Twenty-First Annual Reports*, tables 1 and 2, I and II, IV and XV, and II and XIV, respectively; Bureau of Labor Statistics, *Strikes in the United States 1880–1936*, tables 15 and 37; USA working days lost, Bureau of the Census, *Historical Statistics of the United States: Colonial Times to 1970*, series M112 and M135; USA employment, *ibid.*, series M107 and M130.

behaviour. Michel's study did draw such a distinction, emphasizing the 'local ordinary' and partial strikes which typified relations between workers and employers (1987: 1,668–9). Conceptually, though not statistically, Michel separated 'mining strikes', extensive and organized by trade unions, from 'strikes of miners', which referred to the brief, spontaneous stoppages, sometimes without clear objectives among the participants and which he classified as pre-modern in form (1987: 1,698).

Though major widespread strikes did occur on the Continent from time to time and became more frequent after 1900, Michel perceived no detectable trend in their characteristics. In continental Europe strikes were slow to evolve from the typically spontaneous work stoppages which in motive, form and outcome he equated with absenteeism as a form of traditional, non-rational gesture, 'a means of expression'. A shift towards a perceptibly modern type of industrial action which was organized and more extensive was barely detectable before 1914 (Michel 1987: 1,668–9, 1,679–80, 1,740–3). During the relatively high strike wave in each of the continental European countries beginning in 1899, political influences, sometimes through the formulation of explicit political objectives, were evident in coalmining strikes.

While Michel acknowledged the difference between 'mining strikes' and 'strikes of miners' (1987: 1,698), his focus was limited almost entirely to major strikes. He noted the differences in international strike propensities but he did not pursue the question why the variations existed. Instead, he drew attention to the relationship between trade union weakness and a high strike propensity, underlining the role of centralized trade unions in seeking to control and limit strike activity. However, Michel noted that such a policy in the case of Britain, where levels of organization were greatest and union centralization was the most advanced before 1914, was conspicuously unsuccessful. Furthermore, our research revealed that strike activity was virtually non-existent where union membership at branch level fell below roughly one-third of the work-force, a phenomenon which we have interpreted as indicating that organization was a necessary, though not sufficient, condition for strike action (see chapter 10).

The European context

Like Rimlinger, both Michel and Boll, in seeking explanations for the low levels of strike activity on the Continent by comparison with Britain, have also focused on the role of the state, the institutions through which industrial relations were conducted, whether at national, regional, or local levels, and relations between employers and workers.

The history of the coal industry of Germany, the largest continental producer by far, contains both contrasts and similarities with that of Britain. By 1913 German coal production had reached roughly two-thirds that of Britain, as had the number of mineworkers. This was the result of rapid expansion which began in the 1880s, most of which occurred in the Ruhr, where the average colliery work-force doubled each decade from about 400 in 1880 to more than 2,000 before the First World War (Weisbrod 1990: 140–1). As in Britain, rapid growth was accompanied by organizational changes, though mining remained primarily a semi-skilled manual task. While German and British colliery companies were owned by a mixture of family-dominated enterprises and public companies, the formation of cartels in Germany represented a more cohesive organization than was achieved by the British colliery owners before 1914 (Weisbrod 1990: 140–1). In 1889 miners in Germany mounted a widespread strike, one outcome being the formation of the *Alter Verband*, the social democratic coalminers' union. Thereafter, like their British counterparts, Ruhr miners engaged in militant industrial activity from time to time, demonstrating a capacity to organize and implement solidaristic action (Hickey 1985: 289–90). Why, in view of these similarities, were the strike histories of the two countries so different?

The answer offered in Rimlinger's study was threefold. Initially, the most important determining factor was the difference in the role of the state in the two countries. In Germany state ownership and administration of coal mines only came to an end in 1865. Thereafter, free movement of labour led to the adoption of contractual relations between employers and workers (Weisbrod 1990: 127). This transition was the basis for the first of Rimlinger's arguments, that the authoritarian tradition characteristic of the preceding era had inculcated a deferential attitude among miners towards authority, a weakness which private entrepreneurs and their managers subsequently proceeded to exploit and codify. The miners' acceptance of 'rigorous but fair' disciplinary constraints Rimlinger interpreted as 'an expression of a work ethic and of a deeply rooted, religiously oriented, concept of the master–workman relationship' which persisted after the First World War; during its tumultuous aftermath, miners in the Ruhr 'were noted for their conservatism and willingness to compromise' (Rimlinger 1959: 399). The second factor was the extensive migration of workers from other parts of rural Germany and eastern Europe in response to the expanding demand for labour in the mines. Such workers were accustomed to the 'coercive discipline of a plantation-type capitalism'; they were a repressed and easily disciplined labour force (Rimlinger 1959: 398). The third factor was the existence, swelled by the migrants, of strong ideological orientations, either Socialist or Christian. These orientations, involving beliefs in the creation of a social order 'based on agreed-upon rules administered in an orderly, disciplined fashion', were not consistent with a system of employer–worker relations based on repeated, or continual, tests of strength. Rimlinger maintained that the 'quickie strike' was unusual among German coalminers, a view which Hickey's research suggests might be misleading (Hickey 1985: 291).

Rimlinger's analysis, which emphasized the nature of coalmining and the residential environment which produced solidarity and acted to reinforce conservative values and pacific conduct, is consistent with the picture painted recently by Weisbrod. During the nineteenth century he detected the evolution of a distinctive occupational culture among German colliery workers, 'of self-protection and self-confidence, independent of class tradition and . . . reflected in the "informal structures of solidarity" of daily community life' (Weisbrod 1990: 141). This observation echoes Rimlinger's reference to the 'sense of group solidarity, a certain spirit of independence, and habits of self-defense' which he attributed to British coalminers even before industrialization and which he regarded as one of the fundamental explanations for their exceptionally high strike proneness (Rimlinger 1959: 402).

It is not, however, necessary to resort to a difference in attitude generated by a history of state control and ideological orientations to suggest an alternative, or at least a supplementary, set of explanations for the relative absence of miners' militancy in Germany. The rapid expansion of the industry from the 1880s and the growth in the size of mining enterprises was accompanied by the emergence of a new professional, bureaucratic elite of business managers who had no need for legitimation of their authority by anything other than their ability to achieve success for the enterprise (Spencer 1976; Weisbrod 1990: 150–1). In pursuit of such aims, German employers refused to extend recognition to the trade unions or to entertain the possibility of collective contracts (Weisbrod 1990: 146–7; Feldman 1990). Supplementing non-recognition, extensive company welfare policies were introduced, in part to encourage loyalty to the company but also to discourage trade union membership. Between 1893 and 1914 the proportion of workers living in company housing in the Ruhr rose from an estimated 12 to 35 per cent (Weisbrod 1990: 142), roughly three times the figure in Britain (Church 1986: 600).

Weisbrod associated these two strategies, not with the autonomous patriarchal family business enterprises, but with policies adopted by the second generation of large, hierarchically organized mines associated with a 'new managerial absolutism' (Weisbrod 1990: 130–1). Spencer has questioned how typical the stereotype of the repressive, intransigent mining employer was in the Ruhr. While she confirms that repression and aggression were used by employers to combat the challenge which organized labour began to present to their authority, her research also revealed a trend among some mining employers to move away from paternalistic policies appealing to loyalty, towards an incentive structure offering material rewards (Spencer 1976: 410–11). Colliery employers 'tempered militancy with pragmatism', like the union leaders of the labour movement whom from time to time they confronted (1976: 411).

The absence of an enduring institutional framework for industrial relations distinguishes the German from the British industry in which employers and unions were both well organized and collective bargaining well established, in England by the 1890s and by 1900 in Scotland and South Wales. In Germany the occurrence of major strikes in 1889, 1905 and 1912 was exceptional and concealed both a lack of sustainable high levels of unionization and a disunity between unions which was endemic (Spencer 1976; Hickey 1985: 234, 240;

Weisbrod 1990: 144–52). This is explained by the heterogeneous labour force who, divided by cultural background, religious affiliation, political ideology and in some instances language, formed into four separate, competing unions. A combination of religious and linguistic barriers, and a legacy of social traditions tended to isolate one group of workers from another, particularly from the 'atheistic' social democrats who were in the vanguard of trade unionism. Participation in industrial or political conflict to resist social injustice was less likely to occur among such a section of the population, many of whom worked in coalmines. The loyalties of many German miners remained focused on particular groups, often defined in terms of ethnic origins or religious allegiance, rather than on a broader concept of the workers at large (Hickey 1985: 290–2). Precisely how and how far such characteristics of a learned conservatism and deference alluded to by Rimlinger, though modified in different ways by Weisbrod and Hickey, affected the strike propensity of mineworkers, however, has yet to be demonstrated with more than anecdotal evidence.

While the heterogeneity of the labour force may indeed have inhibited local and partial strike activity, the weakness of trade union organization cannot be assumed to have had an unambiguous effect on German miners' strike propensity, for in Germany, as in other countries, when unions strengthened and centralized, the control and limitation of strikes became an important aspect of union policy (Michel 1987: 1,714, 1,748–50). In order to accumulate fighting funds for major campaigns, to establish their credibility with and their legitimacy in the eyes of the employers, and to consolidate their own positions, trade union leaders tended to oppose local stoppages by increasing centralized control, imposing strict conditions before striking miners might qualify for financial support, and sometimes intervening to stop action already under way (Michel 1987: 1,750–99).

In these respects there were similarities, at least in France, with the policies of the British county unions and later of the MFGB, as exemplified by the development of joint boards of employers and the growth of conciliation. However, in none of the continental European countries was the system of industrial relations as advanced as that in Britain. It might, therefore, seem surprising that the much higher union density in Britain, the greater degree of trade union organizational development, and the more extensive, well-established structure of collective bargaining machinery did not result in a lower level of strike propensity. Such a relationship suggests that the majority of strikes in Britain, which were local and partial, as in foreign coalfields, retained the element of spontaneity in reaction to immediate circumstances at the pit. One plausible supposition is that indirectly the strength of British trade unions provided a basis for miners' self-confidence, as individuals or collectively, at local and pit level, encouraging them to take industrial action more frequently than their continental European counterparts, even though trade union leaders discouraged and denied financial support to those involved in 'wildcat' strikes. It is pertinent to note that, at least before nationalization, British coalmining unions neither disciplined those who went on strike nor, when they had the power, countenanced the victimization of strikers by employers.

Possibly marginally more strike-prone than German coalfields, French mining strikes occurred within a context in which Rimlinger detected similarities with that of Germany. The difference with the turbulent history of mining in Britain, however, is clear. He emphasized the French government's influence on labour–management relations during the nineteenth century, when through regional officials and the *Corps des Mines* 'quasi-military discipline . . . operated not only in the mines but also in the company housing districts', where the government was connected with various paternalistic schemes. One consequence, according to Rimlinger, was that French miners tended to look to government rather than the unions to secure improvements in their working and living conditions (Rimlinger 1959: 400–1). Strict managerial discipline and division between unions based on geography, religion and ideology, resulted in a financially weak and fragmented union structure in which local organizations, often dominated by political activists, operated independently. Under such conditions, though especially during the inter-war period, miners' ordinary grievances became 'hopelessly enmeshed in political issues' (Rimlinger 1959: 401).

Michel's account of industrial relations in the French mining industry is not inconsistent with the broad picture presented by Rimlinger. However, Michel underlines the similarities between the Nord–Pas de Calais region, which by 1912 produced roughly 75 per cent of total French coal output, and the Ruhr. Fewer than a dozen big mining companies dominated production in the Nord where, as in the Ruhr, workers were housed in company dwellings to a considerable extent. In 1913 almost 50 per cent of all workers in the Pas de Calais, the new and rapidly developing part of the North coalfield, lived in company dwellings, a proportion which rose to nearly two-thirds by 1931 (Michel 1990: 272–4, 290). Paternalistic policies took various forms, ranging from the patriarchal to the repressive, often involving moralizing of a narrowly Catholic character. These features of mining life and labour in France were strengthened during the 1920s, a period when 'mining villages closed in on themselves' (Michel 1990: 290). Their significance for strike activity may only be supposed, though the relative absence of strikes suggests that, for the most part, employers succeeded in controlling labour through housing investment and paternalistic policies, though in the late nineteenth century by repressive action.

Following a major strike by miners in the Pas de Calais in 1889, which marked the beginning of mining trade unions formed on a semi-permanent basis, coalmining employers combined in regional associations to confront workers. During the early years of the twentieth century a relatively stable system of employer–union negotiations, which in the Nord led to employers' recognition of trade unions and to collective agreements, resembled the more advanced system of bargaining already established in Britain (Michel 1990: 275–8). However, French unions lacked both the numerical strength and the organizational capabilities of the British mining unions. They were also divided. Even in the Nord the old and the new *syndicats* competed for dominance, a situation which added to the other weaknesses which limited the ability of the French unions to control or prevent strike activity initiated at pit level which was only sporadically successful (Michel 1987: 1,729–40, 1,748).

The potential for industrial conflict increased after the First World War, but particularly from the late 1920s, when the companies carried out a programme of rationalization which involved the concentration of production in large pits, the mining of extensive longwall faces, reorganization of working practices, and the introduction of the Bedaux system. However, to the weaknesses of the unions referred to above was added the effects of an influx of foreign workers, who by 1927 represented 58 per cent of all miners in the Nord, and 20 per cent in Lorraine, Loire and the central coalfields. Migrant workers were discouraged from involvement by the potential threat of deportation so long as they were under consulate supervision. Ethnic, religious and ideological differences added to the difficulties of concerted industrial action by the mineworkers: 'fratricidal hatred between militants sprang up in these years' (Michel 1990: 291).

The strongest reaction to the social consequences of rationalization occurred in 1936 when, following the reunification of the unions in 1935, strikes swept across the coalfields. Employers were compelled to make concessions, not least union recognition and compulsory collective agreements. Yet the increasingly prominent role assumed by Communists, who had secured seats as miners' union representatives, in effect relegated miners' material, local interests and grievances behind their broader political concerns and objectives (Michel 1990: 298–9).

The comparisons drawn above relate largely to major strikes and reflect a limitation of the literature. However, even though the detailed empirical evidence on ordinary local strikes is, in effect, confined to Britain and based on the research reported above, it is possible to infer from the admittedly flawed strike statistics that, contrary to the impression which the literature conveys, small-scale strikes rather than major conflicts were the norm in continental European coalfields as they were in Britain. When the annual working days lost figures are compared over time for each country, the exceptional nature of the major confrontation emerges; in other years the short-lived stoppage, limited in scale, is the typical form of strike activity. While there are differences between the strike propensities of continental European producers they are insignificant when they are compared with the British record. Consequently the similarities between the French and German experience are more prominent in our survey than the differences. Among the conclusions to emerge from our detailed analysis of British coalmining strikes before nationalization was that large mines under family or personal ownership and control were the most strike-prone, and that regional differences were the product of historical, institutional, and particularly organizational factors, notably the ability of miners to establish a substantial *local* trade union membership of at least one-third of the work-force.

While the specific formulae we have sketched out for the most strike-prone British collieries differ from those to which Rimlinger attached particular importance, nevertheless our conclusion concerning regional differences is consistent with Rimlinger's interpretation of the differential strike propensities of miners in various countries in terms of political, social, and cultural, as well as economic factors.

Shorter and Tilly's study of French strikes showed the coal industry to have been less strike-prone than several other industries (Shorter and Tilly 1974: tables 5.2, 8.2, 9.3). None the less, Shorter and Tilly described the characteristics of French coalminers before the advent of automatic cutter-ripper machines after the Second World War as having possessed special qualities and capacities which reflected their work and environment:

The technology of mining . . . places the worker in direct control with his raw materials, evoking from him great skill and effort if the coal is to be smoothly manipulated from the seam face to conveyor buckets. So miners take pride in their professional traditions, and the web of organization within the pits, both friendship groups and regular unions, give them a powerful capacity for collective enterprise.

Compared with other artisanal workers, 'the miners are more at the mercies of economic fluctuation, liable to lay-offs and pay slashes. Yet in other key respects they are identical' (Shorter and Tilly 1974: 13). Others have emphasized the peculiarities of coalmining which differentiate miners from other workers. Remarking on the discrepancies between the international industrial history of mining trade unions and the international record of the political orientation and activity of miners, Holton concluded that 'French, German, or British miners . . . may be seen as sharing more behavioural characteristics in common than the various components of each individual national labour movement' (Holton 1985: 266).

However much similarities in working experience and in mining communities affected miners in all countries, outcomes were different. Large-scale operations and family ownership were characteristics of the major British coalfields, of the Ruhr and the Nord, and paternalistic policies were found in each, yet contrasting strike levels are evident. One important difference appears to have been the extent and nature of paternalistic management strategies which were on a much wider scale in France and Germany than in Britain; another is the degree to which employers on the Continent were successful in resisting union recognition and refusing to enter into collective bargaining at all before the 1890s and crushing strikes with force. A comparable reluctance to negotiate combined with a readiness to deal with strikers aggressively was identified among the coalowners of Scotland and South Wales, Britain's two most militant coalfields before the 1930s. Yet while trade union development was late to develop in those regions (as in France and Germany) strikes were frequent in the two British coalfields, partly the consequence of attempts to gain recognition on the part of the unions and resistance mounted by employers.

Such a situation did not result in high strike activity on the Continent, where employers were even more proscriptive but also where the absence of successful mining trade unions as models and sources of support may have inhibited miners' aspirations towards organization. In this respect our impression is that labour organization at local level on the Continent failed to achieve the critical mass of union membership. It is also possible that because of the greater political element characteristic of union activity on the Continent towns rather than collieries were the principal centres around which organized worker activity occurred.

Clearly, the asymmetric evidence from these comparisons strengthens the suspicion that explanations for the differences between the strike records of Britain and the Continental countries are not to be found in structural factors, except in one important respect. Well before the mid-nineteenth century, Britain was already a large coal producer which, unlike the smaller industries in France and Germany, was based on a capitalistic structure and organization in which contracts between miners and employers were increasingly affected by market forces (Carol Jones 1985). The establishment of ephemeral local mining unions during the first half of the century was succeeded by the formation of permanent unions in several of the major coalfields beginning in the 1880s, though both in the North East and Yorkshire continuous unions dated from the early 1860s. Orderly collective bargaining through joint boards of conciliation and arbitration were functioning in several regions from the 1870s (chapter 3). By the time that coal production resumed rapid expansion during the 1890s, institutional structures had thus been established, developed and adapted to capitalistic organization and market conditions. It seems paradoxical that the relatively advanced development of free collective bargaining and the establishment of collective agreements negotiated by unions, which in 1910 covered one-half of all British coalminers, was accompanied also by the highest strike rates of any country (chapter 3).

Both the later development of their coal industries and the institutional forms through which bargaining and protest occurred contributed to the contrasting levels of strike activity in Britain compared with France and Germany. Important differences in the continental European countries were low levels of formal collective bargaining and the frequent absence of negotiations prior to strikes, the activities of Communist and Syndicalist unions which sometimes engaged in strikes for non-economic reasons, and even greater state intervention in industrial relations than in Britain, one effect of which in those countries was to link strike activity to political rather than economic developments.

The contrasting histories of the role played by the state, the composition of labour forces, the strength and policies of trade unions and employers' organizations, the influences of religion, ideology and political organizations, underline the differences which contributed to contrasting levels of strike activity. In both France and Germany state involvement affected mineworkers' lives and attitudes during the period preceding the rapid growth of the coal industry beginning in the 1880s. Policies of 'oppressive paternalism' applied by employers inside colliery communities and repressive policies against unions and strikers appear to have been more extensive and more extreme, on the whole, than in Britain (Michel 1992: 58–84, 294). In both countries the mining population became increasingly heterogeneous, especially in Germany, where a 'fluid, unstable, and divided' work-force contributed to the formation of competing, and sometimes conflicting, unions based on ethnicity, religion or ideology, rather than on the basis of occupation and geography (Hickey 1985: 292).

The presence in each of the countries of similarities which created a relatively high strike potential do not conceal the contrasting strike patterns in British compared with continental European coalfields. Socio-political and cultural factors were clearly important in contributing to international differences in the strike propensity of coalminers. However, our research on coalmining strikes in Britain suggests that the critical influence of these factors was in inhibiting the development of organization among mineworkers, for it is in this respect, important because of the link we have identified between organization and strike activity, that the British experience differed most from that of continental European countries.

Euro-American comparisons: limitations and possibilities

Britain and the USA possessed the most strike-prone coalfields of all, a conjunction which placed together the two most most advanced capitalistic, market-oriented countries in the world. In both Britain and the USA miners struck with exceptional frequency compared with their compatriots. In most years the percentage of miners on strike in the bituminous coal industry was roughly twice that of other industrial workers, and higher still for anthracite workers during the limited period for which separate figures are available (Fishback 1992: 199–200). Rimlinger attributed the high American strike propensity to the clash between the miners' 'heritage of independence and self-assurance' and the 'ruthlessly competitive' employers. The issue was that of 'rights', vaguely understood by miners who, none the less, believed them to have been guaranteed by the Constitution and determined to defend them against usurpation by their employers (Rimlinger 1959: 405).

Rimlinger thought these ideas distinguished American from British miners for whom the political motivation to defend constitutional rights did not exist because they had none, and who were at the same time subjugated within a class-based society (Rimlinger 1959: 404). However, this particular Anglo-American comparison is not only of dubious relevance to an explanation of the causes of strike propensity; it does not advance the possibility of explaining the differences in coal strike proneness in the two countries. Rimlinger's scant attention to chronology overlooks the possibility that the factors which contributed to mining strikes in one period may have been different from those which were influential in another. Furthermore, while the limitation of the statistical series he used ruled out regional comparisons, the coalmining regions of the US were so large and so diverse in character that this omission represents a serious gap in his analysis.

There were similarities and differences between British and American coalfields. Brody drew attention to the differences in the economics of the coal industry in the two countries. Whereas in Britain supply from deep mining operations was inelastic in the short term during an upswing, which favoured labour's market position, in the USA ease of entry effected by driving shallow drifts and levels led to a rapid response to demand. The result, he argued, was that the secular growth in demand for coal in the USA from the 1880s was accompanied nevertheless by over-capacity and fierce competition at low prices (Brody 1990: 75). Fishback, too, stressed the essentially competitive structure of an industry in which rapidly expanding demand was met by an increase in production capacity, which was reflected by the slower rise of coal prices compared with the general wholesale price index before 1914 (Fishback 1992: 20–1). Brody emphasized an over-supply of labour and extensive under-employment (Brody 1990: 82), which implied a downward pressure on wages. Despite these factors, Fishback has shown that between 1890 and 1913 the annual earnings of bituminous miners grew more quickly than those for American manufacturing workers (Fishback 1992: 21). Like British miners, American miners struck mainly to secure higher pay or fewer hours (Fishback 1992: 216). On his evidence it appears that economistic objectives were far more important in the coalfields of the USA than in continental Europe, though the similarities with strikes in British coalfields are evident – a conclusion which also tends to invalidate Rimlinger's interpretation rooted in the defence of constitutional rights.

There were also, however, major differences. Shortly before the First World War, American mine operators were described by a contemporary mines inspector as 'a great army of antagonistic elements and unorganised forces . . . [who] continue to indulge in a cut-throat warfare' (quoted by Graebner 1974: 50). Labour relations on the American coalfields were much more violent than those even in the coalfields of Scotland and South Wales (Fagge 1992: 105–23). However, unions in the central coalfields of Ohio, western Pennsylvania, Indiana and Illinois achieved recognition and also, to some degree, tacit support from coal operators in those coalfields. It was in the central coalfields that permanent unionization in the USA began in 1890 with the formation of the United Mine Workers of America (UMWA).

In the large, historically important, anthracite coalfield in Pennsylvania unionization and strike activity proved difficult, partly because of the composition of the mining work-forces which consisted of immigrant miners of peasant origins from eastern and southern Europe, but also as a consequence of coal operators' determination to exclude unions from their companies, which went to the point of deploying armed security personnel and armed posses in the command of local sheriffs (Miller and Sharpless 1985: 234). The English-speaking mining population in this area declined from 90 per cent in 1880 to below 52 per cent by 1900 (Miller and Sharpless 1985: 181), the mostly Slav mining work-force accepting the mine operators' determined opposition to unionization until 1897, and not until 1902, after two bloody confrontations with the operators, did the union secure recognition (Miller and Sharpless 1985: 223–83). When the anthracite miners' union affiliated to the UMWA in 1897 its members were divided into six ethnic groups, underlining the conflicting loyalties of the work-force (Miller and Sharpless 1985: 223).

A successful strike supported by miners in the central coalmining states in 1897 marked the inauguration of an interstate joint conference, which for nearly thirty years was the institution through which collective bargaining relations in the industry were conducted (Brody 1990: 83–4). The central principle upon which wage agreements were negotiated was that of 'competitive equality'. The formula which was intended to achieve 'competitive equality' was built on a system in which 'basing points', determined by 'average' conditions in the coalfield, set 'standard' tonnage rates across the coalfields. Departures from 'the standard' were sanctioned by the interstate conference after special adverse factors could be shown to justify variations from it. In return for the agreement to this system of price collusion among operators, the UMWA achieved recognition and some degree of control over terms and conditions of employment across the coalfields (Brody 1990: 85–6).

Bowman's research helps to explain why, despite the mutual antagonism which clearly existed between American coal operators and workers within a highly competitive industrial structure, there was collusion in the form of the agreements reached at the 1898 joint conference. Coal proprietors were anxious to establish an enforceable wage level in the industry which would undermine the low wage competitive basis which had enabled coal proprietors in the southern Appalachian coalfield to undercut the price of coal mined in the central coalfield (Bowman 1989: 107). Bowman detected an element of tacit collusion between the central coalfield mine owners and the UMWA, which continued, with variable success, until the 1920s. Such a policy, which also included an agreement by employers to a 'check off' (deductions from wages for union dues) (Bowman 1989: 107) might justify the description 'rational', but is at odds with the predominant portrait of American coal operators as almost uniformly anti-union both on authoritarian and ideological grounds. Bowman's study also raises the question whether the degree of unionization in the American coal industry was much more dependent upon the attitudes of individual coalowners acting in concert in the central coalfields between the late 1890s and 1920s than on the ethnic divisions which most American historians of labour and of the coal industry have tended to emphasize.

The collusive option which appears to have been pursued by coal operators in the central coalfields of the US was not open to British coalowners. For unlike their American counterparts, before 1914 British coal producers were dependent to a high degree upon overseas markets. However, both in Britain and the USA an intensely competitive industrial structure was accompanied by similar forms of organization and a pre-modern labour process, to the extent that in 1920 Carter Goodrich described mining in the USA as 'in a way a "cottage" industry' (Goodrich 1926: 13). Taking a different path from British coalowners, mechanization in the US was absorbed within existing working practices. The room and pillar system, which accounted for no more than roughly one-quarter of coal produced in Britain in the inter-war years (Supple 1987: 30), in the USA permitted the retention of contracting and tonnage piece-rates (Goodrich 1926: 29–31). In the 1920s American mines were smaller than those in Britain. Out of a total of 9,000 bituminous mines, barely 700 of the largest mines employed an average of 300 workers, whereas fewer than 35 per cent of British miners worked in mines below 500 (Brody 1990: 77; Supple 1987: 364).

There is some similarity between the history of the British system of collective agreements and those adopted in the main central and western coalfields of the USA. From their inception collective agreements in the main central and western coalfields of the USA were under almost constant threat of disintegration, a situation which was exacerbated by the Great Depression. The destabilizing influences were twofold. One was the uneven effect of interstate mining legislation; the other was the rapidly growing competition from the expanding, non-union, southern coalfields of West Virginia and Kentucky. Together, these supplied 20 per cent of total USA coal output by 1913 (Brody 1990: 86–9).

This substantial proportion threatened to destabilize the 'competitive equality' which the central coalfields attempted to preserve. That potential was translated into reality by the mining population of West Virginia, which consisted of rural migrants from within the South, black and white, and from southern and eastern Europe. In 1909, 13 per cent of the work-force was Italian, 6 per cent Hungarian and 3 per cent Polish (Fagge 1992: 109). The cultural background and lack of union experience of this work-force contrasted with those of the many migrant British miners working in the coalfields to the north, and who had been conspicuous during the early history of the UMWA. Before 1919 the miners of West Virginia showed little interest either in union organization or strikes, particularly those urged upon them by the UMWA (Corbin 1981: 27–9), though that is hardly surprising in view of the aggressive opposition undertaken by the operators. Bowman described their action to prevent the UMWA from organizing workers in the south Appalachian coalfields in the 1890s as 'the bloodiest struggle in US labor history' (Bowman 1989: 120). There it seems, where the level of unionization barely reached 20 per cent (Fishback 1992: 24), the lack of organization was accompanied by high levels of violence but relatively few strikes. In contrast, on the central coalfields, where membership exceeded an average of 75 per cent between 1899 and 1923 (Fishback 1992: 24, table 3.2), the period between 1897 and the late 1920s appears to have been one of relative industrial peace.

It is not possible to be more precise concerning the nature of those underlying factors explaining the shape and frequency of strikes, because the literature on industrial relations in the industry is not, on the whole, helpful to an analysis of strikes. Historians who have focused on strikes have either examined aggregate strike activity or, more frequently, have explored the strike history either of a state, an individual colliery or company, or described the history of individual strikes. Yet the acute differences of operators' and miners' experiences at regional level suggests the possibility of similar disparities in strike patterns at local level in the frequency, scale and intensity of the 'normal' strike activity which was the central focus of our research on colliery conflict in Britain.

Before 1920, employers and workers in the coalfields outside the South operated within a framework of relatively orderly competition under collective agreements. In the southern coalfields, where low wage costs were a necessary condition of competitiveness with the coal mined in the other large coalfields, competition was unrestrained, allowing the large number of small mine operators to impose low-wage, high-risk working conditions on a labour force which for the most part was tied into company housing in company towns and which was intimidated into an anti-union, no-strike position (Brody 1990: 81–8).

Mine operators in West Virginia, in attempting to prevent unionization among miners, created a 'paternalist' environment for their workers which was more sustained in its repression and more overtly aggressive than even that created by French and German employers. Such extreme policies, which stemmed from control not only of colliery but of township, were possible because of the locations of the new mining settlements, which were remote to a degree unparalleled on the coalfields of western Europe. In 1924 it was estimated that roughly 80 per cent of all miners working in the state of West Virginia lived in company towns and in Kentucky the figure was 64 per cent; in both cases a multiple of the proportion of miners in the central states inhabiting company dwellings. Added to this isolation and dependence of the workers was the vulnerability to the virtually unlimited political powers exercised by the landowning operators (Fagge 1992: 110). The strategies implemented by mine operators included not only those adopted by continental European and some British employers – tied housing, prescriptive education, religious influence and the provision of community facilities for sport and other forms of 'rational' recreation – but also simultaneously mobilized private policing systems, which involved armed intervention to break up, or to prevent, strikes (Corbin 1981: 50–1). Fagge's comparison between the militancy of miners (and coalowners and operators) in West Virginia with that in the South Wales coalfield revealed a world of difference between the experience, assumptions and attitudes of miners and employers in the two locations. The importance attached in the contemporary discourse of labour leaders to 'notions of feudalism' and an escape through asserting 'American values' (Fagge 1992: 105–18), reflected a society in which militancy was a latent force which derived from the values and aspirations emerging from a society which displayed elements of a quasi-feudalism.

The First World War marked a turning point in two important respects. First, the strategic importance of the nation's coal supply for mechanical energy, to which West Virginia's high quality smokeless coal contributed 25 per cent, gave to the miners, but especially to those working in Southern mines, a sense of indispensability. Exempted from military conscription, the miners were exposed to the government's propaganda which appealed to their patriotism and, by highlighting the difference between the autocracy and militarism of Germany and the centrality of the principles of liberty, democracy and classlessness to the American creed, conveyed a powerful radical political ideology (Corbin 1981: 176–9). A recognition both of the high regard in which they were held by the government and the general public, a newly awakened consciousness of their virtual disenfranchisement by the operators as American citizens, precipitated three years of wildcat strikes and 'bitter bloody warfare' (Corbin 1981: 195–224).

The second respect in which war involved a process of political education of the miners of West Virginia was the approach adopted by the government's Fuel Administration (FA), which imposed tight regulations on the industry. In addition to enforcing the installation of weighing scales and paying increased wages in accordance with the Washington agreement between the FA and the UMWA, the miners of West Virginia were expressly allowed to organize (Corbin 1981: 184). It was not, however, until the Appalachian Agreement of 1933 that the union came to be firmly established in that region and that the non-union threat to the northern coalfields from the South was removed (Brody 1990: 101–3).

Historians of industrial relations in the American coal industry have described and analysed the institutional changes, the major strikes, and spectacularly violent battles which have punctuated its history on a scale rarely found in western Europe. Yet none has related these developments and events to the longer-term history of strikes as phenomena. Such strike statistics as are available indicate relatively high levels of strike activity, but explaining in detail why that should have been the case, or whether and why collieries experienced differences in levels of strike activity, is not possible in the present state of research. The sharp contrasts between the conduct of industrial relations in the northern and southern coalfields before the First World War suggest that differences in strike propensities may have also existed. Yet to test such a proposition would require the computation and analysis of strike statistics disaggregated by state and for the abundant discursive evidence to be reviewed in the light of the data.

The British and continental European experience does not offer the basis for a confident supposition that a more regulated system of industrial relations would necessarily have resulted in a low strike-proneness, as the British case shows. The same is true of the possible significance of large mines, owner-controlled companies, and paternalistic policies. Unlike the British experience, such a combination produced a low level of strike activity in the rest of Europe, though unlike coalminers in Britain and the USA, political considerations, at least among the organizers, were prominent in the major strikes in continental Europe. However,

the character of 'paternalism' imposed in the frontier company towns of West
Virginia was very different from that found on coalfields in most of Europe, both
in form and extent. Historians of the European experience tend to interpret the
role of a heterogeneous work-force as that of inhibiting labour organization and
strikes. Did the combination of a large proportion of migrant labour in the
predominantly small, typically remote, mining communities in the numerous
company towns of West Virginia produce a high or low level of strike propensity?

A comparison by Roger Fagge between miners' behaviour in South Wales
with that in West Virginia was based on an impression of similar and broadly
simultaneous levels of militancy in both regions. Fagge's explanation for these
similarities in the form of militant conduct was in terms less related to industrial
structure and organization than to the emergence of different cultural identities,
of contrasting social, regional and national environments, and of dissimilar
political orientations (Fagge 1992: 111–18). Whereas in the mining communities of South Wales miners were considered to have created an identity as
coalminers, in West Virginia those who flocked to the mines did not, on the
whole, possess or generate a strong occupational identity. Regarding themselves
as residents and miners on a temporary basis, Fagge perceived the 'transitional
culture' to have been central to the explanation of militancy in West Virginia
(Fagge 1992: 111). Corbin's view was that after the First World War the
transitional culture was transformed into an intensely specific class consciousness, the basis for the mobilization of miners in a militant campaign for the
union, and freedom from oppression by operators (Corbin 1981: 245–71).
Elsewhere, however, American miners struck to secure economic gains, which
the post-war coal shortage encouraged and briefly enabled them to succeed
(Fishback 1992: 21), before Depression engulfed them, as it did miners in all
coal producing countries.

The literature we have reviewed above demonstrates the difficulties in attempting to draw comparisons between strike propensities in different countries
and continents. The available statistical basis is inadequate particularly in its
lack of detail mainly because the question of strike propensity has been virtually
ignored since Rimlinger's article was published in the 1950s. Apart from rein-
forcing his assertion that miners' militancy defined in terms of frequency and
duration was essentially an Anglo-American phenomenon, explanations for
international differences remain as puzzling now as they were to Rimlinger. The
British experience appears to have been exceptional in almost every respect:
economic, geographical and geological, social, political and cultural, when
compared with continental Europe and with the USA. Yet the extreme contrasts
in strike activity in the coalfields of continental Europe compared with those in
the USA appear to have existed despite some similarities. The complexity
displayed by our attempt to draw conclusions concerning strike proneness and
miners' militancy on the basis of international comparisons reveals some of the
difficulties which are presented in such an exercise. Much of the research on
strikes as a central factor in industrial relations has treated coalmining strikes

only tangentially. Until, however, historians can present detailed statistics of coalmining strikes at regional and local levels international comparisons of colliery conflict will continue to be, at best, general and inconclusive. Until the data are improved, the analysis of structure and organization and the reinterpretation of narrative in the specific context of coalmining strikes is unlikely to throw more light on international differences in the propensity to strike. While it is possible to reject the static determinism of the principal models applied to explain this problem, convincing and empirically researched alternatives remain to be explored.

14 Myths and realities: strikes, solidarity and 'militant miners'

Some of the conclusions reached in the preceding chapters indicate the need to revise a number of received views regarding coalmining strikes and miners' 'militancy'. We readily acknowledge that strikes on a large scale, which extended across regions or the entire country have been an especially important feature of the British coal industry since the mid-nineteenth century. However, by concentrating upon these, often to the exclusion of other types of strike activity, historians have tended to obscure the study of the far more typical domestic and local strikes. We have described the distinguishing characteristics of these as limited in scale and of short duration; features which persisted both under private and public ownership. These 'ordinary' strikes, which comprised the majority by far, formed the primary focus for our analysis.

Our study reinforced the perception of well-established differences in regional strike propensities, underlining the enduringly conflictual nature of industrial relations in Scotland and South Wales and, in the 1890s though especially after the Second World War, in Yorkshire; in these regions strikes were typically both much more prevalent and of greater frequency. None the less, one of the most important conclusions, which applies to collieries in the most strike-prone regions as to others both before and after nationalization, is that a large proportion of domestic and local strikes occurred at a relatively small number of collieries and places. The typical British colliery was free from recorded domestic strikes in any given year before the 1950s. Other than participation in the relatively small number of widespread stoppages in the industry, many collieries experienced no recorded strike activity at all in the inter-war period. Even in certain pits and places where strike action was frequent, it was almost always a short-lived phenomenon. The especially strike-prone history of the coalfields of Scotland and South Wales, where before 1940 roughly one-third of coalminers in Britain lived, may appear to strengthen the validity of the concept of the 'militant miner'. We drew attention to the view expressed by some historians that the important cultural and historical differences which those coalfields shared contrasted with conditions, attitudes and actions in English coalfields, and that the influence of distinctive Celtic cultural influences may help to explain the highly solidaristic behaviour and the especially high strike propensity exhibited by Scots and Welsh miners compared with their English counterparts.

The emergence of a more militant Yorkshire weakens this interpretation. More-over, even in Scottish and Welsh collieries extreme strike frequency was usually a transient experience and there, too, many collieries remained free of recorded domestic strikes. These conclusions justify rejecting the characterization of the coalminer as the archetypal, militant artisan or proletarian worker, programmed by working experience and isolation in occupational communities to strike hard and often.

After the formation of the National Union of Mineworkers (NUM) and the nationalization of the collieries, the stronger organizational basis affected union membership levels and the forms of collective bargaining at local, area, and national levels. However, whatever the effect of these developments on indus-trial action at national and regional levels, domestic strikes increased in fre-quency and their pre-nationalization characteristics persisted or, indeed, be-came even more marked. In none of this history could we detect a movement from 'early' to 'modern' forms of strike action.

If it is misleading to describe miners as uniformly and consistently militant, it is also pertinent to ask whether it is valid, none the less, to accept the portrayal of miners as possessing an exceptional capacity for solidaristic action, the other attribute commonly associated with miners' militancy. The answer is yes and no. Descriptions of the scale and duration of solidarity which accompanied regional and national coal strikes abound in the literature. The mobilization of miners in these instances (though relatively few in number), on most occasions broadly in support of agreed objectives, distinguished miners from those in other occupa-tions. Coalminers' solidarity was a remarkable historical phenomenon, lasting for a century and defying the forces of modernity. Even in this respect it was necessary to register serious reservations in answer to the questions of whether that solidarity was permanent, or at least permanently latent, and whether when solidaristic action did take place it was spontaneous or a socio-cultural construc-tion. The assumption that the common class position of British coalminers, the similarity of their living standards, working and life experiences, led to coalfield solidarity implies the existence of values which were strongly developed and widely shared as part of a collective consciousness. Our review of the structures and the organization of the industry, however, underlined the fracturing divi-sions derived from differences in pay, working practices, colliery ownership, regional location and local economic and social history. Any one or more of these factors was as likely to result in a conflict of codes and to conflicts of interest among the mining population as to co-operation and solidarity.

The fact of miners' solidarity during the regional and national strikes before 1940 was explained to some extent by ideological and political campaigning undertaken by the Miners' Federation of Great Britain (MFGB). Partly through the exercise of central or district union power, financial, political or both, the MFGB implemented measures designed to reinforce, or establish, common values and shared understandings across regions or throughout the entire indus-try. We argued that the means of achieving solidarity, exemplified by those adopted by the MFGB, involved co-operation rather than social exchanges. Mutually supportive exchanges, whether formal or informal, played little part in the process by which trans-local and trans-regional solidarity was created; organization, coalition-building, through issue transformation and rhetoric, were keys to motivation. The price exacted from regional and county unions for refusal to participate in joint action was exclusion from the collective union undertaking. After nationalization, the orchestration of solidarity was simplified by the formation of the NUM.

We argued that an important contributory element in socially constructed solidarity was that of local cultural and social capital. A paucity of evidence at local level makes it difficult to offer confident generalizations concerning the nature and causes of local solidarity. The data we have assembled on a small number of episodes suggests a reality considerably more complex than the myth of miners' solidarity would allow. These episodes indicate that at a local level, as well as at the regional and national level, solidarity can be understood as the outcome of deliberate social action, not simply as a reflex action carried out according to the dictates of a cultural norm. The social construction of solidarity at this level was based on the use of cultural and social capital. Through the sharing of knowledge about local social networks and institutions, of skills which facilitated communication between groups and organizations, local activists helped to consolidate and extend support for those directly involved in industrial action. Miners' Institutes, co-operative societies, chapels and churches, and individual men and women were seen to have played important formal and informal roles in solidary processes of which the most obvious manifestations were the local strike and distress committees. But underlying this form of deliberate social action were other, more 'taken for granted' attitudes and actions which formed a firm site for the social construction of solidarity. These attitudes and actions conformed closely to Durkheim's model of 'mechanical solidarity' based on the homogeneity of life experiences and embodied in collectively held values the transgression of which was punished 'in a diffuse way by everyone'. These collectively held values enjoined mutually supportive actions which took place in a dense network of kin and neighbours on the basis of a generalized reciprocity. The petty but expressive and necessary exchanges of aid and support provided the essential background to the production of solidary action by activists utilizing the local cultural and social capital.

To be helpful, concepts of social solidarity must explain the absence of social solidarity as well as its construction and presence. Where local cultural capital was poorly developed or absent, perhaps because the local village or neighbourhood was of recent origin, housed an unstable population of transients or perhaps through divisions rooted in religion, ethnicity, language, nation or ideology we would expect solidarity to be a rare achievement. Seen in such a context, the Scottish mining community of Coatbridge, riven by sectarian animosities and a byword for non-unionism in the mid-nineteenth century, should occasion no surprise. Where the local cultural capital was in the control of coalowners or others hostile to the achievement of working-class solidarity, as in the company-built village of Creswell we described in chapter 8, we would also expect difficulties to have dogged the path of any seeking to achieve economic, social and political objectives through solidary action. Similarly, it is easy to imagine circumstances in which conditions for mechanical solidarity were absent and solidarity failed, economic, social and political heterogeneity destroying any sense of sharing widely held values within local society.

These conditions might suffice to explain long-term absences of social solidarity, but one of our most puzzling discoveries was that industrial solidarity as measured by the domestic strike participation rate fluctuated rapidly over time. The construction of domestic strike solidarity which the literature suggests to have been frequently attempted often failed though it sometimes succeeded. We can only speculate on the reasons which might explain this phenomenon, though our starting point is a confident assertion: whatever values were shared by the typical colliery work-force they did not include the view that if one struck all should strike. The records show strike after strike in which very few men were directly involved and none were involved indirectly; the majority of the work-force carried on working. 'One out, all out' was a myth. With equal confidence we can say that in some strikes and lock-outs, most obviously the national strikes and lock-outs of the 1912–26 period, working while others were striking or locked-out was widely and greatly deprecated. This contrast prompts the speculation that the values underlying industrial solidarity among the miners were more subtle than is normally assumed. We speculated that the values distinguished sectional from general conflicts: that it was felt that sections might pursue their own 'private' struggles but could not expect active, general support; that active, general support was accorded only to general actions. This was the distinction which made the social construction of strike solidarity necessary and accounts for the most common process to be observed in that production process, the transformation of the issues in dispute from the private, the domestic and the parochial towards the public, the industrial and national.

The dynamic role which we attributed to localities in this process by which national and regional strikes were sustained is an interpretation which, it should be emphasized, in its original and somewhat different form, has attracted criticism of the most extreme kind. The Kerr–Siegel 'isolated mass' hypothesis sought to explain miners' high strike propensity in terms of their capacity to behave solidaristically. Our empirical inquiry, the first to subject the hypothesis to rigorous empirical testing based on a quantitative analysis, also rejected the hypothesis in the crude, structurally deterministic form that has been employed by some subsequent commentators on mining, miners and miners' communities. Even so, our research pointed to a connection between isolated massness as a 'facilitating' or 'predisposing' condition for the existence of an unusually high frequency of local strike activity.

Having rejected the cruder form of the isolated mass hypothesis with its emphasis on geographical location and rural environment, we explored the residual truth which our empirical testing indicated, namely that while solidarity was not an inevitable consequence of isolated massness a link did appear to exist between massness and strike propensity. An examination of massness in collieries, companies and local union organizations pointed to the conclusion that it was not only the degree of occupational density but also colliery size which was an important part of the process generating high levels of strike activity. The key to understanding the 'size effect' on colliery strikes was given by the facts that larger collieries had about the same number of strikes per thousand workers as did smaller collieries, but that larger collieries lost far more working days per thousand workers from strikes than did smaller collieries. We argued that these facts suggested that bigger collieries did not generate proportionately more grievances, nor were their officials and managers noticeably less adept at resolving disputes before (or after) they became strikes. Instead, strikes at larger collieries sometimes managed to secure the active support of other work groups in the colliery and in this way large colliery scale led to large-scale losses of working days.

Given the impossibility, because of the lack of qualitative information on local strikes, of assembling large numbers of qualitative strike histories as a basis for testing these general propositions – and possibly formulating others – a combination of modelling and traditional historical method produced complementary evidence which enabled us to reject or emphasize various factors adduced in the literature to explain miners' high strike propensity. Such an approach, which was indicative rather than conclusive, resulted in an argument presented in the form of probabilities rather than certainties. Ample evidence underlined the origins of disputes at the point of production; yet, without an explanation of how and why, such an observation remains almost without content. The likelihood of disagreement between workers and supervisory and managerial officials was greater than in many other industries, partly because miners' capacity to earn depended to an exceptionally high degree on variable natural conditions dictated by geology and partly because the cyclicity in the demand for the product was more extreme than in most other industries. Those employed in the industry experienced major changes. The very large secular expansion that took place between the 1880s and 1918 was followed by depression and secular decline until the mid-1930s; war-induced growth and post-war expansion marked the third major secular phase, lasting until the 1960s. These dramatically altered circumstances necessitated some kind of adaptive responses from coalowners, who especially after the First World War faced intense competition. Within such a context, which involved changes in investment, corporate scale, colliery size, technology, organization, working practices and payment systems, the geological characteristics of the industry created a high level of dispute opportunities during the process of implementation by managers. Whether grievances that arose as a result developed into strikes depended partly on the level and role of trade unions and of coalowners' associations, particularly at the regional level in Scotland and South Wales, but more critically at local level, on the competence and personalities of local managers and the strength and character of organized labour in the locality. The absence of union rivalry and the presence at pit level of established formal or informal procedures associated with a culture of consultation and compromise were important elements in a formula for pacific labour relations. In these respects, by comparison with English coalfields, conditions in Scotland and South Wales were more conducive to militancy than to peace, though even on these traditional battlegrounds we showed that relatively few collieries experienced persistent local strikes and that local strikes remained brief and attracted low levels of participation.

Whereas much of the literature has placed labour at the centre of discussions of collective action, stressing either the critical role of lodge officials or, alternatively, a militant rank and file (to both of which our study also attaches some importance), we emphasized the role of pit culture, the outcome of interaction between working miners, unionized or not, and colliery officials and managers, particularly those directly responsible for managing work and setting the tone of labour relations underground. Our evidence suggested that indifference to labour management at boardroom level, a lack of managerial control over the conduct of supervisory officials underground or ineptness on their part, should be seen as potentially strike-precipitating factors down the pit because such circumstances were more likely to create and exacerbate grievances and to encourage their resolution by a resort to strike action. This conclusion may also be seen as a corollary of our rejection of the 'militant miner' as the role of principal, if not exclusive, originator of industrial action.

Whether individual grievances and disputes were resolved peacefully or turned into full-blown strikes, and whether some collieries became for a time highly strike-prone or not, depended upon a variety of factors the importance of which varied in time and place, partly because they were present in different combinations. Our evidence (particularly the testimonies of those involved at the time, as reported by Paterson and Willett, Goffee, Krieger and ourselves (chapter 11, above)) also underlined the relevance of Gouldner's emphasis on the meanings, possibly different and conflicting, which workers and managers attached to the events which formed the immediate trigger precipitating any particular strike. These meanings derived in part from a range of experience outside the workplace, from pit culture and from historical events and interactions. The implication that an individual strike might have no immediate cause but occurred when diverse and cumulative grievances produced the occasion for industrial action to take place underlines the importance of specific workplace and local histories if any particular industrial action is to be fully understood. However valuable such a perspective, emphasizing the role of 'consciousness' in a concrete context of a closely observed and analysed strike, may be, the approach possesses limitations for those concerned to generalize. Gouldner's insights are valuable in helping us to appreciate the character of strikes, but they are less helpful to our intention of constructing an interpretation which explains why, in the event of a grievance arising, a strike was more likely in

collieries and places which exhibited certain combinations of objective characteristics and historical experiences.

We argued that in the pre-nationalization period strikes were more likely at
those collieries which were family owned and remotely managed. It is possible to
interpret the last of these as a sign of distancing from the work-force, one
possible consequence of which might have been a greater degree of discretion in
the hands of subordinates in the conduct of industrial relations. This would be
consistent with our conclusion, supported by the oral evidence of ex-miners,
that, at least in the English coalfields, a high turnover of underground mine
managers was associated with highly strike-prone pits, and that managers played
a major role in creating a climate of conflict or harmony underground where
most disputes originated. Those pits in which miners belonged to an independent trade union organizing a higher proportion of the work-force than others
were, other conditions being similar, more likely to experience a period when
they were highly strike-prone. Relatively high union density (exceeding one-
third) at local level combined with low union density at district level appears to
have been an important condition likely to culminate in industrial action.

After nationalization colliery ownership was no longer a variable in affecting
industrial relations. Likewise, after the formation of the NUM membership
levels ceased to be an important variable in that context, while union recognition
and non-unionism, running sores for so long in Scotland and South Wales and a
frequent ground for conflict, also ceased to be issues. None the less, strikes
became more, rather than less, numerous and more widespread. As under
private ownership, structural developments in the form of greater industrial
concentration and growth in pit size, mechanization, and changes in work
organization and working practices produced continuous change in the industry
between the 1930s and 1960s. For managers and workers in the industry,
continuous flux was the context and experience in their working lives. Nowhere
was this more true than in Yorkshire, which after the Second World War
emerged as one of the most rapidly growing coalfields and the largest coal
producing region. Yorkshire was also one of the most strike-prone regions, a
development which also owed much to a combination of trade union politics,
organization, ideology and personalities at local level. Under public as under
private ownership, inter-colliery variation in strike activity was a persistent
feature; so too was the usually temporary character of high strike proneness in
individual collieries. After 1947, as before, structural characteristics by themselves (colliery size, working conditions and isolation) do not provide an adequate explanation, nor do organizational factors (work organization and collective bargaining arrangements) offer a convincing interpretation of differential
strike propensities. Neither is an explanation expressed solely in terms of 'vol-
untarism' which gives special emphasis to the role of personalities, lodge leaders
or managers, or politics. The continuities in strike patterns after nationalization
point to the persistence of long-established determining structures which survived the overarching structural changes following the Second World War. After
1947, as before, strike propensities were determined by action undertaken by

organizations and individuals but, as before, they were undertaken within structures, some of which were more likely to produce conflict than others and the characteristics of which we have described above.

The lack of international comparisons of mining strikes on a comparable statistical basis rules out the possibility of drawing more than tentative conclusions from an international survey, emphasizing the large research agenda which even our cursory survey has exposed. The distinction which Rimlinger drew between the highly strike-prone Anglo-Saxon countries and the relatively peaceful coalfields of continental Europe remains valid (*Germinal* notwithstanding). The importance of migrants, particularly peasants holding religious or other ideological convictions antithetical to industrial militancy, has been one major theme in the literature. More recently the importance of the attitudes and policies of coalowners, vigorously pursuing a repressive paternalism coupled with anti-unionism has received greater emphasis. Continental employers tended to be more successful in imposing proscriptive policies on workers, while labour organizations at local level appear to have failed to reach a critical mass of trade union membership. The possibility also exists that because of the greater political element characteristic of union activity on the Continent, which was not directly related to the advance of coalminers' sectional interests, towns rather than collieries became the principal focal points around which workers' actions were concentrated.

A major issue raised in the literature is the extent to which the economics of coalmining and the occupational characteristics of coalminers were more or less important in explaining differential strike propensities, or whether international differences in politics, society and culture were the critical factors. The state of research scarcely encourages confident generalization. Shorter and Tilly's study, which was based on strikes in all industries in France, gave little space to conflict in the coalfields, but we endorse their general conclusion, that organization was a precondition for large-scale collective action. In the British coal industry, too, large strikes were never 'spontaneous'. As for local strikes, the level of local union organization was a critical influence on differential patterns of strike propensity. This being the case, and given that, compared with Britain, the size of collieries was greater and employment in relatively large collieries more prevalent on the Continent, the factors which inhibited the development of trade union organization in those countries should be a fruitful avenue for further research.

The same applies to comparisons with the US coal industry, though the extreme regional contrasts in the experience of American employers and workers render generalization even more problematical. The same factors which have been adduced to explain relative quiescence on the continental European coalfields (culturally determined attitudes of employers and workers, repressive and authoritarian paternalism, extensive migrant labour, inter-union rivalry) have also been deployed in accounting for the highly strike-prone history of the American industry.

The indeterminate outcome of the international comparisons attempted in chapter 13 underlines the limitation of approaches by social scientists which hitherto have been more sociological than historical, which have sought certainties rather than accepting ambiguities, and which have paid insufficient attention either to chronology or to the possibility of the reversibility of processes and the decomposition of syndromes. The limitations also reflect historians' neglect of conceptual frameworks and detailed quantitative data in forms suitable for effective international comparisons. Without these, none of the questions to which we have supplied answers (however provisional some of them may be) in respect of the British coal industry can be explored in this and other industries within an international framework.

The final implication of our work is that it demonstrates the possibility of a new and redefined approach to labour studies. Through the methodology we have devised, eclectic but systematic, combining concepts and theories with a use of evidence from a variety of sources which captures the reality of work and working lives at all levels at different times and in different localities, we have offered a route to the development of greater and more concrete understandings of the origins, processes and outcomes of industrial conflict – and of industrial harmony. We do not insist that strikes are the most important aspect of industrial relations but, considered in the broadest perspective, they have resulted from aspects of modernity which have defined the pattern and nature of work and generated the institutional and cultural frameworks within which relations between employers and workers, employers and employers, workers and workers, both at work and beyond the pithead or factory gates, took their course. We have shown in one industry how subtle, varied and changing forms and levels of interactions between these groups occurred, a picture which affects our appreciation of class formation and its significance as well as the course of labour relations. Because of this we regard the historical study of industrial relations to be vital if we are to increase our understanding of social change in modern societies.

General appendix

The first section of this appendix describes and evaluates the official records of strikes collected by the Board of Trade Labour Statistical Bureau and its successor departments and Ministries since 1888. It should be read in conjunction with our comments in chapter 1. The second section indicates how we have defined and named collieries.

THE BOARD OF TRADE AND MINISTRY OF LABOUR RECORDS OF COALMINING STRIKES

From 1901 these records exist as a series of manuscript ledgers catalogued by the Public Record Office as *Trade Disputes: Record Books, Strikes and Lock-outs in 1901*, etc. These are referred to in what follows as the *Record Books*. The ledgers for 1916–46 have been published on microfilm (Lowe 1985). For years prior to 1901 only the details published in the *Report on the Strikes and Lock-outs of 1888 by the Labour Correspondent of the Board of Trade* and subsequent annual *Reports* (later revised and collected in the Board of Trade *Abstracts of Labour Statistics of the United Kingdom*) and in the Board of Trade *Labour Gazette* survive. Our machine-readable coding of these data is available to other researchers at the ESRC's Data Archive held at Essex University. Readers who are considering using these sources or our coding of them for their own purposes may also wish to consult the *Guide* to this data set held at the Data Archive (Outram 1997). While this appendix focuses on the records covering the first forty years of the twentieth century the general principles governing the statistical recording of strikes have remained remarkably stable from the early 1890s and much of what we have to say pertains to the entire period since that time.

The sources on which the following comments are based are primarily the records themselves and the early annual reports. No detailed official guide to the sources and methods used in the compilation of these statistics has ever been published. What published official material is available is not adequate and almost all of it relates to the era before 1914. In what follows the *Report on the Strikes and Lock-outs of 1888 by the Labour Correspondent of the Board of Trade* and succeeding volumes are referred to as the *Report* for 1888, etc.

ORGANIZATION

A resolution, proposed by Charles Bradlaugh, calling for the 'full and accurate publication of Labour Statistics' was adopted by the House of Commons in March 1886 (Schloss 1893: 44; Davidson 1972: 231). The Board of Trade formed a Labour Statistical Bureau to perform this task and started to collect statistics on, *inter alia*, strikes and lock-outs in all industries in the UK in early 1888. The work of the Bureau was significantly hampered by the inadequacy of the resources at its disposal until its reorganization as the Board of Trade Labour Department in 1893. The *Report* for 1893 implied that 'many disputes' had previously escaped observation and this is one reason for the widespread dis-counting of the data collected before 1893. We have followed that practice here (Board of Trade, *Copy of Memorandum on the Progress of the Work of the Labour Department, Board of Trade*: 4–5; Journal of the Royal Statistical Society 1893: 331; Schloss 1893: 46–9; Davidson 1972: 232–8). The functions of the Labour Department were taken over by the Ministry of Labour in 1917. In what follows, references to 'the Bureau', 'the Department' and 'the Ministry' should be taken to include the other two, except where the context demands otherwise.

THE BUREAU'S QUESTIONNAIRES AND RATES OF RESPONSE TO THEM

The methods used to collect statistics of strikes by the Bureau adopted in the middle of 1888 appear to have remained unchanged in principle at least until the end of the period covered by this book. No fundamental changes in the method of collection of these statistics have been noted in the official literature we have surveyed. Internal evidence does not suggest any significant change in method-ology before the end of our period and none is suggested by the fullest survey of which we are aware in the unofficial literature (Winterton 1989: 62–80). The Labour Department kept a watch on 'a number of the most important daily papers from large centres of industry' and all references to strikes and lock-outs were noted. Questionnaires were then sent to the 'employers of labour' and the 'workmen's associations or to workmen representing the strike committee where there was no regular union' requesting information (*Report* for 1888: 34). In 1893 the Department also persuaded a number of trade organizations, including some coalowners' associations, to send details of any strikes which came to their notice without waiting for the Department to send them a questionnaire. It is also known that at some point the National Coal Board began to notify the Ministry of Labour of strikes coming to its attention without waiting for the Ministry to send in a questionnaire. For this reason it has been widely assumed that the Ministry's records of coalmining strikes in the nationalized era are unusually complete (Clegg 1976: 312; Winterton 1989: 224–6). The provision of information to the Ministry was on an entirely voluntary basis, however, and has remained so.

Investigations based on postal questionnaires are affected by a number of difficulties inherent in the methodology. There is no incentive to fill in the forms carefully or completely, or, indeed, at all. It is thus not surprising to find that of the forms returned 'many . . . [were] so incomplete or confused as to be worthless' (Schloss 1893: 49). Respondents are free to interpret the questions in their own manner and have no ready opportunity to clarify the meaning of the questions posed. Rates of response to the questionnaires were published by the Board of Trade, in the *First, Second* and *Third Abstracts of Labour Statistics of the United Kingdom* and the earliest *Reports*. The average response rate taking employers, etc. and unions, etc. together was 54.8 per cent in the period up to 1893 and 53.2 per cent in the years 1893 to 1895. (Data for 1896 and the following years were not published.) In addition, as we have noted, the Department also received information directly from various coalowner organizations and later the NCB. Nevertheless, these response rates have to be regarded as rather low. After 1893 the number of forms returned increased to an average of 1.5. It is likely that no completed questionnaire was received in a considerable number of cases. In this situation the practice was to 'take such information as may be otherwise available' (Schloss 1893: 49). Schloss took this locution to be 'an euphemism covering the free use of newspaper paragraphs which, if I may borrow the official language, are not in all cases written "with such care and completeness as is desirable" ' (*ibid.*).

PRODUCTION OF OFFICIAL RECORDS

The questionnaires received by the Department and the other 'case papers' such as newspaper clippings and correspondence have long since been destroyed. Apart from the published statistics what survive are the Department's *Record Books*. The entries in these *Record Books* admit of no ambiguity or disagreement about the 'facts' of a case: if employer and union disagreed about the 'cause or object' of the strike, for instance, and this was reflected in the answers they gave on the questionnaires sent to them that disagreement is now lost in oblivion. The Department claimed in 1895 that if the returned Inquiry Forms differed attempts were made 'so far as [was] possible to reconcile important discrepancies' (*Report* for 1895: 9). There was thus some safeguard against carelessly, mistakenly, or misleadingly answered questionnaires. But the Department's statisticians had a considerable role in producing an unambiguous account of a strike from materials which may have been incomplete and contradictory. Perhaps the most potentially controversial aspect of the officials' accounts were the classifications of the 'result' of the strike. This was not a matter on which the officials sought the opinions of the parties involved. Instead, they asked for the 'terms of settlement' and made their own assessments in the light of the information received. This is only the most obvious of the examples in which the officials recorded what they thought rather than what they had been told.

COVERAGE

The nature of any biases in the Department's strike statistics are difficult to even guess at except in one respect. This is that there was and is a bias against small strikes. This bias takes two forms; one is an intentional bias produced by the operation of 'inclusion criteria', the second is an unintentional bias arising from the higher probability of larger strikes coming to the notice of the Department. The intentional bias against the smallest strikes is routinely noted in the modern literature (for example, Knowles 1952: 301–2; Clegg 1979: 261; Winterton 1989: 65–8). The unintentional bias is noted less often but it was acknowledged by the Ministry of Labour's *Written Evidence* to the 1968 Royal Commission on Trade Unions and Employers' Associations (38n). Detailed case studies of industrial conflict in particular establishments, firms or industries (e.g. Scott *et al.* 1963: 44–5; Turner *et al.* 1967: 52–3; Winterton 1989) typically remark on the relatively large number of strikes that occur which are too small to satisfy the inclusion criteria. Knowles (1952: 303–4) commented on the differences between the NCB data on stoppages in coalmining as reported to the NCB's regional directors and as reported to the Ministry of Labour. However, there is no obvious jump in the number of officially recorded strikes or any other obvious change in the data recorded in the Ministry's *Record Books* immediately after nationalization and it would appear therefore that by the late 1940s the great majority of officially unrecorded strikes were strikes too small to satisfy the Ministry's inclusion criteria.

UNIT OF ENUMERATION

Those who count strikes sometimes count strikes and sometimes count plants, firms, towns or states *affected by* strikes. Until the *Report* for 1890, the 'establishment [was] taken as the unit of enumeration. [In 1890] it [was] determined to make the strike, whether a general or merely a local one, the unit, providing also a separate column showing the number of establishments which were concerned in each dispute' (*Report* for 1890: 9). This practice has been maintained consistently ever since.

INDUSTRY

From the occupational details given in the *Record Books*, it is clear that coke-oven and by-product works were included in the definition of the coalmining industry. The few strikes that occurred in coke-oven and by-product works are not separately distinguished in the text tables above until after 1940. Mining other than coalmining, e.g. iron-stone mining, was excluded, as was quarrying, although fireclay miners appear once or twice; fireclay was commonly found with coal.

GEOGRAPHICAL COVERAGE

The *Record Books* include details of strikes in what is now the Republic of Ireland until the end of 1921. There were a small number of coal mines in the twenty-six counties but there has never been any coal mine in what is now Northern

Ireland. Irish strikes are excluded from our data sets which thus refer to Great
Britain throughout.

COMPANY NAME AND COLLIERY NAME

From 1921 onwards the *Record Books* usually give the name of the company or
companies and/or the name of the colliery or collieries involved in the strike. The
referent of the name is sometimes uncertain: names were assumed to be colliery
names, not company names, unless there was evidence to the contrary. Thus
'Valleyfield' was assumed to mean 'Valleyfield Colliery' not the 'Valleyfield
Colliery Company Limited'. No attempt has been made to ascertain the ultimate ownership of the companies given as the colliery owners in the *Record
Books*. In practice few problems arose from this. For example, Yorkshire Amal-
gamated Collieries, an ultimate owner of many collieries, never appears in the
Record Books as the company involved, only its operating subsidiaries, Cadeby
Main Collieries Ltd, the Maltby Main Colliery Company, etc.

COLLIERIES

The annual *Lists of Mines* published by the Home Office and later the Mines
Department and the Ministry of Fuel and Power give an authoritative listing of
every mine operating under the Coal Mines Acts. They were compiled from
statutory returns to the Mines Inspectorate. They number and name each mine
and give some further information about each including its owners, its location
and the numbers employed. The privately published annual *Guides to the Coalfields* give similar information to the *Lists* and appear to be based on Mines
Inspectorate information. For the period after 1950, when the last *List* was
published, we have used the *Guides* in the same way as the *Lists*. Our basic
definition of a 'colliery' is 'that which is numbered and named by the *List of
Mines* or the *Guide to the Coalfields*'. However, this obviously begs some questions. Furthermore the way the compilers of the *Lists of Mines* and the *Guides*
defined a colliery was not always in conformity with the general usage reflected
in the *Record Books* and this has led to a number of difficulties.

DEFINITION OF A COLLIERY

There is no official guidance on how the *Lists of Mines* defined a colliery.
However, the *Lists* were compiled by the Mines Inspectorate and the prime
function of the Mines Inspectorate was the enforcement of the Coal Mines and
Metalliferous Mines Regulation Acts. It is safe to assume that the definition of
collieries was influenced by statutory provisions and legal decisions. The Coal
Mines Act 1911, the principal statute regulating matters of health and safety in
coal mines in the inter-war period, provided, effectively, that each mine had to
be under the daily personal supervision of a manager. Where a manager
managed two or more mines each mine had to be under the supervision of a

separate under-manager (MacSwinney and Lloyd-Greame 1912: 1–2). This suggests the *Lists* used the following definition: a mine is that system of workings for which an under-manager or, where there is no under-manager, a manager is responsible. A legal decision of 1920 indicated that the factors to be taken into account in deciding whether or not workings comprised one or more 'systems' were primarily the separation or integration of underground systems of ventilation, drainage, roads, haulage and winding (Mines Department, *Mines and Quarries: General Report with Statistics for 1920: Part II Labour*: 36–7). This definitional practice had the consequence that some collieries customarily referred to as such were treated by the compilers of the *List of Mines* as only parts of collieries. Conversely, some collieries customarily referred to as single entities were treated as several separate collieries. For example 'Polmaise Colliery' near Stirling was treated as two separate collieries: Polmaise Nos. 1 & 2 under one manager and Polmaise Nos. 3 & 4 under another. This has the unfortunate effect of making it impossible to link strikes recorded at 'Polmaise Colliery' with a specific colliery and they accordingly appear in our data set as strikes at unidentified collieries.

We were also forced to treat some pairs and, very rarely, larger sets of separate collieries as if they were single collieries when the *List of Mines* or the *Guide* gave employment data only for the set and not for each individual member.

TREATMENT OF LISTING CHANGES

The definition of a given system of workings as a single colliery was not always maintained consistently from year to year by the *Lists of Mines* or the *Guides*. Presumably in response to changes in systems of ventilation, haulage, etc., as collieries were extended or contracted, workings which one year appear as separate collieries appear as merely parts of collieries in subsequent years and vice versa. Because of our interest in histories of colliery strikes, we thought it appropriate to keep a given set of colliery workings together under one name throughout the period of investigation and to treat that set as a single colliery. For most of our analyses, therefore, we standardized the definition of the colliery on the smallest entity for which employment data was consistently available in the annual *Lists of Mines*. This usually, but not always, led us to treat collieries which merged at some point in the 1921–40 period or the 1943–63 period as single collieries *throughout* those periods. Such collieries we term 'subsequently merged' collieries.

The collieries in the colliery sample were treated differently, however. For the purposes of that sample it would have been artificial and misleading to attempt any standardization and we therefore followed all mergers and splits ('demergers'), treating the colliery in any one year as it was defined in that year. After a merger the new colliery was defined as the whole of the merged entity, not just the pit or pits which corresponded to the old colliery. After a split, where two or more new collieries were formed out of the old colliery, we followed one of the new collieries, choosing the colliery to follow at random. This procedure avoids the introduction of any bias into the sample; to have followed the biggest of the new collieries, for example, would have introduced a bias in the sample towards large collieries.

COLLIERY NAMING CONVENTIONS

Although in the text we often refer to collieries informally, in the tables we refer to collieries by their *List of Mines* or *Guide* name whenever possible. It is not possible to do so in three sets of cases. The first is where the *List* gives a single number to, and thus treats as a single mine, a collection of entities ('pits') each of which is given a separate name. In these cases we invented a colliery name by concatenating the pit names with addition signs and terminating the whole with 'Colliery'. For example: 'Bamfurlong No. 1 + Bamfurlong No. 3 + Bamfurlong No. 4 Colliery'. The second set of cases consist of 'subsequently merged' collieries which we have treated as if they had been merged at all points in the 1921–40 or 1943–63 periods. The third set consist of sets of collieries for which the *Lists of Mines* or the *Guides* gives only their total, joint employment. In both these latter two cases we have given the aggregate of collieries concerned a name which consists of all the component names concatenated by pairs of addition signs, for example: 'Carberry Colliery ++ Wallyford Colliery'.

IMPLICATIONS OF PROCEDURES

The upshot of all this is that the definition of 'colliery' implicit in our work is based on mine engineering and mine management features as reflected in statutory provisions and legal decisions and has also been constrained by data limitations. The resulting definitions sometimes depart from normal usage. This has affected our measurements at various points but we do not think this imparts any noticeable bias to our work. One measure obviously affected by our identification procedures is the number of strikes which involved more than a single colliery. In some cases strikes which our definitions imply were 'multi-colliery' strikes would be classified as single colliery strikes on other, reasonable, definitions. For example, the three collieries (on our definitions) at Gwaun-cae-Gurwen in South Wales often struck together and these strikes thus appear as rare examples of strikes extending beyond the confines of the colliery. Had we followed some usages and regarded the East, Maerdy and Steer collieries at Gwaun-cae-Gurwen as parts of a single 'colliery' then our count of the number of multi-colliery strikes would have been lower. Our identification of the most strike-prone collieries also depends on our prior definition of those collieries and different definitions generate different results. For example, in constructing table 5.10 we have treated Polmaise Nos. 1 & 2 colliery as separate from Polmaise Nos. 3 & 4 Colliery; each was fairly strike prone in the late 1930s but not sufficiently so to enter table 5.10; had they been treated as a single colliery they might well have done so.

References

ARCHIVAL SOURCES

CLWYD RECORD OFFICE (CRO)

North Wales Miners' Association, *Statement of Accounts*, 1930, D/NM/66.
North Wales and Border Counties Mineworkers' Association, *Statement of Accounts*, 1935, D/NM/79–97.

DERBYSHIRE RECORD OFFICE (DeRO)

Derbyshire Miners' Association, *Minutes*, 1930 and 1935, N3.

DURHAM RECORD OFFICE (DuRO)

Durham Miners' Association, *Records of Membership*, 1930 and 1935, D/DMA 1–30.

NATIONAL LIBRARY OF SCOTLAND

Lanarkshire Mine Workers' Union, *Statements of Dues and Funeral Claims*, 1930 and 1935, NLS Dep. 227/45a.

NATIONAL UNION OF MINEWORKERS, SHEFFIELD

Miners' [*after 1933* Mineworkers'] Federation of Great Britain, *Minutes of Proceedings*, 1920–38.

NATIONAL UNION OF MINEWORKERS, YORKSHIRE AREA, BARNSLEY

Yorkshire Mine Workers' Association, *Balance Sheets and General Statements*, 1930 and 1935.

NATIONAL UNION OF MINEWORKERS, NORTH STAFFORDSHIRE DISTRICT, STOKE-ON-TRENT

North Staffordshire Miners' Federation, *Official Statements of Accounts*, 1930 and 1935.

NORTHUMBERLAND RECORD OFFICE (NuRO)

Northumberland Coal Owners' Association, *Cramlington Colliery Co. Ltd.*, NCB 1274/49.

276

Northumberland Miners' Mutual Confident Association, *Balance Sheets*, 1930 and 1935, NRO 759/68.
Burradon Colliery Branch Executive Committee Minutes, NRO 759/21.
Burradon Colliery Branch Minutes, NRO 3013.

NOTTINGHAMSHIRE RECORD OFFICE (NuRO)

Nottinghamshire Miners' Association, *General Fund Receipts and Payments Accounts*, 1930 and 1935.

PUBLIC RECORD OFFICE, KEW, LONDON (PRO)

Board of Trade, *Trade Disputes: Record Books, Strikes and Lock-outs in 1901*, and subsequent volumes to 1916, PRO LAB 34/1–16.
Ministry of Labour, *Statistics, Industrial Disputes: Sectional Instructions on the Compilation of Statistics of Stoppages, Definition of Strikes and Lockouts*, PRO LAB 17/325.
Ministry of Labour, *Trade Disputes: Record Books, Strikes and Lock-outs of 1917*, and subsequent volumes, PRO LAB 34/17–.
National Coal Board
  Registration of Assets: Estimates of Value:
    Cumberland Coal Co. (Whitehaven) Ltd., PRO COAL 37/121.
    Mitchell Main Colliery Co. Ltd., PRO COAL 37/256–60.
    Moresby Coal Co. Ltd., PRO COAL 37/265.
    Wharncliffe Silkstone Colliery Co. Ltd., PRO COAL 37/372–5.
  Stoppages and Restrictions due to Trade Disputes: Policy, 1946–49, PRO COAL 26/89.

SALFORD MINING MUSEUM

Lancashire and Cheshire Miners' Federation, *Monthly Statements of Accounts*, 1930 and 1935.

SHEFFIELD CITY ARCHIVES

Doncaster Amalgamated Collieries Ltd:
  Hickleton Main Colliery, Deputations Book, NCB 1137/1.
  Hickleton Main Colliery, Deputations Book, NCB 1137/9.
  Hickleton Main Colliery, Reports to Directors, 1937–46, NCB 1820.
South Yorkshire Coal Owners' Association, *Minutes*, 1887–1925, MD 2699/1–25.

SOUTH WALES COALFIELD ARCHIVE, SWANSEA UNIVERSITY COLLEGE LIBRARY

South Wales Miners' Federation, *Average Membership and Vote Entitlement of SWMF Lodges 1933–40*, SWMF/NUM Misc. Office Papers F(22).

UNIVERSITY OF GLASGOW ARCHIVES

Scottish Coal Owners' Association, *Minutes*, UGD/159/1.

OFFICIAL PUBLICATIONS

BOARD OF TRADE

[*Annual Abstracts of Labour Statistics*] *Report on the Work of the Labour Department of the Board of Trade (1893–94) with Supplement containing Abstract of Labour Statistics* [i.e. the First Annual Abstract of Labour Statistics] (C. 7565), 1894 lxxx 397;

Second Annual Report of the Labour Department of the Board of Trade (1894–95) with Abstract of Labour Statistics (C. 7900), 1895 xcii 1; *Third* [similarly] (C. 8230), 1896 lxxx (Pt. 2) 1;

Fourth Annual Report of the Labour Department of the Board of Trade (1896–97) with Abstract of Labour Statistics of the United Kingdom (C. 8642), 1897 lxxxiv 1;

Fifth Annual Abstract of Labour Statistics of the United Kingdom 1897–98 (C. 9011), 1898 lxxxviii 695; *Sixth* (Cd. 119), 1900 lxxxiii 1; *Seventh* (Cd. 495), 1901 lxxiii 1; *Eighth* (Cd. 1124), 1902 xcvii 1; *Ninth* (Cd. 1755), 1903 lxvii 1; *Tenth* (Cd. 2491), 1905 lxxvi 139; *Eleventh* (Cd. 3690), 1907 lxxx 515; *Twelfth* (Cd. 4413), 1908 xcviii 325; *Thirteenth* (Cd. 5041), 1910 cx 1; *Fourteenth* (Cd. 5458), 1910 cx 307;

Fifteenth Abstract of Labour Statistics of the United Kingdom (Cd. 6228), 1912–13 cvii 517; *Sixteenth* (Cd. 7131), 1914 lxxx 301; *Seventeenth* (Cd. 7733), 1914–16 lxi 295; *Eighteenth* (Cmd. 2740) 1926 xxix 1; *Nineteenth* (Cmd. 3140), 1928 xxv 495; *Twentieth* (Cmd. 3831), 1930–1 xxxii 453;

Twenty-First Abstract of Labour Statistics of the United Kingdom (1919–1933) (Cmd. 4625), 1933–4 xxvi 911;

Twenty-Second Abstract of Labour Statistics of the United Kingdom (1922–1936) (Cmd. 5556), 1936–7 xxvi 869.

Copy of Memorandum on the Progress of the Work of the Labour Department, Board of Trade (HC 194), 1893–4 lxxxii 363.

The Labour Gazette: The Journal of the Labour Department of the Board of Trade (May 1893 to January 1905); continued as: *The Board of Trade Labour Gazette* (February 1905 to June 1917); continued by Ministry of Labour as: *The Labour Gazette*.

Report on Collective Agreements between Employers and Workpeople in the United Kingdom (Cd. 5366), 1910 xx 1.

Report on Rules of Voluntary Conciliation and Arbitration Boards and Joint Committees, 1908 (Cd. 3788), 1908 xcviii 1; *Second Report on Rules of Voluntary Conciliation and Arbitration Boards and Joint Committees*, 1910 (Cd. 5346), 1910 xx 543.

Report on the Strikes and Lock-outs of 1888, by the Labour Correspondent to the Board of Trade (C. 5809) 1889 lxx 703; *of 1889* (C. 6176), 1890 lxviii 445; *of 1890* (C. 6476), 1890–1 lxxviii 689; *of 1891* (C. 6890), 1893–4 lxxxiii (Pt. 1) 461;

Report by the Chief Labour Correspondent on the Strikes and Lock-outs of 1892 (C. 7403), 1894 lxxxi (Pt. 1) 1; *of 1893* (C. 7566), 1894 lxxxi (Pt. 1) 409; *of 1894* (C. 7901), 1895 xcii 211; *of 1895* (C. 8231), 1896 lxxx (Pt. 1) 441;

Report by the Chief Labour Correspondent on the Strikes and Lock-outs of 1896 with Statistical Tables, (C. 8643), 1897 lxxxiv 239; *of 1897* (C. 9012), 1898 lxxxviii 423; *of 1898* (C. 9437), 1899 xcii 277; *of 1899* (Cd. 316), 1900 lxxxiii 383; *of 1900* (Cd. 689), 1901 lxxiii 591;

Report on Strikes and Lock-outs in the United Kingdom in 1901, and on Conciliation and Arbitration Boards, (Cd. 1236), 1902 xcvii 241; *in 1902* (Cd. 1623), 1903 lxvi 1175; *in 1903* (Cd. 2112), 1904 lxxxix 699; *in 1904* (Cd. 2631), 1905 lxxvi 707; *in 1905* (Cd. 3065), 1906 cxii 897; *in 1906* (Cd. 3711), 1907 lxxx 111; *in 1907* (Cd. 4254), 1908 xcviii 599; *in 1908* (Cd. 4680), 1909 xlix 1; *in 1909* (Cd. 5325), 1910 lviii 389;

in 1910 (Cd. 5850), 1911 xli 411; *in 1911* (Cd. 6472), 1912–13 xlvii 43; *in 1912* (Cd. 7089), 1914 xlviii 363; *in 1913* (Cd. 7658), 1914–16 xxxvi 489.

BUREAU OF LABOR STATISTICS (USA)

Strikes in the United States 1880–1936, by Florence Peterson (Bulletin No. 651 of the United States Department of Labor Bureau of Labor Statistics), Government Printing Office, Washington, 1938.

BUREAU OF THE CENSUS (USA)

Historical Statistics of the United States: Colonial Times to 1970 (Bicentennial Edition), Washington, 1975.

CENSUS

Census of England and Wales 1931.
Census of Scotland 1931.

[COMMISSION ON COAL SUPPLY] COMMISSIONERS APPOINTED TO INQUIRE INTO THE SEVERAL MATTERS RELATING TO COAL IN THE UNITED KINGDOM

General Minutes, and Proceedings of Committees A, B, C, D. &c., (C. 435–I.), 1871 xviii 199.

COMMISSION OF ENQUIRY INTO INDUSTRIAL UNREST

Report on No. 7 Division (Wales and Monmouthshire) (Cd. 8668), 1917–18 xv 83.

[COMMISSIONER APPOINTED . . . TO INQUIRE . . . INTO THE STATE OF THE POPULATION IN THE MINING DISTRICTS] COMMISSIONER APPOINTED UNDER THE PROVISIONS OF THE ACT 5 & 6 VICT., c. 99, TO INQUIRE INTO THE OPERATION OF THAT ACT, AND INTO THE STATE OF THE POPULATION IN THE MINING DISTRICTS

Report, 1847 (844), 1847 xvi 401.

COMMISSIONER OF LABOR (USA)

Third Annual Report of the Commissioner of Labor 1887: Strikes and Lockouts, Government Printing Office, Washington, 1888.
Tenth Annual Report of the Commissioner of Labor 1894: Strikes and Lockouts, Government Printing Office, Washington, 1896.
Sixteenth Annual Report of the Commissioner of Labor 1901: Strikes and Lockouts, Government Printing Office, Washington, 1901.
Twenty-First Annual Report of the Commissioner of Labor 1905: Strikes and Lockouts, Government Printing Office, Washington, 1907.

[COMMITTEE ON TRUSTS] COMMITTEE OF THE MINISTRY OF RECONSTRUCTION ON TRUSTS

Report (Cd. 9236), 1918 xiii 789.

DEPARTMENT OF EMPLOYMENT

Strikes in Britain: a Research Study of Industrial Stoppages in the United Kingdom, by C. T. B. Smith, Richard Clifton, Peter Makeham, S. W. Creigh, and R. V. Burn (Manpower Paper No. 15), Department of Employment, 1978.

DEPARTMENT OF EMPLOYMENT AND PRODUCTIVITY

British Labour Statistics: Historical Abstract 1886–1968, 1971.

HOME OFFICE

List of Mines in the United Kingdom of Great Britain and Ireland and the Isle of Man. For the Year 1896; and similarly, annually until: *List of Mines in the United Kingdom and the Isle of Man: 1902*; then similarly, annually until 1919. Continued by the Mines Department from 1920.

Mines and Quarries: General Report and Statistics. For 1897. Part III. Output. (C. 9098), 1899 cvii 175; *for 1898* (C. 9527), 1899 cvii 607; *for 1899* (Cd. 387), 1900 cii 261; *for 1900* (Cd. 818), 1902 cxvi (Pt. 2) 377; *for 1901* (Cd. 1307), 1902 cxvi (Pt. 2) 537; *for 1902* (Cd. 1817), 1904 cvi 99; *for 1903* (Cd. 2283), 1905 xcviii 101; *for 1904* (Cd. 2745), 1906 cxxxiv 289; *for 1905* (Cd. 3196), 1906 cxxxiv 891; *for 1906* (Cd. 3774), 1908 cxxii 325; *for 1907* (Cd. 4343), 1908 cxxii 795; *for 1908* (Cd. 4937), 1909 ciii 523; *for 1909* (Cd. 5413), 1910 cix 855; *for 1910* (Cd. 5977), 1911 cii 699; *for 1911* (Cd. 6550), 1912–13 cvii 371; *for 1912* (Cd. 7197), 1914 xcix 741; *for 1913* (Cd. 7741), 1914–16 lxxx 677; *for 1914* (Cd. 8141), 1914–16 lxxx 921; *for 1915* (Cd. 8444), 1917–18 xxxvii 423; *for 1916* (Cd. 8885), 1917–18 xxxvii 549; *for 1917* (Cmd. 4), 1919 li 583; *for 1918* (Cmd. 531), 1920 1 703; *for 1919* (Cmd. 1035), 1920 1 983.

Report on the Causes of and Circumstances Attending an Explosion and Underground Fire which Occurred at the Wellington Pit, Whitehaven Colliery on the 11th May, 1910 by R. A. S. Redmayne, H. M. Chief Inspector of Mines, and Samuel Pope, Barrister-at-Law (Cd. 5524), 1911 xxii 293.

[Report on an Explosion at Wharncliffe Silkstone Colliery] Report to the Right Honourable the Secretary of State for the Home Department on the Circumstances Attending an Explosion which Occurred at the Wharncliffe Silkstone Colliery on the 30th May, 1914 by Samuel Pope (Barrister-at-Law), and Thomas H. Mottram (One of His Majesty's Divisional Inspectors of Mines) (Cd. 7720), 1914–16 xxi 131.

Summaries of Statistics Relating to Mines and Minerals obtained by Her Majesty's Inspectors of Mines . . . Year 1893 (C. 7328), 1894 xciv 547; *Summaries of Statistics Relating to Mines and Minerals of the United Kingdom of Great Britain and Ireland, with the Isle of Man, obtained by Her Majesty's Inspectors of Mines . . . Year 1894* (C. 7666), 1895 cvii 519; *Summaries of Statistics Relating to the Mines and Quarries in the United Kingdom and the Isle of Man, obtained by Her Majesty's Inspectors of Mines . . . Year 1895* (C. 8113), 1896 xciii 241; and similarly, *Year 1896* (C. 8460), 1897 xcix 241.

INTERNATIONAL LABOUR OFFICE

Methods of Compiling Statistics of Industrial Disputes (Studies and Reports: Series N (Statistics) No. 10), Geneva, and London, P. S. King for the International Labour Office (League of Nations), 1926.

MINES DEPARTMENT

Annual Report of the Secretary for Mines, First, 1921, to *Eighteenth* and final, 1938.
List of Mines in the United Kingdom and the Isle of Man: 1920 and similarly, annually until 1938. Continued by the Ministry of Fuel and Power from 1945.
Mines and Quarries: General Report with Statistics for 1920: By H. M. Chief Inspector of Mines: Part II.—Labour, (HC 239), 1921 xli 867.
Royal Commission on the Coal Industry (1925): Minutes & Appendices, 1926.
Statistical Summary of Output and of the Costs of Production, Proceeds and Profits of the Coal Mining Industry as a Whole, and for the Various Districts, in respect of the Three Months ended on 30th September, 1920 (Cmd. 1080), 1920 xlix 95.

MINISTRY OF FUEL AND POWER

List of Mines in Great Britain and the Isle of Man 1945, and similarly for *1950.*
Statistical Digest from 1938 (Cmd. 6538), 1943–4 viii 151; *Statistical Digest 1944* (Cmd. 6639), 1944–5 x 153; *1945* (Cmd. 6920), 1945–6 xxi 99; *for the Years 1946 and 1947* (Cmd. 7548), 1948–9 xxix 595.
Statistical Digest 1948 and 1949 (non-Parliamentary); *Statistical Digest 1950*; and similarly, annually until 1955. Continued by Ministry of Power.

MINISTRY OF LABOUR

The Labour Gazette (July 1917 to May 1922); continued from *The Board of Trade Labour Gazette* and continued as: *The Ministry of Labour Gazette* (June 1922 to May 1968).
Report on Collective Agreements between Employers and Workpeople in Great Britain and Northern Ireland. Vol. I: *Mining and Quarrying Industries . . . [etc.],*1934.

MINISTRY OF POWER

Statistical Digest 1956; and similarly, annually until 1966.

MINISTRY OF TECHNOLOGY

Management and Technology (Problems and Progress in Industry No. 3), by Joan Woodward, 1958.

NATIONAL COAL BOARD

Annual Report and Statement of Accounts for the Year Ended 31st December 1946 (HC 174), 1947–8 x 351; *for the Year Ended 31st December 1947* (HC 175), 1947–8 x 387; *for the Year Ended 31st December 1948* (HC 187), 1948–9 xiii 21; *for the Year Ended 31st December 1954* (HC 1), 1955–6 xii 1; *for the Year Ended 3rd January 1959.* Vol. I: *Report* (HC 158), 1958–9 ix 365. Vol. II: *Accounts and Statistical Tables* (HC 159), 1958–9 ix 431; *Report and Accounts 30th December, 1962 – 28th March, 1964.* Vol. I: *Report* (HC 317), 1963–4 x 31. Vol. II: *Accounts and Statistical Tables* (HC 318), 1963–4 x 91.

REGISTRAR OF FRIENDLY SOCIETIES

Annual Report of the Chief Registrar of Friendly Societies for 1925: part IV *Trade Unions* (HC 138), 1926 xxii 621.

Annual Report of the Chief Registrar of Friendly Societies for 1926: part IV *Trade Unions* (HC 73), 1927 ix 299.

ROYAL COMMISSION ON THE COAL INDUSTRY (1925)

Report (Cmd. 2600), 1926 xiv 1.
Minutes & Appendices: see Mines Department.

ROYAL COMMISSION ON LABOUR

[Majority Report] Fifth and Final Report: part I: *The Report* (C. 7421), 1894 xxxv 9.

ROYAL COMMISSION ON SAFETY IN COAL MINES

Report (Cmd. 5890), 1938–9 xiii 263.

ROYAL COMMISSION ON TRADE UNIONS AND EMPLOYERS' ASSOCIATIONS 1965–1968

Disputes Procedures in Britain (Research Papers, 2 (part 2)), by A. I. Marsh and W. E. J. McCarthy, 1968.
Minutes of Evidence: 4: Tuesday 16th November 1965: Witness: National Coal Board, 1966.
Written Evidence of the Ministry of Labour, 1965.

SECONDARY SOURCES

Ackers, Peter (1994) 'Colliery deputies in the British coal industry before nationalization', *International Review of Social History*, 39(3), 383–414.
    (1996) 'Life after death: mining history without a coal industry', *Historical Studies in Industrial Relations*, 1, 159–170.
Acton Society Trust (1953) *Size and Morale: a Preliminary Study of Attendance at Work in Large and Small Units*, London, Acton Society Trust.
    (1957) *Size and Morale: Part II: a Further Study of Attendance at Work in Large and Small Units*, London, Acton Society Trust.
Allen, V. L. (1964) 'The origins of industrial conciliation and arbitration', *International Review of Social History*, 9(2), 237–54.
    (1971) *The Sociology of Industrial Relations: Studies in Method*, London, Longman.
    (1981) *The Militancy of British Miners*, Shipley, The Moor Press.
Anthony-Jones, W. J. (1959) 'Labour relations in the South Wales coal mining industry, December 1926 – September 1939', doctoral thesis, University College of Wales, Aberystwyth.
Arnot, R. Page (1926) *The General Strike: May 1926: its Origin and History*, London, Labour Research Department.
    (1949) *The Miners: a History of the Miners' Federation of Great Britain (1889–1910)*, London, George Allen and Unwin.
    (1953) *The Miners: Years of Struggle: a History of the Miners' Federation of Great Britain (from 1910 onwards)*, London, George Allen and Unwin.
    (1955) *A History of the Scottish Miners: from the Earliest Times*, London, George Allen and Unwin.

(1961) *The Miners in Crisis and War: a History of the Miners' Federation of Great Britain (from 1930 onwards)*, London, George Allen and Unwin.

(1967) *South Wales Miners: Glowyr de Cymru: a History of the South Wales Miners' Federation (1898–1914)*, London, George Allen and Unwin.

(1975) *South Wales Miners: Glowyr de Cymru: a History of the South Wales Miners' Federation (1914–1926)*, Cardiff, Cymric Federation Press.

(1979) *The Miners: One Union, One Industry: a History of the National Union of Mineworkers 1939–46*, London, George Allen and Unwin.

Ashworth, William, with the assistance of Pegg, Mark (1986) *The History of the British Coal Industry*. Vol. V: *1946–1982: The Nationalized Industry*, Oxford, Clarendon Press.

Askwith, Lord (1920/1974) *Industrial Problems and Disputes*, Brighton, Harvester Press, 1974 (first edition: London, John Murray, 1920).

Babbage, Charles (1832/1989) *On the Economy of Machinery and Manufactures* (Campbell-Kelly, Martin (ed.), *The Works of Charles Babbage*. Vol. VIII), London, William Pickering (Pickering and Chatto (Publishers)), 1989 (first edition: 1832). Page references are to the 1989 edition which reproduces that of the original edition.

Bain, George Sayers (ed.) (1983) *Industrial Relations in Britain*, Oxford, Basil Blackwell.

Baldwin, George B. (1955) *Beyond Nationalization: the Labor Problems of British Coal*, Cambridge, Harvard University Press.

Barnett, Correlli (1986) *The Audit of War: the Illusion and Reality of Britain as a Great Nation*, London, Macmillan.

Barry, E. Eldon (1965) *Nationalisation in British Politics: the Historical Background*, London, Jonathan Cape.

Batstone, Eric, Boraston, Ian, and Frenkel, Stephen (1978) *The Social Organization of Strikes*, Oxford, Basil Blackwell.

Baylies, Carolyn (1993) *The History of the Yorkshire Miners 1881–1918*, London, Routledge.

Bellamy, Joyce M., and Saville, John, *Dictionary of Labour Biography*. Vol. I, London, Macmillan, 1972; Vol. II, 1974; Vol. III, 1976; Vol. IV, 1977; Vol. V, 1979; Vol. VI, 1982; Vol. VII, 1984; Vol. VIII, with assistance from David E. Martin, 1987; Vol. IX, with assistance from David E. Martin, 1993.

Belloc, Hilaire (1913) *The Servile State*, London, Constable.

Benson, John (1980) *British Coalminers in the Nineteenth Century: a Social History*, Dublin, Gill and Macmillan.

Bevan, G. Phillips (1880) 'The strikes of the past ten years', *Journal of the Royal Statistical Society*, 43, 35–54.

Beynon, Huw (1985) *Digging Deeper: Issues in the Miners' Strike*, London, Verso.

Beynon, Huw, and Austrin, Terry (1994) *Masters and Servants: Class and Patronage in the Making of a Labour Organisation: the Durham Miners and the English Political Tradition*, London, Rivers Oram Press.

Blanchflower, David, and Cubbin, John (1986) 'Strike propensities at the British workplace', *Oxford Bulletin of Economics and Statistics*, 48(1), 19–39.

Blauner, Robert (1960) 'Work satisfaction and industrial trends in modern society', in Galenson, Walter, and Lipsett, Seymour Martin (eds.), *Labor and Trade Unionism: an Interdisciplinary Reader*, New York, John Wiley, 339–60.

(1964) *Alienation and Freedom: the Factory Worker and his Industry*, Chicago, University of Chicago Press.

Boll, Friedhelm (1985) 'International strike waves: a critical assessment', ch. 4 of Mommsen, Wolfgang J., and Husung, Hans-Gerhard (eds.), *The Development of Trade*

Unionism in Great Britain and Germany, 1880–1914, London, George Allen and Unwin, 78–99.

Bougen, P. D., Ogden, S. G., and Outram, Q. (1988) 'Profit sharing and the cycle of control', *Sociology*, 22(4), 607–29.

(1990) 'The appearance and disappearance of accounting: wage determination in the UK coal industry', *Accounting, Organizations and Society*, 15(3), 149–70.

Bowman, John R. (1989) *Capitalist Collective Action: Competition, Cooperation, and Conflict in the Coal Industry*, Cambridge, Cambridge University Press and Paris, Editions de la Maison des Sciences de l'Homme.

Boyns, Trevor R. (1989) 'Of machines and men in the 1920s', *Llafur*, 5(2), 30–9.

(1992) 'Powell Duffryn: the use of machinery and production planning techniques in the South Wales coalfield', in Tenfelde, Klaus (ed.), *Towards a Social History of Mining in the 19th and 20th Centuries: Papers Presented to the International Mining History Congress Bochum, Federal Republic of Germany, September 3rd–7th, 1989*, Munich, Verlag C. H. Beck, 370–86.

Bradshaw's April 1910 Railway Guide: a New Edition of the April 1910 Issue of Bradshaw's Railway and Steam Navigation Guide for Great Britain and Ireland (1968) Newton Abbot, David and Charles Reprints.

Braverman, Harry (1974) *Labor and Monopoly Capital: the Degradation of Work in the Twentieth Century*, New York, Monthly Review Press.

Briggs, Asa (1966) 'Trade union history and labour history', *Business History*, 8(1), 39–47.

Brody, David (1989) 'Labor history, industrial relations, and the crisis of American labor', *Industrial and Labor Relations Review*, 43, 7–18.

(1990) 'Labour relations in American coal mining: an industry perspective', ch. 3 of Feldman, Gerald D., and Tenfelde, Klaus (eds.), *Workers, Owners and Politics in Coal Mining: an International Comparison of Industrial Relations*, New York, Berg, 74–117.

Brown, Harold (1981) *Most Splendid of Men: Life in a Mining Community, 1917–25*, Poole, Blandford Press.

Brown, K. (1987) 'The lodges of the Durham Miners' Association, 1869–1926', *Northern History*, 23, 138–52.

Brown, R. K., Brannen, P., Cousins, J. M., and Samphier, M. L. (1972) 'The contours of solidarity: social stratification and industrial relations in shipbuilding', *British Journal of Industrial Relations*, 10(1), 12–41.

Bulman, H. F. (1920) *Coal Mining and the Coal Miner*, London, Methuen.

Bulman, H. F., and Redmayne, R. A. S. (1896) *Colliery Working and Management: Comprising the Duties of a Colliery Manager, the Superintendence & Arrangement of Labour & Wages and the Different Systems of Working Coal Seams*, London, Crosby Lockwood and Son.

(1906) *Colliery Working and Management . . .* , second edition, revised and enlarged, London, Crosby Lockwood & Son.

(1925) *Colliery Working and Management . . .* , fourth edition, thoroughly revised and much enlarged, London, Crosby Lockwood & Sons.

(1951) *Colliery Working and Management . . .*, fifth edition, enlarged, etc., Kingston Hill, Technical Press.

Bulmer, Martin I. A. (1975a) 'Sociological models of the mining community', *Sociological Review* (New Series), 23(1), 61–92.

Bulmer, Martin I. A. (ed.) (1975b) *Working-Class Images of Society*, London, Routledge and Kegan Paul.

Burgess, Keith (1975) *The Origins of British Industrial Relations: the Nineteenth Century Experience*, London, Croom Helm.

Calhoun, C. J. (1978) 'History, anthropology and the history of communities: some problems in MacFarlane's proposal', *Social History*, 3, 363–72.

Campbell, Alan B. (1978) 'Honourable men and degraded slaves: a comparative study of trade unionism in two Lanarkshire mining communities c. 1830–1874', ch. 3 of Harrison, Royden (ed.), *Independent Collier: the Coal Miner as Archetypal Proletarian Reconsidered*, Hassocks, Harvester Press, 75–113.

(1979) *The Lanarkshire Miners: a Social History of their Trade Unions, 1775–1974*, Edinburgh, John Donald.

(1984) 'Colliery mechanisation and the Lanarkshire miners', *Bulletin of the Society for the Study of Labour History*, 49, 37–43.

(1989a) 'From independent collier to militant miner: tradition and change in the trade union consciousness of the Scottish miners, 1874–1929', *Scottish Labour History Society Journal*, 24, 8–23.

(1989b) 'Tradition and generational change in the Scots miners' unions, 1874–1929' in Blok, Aad, Damsma, Dirk, Diederiks, Herman, and van Voss, Lex Heerma (eds.), *Generations in Labour History: Papers Presented to the Sixth British-Dutch Conference on Labour History: Oxford 1988*, Amsterdam, Stichting beheer IISG, 23–37.

(1992) 'Communism and trade union militancy in the Scottish coalfields', in Tenfelde, Klaus (ed.), *Towards a Social History of Mining in the 19th and 20th Centuries: Papers Presented to the International Mining History Congress Bochum, Federal Republic of Germany, September 3rd-7th, 1989*, Munich, Verlag C. H. Beck, 85–104.

(1995) 'The Communist Party in the Scots coalfield in the inter-war period', in Andrews, Geoff, Fishman, Nina, and Morgan, Kevin (eds.), *Opening the Books: Essays on the Social and Cultural History of British Communism*, London, Pluto Press, 44–63.

Campbell, Alan, B., and Reid, Fred (1978) 'The independent collier in Scotland', ch. 2 of Harrison, Royden (ed.), *Independent Collier: the Coal Miner as Archetypal Proletarian Reconsidered*, Hassocks, Harvester Press, 54–74.

Carr, Bill (1976) 'From the Yorkshire coalfield', in Skelley, Jeffrey (ed.), *The General Strike: 1926*, London, Lawrence and Wishart, 340–51.

Carr-Saunders, A. M., and Wilson, Paul Alexander (1933) *The Professions*, Oxford, Clarendon Press.

Carvel, John L. (1948) *The Coltness Iron Company: a Study in Private Enterprise*, London, Constable.

Cawley, Roger (1984) 'British coal owners, 1881–1893: the search for structure', doctoral thesis, State University of New York at Binghamton.

Challinor, Raymond (1972) *The Lancashire and Cheshire Miners*, Newcastle-upon-Tyne, Frank Graham.

Chaplin, Helen Louise (1992) 'The 1905 Kinsley evictions: a study of a Yorkshire coalmining community', MA dissertation, School of History, University of Leeds.

Charemza, Wojciech W., and Deadman, Derek. F. (1992) *New Directions in Econometric Practice*, Aldershot, Edward Elgar.

Church, Roy (1987) 'Edwardian labour unrest and coalfield militancy, 1890–1914', *The Historical Journal*, 30(4), 841–57.

(1990) 'Employers, trade unions and the state, 1889–1987: the origins and decline of tripartism in the British coal industry', ch. 2 of Feldman, Gerald D., and Tenfelde, Klaus (eds.), *Workers, Owners and Politics in Coal Mining: an International Comparison of Industrial Relations*, New York, Berg, 12–73.

Church, Roy, with the assistance of Hall, Alan, and Kanefsky, John (1986) *The History of the British Coal Industry*. Vol. III: *1830–1913: Victorian Pre-eminence*, Oxford, Clarendon Press.

Church, Roy, Outram, Quentin, and Smith, David N. (1989a) 'Towards a history of British miners' militancy', *Bulletin of the Society for the Study of Labour History*, 54(1), 21–36.

(1989b) 'British coal mining strikes: 1893–1940: dimensions and distributions', University of Leeds, *School of Business and Economic Studies Discussion Paper Series*, No. 89/7.

(1990) 'British coal mining strikes, 1893–1940: dimensions, distribution and persistence', *British Journal of Industrial Relations*, 28(3), 329–49.

(1991a) 'The militancy of British miners 1893–1986: interdisciplinary problems and perspectives', *Journal of Interdisciplinary History*, 22(1), 49–66.

(1991b) 'The "isolated mass" revisited: strikes in British coal mining', *Sociological Review* (New Series), 39(1), 55–87.

(1992) 'Theoretical orientations to miners' strikes', in Tenfelde, Klaus (ed.), *Towards a Social History of Mining in the 19th and 20th Centuries: Papers Presented to the International Mining History Congress Bochum, Federal Republic of Germany, September 3rd–7th, 1989*, Munich, Verlag C. H. Beck, 565–81.

(1995) 'Down and out in Wigan and Barnsley: British coal mining strikes under private ownership', *Scottish Journal of Political Economy*, 42(2), 127–51.

Citrine, Lord (1964) *Men and Work: an Autobiography*, London, Hutchinson.

Clarke, J. F. (1969) 'An interview with Sir William Lawther', *Bulletin of the Society for the Study of Labour History*, 19, 14–21.

Clegg, Hugh Armstrong (1976) *The System of Industrial Relations in Great Britain*, third edition, Oxford, Basil Blackwell.

(1979) *The Changing System of Industrial Relations in Great Britain*, Oxford, Basil Blackwell.

(1985) *A History of British Trade Unions Since 1889*. Vol. II: *1911–1933*, Oxford, Clarendon Press.

Clegg, Hugh Armstrong, and Chester, T. E. (1953) *The Future of Nationalization*, Oxford, Basil Blackwell.

Clegg, Hugh Armstrong, Fox, Alan, and Thompson, A. F. (1964) *A History of British Trade Unions Since 1889*. Vol. I: *1889–1910*, Oxford, Clarendon Press.

Cliff, Dave (1986) 'Memoir: North Staffs, a tale of two pits', in Samuel, Raphael, Bloomfield, Barbara, and Boanas, Guy (eds.), *The Enemy Within: Pit Villages and the Miners' Strike of 1984–5*, London, Routledge and Kegan Paul, 86–92.

Coates, Ken (ed.) (1974) *Democracy in the Mines: Some Documents of the Controversy on Mines Nationalisation up to the Time of the Sankey Commission*, Nottingham, Bertrand Russell Peace Foundation for Spokesman Books.

Cole, G. D. H. (1913) *The World of Labour: a Discussion of the Present and Future of Trade Unionism*, London, G. Bell and Sons.

(1923) *Labour in the Coal-Mining Industry, (1914–1921)*, (Carnegie Endowment for International Peace, Division of Economics and History, Economic and Social History of the World War, British Series), Oxford, Clarendon Press.

(1927) *A Short History of the British Working Class Movement 1789–1927*. Vol. III: *1900–1927*, London, George Allen and Unwin and the Labour Publishing Co.

(1949) *The National Coal Board, its Tasks, its Organisation and its Prospects*, Revised edition, (Fabian Research Series No. 129), London, Fabian Publications and Gollancz.

The Colliery Guardian, weekly, London, The Colliery Guardian Co.

The Colliery Year Book and Coal Trades Directory, annually, London, The Louis Cassier Co.

Colls, Robert (1987) *The Pitmen of the Northern Coalfield: Work, Culture, and Protest,*

1790–1850, Manchester, Manchester University Press.

Cooke, Philip (ed.) (1989) *Localities: the Changing Face of Urban Britain*, London, Unwin Hyman.

Corbin, David A. (1981) *Life, Work, and Rebellion in the Coal Fields: the Southern West Virginia Miners, 1880–1922*, Urbana, University of Illinois Press.

Court, W. H. B. (1951) *Coal*, (History of the Second World War: United Kingdom Civil Series), London, HMSO and Longmans, Green.

Cousins, J. M., and Davis, R. L. (1974) ' "Working class incorporation"—a historical approach with reference to the mining communities of S. E. Northumberland 1840–1890', in Parkin, Frank (ed.), *The Social Analysis of Class Structure*, London, Tavistock Publications, 275–97.

Cowling, Maurice (1971) *The Impact of Labour, 1920–1924: the Beginning of Modern British Politics*, Cambridge, Cambridge University Press.

Crew, David F. (1986) 'Class and community: local research on working-class history in four countries', in Tenfelde, Klaus (ed.), *Arbeiter und Arbeiterbewegung im Vergleich: Berichte zur Internationalen historischen Forschung*, (*Historische Zeitschrift*, Sonderhefte, 15), Munich, Oldenbourg, 279–336.

Cronin, James E. (1979) *Industrial Conflict in Modern Britain*, London, Croom Helm.

(1982) 'Strikes, 1870–1914', in Wrigley, Chris (ed.), *A History of British Industrial Relations 1875–1914*, Brighton, Harvester Press.

(1985) 'Strikes and the struggle for union organization: Britain and Europe', ch. 3 of Mommsen, Wolfgang J., and Husung, Hans-Gerhard (eds.), *The Development of Trade Unionism in Great Britain and Germany, 1880–1914*, London, George Allen and Unwin, 55–77.

(1989) 'The "rank and file" and the social history of the working class', *International Review of Social History*, 34, 78–88.

Crook, Wilfrid Harris (1931) *The General Strike; a Study of Labor's Tragic Weapon in Theory and Practice*, Chapel Hill, University of North Carolina Press.

Daunton, M. J. (1980) 'Miners' houses: South Wales and the Great Northern coalfield, 1880–1914', *International Review of Social History*, 25(2), 143–75.

(1981) 'Down the pit: work in the Great Northern and South Wales coalfields, 1870–1914', *Economic History Review* (Second Series), 34(4), 578–97.

Davidson, Roger (1972) 'Llewellyn Smith, the Labour Department and government growth 1886–1909', ch. 9 of Sutherland, Gillian (ed.), *Studies in the Growth of Nineteenth-Century Government*, London, Routledge and Kegan Paul, 227–62.

Davies, Paul (1987) *A. J. Cook*, Manchester, Manchester University Press.

Dennis, Norman, Henriques, Fernando, and Slaughter, Clifford (1956) *Coal is Our Life: an Analysis of a Yorkshire Mining Community*, London, Eyre and Spottiswoode.

Dintenfass, Michael (1985) 'Managing industrial decline: four British colliery companies between the wars', doctoral thesis, Columbia University.

Dobb, Maurice (1963) *Studies in the Development of Capitalism*, revised edition, London, Routledge and Kegan Paul (first edition: 1946).

Douglass, Dave (1972) *Pit Life in County Durham: Rank and File Movements and Workers' Control*, (*History Workshop* Pamphlet No. 6), Oxford, Ruskin College. (Reprinted as Douglass 1977).

(1977) 'The Durham pitman', part 4 of Samuel, Raphael (ed.), *Miners, Quarrymen and Saltworkers*, London, Routledge and Kegan Paul, 205–95.

Downing, J. M., and Gore, Van (1983) 'Company paternalism and the butty system: conversation with Creswell residents', *Bulletin of the Society for the Study of Labour History*, 46, 21–9.

Duncan, Robert (1986) *Bothwellhaugh: a Lanarkshire Mining Community, 1884–1965*, Bothwellhaugh, Workers' Educational Association.

Durcan, J. W., McCarthy, William E. J., and Redman, G. P. (1983) *Strikes in Post-War Britain: a Study of Stoppages of Work due to Industrial Disputes, 1946–1973*, London, George Allen and Unwin.

Durkheim, Emile (1893/1984) *The Division of Labour in Society*, (trans. Halls, W. D.) London, Macmillan (first French edition: 1893).

Edwards, Christine (1978) 'Measuring union power: a comparison of two methods applied to the study of local union power in the coal industry', *British Journal of Industrial Relations*, 16(1), 1–15.

Edwards, Christine, and Heery, Edmund (1985) 'Formality and informality in the working of the National Coal Board's incentive scheme', *British Journal of Industrial Relations*, 23(1), 25–45.

Edwards, Clem (1893) 'The lock-out in the coal trade', *Economic Journal*, 3(4), 650–7.

Edwards, Ness (1938) *History of the South Wales Miners' Federation*. Vol. I, London, Lawrence and Wishart.

Edwards, P. K. (1977) 'A critique of the Kerr-Siegel hypothesis of strikes and the isolated mass: a study of the falsification of sociological knowledge', *Sociological Review* (New Series), 23(3), 551–74.

(1980) 'Size of plant and strike-proneness', *Oxford Bulletin of Economics and Statistics*, 42(2), 145–56.

(1981) *Strikes in the United States 1881–1974*, Oxford, Basil Blackwell.

(1983) 'The pattern of collective industrial action', ch. 9 of Bain, George Sayers (ed.), *Industrial Relations in Britain*, Oxford, Basil Blackwell, 209–34.

(1986) *Conflict at Work: a Materialist Analysis of Workplace Relations*, Oxford, Basil Blackwell.

(1988) 'Patterns of conflict and accommodation', ch. 7 of Gallie, Duncan (ed.), *Employment in Britain*, Oxford, Basil Blackwell, 187–217.

Edwards, P. K., and Scullion, Hugh (1982) *The Social Organization of Industrial Conflict: Control and Resistance in the Workplace*, Oxford, Basil Blackwell.

Edwards, Richard C. (1979) *Contested Terrain: the Transformation of the Workplace in the Twentieth Century*, New York, Basic Books.

Eisele, C. Frederick (1974) 'Organization size, technology, and frequency of strikes', *Industrial and Labor Relations Review*, 27(4), 560–71.

Eldridge, J. E. T. (1968) *Industrial Disputes: Essays in the Sociology of Industrial Relations*, London, Routledge and Kegan Paul.

Evans, David (1911) *Labour Strife in the South Wales Coalfield 1910–1911: a Historical and Critical Record of the Mid-Rhondda, Aberdare Valley and other Strikes*, Cardiff, Educational Publishing Co, 1911 (Reprinted, Cardiff, Cymric Federation Press, 1963).

Evans, E. W. (1961) *The Miners of South Wales*, Cardiff, University of Wales Press.

Fagge, Roger J. (1992) 'A comparison of the miners of South Wales and West Virginia, 1900–1922: patterns of militancy', in Tenfelde, Klaus (ed.), *Towards a Social History of Mining in the 19th and 20th Centuries: Papers Presented to the International Mining History Congress Bochum, Federal Republic of Germany, September 3rd-7th, 1989*, Munich, Verlag C. H. Beck, 105–22.

Farman, Christopher (1972) *The General Strike: May 1926*, London, Rupert Hart-Davis.

Feinstein, C. H. (1972) *National Income, Expenditure and Output of the United Kingdom, 1855–1965*, Cambridge, Cambridge University Press.

Feldman, Gerald D. (1990) 'Industrial relations in the coal industry in twentieth-century Europe and the USA: a historical and comparative perspective', ch. 8 of Feldman,

Gerald D. and Tenfelde, Klaus (eds.), *Workers, Owners and Politics in Coal Mining: an International Comparison of Industrial Relations*, New York, Berg, 361–94.

Feldman Gerald D., and Tenfelde, Klaus (eds.) (1990) *Workers, Owners and Politics in Coal Mining: an International Comparison of Industrial Relations*, New York, Berg.

Fine, Ben, O'Donnell, Kathy, and Prevezer, Martha (1985a) 'Coal before nationalisation', ch. 11 of Fine, Ben, and Harris, Laurence, *The Peculiarities of the British Economy*, London, Lawrence and Wishart, 285–319.

(1985b) 'Coal after nationalisation', ch. 6 of Fine, Ben and Harris, Laurence, *The Peculiarities of the British Economy*, London, Lawrence and Wishart, 1985, 167–202.

Fishback, Price V. (1992) *Soft Coal, Hard Choices: the Economic Welfare of Bituminous Coal Miners, 1890–1930*, New York, Oxford University Press.

Fisher, Chris (1981) *Custom, Work and Market Capitalism: the Forest of Dean Colliers, 1788–1888*, London, Croom Helm.

Fisher, Chris, and Smethurst, John (1978) ' "War on the law of supply and demand": the Amalgamated Association of Miners and the Forest of Dean colliers, 1869–1875', ch. 4 of Harrison, Royden (ed.), *Independent Collier: the Coal Miner as Archetypal Proletarian Reconsidered*, Hassocks, Harvester Press, 114–55.

Fishman, Nina (1991) 'The British Communist Party and the trade unions, 1933–1945: the dilemmas of revolutionary pragmatism', doctoral thesis, University of London.

(1995) *The British Communist Party and the Trade Unions, 1933–45*, Aldershot, Scolar Press.

Fitzgerald, Robert (1988) *British Labour Management and Industrial Welfare 1846–1939*, London, Croom Helm.

Fitzpatrick, John S. (1980) 'Adapting to danger: a participant observation study of an underground mine', *Sociology of Work and Occupations*, 7(2), 131–58.

Foster, John (1976) 'British Imperialism and the labour aristocracy', ch. 1.1 of Skelley, Jeffrey (ed.), *The General Strike: 1926*, London, Lawrence and Wishart, 3–57.

Francis, Hywel (1973) 'The anthracite strike and disturbances of 1925', *Llafur*, 1(2), 15–28.

(1980) 'The secret world of the South Wales miner: the relevance of oral history', in Smith, David (ed.), *A People and A Proletariat: Essays in the History of Wales: 1780–1980*, London, Pluto Press in association with Llafur, the Society for the Study of Welsh Labour History, 166–80.

Francis, Hywel, and Rees, G. (1989) 'No surrender in the villages: the 1984–85 miners' strike in South Wales', *Llafur*, 5(2), 41–71.

Francis, Hywel, and Smith, David (1980) *The Fed: a History of the South Wales Miners in the Twentieth Century*, London, Lawrence and Wishart.

Freeman, Daniel H. (1987) *Applied Categorical Data Analysis*, New York, Marcel Dekker.

Friedman, Andrew L. (1977) *Industry and Labour: Class Struggle at Work and Monopoly Capitalism*, London, Macmillan.

(1987) 'The means of management control and labour process theory: a critical note on Storey', *Sociology*, 21(2), 287–94.

Fynes, Richard (1873/1972) *The Miners of Northumberland and Durham*, Newcastle, Cooperative Press Printing Society Group, 1972 (first edition: Sunderland, Thomas Sumerbell, 1873).

Gallacher, William (1906) 'Coal cutting machinery in Lanarkshire mines', in *Report of the Lanarkshire Miners' County Union for the period ending 31 December, 1906*, 14–19, National Library of Scotland Deposit 227(29). (Reprinted in *Bulletin of the Society for the Study of Labour History*, 49, 43–5 (1984). Page references are to the reprint).

Gallie, Duncan (1978) *In Search of the New Working Class: Automation and Social Integration within the Capitalist Enterprise*, Cambridge, Cambridge University Press.

Garside, W. R. (1971) *The Durham Miners 1919–1960*, London, George Allen and Unwin.

Geary, Dick (1981) *European Labour Protest 1848–1939*, London, Croom Helm.

(1986) 'Protest and strike: recent research on "collective action" in England, Germany, and France', in Tenfelde, Klaus (ed.), *Arbeiter und Arbeiterbewegung im Vergleich: Berichte zur Internationalen historischen Forschung*, (*Historische Zeitschrift*, Sonderhefte, 15), Munich, Oldenbourg, 363–87.

Giddens, Anthony (1979) *Central Problems in Social Theory: Action, Structure and Contradiction in Social Analysis*, London, Macmillan.

Gilbert, David (1992) *Class, Community, and Collective Action: Social Change in Two British Coalfields, 1850–1926*, Oxford, Clarendon Press.

Goffee, Robert E. (1977) 'The butty system and the Kent coalfield', *Bulletin of the Society for the Study of Labour History*, 34, 41–55.

(1981) 'Incorporation and conflict: a case study of subcontracting in the coal industry', *Sociological Review* (New Series), 29(3), 475–97.

Goldthorpe, John H. (1959) 'Technical organization as a factor in supervisor-worker conflict: some preliminary observations on a study made in the mining industry', *British Journal of Sociology*, 10(3), 213–30.

Goodrich, Carter L. (1920/1975) *The Frontier of Control: a Study in British Workshop Politics*, London, Pluto Press, 1975 (first edition: London, G. Bell, 1920).

(1926) *The Miner's Freedom: A Study of the Working Life in a Changing Industry*, New York, Workers' Education Bureau of America.

Gospel, Howard F. (1992) *Markets, Firms, and the Management of Labour in Modern Britain*, Cambridge, Cambridge University Press.

Gospel, Howard F. and Littler, Craig R. (1983) *Managerial Strategies and Industrial Relations: an Historical and Comparative Study*, London, Heinemann Educational.

Gouldner, Alvin W. (1954) *Wildcat Strike: a Study in Worker-Management Relationships*, Yellow Springs, Antioch Press.

Graebner, William (1974) 'Great expectations: the search for order in bituminous coal, 1890–1917', *Business History Review*, 48(1), 49–72.

Greasley, David (1982) 'The diffusion of machine cutting in the British coal industry, 1902–1938', *Explorations in Economic History*, 19(3), 246–68.

(1995) 'The coal industry: images and realities on the road to nationalisation', ch. 3 of Millward, Robert, and Singleton, John (eds.), *The Political Economy of Nationalisation in Britain 1920–1950*, Cambridge, Cambridge University Press, 37–64.

Greene, William H. (1987–92) *LIMDEP: Version 6.0: User's Manual*, Bellport, Econometric Software, Inc.

Greenwell, Herbert (1933) 'The employer's point of view: II: the man and the machine', *The Human Factor*, 7(9), 300–6.

Gregory, Derek, and Urry, John (eds.) (1985) *Social Relations and Spatial Structures*, Basingstoke, Macmillan.

Gregory, Roy (1968) *The Miners and British Politics 1906–1914*, London, Oxford University Press.

Griffin, Alan. R. (1962) *The Miners of Nottinghamshire 1914–1944: a History of the Nottinghamshire Miners' Unions*, London, George Allen and Unwin.

(1971) *Mining in the East Midlands 1550–1947*, London, Frank Cass.

(1977) '[Letter]', *Bulletin of the Society for the Study of Labour History*, 35, 30–1.

(1978) '[Letter] Non-political or company unionism', *Bulletin of the Society for the Study of Labour History*, 37, 13.

Griffin, Alan R., and Griffin, Colin P. (1977) 'The non-political trade union movement', in Briggs, Asa, and Saville, John (eds.), *Essays in Labour History, 1918–1939*. [Vol. III], London, Croom Helm, 133–62.

Griffin, Colin P. (1987) 'Conciliation in the coal mining industry before 1914: the experience of the Leicestershire coalfield', *Midland History*, 12, 67–84.

([1982]) *The Leicestershire and South Derbyshire Miners*. Vol. I: *1840–1914*, Coalville, National Union of Mineworkers Leicester Area.

(1984) *Nottinghamshire Miners between the Wars: the Spencer Union Revisited*, Nottingham, University of Nottingham, Department of Adult Education, Centre for Local History.

Griffin, Colin P. (ed.) (1990) *The Nottinghamshire Miners' Industrial Union: Rufford Branch Minutes 1926–36; District Minutes 1926–7*, (Thoroton Society Record Series, Vol. xxxviii), Nottingham, Thoroton Society.

Gregory, Roy (1968) *The Miners and British Politics 1906–1914*, Oxford, Oxford University Press.

Guide to the Coalfields, annually, London, The Colliery Guardian Co. Ltd.

Hair, P. E. H. (1955) 'The social history of the British coal miners, 1800–45', doctoral thesis, Oxford University.

Handy, L. J. (1981) *Wages Policy in the British Coalmining Industry: a Study of National Wage Bargaining*, Cambridge, Cambridge University Press.

Hare, A. E. C. (1940) *The Anthracite Coal Industry of the Swansea District*, (University College of Swansea, Social and Economic Survey of Swansea and District, Pamphlet no. 5), Cardiff, University of Wales Press Board.

Hausman, Jerry A., and Wise, David A. (1979) 'Attrition bias in experimental and panel data: the Gary income maintenance experiment', *Econometrica*, 47(2), 455–73.

Hayes, Beth (1984) 'Unions and strikes with asymmetric information', *Journal of Labor Economics*, 2(1), 57–83.

Hechter, M. (1975) *Internal Colonialism: the Celtic Fringe in British National Development, 1536–1966*, London, Routledge and Kegan Paul.

Hickey, S. H. F. (1985) *Workers in Imperial Germany: the Miners of the Ruhr*, Oxford, Clarendon Press.

Hicks, J. R. (1932) *The Theory of Wages*, London, Macmillan.

Hobsbawm, Eric J. (1964) 'Trade union historiography', *Bulletin of the Society for the Study of Labour History*, 8, 31–6.

Hodges, Frank (1920) *Nationalization of the Mines*, London, Leonard Parsons.

([1925]) *My Adventures as a Labour Leader*, London, George Newnes.

Holton, Bob [Robert J.] (1976) *British Syndicalism, 1900–1914: Myths and Realities*, London, Pluto Press.

Holton, Robert J. (1985) 'Revolutionary Syndicalism and the British labour movement', ch. 15 of Mommsen, Wolfgang J., and Husung, Hans-Gerhard (eds.), *The Development of Trade Unionism in Great Britain and Germany, 1880–1914*, London, George Allen and Unwin, 266–82.

Hopper, Trevor, Cooper, David, Lowe, Tony, Capps, Teresa, and Mouritsen, Jan (1986) 'Management control and worker resistance in the National Coal Board: financial controls in the labour process', ch. 6 of Knights, David and Willmott, Hugh (eds.), *Managing the Labour Process*, Aldershot, Gower, 109–41.

Horner, Arthur (1960) *Incorrigible Rebel*, London, MacGibbon and Kee.

Howell, David (1983) *British Workers and the Independent Labour Party 1888–1906*, Manchester, Manchester University Press.

Howells, Kim (1979) 'The South Wales miners, 1937–1957: a view from below', doctoral thesis, University of Warwick.

Hutt, Allen (1937) *The Post-War History of the British Working Class*, London, Victor Gollancz.

Hyman, Richard (1972) *Strikes*, Glasgow, Fontana, William Collins Sons and Co.

(1975) *Industrial Relations: a Marxist Introduction*, London, Macmillan.

(1984) *Strikes*, third edition, no place, Fontana.

Ingham, Geoffrey K. (1970) *Size of Industrial Organization and Worker Behaviour*, Cambridge, Cambridge University Press.

Jencks, Clinton E. (1966) 'British coal: labor relations since nationalization', *Industrial Relations* [California], 6(1), 95–110.

Jenkins, Roy (1960) 'Not really a rebel', *The Observer*, 18 December.

Jevons, H. Stanley (1915/1969) *The British Coal Trade*, Newton Abbot, David and Charles Reprints 1969 (first edition: London, Kegan Paul Trench Trubner, 1915).

Jones, Carol (1985) 'The industrial relations of the Northumberland and Durham coal industry 1825–1845', doctoral thesis, Sunderland Polytechnic.

Jones, J. Harry, Cartwright, G., and Guénault, P. H. (1939) *The Coal-Mining Industry: an International Study in Planning*, London, Sir Isaac Pitman.

Jones, Joseph (1936) *The Coal Scuttle*, London, Faber.

Jones, Lewis (1937/1978) *Cwmardy: the Story of a Welsh Mining Valley*, London, Lawrence and Wishart, 1978 (first edition: London, Lawrence and Wishart, 1937).

Journal of the Royal Statistical Society (1893) 'Miscellanea: VI. The Labour Department and the Labour Gazette', *Journal of the Royal Statistical Society*, 56(2), 330–3.

Joyce, Patrick (1980) *Work, Society and Politics: the Culture of the Factory in Later Victorian England*, Brighton, Harvester Press.

Kahn, Margaret Felicia (1984) 'The National Union of Mineworkers and the revival of industrial militancy in the 1970s', doctoral thesis, University of California, Berkeley.

Kahn, Peggy (1982) '[Tommy Mullany]', *Bulletin of the Society for the Study of Labour History*, 44, 49–58.

Kerr, Clark, and Siegel, Abraham (1954) 'The interindustry propensity to strike—an international comparison', ch. 14 of Kornhauser, Arthur, Dubin, Robert, and Ross, Arthur M. (eds.), *Industrial Conflict*, New York, McGraw-Hill, 189–212.

Kirby, M. W. (1977) *The British Coalmining Industry, 1870–1946: a Political and Economic History*, London, Macmillan.

Knights, David, Willmott, Hugh, and Collinson, David (eds.) (1985) *Job Redesign: Critical Perspectives on the Labour Process*, Aldershot, Gower.

Knowles, K. G. J. C. (1952) *Strikes: a Study in Industrial Conflict: with Special Reference to British Experience between 1911 and 1947*, Oxford, Basil Blackwell.

Krieger, Joel (1984) *Undermining Capitalism: State Ownership and the Dialectic of Control in the British Coal Industry*, Pluto Press, London (first edition: Princeton, Princeton University Press, 1983).

Lancaster Regionalism Group (1985) *Localities Class and Gender*, London, Pion Press.

Laslett, Peter (1983) *The World We Have Lost: Further Explored*, third edition, London, Methuen.

Lawson, Jack (1941) *The Man in the Cap: the Life of Herbert Smith*, London, Methuen.

Lawther, Will (1927) 'One miners' union – now', *Plebs*, 19, 124–7.

Lee, C. H. (1979) *British Regional Employment Statistics 1841–1971*, Cambridge, Cambridge University Press.

Lee, W. A. ([1924]) 'The history of organisation in the coal industry', ch. 23 of Mining Association of Great Britain, *Historical Review of Coalmining*, London, Fleetway Press, 351–77.

Lewis, Evan David (1959) *The Rhondda Valleys: a Study in Industrial Development: 1800 to the Present Day*, London, Phoenix House.

Lincoln, James R. (1978) 'Community structure and industrial conflict: an analysis of strike activity in SMSAs', *American Sociological Review*, 43, 199–220.

Lockwood, David (1966) 'Sources of variation in working-class images of society', *Sociological Review* (New Series), 14(3), 249–67. (Reprinted as ch. 2 of Bulmer, Martin I. A. (ed.) (1975) *Working-Class Images of Society*, London, Routledge and Kegan Paul, 16–31. Page references are to the reprint).

Long, Paul Brook (1978) 'The economic and social history of the Scottish coal industry, 1925–1939, with particular reference to industrial relations', doctoral thesis, University of Strathclyde.

Lowe, Rodney (ed.) (1985) *Conflict and Consensus in British Industrial Relations, 1916–1946*, Brighton, Harvester Microform.

Lyddon, Dave and Smith, Paul (1996) 'Editorial: industrial relations and history', *Historical Studies in Industrial Relations*, 1, 1–10.

MacDougall, J. D. (1927) 'The Scottish coalminer', *The Nineteenth Century and After*, 102, 762–81.

MacFarlane, James (1972) 'Denaby Main: a South Yorkshire mining village', *Bulletin of the Society for the Study of Labour History*, 25, 82–100.

(1976a) 'One association – the Yorkshire Miners' Association: the Denaby Main Lock-out of 1885', ch. 5 of Pollard, Sidney and Holmes, Colin (eds.), *Essays in the Economic and Social History of South Yorkshire*, Sheffield, Recreation, Culture and Health Department, South Yorkshire County Council. (Copy in Leeds City Public Libraries).

(1976b) 'Denaby Main: a South Yorkshire mining village', ch. 6 of Benson, J., and Neville, R. G. (eds.), *Studies in the Yorkshire Coal Industry*, Manchester, Manchester University Press, 109–44.

Macfarlane, L. J. (1966) *The British Communist Party: its Origin and Development until 1929*, London, MacGibbon and Kee.

Machin, Frank (1958) *The Yorkshire Miners: a History*. Vol. I, Barnsley, National Union of Mineworkers (Yorkshire Area).

Macintyre, Stuart (1980a) *Little Moscows: Communism and Working-Class Militancy in Inter-war Britain*, London, Croom Helm.

(1980b) *A Proletarian Science: Marxism in Britain, 1917–1933*, Cambridge, Cambridge University Press.

MacIver, R. M., and Page, Charles H. (1950) *Society: an Introductory Analysis*, London, Macmillan Co.

MacSwinney, Robert Foster, and Lloyd-Greame, P. (1912) *The Coal Mines Act 1911: and Other Acts Affecting Mines and Quarries: with a Commentary*, London, Sweet and Maxwell.

Maddala, G. S. (1977) *Econometrics*, Tokyo, McGraw-Hill Kogakusha.

Manley, E. R. (1947) *Meet the Miner: a Study of the Yorkshire Miner at Work, at Home and in Public Life*, Lofthouse, the author.

Marginson, Paul M. (1984) 'The distinctive effects of plant and company size on workplace industrial relations', *British Journal of Industrial Relations*, 22(1), 1–14.

Marsh, Arthur, and Ryan, Victoria (1984) *Historical Directory of Trade Unions*. Vol. II, Aldershot, Gower.

Martin, Roderick (1969) *Communism and the British Trade Unions 1924–1933: a Study of the National Minority Movement*, Oxford, Clarendon Press.

Marx, Karl (1847/1976) *The Poverty of Philosophy: Answer to the* Philosophy of Poverty *by M. Proudhon*, in Marx, Karl, and Engels, Frederick, *Collected Works*. Vol. VI: *Marx and Engels: 1845–48*, London, Lawrence and Wishart, 1976, 105–212 (first French edition: 1847).

   (1867/1976) *Capital: a Critique of Political Economy: Volume One* (trans. Ben Fowkes) Harmondsworth, Penguin Books in association with New Left Review, 1976 (first German edition: 1867).

Mason, Anthony (1970) *The General Strike in the North East*, (University of Hull Occasional Papers in Economic and Social History No. 3), Hull, University of Hull Publications.

Massey, Doreen (1984) *Spatial Divisions of Labour: Social Structures and the Geography of Production*, London, Macmillan.

Mavor, S. (1924) 'The problems of mechanical coal mining', *Colliery Guardian*, 129 (3311), 1510–11 (13 June).

McCormick, Brian J. (1969) 'Strikes in the Yorkshire coalfield, 1947–1963', *Economic Studies*, 4(1/2), 171–97. (Reprinted in Kelly, David M., and Forsyth, David. J. C. (eds.) (1969) *Studies in the British Coal Industry*, London, Pergamon Press, 171–97).

   (1979) *Industrial Relations in the Coal Industry*, London, Macmillan.

Melling, Joseph (1979) 'Industrial strife and business welfare philosophy: the case of the South Metropolitan Gas Company from the 1880s to the war', *Business History*, 21(2), 163–79.

   (1981) 'Employers, industrial housing and the evolution of company welfare policies in Britain's heavy industry: west Scotland, 1870–1920', *International Review of Social History*, 26, 255–301.

Michel, Joël (1987) 'Le Mouvement ouvrier chez les mineurs d'Europe occidentale (Grand-Bretagne, Belgique, France, Allemagne): étude comparative des années 1880 à 1914' (6 volumes), Thèse d'Etat, Université de Lyon II.

   (1990) 'Industrial relations in French coal mining from the late nineteenth century to the 1970s', ch. 6 of Feldman, Gerald D., and Tenfelde, Klaus (eds.), *Workers, Owners and Politics in Coal Mining: an International Comparison of Industrial Relations*, New York, Berg, 271–314.

   (1992) 'Bergarbeiter-Kommunen und Patriarchalismus in Westeuropa vor 1914', in Tenfelde, Klaus (ed.), *Towards a Social History of Mining in the 19th and 20th Centuries: Papers Presented to the International Mining History Congress Bochum, Federal Republic of Germany, September 3rd–7th, 1989*, Munich, Verlag C. H. Beck, 58–84.

Miller, Donald L., and Sharpless, Richard E. (1985) *The Kingdom of Coal: Work, Enterprise, and Ethnic Communities in the Mine Fields*, Philadelphia, University of Pennsylvania Press.

Mitchell, B. R. (1984) *Economic Development of the British Coal Industry 1800–1914*, Cambridge, Cambridge University Press.

Montgomery, David (1991) 'The limits of union-centered history: responses to Howard Kimeldorf', pp. 110–16 of Kazin, M., 'The limits of union-centered history: response', *Labor History*, 32, 104–27.

Morgan, John E. ([1956]) *A Village Workers' Council and What it Accomplished, being a Short History of the Lady Windsor Lodge, S. W.M.F.*, Pontypridd, Celtic Press.

Morgan, Kenneth O. (1972–3) 'The new Liberalism and the challenge of Labour: the Welsh experience, 1885–1929', *Welsh History Review*, 6, 288–312.

   (1975) 'Socialism and syndicalism: the Welsh miners' debate, 1912', *Bulletin of the Society for the Study of Labour History*, 30, 22–37.

(1981) *Wales 1880–1980: Rebirth of a Nation*, Oxford, Clarendon Press.

(1985) 'A time for miners to forget history', *New Society*, 71, 283–5 (21 February).

(1987) *Labour People: Leaders and Lieutenants: Hardie to Kinnock*, Oxford, Oxford University Press.

Mór-O'Brien, Anthony (1984–5a) 'Patriotism on trial: the strike of the South Wales miners, July 1915', *Welsh History Review*, 12, 76–104.

(1984–5b) 'The Merthyr Borough election, November 1915', *Welsh History Review*, 12, 538–66.

Morris, J. H. and Williams, L. J. (1957) 'The discharge note in the South Wales coal industry, 1841–1898', *Economic History Review* (Second Series), 10(2), 286–93.

(1958) *The South Wales Coal Industry 1841–1875*, Cardiff, University of Wales Press.

Morris, Julia, Sapsford, David, and Turnbull, Peter (1994) 'Persistent militants and quiescent comrades: intra-industry strike activity on the docks, 1947–89', unpublished paper, University of Leeds, School of Business & Economic Studies.

Morris, Margaret (1976) *The General Strike*, Harmondsworth, Penguin Books.

Munro, J. E. Crawford (1885) *Sliding Scales in the Coal Industry: a Paper Read before the British Association, Section F, Aberdeen, 1885*, Manchester, John Heywood. (Copy in Brotherton Library, University of Leeds).

Neuman, Andrew Martin (1934) *Economic Organization of the British Coal Industry*, London, George Routledge.

Neville, Robert G. (1974) 'The Yorkshire miners 1881–1926: a study in labour and social history' (2 volumes), doctoral thesis, University of Leeds.

(1976) 'In the wake of Taff Vale: the Denaby and Cadeby miners' strike and conspiracy case, 1902–06' ch. 7 of Benson, J., and Neville, R. G. (eds.), *Studies in the Yorkshire Coal Industry*, Manchester, Manchester University Press, 145–62.

Newton, Kenneth (1969) *The Sociology of British Communism*, London, Allen Lane, The Penguin Press.

Outram, Quentin (1982) 'The British coal mining industry: the 1924 National Wages Agreement', University of Leeds, *School of Economic Studies Discussion Paper*, no. 117.

(1997) 'The Ministry of Labour records of coalmining strikes 1903–1940: a guide to the dataset deposited in the ESRC Data Archive', unpublished paper held at ESRC Data Archive, Essex University.

Park, Robert Ezra (1952) *Human Communities: the City and Human Ecology*, Glencoe, Illinois, The Free Press.

Paterson, T. T. (1956) 'Scale factors in coal-mining labour indices', *Operational Research Quarterly*, 7(4), 155–64.

Paterson, T. T., and Willett, F. J. (1951) 'Unofficial strike', *Sociological Review* [First Series], 43 (Section 4), dual pagination: pp. 1–38 of article printed at pp. 57–94 of journal.

Paynter, Will (1972) *My Generation*, London, George Allen and Unwin.

The People of Thurcroft (1986) *Thurcroft: a Village and the Miners' Strike: an Oral History* (eds. Peter Gibbon and David Steyne), Nottingham, Spokesman.

Petras, James, and Zeitlin, Maurice (1967) 'Miners and agrarian radicalism', *American Sociological Review*, 32, 578–86.

Phelps Brown, E. H. (1959) *The Growth of British Industrial Relations: a Study from the Standpoint of 1906–14*, London, Macmillan.

(1986) *The Origins of Trade Union Power*, revised edition, Oxford, Oxford University Press.

Phillips, Elizabeth (1925) *A History of the Pioneers of the Welsh Coalfield*, Cardiff, Western Mail.

Phillips, G. A. (1976) *The General Strike: the Politics of Industrial Conflict*, London, Wiedenfeld and Nicolson.

Pick, J. B. (1946) *Under the Crust*, London, John Lane.

Pitt, Malcolm (1979) *The World on Our Backs: The Kent Miners and the 1972 Miners' Strike*, London, Lawrence and Wishart.

Piore, Michael J. and Sabel, Charles F. ([1984]) *The Second Industrial Divide: Possibilities for Prosperity*, New York, Basic Books.

Porter, J. H. (1970) 'Wage bargaining under conciliation agreements, 1860–1914', *Economic History Review* (Second Series), 23(3), 460–75.

  (1971) 'Wage determination by selling price sliding scales 1870–1914', *Manchester School of Economic and Social Studies*, 39(1), 13–21.

Prais, S. J., with the collaboration of Daly, Anne, Jones, Daniel T., and Wagner, Karin (1976) *Productivity and Industrial Structure: a Statistical Study of Manufacturing Industry in Britain, Germany and the United States*, Cambridge, Cambridge University Press.

Price, Richard (1989) ' "What's in a name?" Workplace history and "rank and filism" ', *International Review of Social History*, 34, 62–77.

Redfield, Robert (1947) 'The folk society', *American Journal of Sociology*, 52(4), 293–308.

Redmayne, Sir Richard A. S. (1942) *Men, Mines, and Memories*, London, Eyre and Spottiswoode.

Rees, Gareth, Bujra, Janet, Litlewood, Paul, Newby, Howard, and Rees, Teresa L. (eds.) (1985) *Political Action and Social Identity: Class, Locality and Ideology*, London, Macmillan.

Reid, Fred (1978) *Keir Hardie: the Making of a Socialist*, London, Croom Helm.

Renshaw, Patrick (1975) *The General Strike*, London, Eyre Methuen.

Revans, R. W. (1955) 'Scale factors in the management of coal mines', *Operational Research Quarterly*, 6(3), 91–107.

  (1956) 'Industrial morale and size of unit', *Political Quarterly*, 27, 303–11.

  (1958) 'Human relations, management and size', ch. 7 of Hugh-Jones, E. M. (ed.), *Human Relations and Modern Management*, Amsterdam, North-Holland, 177–220.

Rigg, Paul (1987) 'Miners and militancy: a study of branch union leadership', *Industrial Relations Journal* [Nottingham], 18(3), 189–200.

Rimlinger, Gaston V. (1959) 'International differences in the strike propensity of coal miners: experience in four countries', *Industrial and Labor Relations Review*, 12(3), 389–405.

Rowe, J. W. F. (1923) *Wages in the Coal Industry*, London, P. S. King & Son.

Rubinstein, David (1978) 'The Independent Labour Party and the Yorkshire miners: the Barnsley by-election of 1897', *International Review of Social History*, 23, 102–34.

Rutledge, I. (1977) 'Changes in the mode of production and the growth of "mass militancy" in the mining industry 1954–74', *Science and Society*, 41, 410–29.

Sack, Robert David (1980) *Conceptions of Space in Social Thought: a Geographic Perspective*, London, Macmillan.

Samuel, Raphael (1977) 'Mineral workers', part 1 of Samuel, Raphael (ed.), *Miners, Quarrymen and Saltworkers*, London, Routledge and Kegan Paul, 1–97.

Samuel, Raphael, Bloomfield, Barbara, and Boanas, Guy (eds.) (1986), *The Enemy Within: Pit Villages and the Miners' Strike of 1984–5*, London, Routledge and Kegan Paul.

SAS Institute Inc. (1985) *SAS User's Guide: Statistics: Version 5 Edition*, Cary, North Carolina, SAS Institute Inc.

Saunders, Peter (1981) *Social Theory and the Urban Question*, London, Hutchinson.

Saville, John (1971) 'Notes on ideology and the miners before World War I', *Bulletin of the*

Society for the Study of Labour History, 23, 25–7.

Scargill, Arthur (1975) 'The new unionism', *New Left Review*, 92, 3–33.

Schloss, David F. (1893) 'The reorganisation of our Labour Department', *Journal of the Royal Statistical Society*, 56(1), 44–70.

Scott, W. H., Mumford, Enid, McGivering, I. C., and Kirkby, J. M. (1963) *Coal and Conflict: a Study of Industrial Relations at Collieries*, Liverpool, Liverpool University Press.

Seddon, Vicky (ed.) (1986) *The Cutting Edge: Women and the Pit Strike*, London, Lawrence and Wishart.

Shorter, Edward, and Tilly, Charles (1974) *Strikes in France 1830–1968*, Cambridge, Cambridge University Press.

Silverman, David (1970) *The Theory of Organisations: a Sociological Framework*, London, Heinemann.

Skelley, Jeffrey (ed.) (1976) *The General Strike: 1926*, London, Lawrence and Wishart.

Slaughter, Clifford (1958) 'The strike of Yorkshire mineworkers in May, 1955', *Sociological Review* (New Series), 6(2), 241–59.

Smith, Adam (1776/1976) *An Inquiry into the Nature and Causes of the Wealth of Nations* (eds. Campbell, R. H., Skinner, A. S., and Todd, W. B.), (2 volumes), Oxford, Clarendon Press, 1976 (first edition: London, W. Strahan, 1776).

Smith, C. S. (1960) 'Planned transfer of labour, with special reference to the coal industry', doctoral thesis, University of London.

Smith, David (1972–3) 'The struggle against company unionism in the South Wales coalfield, 1926–1939', *Welsh History Review*, 6, 354–78.

   (1978) '[Letter] Non-political or company unionism?', *Bulletin of the Society for the Study of Labour History*, 36, 22–3.

Smith, David (ed.) (1980) *A People and A Proletariat: Essays in the History of Wales: 1780–1980*, London, Pluto Press in association with Llafur, the Society for the Study of Welsh Labour History.

Spaven, Pat (1978) 'Main gates of protest: contrasts in rank and file activity among the South Yorkshire miners 1858–1894', ch. 7 of Harrison, Royden (ed.), *Independent Collier: the Coal Miner as Archetypal Proletarian Reconsidered*, Hassocks, Harvester Press, 201–31.

Spencer, Elaine Glovka (1976) 'Employer response to unionism: Ruhr coal industrialists before 1914', *Journal of Modern History*, 48(3), 397–412.

Stacey, Margaret (1969) 'The myth of community studies', *British Journal of Sociology*, 20, 134–45.

Stead, Peter (1972–3) 'Working-class leadership in South Wales, 1900–1920', *Welsh History Review*, 6, 329–53.

   (1973) 'The Welsh working class', *Llafur*, 1(2), 42–54.

Stearns, Peter N. (1975) *Lives of Labour: Work in a Maturing Industrial Society*, London, Croom Helm.

Storey, John (1985) 'The means of management control', *Sociology*, 19(2), 193–211.

Storm-Clark, Christopher (1971) 'The miners, 1870–1970: a test-case for oral history', *Victorian Studies*, 15(1), 49–74.

Sunley, Peter (1988) 'Broken places: towards a geography of the 1926 coal dispute', ch. 1 of Heffernan, Mike, and Gruffud, Pyrs (eds.), *'A Land Fit for Heroes': Essays in the Human Geography of Inter-War Britain*, (Loughborough University Department of Geography Occasional Paper No. 14), Loughborough, Loughborough University of Technology, 5–36.

Supple, Barry (1984) ' "No bloody revolutions but for obstinate reactions"? British coalowners in their context, 1919–20', ch. 13 of Coleman, D. C., and Mathias, Peter (eds.), *Enterprise and History: Essays in Honour of Charles Wilson*, Cambridge, Cambridge University Press, 212–36.

(1986) 'Ideology and necessity: the nationalisation of coal mining, 1916–1946', in McKendrick, N., and Outhwaite, R. B. (eds.), *Business Life and Public Policy: Essays in Honour of D. C. Coleman*, Cambridge, Cambridge University Press.

(1987) *The History of the British Coal Industry*. Vol. IV: *1913–1946: The Political Economy of Decline*, Oxford, Clarendon Press.

Symons, Julian (1957) *The General Strike: a Historical Portrait*, London, The Cresset Press.

Tailby, Stephanie (1990) 'Labour utilization and labour management in the British coalmining industry, 1900–1940', doctoral thesis, University of Warwick.

Tawney, R. H. (1943) 'The abolition of economic controls, 1918–1921', *Economic History Review* [First Series], 13(1/2), 1–30.

Taylor, Andrew J. (1984a) ' "The pulse of one fraternity": non-unionism in the Yorkshire coalfield, 1931–8', *Bulletin of the Society for the Study of Labour History*, 49, 46–56.

(1984b) *The Politics of the Yorkshire Miners*, London, Croom Helm.

Taylor, A[rthur] J. (1960) 'The sub-contract system in the British coal industry', ch. 9 of Pressnell, L. S. (ed.), *Studies in the Industrial Revolution: Presented to T. S. Ashton*, London, Athlone Press, 215–35.

Tenfelde, Klaus (ed.) (1986) *Arbeiter und Arbeiterbewegung im Vergleich: Berichte zur Internationalen historischen Forschung*, (*Historische Zeitschrift*, Sonderhefte, 15), Munich, Oldenbourg.

(1992) *Towards a Social History of Mining in the 19th and 20th Centuries: Papers Presented to the International Mining History Congress Bochum, Federal Republic of Germany, September 3rd-7th, 1989*, Munich, Verlag C. H. Beck.

Thomas, Ralph (1986) *Oakdale: the Model Village*, Cwmbran, Village.

Thurley, Keith, and Wood, Stephen (eds.) (1983) *Industrial Relations and Management Strategy*, Cambridge, Cambridge University Press.

Tilly, Charles ([1978]) *From Mobilization to Revolution*, Reading, Addison-Wesley.

(1995) *Popular Contention in Great Britain: 1758–1834*, Cambridge, Harvard University Press.

Treble, John G. (1987) 'Sliding scales and conciliation boards: risk-sharing in the late 19th century British coal industry', *Oxford Economic Papers*, 39, 679–98.

Trist, E. L., and Bamforth, K. W. (1951) 'Some social and psychological consequences of the longwall method of coal-getting: an examination of the psychological situation and defences of a work group in relation to the social structure and technological content of the work system', *Human Relations*, 4(1), 3–38.

Trist, E. L., Higgin, G. W., Murray, H., and Pollock, A. B. (1963) *Organisational Choice: Capabilities of Groups at the Coal Face under Changing Technologies: The Loss, Rediscovery & Transformation of a Work Tradition*, London, Tavistock Publications.

Turner, H. A. (1963) *The Trend of Strikes: an Inaugural Lecture*, Leeds, Leeds University Press.

Turner, H. A., Clack, Garfield, and Roberts, Geoffrey (1967) *Labour Relations in the Motor Industry: a Study of Industrial Unrest and an International Comparison*, London, George Allen and Unwin.

Unofficial Reform Committee (1912/1974) *The Miners' Next Step*, in Coates, Ken (ed.), *Democracy in the Mines: Some Documents of the Controversy on Mines Nationalisation up to the Time of the Sankey Commission*, Nottingham, Bertrand Russell Peace Foundation for Spokesman Books, 1974, 16–30 (first edition: Tonypandy, Robert Davies & Co. 1912).

Vernon, Frank (1984) *Pride and Poverty: Memories of a Mexborough Miner*, Doncaster, Doncaster Library Services, Doncaster Metropolitan Borough Council. (Copy in Leeds City Public Libraries).

Waddington, David, Wykes, Maggie, and Critcher, Chas, with Hebron, Sandra (1991) *Split at the Seams? Community, Continuity and Change after the 1984–5 Coal Dispute*, Milton Keynes, Open University Press.

Waller, Robert J. (1983) *The Dukeries Transformed: the Social and Political Development of a Twentieth Century Coalfield*, Oxford, Clarendon Press.

(1987) 'Sweethearts and scabs: irregular trade unions in Britain in the twentieth century', ch. 9 of Waller P. J. (ed.), *Politics and Social Change in Modern Britain: Essays Presented to A. F. Thompson*, Brighton, Harvester, 213–28.

Warwick, Dennis, and Littlejohn, Gary (1992) *Coal, Capital and Culture: a Sociological Analysis of Mining Communities in West Yorkshire*, London, Routledge.

Webb, Sidney (1921) *The Story of the Durham Miners (1662–1921)*, London, The Fabian Society and the Labour Publishing Co.

Weber, Max (1922/1968) *Economy and Society: an Outline of Interpretive Sociology* (ed. Roth, Guenther, and Wittich, Claus; trans. Fischoff, Epphraim, *et al.*), New York, Bedminster Press, 1968 (first German edition: 1922).

Weisbrod, Bernd (1990) 'Entrepreneurial politics and industrial relations in mining in the Ruhr region: from managerial absolutism to co-determination', ch. 4 of Feldman Gerald D., and Tenfelde, Klaus (eds.), *Workers, Owners and Politics in Coal Mining: an International Comparison of Industrial Relations*, New York, Berg, 118–202.

Welbourne, E. (1923) *The Miners' Unions of Northumberland and Durham*, Cambridge, Cambridge University Press.

Wellisz, Stanislas (1953) 'Strikes in coal-mining', *British Journal of Sociology*, 4(4), 346–66.

White, Joseph (1990) 'Syndicalism in a mature industrial setting: the case of Britain', ch. 6 of van der Linden, Marcel, and Thorpe, Wayne (eds.), *Revolutionary Syndicalism: an International Perspective*, Aldershot: Scolar Press, 101–18.

Williams, D. J. (1924) *Capitalist Combination in the Coal Industry*, London, The Labour Publishing Co.

Williams, J. (1985) 'Miners and the law of contract', *Llafur*, 4(2), 36–49.

Williams, J. E. (1962a) 'Labour in the coalfields', *Bulletin of the Society for the Study of Labour History*, 4, 24–32.

(1962b) *The Derbyshire Miners: a Study in Industrial and Social History*, London, George Allen and Unwin.

Williamson, Bill (1982) *Class, Culture and Community: a Biographical Study of Social Change in Mining*, London, Routledge and Kegan Paul.

Wilson, Reverend Jesse (1904) *The Story of the Great Struggle 1902–3*, London, Christian Commonwealth Co. Ltd.

Wilson, Trevor (1986) *The Myriad Faces of War: Britain and the Great War, 1914–1918*, Cambridge, Polity Press.

Winchester, David (1983) 'Industrial relations research in Britain', *British Journal of Industrial Relations*, 21(1), 100–14.

Winterton, Jonathan Charles (1981) 'The trend of strikes in coal mining, 1949–1979', *Industrial Relations Journal* [Nottingham], 12(6), 10–19.

(1989) 'An inter-industry analysis of UK strike activity 1949–1976', doctoral thesis, University of Leeds.

Winterton, Jonathan Charles and Winterton, Ruth (1989) *Coal, Crisis and Conflict: the 1984–85 Miners' Strike in Yorkshire*, Manchester, Manchester University Press.

Wirth, Louis (1938) 'Urbanism as a way of life', *American Journal of Sociology*, 44(1), 1–24.

Wood, Oliver (1988) *West Cumberland Coal 1600–1982/3*, (Extra Series 24), [Kendal], Cumberland and Westmorland Antiquarian and Archaeological Society.

Woodward, Joan (1965) *Industrial Organization: Theory and Practice*, London, Oxford University Press.

Wyncoll, Peter (1976) 'The East Midlands', ch. 2.4 of Skelley, Jeffrey (ed.), *The General Strike: 1926*, London, Lawrence and Wishart, 173–92.

Youngson Brown, A. J. (1953) 'Trade union policy in the Scots coalfields, 1855–1885', *Economic History Review* (Second Series), 6(1), 35–50.

Zeitlin, Jonathan (1989) ' "Rank and filism" and labour history: a rejoinder to Price and Cronin', *International Review of Social History*, 34, 89–102.

Zieger, Robert H. (1983) 'Industrial relations and labor history in the Eighties', *Industrial Relations* [California], 22, 58–70.

Zweig, F. (1948) *Men in the Pits*, London, Victor Gollancz.

Zweiniger-Bargielowska, I. M. (1990) 'Industrial relationships and nationalization in the South Wales coal mining industry', doctoral thesis, University of Cambridge.

(1992–3) 'Miners' militancy: a study of four South Wales collieries during the middle of the twentieth century', *Welsh History Review*, 16, 356–83.

INTERVIEWS

Mr R. Brownsword, re Norton Colliery, Norton-le-Moors, Stoke-on-Trent, 5 March 1990.

Mr I. Ellwood, re Whitburn Colliery, Castletown, South Shields, 28 May 1990.

Mr J. Errington, re Hylton Colliery, Castleton, Sunderland, 12 March 1990.

Mr J. S. McKenna, re Rossington Colliery, New Rossington, Yorkshire, 5 June 1990.

Mr J. Shaw, re Norton Colliery, Norton-le-Moors, Stoke-on-Trent, 5 March 1990.

Mr W. Spencer, re Hapton Valley Colliery, Burnley, 1 February 1990.

Mr J. Timson, re Hylton Colliery, Castleton, Sunderland, 12 March 1990.

Mr J. Whatmore, re Whitfield Colliery, Stoke-on-Trent, 28 March 1990.

Mr A. Wilde, re Rossington Colliery, New Rossington, Yorkshire, 5 June 1990.

Index

Unofficial Reform Committee, 61, 68
  see also Syndicalism

Vernon, Frank, on 'going home', 12
victimization, *see* strikers
viewers, *see* management
villages, colliery, *see* communities,
  coalmining

wages and earnings
  allowances, and 1912 National Strike, 113
  allowances, after nationalization, 223
  'basis' or 'standard', 44
  and coal prices, 38–9, 41–3, 46, 49; link
    with, broken, after 1926, 50
  day wage structure (1955), 223
  deductions from, issue in 'bag dirt' strike
    (1902), 109
  instability of, 38, 43
  'living', 42, 43, 45, 49
  minimum, and 1912 National Strike, 45,
    114–15; under conciliation boards, 43;
    under sliding scales, 42
  after nationalization, 223–4
  NPLA, 10, 37, 219, 224
  piece-rate, after nationalization, 223
  'standard' or 'basis', 44

and strikes, 224
walkouts, 'spontaneous', 12
Warwick, Dennis, and Littlejohn, Gary, on
  'local cultural capital', 117
Weber, Max, on size of enterprise, 159, 162
  see also meanings
West Yorkshire Coal Owners' Association,
  47
Williams, D. J., *Capitalist Combination*,
  160–1
Williams, Evan (president, MAGB,
  1919–44), puts nationalization to sleep,
  50
Wilson, Rev. Jesse, of Denaby, 111
Winstone, James (president, SWMF,
  1920–1), 62
Wirth, Louis, sociology of the city, 141–2
work groups, coalmining, size of, 169
  see also 'labour process'

Yorkshire Miners' [*from 1922* Mine
  Workers'] Association
  attacks unofficial strikes (1945), 222
  and Denaby strike (1902), 110–11

Zweiniger-Bargielowska, I. M., studies by,
  58, 196–7, 238–9